A
ssage
to
gland

Austin Pilgrim, Brixton, 1960

JOHN WESTERN

A *Passage* *to* *England*

BARBADIAN LONDONERS SPEAK OF HOME

Foreword by
Robert Coles

UNIVERSITY OF MINNESOTA PRESS
MINNEAPOLIS

W. H. Auden, excerpt from "On This Island," reprinted by permission of Random House, Inc., from *W. H. Auden: Collected Poems* by W. H. Auden, edited by Edward Mendelson, copyright 1937 and renewed 1965 by W. H. Auden; by permission of Faber and Faber, Ltd. ("Look Stranger at This Island") from *Collected Poems* by W. H. Auden. John Betjeman, "In Westminster Abbey," reprinted by permission of John Murray (Publishers) Ltd. from *Collected Poems* by John Betjeman, fourth edition, copyright 1979 by John Betjeman. T. S. Eliot, excerpt from *Murder in the Cathedral*, reprinted by permission of Harcourt Brace Jovanich, Inc., 1963; by permission of Faber and Faber, Ltd., copyright 1935. Excerpts from "Home from Home" printed by permission of British Broadcasting Corporation from BBC Radio 4 program, "Home from Home," Rita Payne, producer, transmitted May–June 1988. Ken Pyne cartoon, reproduced from *Punch* magazine, July 28, 1982, by permission of *Punch*. Excerpt from *Another Life* by Derek Walcott, copyright 1972, 1973 by Derek Walcott. Reprinted by permission of Farrar, Straus and Giroux, Inc.

Published by the University of Minnesota Press
2037 University Avenue Southeast, Minneapolis, MN 55414
Printed in the United States of America on acid-free paper

Library of Congress Cataloging-in-Publication Data

Western, John.
 A passage to England : Barbadian Londoners speak of home / John Western.
  p.   cm.
 Includes index.
 ISBN 0-8166-1984-0 (hc). — ISBN 0-8166-1985-9 (pbk)
  1. West Indians—England—London—Social life and customs.
 2. Barbados—Emigration and immigration. 3. Barbados—Social life
 and customs. 4. London (England)—Race relations. I. Title.
 DA676.9.W4W47   1992
 942.1'00496972981—dc20   91-25920
                                                                 CIP

The University of Minnesota is an
equal-opportunity educator and employer.

to my mother

to Patricia

and in memory of my father
Charles Western (1906–87), printer
A good man

We do return and leave and return again, criss-crossing the Atlantic, but whichever side of the Atlantic we are on, the dream is always on the other side.

Pauline Melville, *Shape-Shifter: Stories*, 1989

Modernity has indeed been liberating. . . . It has opened up for the individual previously unheard-of options and avenues of mobility. . . . However, these liberations have had a high price. Perhaps the easiest way to describe it is . . . as "home-lessness."

Peter Berger, Brigitte Berger, and
Hansfried Kellner, *The Homeless Mind*, 1973

Contents

Illustrations

Foreword

Robert Coles

I first met John Western in South Africa during August of 1974. I had gone there with my father, a Yorkshireman who as a young man had crossed the Atlantic to live in America, and my son, then ten years old. John was in the midst of his study of Cape Town's "Coloured" population—the travail of a mixed-race people caught in the perversities of apartheid. I still remember my father's impressions of John: "a bright, energetic, decent, thoughtful lad," the words spoken, I noticed, with a bit more of the English cadence than was usually the case—a nod of familiarity, perhaps, to a young man who also hailed from the "old country," as Dad often called his nation of birth. That description (save the last word) still serves as a useful preliminary one for the author of this book, though now, with these pages, so wonderfully informative, so beautifully written, the author, in his early middle age, threatens to become a most distinguished social essayist, someone with a lot to teach all of us who are, in these final years of the twentieth century, and second millennium, still, alas, struggling with what George Eliot called "the old Adam" in ourselves—the racial and national fears, doubts, suspicions that, among other matters, this book documents so tellingly.

Not that the reader is in for a discussion of sociological or psychological abstractions. This is a book about particular men, women, children—their memories, their experiences, their hopes, worries, apprehensions. They have in common, of course, a certain heritage: they are black and they hail from Barbados, even as now they live in England's capital city. As the author, a careful and affectionate observer of them, a chronicler of their lives, reminds us, they left an island in order to seek an island—and to a degree, speaking metaphorically, they are part of yet another island: inhabitants of a community in London, yet not integrated into its midst the way others have come to be. We are brought by a writer's skill, his narrative will and judgment, into the company of these interesting people—individuals whose ideas and opinions teach us a good deal, and whose experiences grow upon us, amuse and edify us, and cumulatively enlarge our own sensibilities, even as we come to know of theirs. In a sense, then, their "passage to England" becomes the reader's as well. These are stories that become part of our own stories—what happens to us as we meet through words our fellow human beings.

I hope very much the reader will also take advantage of the opportunity the author provides with respect to himself—that we who come to this book make his acquaintance. He is a social geographer, a scholar and researcher, a book writer, an intermediary with respect to the individuals whose lives we meet on the pages that follow. But he is also his own interesting, provocative self, and his English life, his American life, his life as a particular kind of fieldworker—all of that is well worth our attention. The way he writes about himself (and of course, the way he writes about his manner of doing his work, his research) tells us a lot about the way he got along with the people who become, here, our teachers, maybe even friends of sorts, even as they became his.

I must note here how entranced I was by the discussion, early on, of the advantages and burdens of the tape recorder as a modern instrument of documentary research. With delightful candor one social scientist, at last, dares acknowledge his decision to rely upon old-fashioned memory rather than the whirl of contemporary technology, and for reasons any number of us well know—the tape recorder not only as an utterly accurate listener, but a formidably shaping presence: a major player, as it were, in what happens between an observer and the observed, hence, ironically, an intrusion or distortion that is potentially more significant or substantial than any lapse of memory may turn out to be, or any spell of subjectivity as it determines what is written about what was heard. I recall, in my own early work, interviews in which both the children or parents with whom I was conversing and I were so preoccupied with the workings and implications of the Sony machine I carried with me that we seemed, often, to be talking to it, addressing nervously and all too conscientiously its demanding company. Lord knows what we didn't say, wouldn't think of saying, so long as its small red light sent its psychological and moral signal to us, as well as its announcement that all goes well with a major symbol of what these days gets called "science." I well remember, too, when (with some trepidation) I one day told myself as well as those I was meeting that I was prepared to risk a plain old talk, with no tapes, no machine nearby, and later, risk my impressions, my power of recall, as I tried to get down what had transpired in this or that room with one or another person. I have never, though, written about such matters with the bold and delightful personal openness that characterizes John Western's early expository pages of this book; and so I thank him for what he dares tell (and teach) some of us who are his colleagues, even as I thank and applaud him for yet another wonderfully suggestive and informative book—its richly textured stories, with their ambiguities and subtleties and complexities and nuances thoroughly intact, a real gift to us readers, and a gift, as well, to the tradition of humane, sensitive, social science research.

Preface

Pure chance, really. My first arrival at Syracuse University for the fall se-
mester of 1984 happened to coincide with the arrival of a Barbadian
graduate student at the same department of the university: the first Barbadian I'm aware of having met. She chose me as one of her two advisors.
We got on very well. The academic year done, my wife and I went to Barbados (we'd never before been in the Caribbean) and met the student's
family. Her mother then came and stayed with us. "My brother lives in
England. He drives buses in London," said she. Thus was planted in my
mind the spore of this project, a project that deals with fuzzy but fascinating universal concepts like home, belonging, identity, culture, and place,
all in the context of Barbadian migration to a British society that has vastly
changed over the past thirty-five years.

In summer 1986 while visiting my parents in Kent I went off to see the
brother in Southall, west London. We met two or three times, and he also
introduced me to a couple of his friends. The brother had been recruited
in Barbados by London Transport in 1957. As it was he who set me off
on the track of those who became my "sample," it should not surprise
that, among the migrant generation members of this sample, eight of the
other eleven men and two of the eleven women were also LT recruits.
London Transport, a public body, had at that time been experiencing a
labor shortage. So had the British National Health Service, for which a
number of the women migrants likewise came to work. These single
young people then met and married, raised children in London (who also
speak in this book), and have stayed in Britain. As the end of their working
lives begins to come into view, they wonder if they should return "home"
to Barbados. They find themselves in a very modern predicament, however: they're in a quandary as to where their "home" actually is . . . a
quandary so many of us share these days. That is what this work is about.
It is their words that tell us about it. Clearly their story is a particular
one—matters of race figure quite prominently—but just as clearly, their
story has a general relevance and resonance.

The summer 1986 reconnaissance convinced me the research was
practicable. The London School of Economics' geography department
generously offered me an institutional pied-à-terre were I to come, Syracuse University then gave me a year's leave, and the National Geographic
Society in Washington, DC, provided me with some funds. Thus, another
year later we came to live on St. Lukes Road in inner west London in order

that I might talk with Barbadian Londoners. Apprised of my impending return, the brother and his friends had let some of *their* friends know of my project. Thus was I afforded amicable introductions of limited threat to potential respondents. My contact-making gathered a moderate momentum; I started in.

It should by now be evident that the aim of this research was not to get some "factual answers" or "right answers" for a social survey. If that had been the case, probably the best way to do it would have been to use some extensive stratified random sample, representative of all identifiable Barbadian Londoners, via the employment of a significant number of trained research assistants. Work has been done in this manner, well and painstakingly done by organizations like the Policy Studies Institute in producing the *Black and White Britain* surveys.

However, my concentration on just a dozen nonrandom families, interviewed a number of times in much greater depth than would be possible in the questionnaire-survey-by-a-stranger mode, reveals a different emphasis. Yes, the aim was still to gain some "factual answers." But more so for me it was really *to ask questions in a particular way,* much as I had in my previous work, with so-called Coloured people[1] in Cape Town. There I had enjoyed doing all my own work, unbeholden to anyone else in some research team. I wished to be an independent researcher again, delving deeper in interviews, searching for richness and texture in responses. Thus in London I would go meet a family, in all but one case in their home, in all but three cases the primary contact person being the man. Sometimes spouses would be present, sometimes not. I went without any researcher's paraphernalia, no briefcase or collar-and-tie or notepad or tape recorder. I went to present myself, to explain about the work I wanted, if permitted, to do with them, and to chat about "things in general."

Two households did not want to take part. One, after a whole pleasant evening's parlor conversation, dissembled. When I tried to set up a second meeting a couple of weeks later, there was further procrastination and then, apologetically, a declining to take part. It turned out there had been a family tragedy not long before. Its nature was to some degree related to the uncertainties about belonging that I was investigating. It was unthinkable to proceed further in order to probe and publish such pain. The other "household" was a widower of high achievement and of thorough politicization. Fate had not dealt kindly with him in some aspects of his life, and a certain bruised disappointment was evident in this sensitive man's conversations with me. My normal sunny manner was not going to melt his resistance; I knew deflection when I felt it.

Having met a family, I would try before too much time elapsed to set up a second meeting. I should interpose here that "family" was in all but one instance parents and offspring. Sometimes a grandmother or cousins from Barbados were also living with them for an indefinite period, or sometimes the couple had no children left in the home. Although appearing to be very straightforward (quasi-) nuclear families, there were of course various complications, as with all families. Some I was told about, some I found out indirectly—when I did, it made other things fall into place—and some of course I don't know about at all. The researcher from whom no secrets are hid does not exist. I cannot claim a greater intimacy with the households than that which I was permitted.

From all these preliminary meetings I wrote down—either right then on public transport as I rode back to our Notting Hill apartment or alone, uninterrupted, with the phone off the hook, in the flat the next morning—what I could remember of the conversation. I believe my memory was well tuned and very retentive. I did not use a tape recorder. There are evident disadvantages in eschewing taping. One loses sometimes the gravid pause, sometimes the subtle inflection. One cannot guarantee verisimilitude. In some of this book's quotations an "um" or "er" has been inserted, I admit that. On the other hand, there are absolutely no composites, no artful molding of two separate interviews into one. In a few of the quotations, mainly very long ones, I've changed sentence order. Willful doctoring, however, has affected only about one in ten of the quotations; I ask the reader to trust me on that. Most of whatever inaccuracies there may be in these quotations will be accidental, not willed. The inaccuracies will be the result of my faulty memory. And that leads straight to what must be the simplest, most important drawback in choosing not to tape: one cannot, if one relies on memory, come back again to the moment itself, for reappraisal and reinterpretation, as one can with tapes. However, this is not the time to add to the already considerable methodological literature about how or how not to use which particular vehicle of inquiry. Not to beat about the bush, I simply don't *like* tape recording my interviews. I know how uncomfortable I would feel if I was being interviewed and saw that everything was going into the record.

Whether everyone feels thus inhibited I of course cannot say. Some very practiced colleagues tell me, not so. But to do good work not only the respondent but also the questioner must be at ease. The interviewer and interviewee are bound to each other; their mien influences each other, back and forth—a mutuality captured in what has become one of the catch phrases of humanistic geography: "Every object an object for some subject." So *I* want to relax as much as is practicable in interviewing; that tape spool turning would unsettle *me* . . . even if such were not also the case for the interviewee.

It was not until after prior meetings that I would come along to administer the questionnaire (having run a first draft of it past two Barbadian Londoners with whom I felt particularly comfortable). This always took at least one hour and usually two or three: an entire evening. I administered it to one of the parents—spouses were not present—in all but two cases to the man first. On a later occasion I came back to give the questionnaire to the other spouse, separately. And still later, I sought out their eldest child, whether male or female, who now lived away, and did the questionnaire with them wherever they were.

Thirty-four interview schedules, with either 94 or 104 questions each (see the Appendix), plus my substantial notes from the other more informal meetings: these constitute my basic data. I believed before I began in London that, simply, I would find this more concentrated yet more open-ended mode of ethnographic research personally satisfying. And although it proved harder work than I had ever anticipated, and although not infrequently I had wearily to draw deep from my personal reserves, the work had indeed ended up giving me a sense of satisfaction by the time I left at the end of August 1988. It was gratifying, when on a seven-day visit to London from America nine months later, that all of the households were pleased that I should phone to say hello. Some indeed invited me round for an evening of drinks or a Barbadian meal, invitations I accepted. I ended up liking virtually all of the people I interviewed. I look forward to appearing on their doorsteps with a copy of this book and saying, "Here, you're in this, this is for you. With my thanks."

I do thank them, very much. They not only told me about themselves and about Barbados and about England, they induced me to think about my own relationship to England. As the reader will shortly discover, the first chapter, "Transatlantic Homes," refers not only to their experiences but also to mine. Up until a generation or so ago the academic practitioner of ethnographic fieldwork (which is what this present study may loosely be labeled) would be expected to maintain an authorial, if not Olympian, detachment from the material. An "objective account" was rendered. The exceptions were very few: *Return to Laughter* (Bowen)[2] is probably the best known. Then it became common to add an afterwordlike chapter about how the work was done, as with classics like *Tally's Corners* (Liebow)[3] or *Soulside* (Hannerz). [4] There was still a hint of "Confessions of a Fieldworker" about this, however. After all, such concerns were relegated to the very end, after the *real* stuff of the book had been conveyed in the approved, coolly measured observational manner: Numbers preceded Revelation.

Most recently there seems to have been a sea change. No longer are manifestations of the fieldworker's personality inadmissible in scholarly accounts.[5] Reflexive social research, coupled with a growing enthusiasm for qualitative modes of inquiry, has permitted the researcher-as-person to honorably occupy the stage along with those persons being studied. Sometimes this takes the form of a double publication: a first presents the findings of the research itself, and a second lays out how the research was done on the ground and how the researcher felt and feels about it. I've decided here to attempt to combine these two aspects in one volume. The most evident combination occurs in the first chapter, wherein the researcher becomes part of the research—clearly, there's a fashionable whiff of the postmodern about this. But thereafter the book becomes more of a storytelling exercise, as much as possible in the words of the Barbadian Londoners themselves. It is only in the conclusion that I as author reappear openly. Throughout the work, however, I suspect my *tone* can be sensed: that those persons in this book—as with any other persons—have something to tell the rest of us, and we should try to listen attentively and with respect. As one of them said to me, "You know, we're not just people who work on the buses and on the trains."

I've been very uncertain about whether to report on this research in this way. The pitfalls of overindulgent autobiographical self-absorption are evident. But the richness of the account—to laypeople, not just to academic colleagues—is, I believe, enhanced. I wish on this occasion to address a broader audience than my own and cognate academic disciplines. Unused to such an attempt at reaching out, I sent a first draft of the first chapter, requesting reactions, to about fifteen colleagues whose acuity I hold in high esteem. Some replied, don't do it this way. An eminent British scholar responded:

> You ask whether you have gone over the top in your autobiographical reminiscences. Well, my answer is that I feel you have. Your Garden of Memories is obviously a lovely (I think I mean "lovesome") place for you to wander in, and nice enough for your friends too, but your other readers won't perhaps want to know such a mass of detail. So I suggest some severe weeding and pruning.

A somewhat greater number of colleagues said yes, proceed . . . but address such and such a shortcoming. Perhaps what really decided me were the urgings of the members of my Syracuse University spring 1989 ethnography/cultural geography graduate seminar.[6] Be up front about your involvement, they insisted, do it. So, trusting that this was not some knavish plot on their part to connive at my professional discomfiture, I did proceed . . . though I did some weeding and pruning, too.

The previous paragraph indicates that there are a lot of people to whom

I am grateful for their help in doing this study—most obviously, the inter-viewees themselves, whom at their request I have not named but to whom I have accorded typical Barbadian names as pseudonyms. As for my many colleagues on both sides of the Atlantic, I shall not name you here either, in part because a long list of acknowledgments can become tiresome, and also because of the implication of guilt by association (how-ever often the predictable disclaimer, "although the errors are of course the author's responsibility alone," is flourished). So—you know who you are—I offer you my thanks here, but I also undertake to say so personally to each of you. I wish to make just two exceptions. David Lowenthal fo-cused tremendous, irresistibly logical criticism, both detailed and more general, upon the manuscript's penultimate draft. And Kay Steinmetz proved a marvelous editor and word processor, who strove manfully to remove gender bias from my writing. I'm really grateful to you both.

The dedication of this book reveals my greatest debts.

The Barbadian Londoners

Orville Alleyne, administrator in a London bus garage
Pauline, his wife, psychiatric nurse and home visitor for a local authority
Gordon, their Barbados-born son, college educated, living and working in central London, member of the gay community

Dotteen Bannister, nurse with a family doctor practice
Jeff, her husband, administrator in the headquarters of the post office

Beverly Brathwaite, recently retired from a metalworking concern
Trevor, her husband, a longtime bus driver
Trevor Jr., their Barbados-born son, a young, confident, and successful businessman in a multinational company
Catherine, his Grenada-born wife, starting up her own beauty business

Charles Eastmond, mail sorter in the principal London post office
Eulie, his wife, a social worker
Meg, their London-born daughter, a word-processor operator in a large east London concern

Ernestine Farley, night-duty nursing assistant and celebrated cake-maker
George, her husband, part-time security guard recently retired from bus conducting
Paula, their Barbados-born daughter, working in central London in the main offices of a large bank

Tony Gill, head of local rolling-stock operations on British Rail's King's Cross lines
Sandra, his wife, formerly a clerical worker with British Rail, now working in the home
Derek, their London-born son, a businessman in a large corporation

Alan Maycock, high-level administrator in the Greater London Council, which was then in the process of being wound down
Althea, his wife, clerical worker in a London public service
Susan, their London-born daughter, at college in northern England, with dreams of going into television afterward

Austin Pilgrim, manager at one of London's flagship Underground stations and an aficionado of cricket

Marie, his wife, recently retired from clerical work at a major multi-national's headquarters in central London

Nigel, their poised London-born son, starting off his career in Liverpool after gaining a B.Sc. at York University

Edward Pilgrim, Austin's elder brother, stores superintendent at a major London hospital and an utter aficionado of cricket

Carol, his Barbados-born daughter, a part-time psychiatric nurse's aid and married to Colin Simmons

Audley Simmons, clerk in a transport firm, after thirty years on the London buses

Edith, his Jamaican wife, clerk in a suburban post office district headquarters

Colleen, their London-born daughter, clerk, lover of reggae music, and a Rastafarian

Ken Wright, her husband, musician and Rastafarian, born in Jamaica

Amelia Simmons, recently retired from nursing at a large London hospital

John, her husband, and elder brother to Audley, team leader of baggage handling at Heathrow Airport, preparing to retire to Barbados

Colin, their Barbados-born son, self-employed businessman in the electronics field, and married to Carol Pilgrim

Frank Springer, an inspector with the Underground, the earliest arrived of all (1956)

Joan, his wife, a traveling ticket inspector with the Underground

Max, their London-born son, a young businessman hauling himself up by his bootstraps with unyielding determination

Plus more occasional contributions from:

Gladstone Codrington, highly placed in a quasi-governmental organ concerned with domestic policy

D'Arcy Holder, a bus driver

Colin Jemmott, in midcareer as a very successful London businessman

Ivan Weekes, highly placed in the administrative headquarters of the British Methodist Church

One
Transatlantic Homes

Through writing—knowledge and curiosity feeding off one another—I had arrived at a new idea of myself and my world. But the world had not stood still. In 1950 in London, in the boarding house, I had found myself at the beginning of a great movement of peoples after the war, a great shaking up of the world, a great shaking up of old cultures and old ideas.

V. S. Naipaul, *The Enigma of Arrival*

This book is about identity—who and what people feel themselves to be. It has been said, "A man is his place." Overstatement perhaps; but certainly, as a geographer, I am interested in the evident role place plays in molding identity. Those whose words fill this book are women and men who have a multiple identity: Barbadian and Londoner, a place of origin and a place of habitation. I sense that, at least in the industrialized countries, the world is going to see more and more persons who have to wrestle with such complex identities, combinations undreamed of less than two generations ago: Turkish Germans, Assyrian Swedes, Arab French. What of the possibility, once January 1, 1993, has brought greater economic integration and internal labor mobility to the EEC, of Irish Germans or Irish Italians? And how long can that putatively "homogeneous" industrial state, Japan, maintain its distance from significant new ethnic admixture?

If these speculations sound a little too ringingly global, they nevertheless are meant to induce the reader to perceive the people interviewed in this book as more than rather oddly complicated, if deserving, objects of study. Instead, think of them as harbingers or examples of what may well be becoming the norm in our societies. People from the world's poorer countries are being drawn to industrial countries where they stand out phenotypically and culturally from the natives. Unlike the predominantly European migrations to the New World over the past centuries, today's migrants are not encountering natives whom they can dismiss as savages,

1

conquer, and even exterminate. Nor do today's newcomers arrive in fluid societies of a New World stamp, when they set foot in an England, Japan, or Italy. They're going to have a tougher time of it, dealing with cultural rejection by the outnumbering natives, and having to achieve some cultural *modus vivendi* with them, on unequal terms. And in the longest term, whether you or I are at present in the Old World or New, rich world or poor, more and more of our descendants are going to encounter complexities of identity such as those the Barbadian Londoners have experienced.

For some of these Londoners, their complex identity was a burden of sorts. Others wore it more lightly, and yet others found in it something to celebrate. And as I worked with them my initial professional, geographer's interest in place-based complex identities began to undergo a change. The issue became no longer only an objectively intriguing academic conundrum, but an examination in part of my own identity. I realized I was asking them things I could just as well have been asking of myself . . . but until then never had. In these first pages I dwell a little on my own experiences as a contrivance, in order to draw readers into engagement with this study. That is, the questions arising from the experience of the Barbadian Londoners are, I would claim, universal in import: questions of identity and of belonging, of "home." I started off looking with curiosity at these "exotic," "different" people, and then realized that in some ways their experiences spoke directly to mine; I was led to look at the path my own life has taken. Similarly, perhaps in turn readers might be drawn to examine themselves, the details and trajectories of their own lives in society, and compare themselves to, contrast themselves with, the Barbadian Londoners. That is at least my hope and intent.

I might start in on this venture by claiming that my own experiences of a complex spatial self-identity seemed not altogether unrelated to those of the Barbadian Londoners. As a young, single, footloose person, as most of them had been at the start, I crossed the Atlantic for greener and especially more extensive pastures; their journeys were made thirty years ago, mine ten years later. Like them, I migrated in a sort of hopeful uncertainty. Like them I had no concrete intent to become a settler. In part I had made the move just because it was "the thing to do"—a phrase that cropped up not infrequently in their conversation. Like them, I stayed, and became— in the terms that fond, distant parents would use (theirs and mine)— "successful." Like them, I found that distant aged parents died or moved away from the village or town that had been the childhood home; for some of them (as for me), it's difficult to say with precision today where "home" is in one's homeland. Indeed, is homeland—land of origin—

"home" now anyway? This is an ambiguous matter, for them as for me. We have ended up with two "homes." We possess transatlantic, or rather, Atlantic-spanning identities. Yes, their complexities were my complexities.

But were they? A white, college-educated, middle-class male should not be too glib in claiming fraternity with the persons in this study. It smacks of posturing to allude to insights based on "common experiences." First of all, the economic pressures on them in Barbados in the late 1950s—whatever anyone said about "adventure" or it simply being "the thing to do"—were considerable. A small overpopulated colonial island with a declining monocultural base in sugar cane spelled few job openings. Some were unemployed, some underemployed, some frustrated at the evident lack of potential for advancement ("dead men's shoes," said a civil service under-clerk). There were forces pushing them out of Barbados. However, there were no economic exigencies propelling me from Britain. In the late 1960s, before the oil crisis and world industrial recession, the country had plenty of openings for a new Oxbridge graduate, or so I fully believed. No, my move away from the land of my birth felt a free choice, a luxury I could afford. Unlike them, I was not going abroad in order to make a larger contribution to hard-pressed family finances. I never had to remit anything out of my meager graduate-student assistantships home, whereas they did, scrimping on their low-paying, entry-level jobs. My assistantships may have been meager, but they held the possibilities of real monetary and career advancement once my apprenticeship had been successfully served; whereas they—starting off as Underground station sweepers, pourers of tea in railway cafeterias, workers in locomotive depots, trainee bus conductors, trainee nurses, or hotel maids—had a probably longer and less rapid climb ahead of them toward relative financial security and social kudos. I and they entered our respective "host societies" at different levels. Furthermore, I was certain I could always return to my original society, employable, whenever I desired.

Second, compare briefly what happened to them, as new arrivals, with what happened to me. I assumed, with a fair basis in fact, that I was welcome at my destinations. Canada accorded me Landed Immigrant status in a trice; I thereby joined, in John Porter's phrase, one of the country's two "charter groups," and, indeed, straightway voted in an Ontario provincial election. When I moved on to California, the welcome was not spelled out quite so unambiguously; this was a far more complex place. But I had not been at the University of California at Los Angeles a year when Wilbur Zelinsky's *Cultural Geography of the United States*[1] came out, and it strongly influenced the crystallization of my first comprehensive notion of what the United States *was* culturally and societally. In it I read that the United States was basically a "neo-British" society—quite believable in Santa Monica (where I stayed), if not in East Los Angeles. And despite my hesitation about possible present-day resonances of the independence struggles against the British 200 years earlier, and despite my cringing when overhearing other expatriate British passing heavy-handedly jocular remarks about "you colonials" to their American hosts, I found that for most Americans I met there was no problem with the British. Americans and their national media tended to concentrate on more recent transatlantic relations, particularly idolizing the heroic Winston Churchill–Franklin Roosevelt Grand Alliance against the princes of evil.

So I rarely if ever experienced rejection solely upon the accident-of-birth basis of my being evidently British. Whereas for one Barbadian, Austin Pilgrim (frontispiece), the accident of birth of being evidently black brought in its train the following experiences:

> We were all so lonely when we first got here. Pubs wouldn't let you in. Dances would say, "No, you've got to be properly dressed." So we took ties in our pockets. Put 'em on when we got near the door. "Sorry," they said, "you've got to be a member." I couldn't understand it—just because I'm black; I began to think, "What's *wrong* with me?" I would get depressed. So we'd go in groups of ourselves, would stick together. My first Christmas Eve [1960] was awful. At home we used to go walking from friends' houses to friends' houses, didn't have to arrange it, to meet and to be friends. Here the streets were empty. It was cold. We were so lonely, so we stuck together . . . [2]

Nor did I ever come to feel stigmatized as unacceptably alien on the basis of my manner of speech. In fact, in America my accent proved to be unquestionably "cute." I did not care to worry overmuch at whatever implied recognition of superiority might skulk there, accorded by some speculated postcolonial cultural uncertainty to this badge of an older, allegedly more poised, tradition. I kept my southern English accent, and more or less keep it still. It is an advantage to me. But the likelihood of the average white Londoner breathlessly stopping a Barbadian in midsentence to tell him or her "I just *love* your accent" would appear to be quite small. Not that it has never happened. It has, but the Barbadian in question was not quite sure to what degree she was being ribbed or with what degree of malice. In America in a few such instances, I too have sensed that I was in the process of being mocked. On most occasions, however, it is instead an unsophisticated "wow, that's neat" reaction to my speech.

Never did I meet the unpleasantness another Barbadian met at his south London bus garage:

> I'll tell you the thing I really didn't like, it was really rude. You'd be talking to an Englishman, and before you even finished the sentence he'd interrupt with "Pardon?" Loudly. It made you feel a fool. I mean, I know how to speak this language, I speak it properly. I don't have a broad accent. But "Pardon?" they'd say, very abruptly. It's not as if *their* accent was easy to understand either. Sometimes I'd pass two of them talking broad Cockney. I could hardly understand a word. 'Course, I gradually got used to it.

Accent was in my case the most immediate signal to Americans that I was not one of them. But I do have the option of disguising myself, Americanizing my speech patterns, and melting into an accepting host society. It isn't just accent that signals the Barbadians' "otherness" in Britain, however. Their *visibility* removes any option, at least in the short- to medium-term, of melting into an accepting host society. And America and Britain are very different "host societies" anyway. Any white foreigner, let's say a Czech whose appearance could fairly pass as British, would find a certain stickiness in getting to be accepted as truly British. This same individual would meet fewer such impediments in assimilating into American society; America is easier to join. It is, after all, a society composed almost entirely of those who have joined . . . although Africans did so involuntarily. America hymns—and, as with the Statue of Liberty centennial, occasionally trumpets—the grit of immigrants taking their chances in a New World. "We are all immigrants," President Kennedy averred; it can well be a term of pride. A conservative President Reagan could say, "Anyone [can be] as good an American as any other."

Britain, instead, thrums to an Old World's theme: "a thousand years of continuity." We the natives have, in situ, gradually down the centuries, molded this society with which we are now well pleased. Our celebrated tolerance will permit outsiders to find a haven, but do not presume to attempt to change us; no "melting pot" ideology here. Saxons and Normans may once have melted, but that was long ago. George Mikes, from Hungary, wrote amusingly but tellingly of such English attitudes in his *How to Be an Alien* of 1946:

> Once a foreigner, always a foreigner. There is no way out for him. He may become British; he can never become English. . . . Magnanimous English people . . . will treat you with condescension, understanding, and sympathy. They will invite you

to their homes. Just as they keep lap-dogs and other pets, they are quite prepared to keep a few foreigners.[3]

Mikes was concerned with a case such as his own: the white foreigner's experience of cultural alterity at the hands of the English. Black foreigners then were few. However, in the decade or so after he wrote, large numbers of darker people came to settle, mostly from the West Indies. These persons became labeled "immigrants," a term of opprobrium reserved particularly for such ever-visible strangers. For blacks, "immigrant" was a term to hold one at arm's length, a term that can be made elastic by the concoction of the logically ridiculous designation "second-generation immigrant" for young black British people, some of whom speak to this issue in the chapters that follow.

In comparing Britain with the United States, I do not wish to give the impression of having swallowed the romantic American Immigrant Saga whole. Nativist riots, the Know-Nothings, the Chinese Exclusion Act of 1882, the quota system from 1921 to 1965, the turning away of German Jewish refugees in 1939, the internment of blameless Japanese-Americans in the wake of Pearl Harbor, the Haitian bodies washed up mutely on south Florida beaches, the six years of wrangling and scratching to produce the 1986 Immigration Act: all these and more point to the gap between the public rhetorical espousal of the richness that immigration brings American life, and the reality of resentment, suspicion, and defensive refusal. But one *can* join, even though in the joining some are more equal than others.

Britain, however, seems less welcoming to prospective joiners. As the *Economist* reported in a review of Jonathon Green's *Them: Voices from the Immigrant Community in Contemporary Britain:*

Being an immigrant is no barrel of laughs wherever you go; it is even tougher when your hosts tend to dislike foreigners on principle, and this, according to Mr Green's sample,[4] is sadly true of the British.

The Barbadians know a lot about this. A man who has been living in Britain now for thirty-three years offered this vignette for consideration:

I'll tell you what the difference is between England and America. I was waiting at a bus stop at Massapequa on Long Island and this old white man was standing waiting too, and he asked me some question. And I didn't know the answer and said so. And he looked at me and said I spoke differently. I said I was from the West Indies. "Ah," he said, "I'd thought you were an American, until you spoke."

And I thought, that's the opposite to England. We've been here for over thirty years, but still people ask us, "Where're you from?" The English assume we can't be English, the way we look. We *still* don't belong.

The rebuff is perhaps yet more stinging because three-quarters of the male interviewees were actually recruited, actively sought out in Barbados by British government officials, and financially assisted with the costs of passage to the United Kingdom where they were to work with London Transport and British Railways. Clearly in some manner they were wanted. In other ways, they sooner or later found out that they were not:

> But we didn't go out much, we worked odd hours [i.e., unsocial hours]. We'd just sit in watching TV. . . . You got rudeness. One morning very soon after we got here [1961] we walked into the room at the garage, they were all sitting around off duty, looking straight at us, the three of us. "Good morning," we said. Absolute silence. "Maycock," said my mate, "no one's replied." "Well, *we* don't say hello to them tomorrow," I said.

Tony Gill was one of the minority of the men in this study who came not as transport industry recruits but as men taking their own chances with British employment once they got here. He told of his reception in June 1960:

> I'd never been unemployed a day in my life. So that very first day, a Monday, I went down to the place . . . with all the notices, you know . . . oh . . . ["the Labour Exchange?"] *Yes,* and that afternoon I had my first interview. I passed it, for an electrician. I asked, "Can I have the job?" The man was noncommittal, just said, "Go off and join the union." So I did but I thought he meant no, so next day I went off for a second job, passed the interview again, got on well with the interviewer. And at the end he said—and he seemed straight with me, he was a nice honest man—he said, "I'd give you the job, but they'll not have you work with them. You're the first black man we've had here, they won't like it, it'll be tough on you. It's not me, it's them. . . . " I believed him, he was a fair man, so I didn't take up the job.[5]
>
> Back to the Labour Exchange, the third day. There was a job on BR [British Railways]. Went down to the Kentish Town offices for the interview. Did well in the electrical test. Then I passed the medical. "You can have the job." It was at Cricklewood sheds. They all threatened to strike, I was the first black man there as an electrician. Cleaners were okay—but not an elec-

trician. But the overseer didn't back down, and they did. And we gradually got to be mates, Alf, and Alan (he's dead now, poor chap). And they told me later they'd thought I'd be a savage. When I talked about Barbados and I told 'em I lived in a proper, separate house on its own little bit of ground and how bad it was now, here, to have to live in just a room, they were surprised. They were so *ignorant*. Now, I don't bear a grudge, I understood how they feel, I don't let it get to me.

Oh, and a week or so later the first job fella phoned and offered me the job—too late!

C. Wright Mills termed it "the sociological imagination": that people may "grasp what is happening to themselves as minute points of the intersection of biography and history within society."[6] A novelist can weave a satisfying pattern out of the events of world history impinging on individual lives and can contrive (as the reader willingly suspends disbelief) their neat concatenation in works such as O. Manning's *Balkan Trilogy,* J. G. Ballard's *Empire of the Sun,* or Salman Rushdie's *Midnight's Children.*[7] In the average real-world life, the intersections are likely to be more partial, less pointed, less symmetrical. Yet as I pursued this study I kept on being led to view those whom I was interviewing in terms of this intersection. The choices made by these persons were in varying ways both broadened and constrained by the historical moment. They were actors allowed a certain deviation from the script written by context. This has been well put by Bonham Richardson in his study of the migration of Caribbean islanders from St. Kitts and Nevis. Talking of the various journeyings of a pseudonymous "Isaac Caines," Richardson wrote, "Caines is a real person, and to point out gratuitously that his case is 'typical' detracts from the individual tenacity, resilience, and aggressiveness that he has shown throughout his life."[8] Nice sentiments; but still, one must resist the temptation to romanticize the triumph of pluck, of caricaturing the interviewees' strivings in some morality play whereby the immigrant's virtue overcometh adversity. But neither should one take too much away from them—to a degree they have through fortitude *made* their chances.

I see Mills's intersection in my own life trajectory too. I am almost precisely a "Midnight's child," born in the spring of 1947, my life coinciding with the era of decolonization. It also coincides with the creation of a significantly multiracial society in a Britain sliding all the while down the world power standings. Childhood memories can take on a certain significance in this light. There was, for example, Archdeacon Jadesimi. While in their twenties my parents had, separately, gone out to the then-British colony of Nigeria to work for an Anglican missionary body. They met and married there, but soon returned to England and eventually set up home in Kent. Twenty or more years later a number of young Yoruba churchpeople they had known were rising in the hierarchy and, in Britain for a conference or whatever, they occasionally visited us in Margate. Such was Jadesimi: the first African a little English boy had ever seen. In the family photo album I, aged five or six, am sitting on his knee. While everyone else looks at the camera, I stare up with admiration outweighed by a frank fascination, into this very black face with its astounding smile.

When I think back, trying to recapture the "golden weather" of childhood, I find a number of names, proper nouns mostly, lodged in my memory. Names from the six o'clock radio news as we ate our tea. Names unrelated to each other; names without pattern, nodules randomly strewn across the sandy floor of a child's mind: Suez, Woomera, General Grivas, Duncan Edwards and Munich, Mr. Nkrumah, Roger Bannister, Lady Docker, Mau Mau, skiffle-group, Wolfenden, Group Captain Peter Townsend, Sputnik . . . and color bar and Notting Hill. When I asked my parents what "color bar" (or, as I well remember, "working class") meant, I was fobbed off; my mother said it was not something we talked about, dear. The Notting Hill antiblack riots coincided precisely with my leaving my neighborhood primary school to go at the end of the 1958 summer to the high school four miles distant. While my preoccupations were getting my new dark-green school uniform, learning how to knot my Junior House tie correctly, and wondering about how and when and with whom to catch the public bus to Ramsgate or how grave an error it would be to run late into Mr. Thompson's French class, a number of the Barbadians were running for their lives in Notting Hill. Joan Springer, then aged twenty-three, recalls:

> We came out at Ladbroke Grove Station (we'd both been working late shifts that evening on the Transport). The whole crowd was shouting. There were two or three policemen outside. I was never so scared in all my life. "Get that yellow nigger," they shouted at Frank.[9] They was after him, not interested in me. The police was with us for a bit, got us through the thick crowd. *Then they left us.* My God, he ran and ran. I only found out later that he'd beaten them to his room and got the door closed. I wasn't so fast. They surrounded me [on the front steps of a house]. Then white people opened the door, the woman called me in, they called the police 999, they're good people, they saved me, I could've been robbed, gang-raped. I was crying. They would've cut Frankie to pieces [she pauses, collects herself, then adds with a laugh] Oh, I was really cross with him! [for leaving her behind in his escape]. It was the worst experience I've

ever had [pauses]. So, you see, the white woman helped me, there's good and bad: I give as I find.

I remind myself again, while this was going on only seventy-five miles away, I was walking nervously for the first time through the arched entrance to Ramsgate boys' grammar school. And here the ethnic homogeneity that had so strikingly marked my local primary school began to become a little less evident. For the first time there were Roman Catholics in the same class as I (they'd had their own primary school in Margate). I also encountered a sprinkling of Jewish and of Greek Cypriot fellow pupils; a Hungarian or two; and Diaz, who was, they said, "Sinhalese," whatever that meant. He and I played on the same school sports teams and, speaking in the same East Kent accents as I, he never seemed as odd as Andy Guard, who had come to our school from Barnstaple and so spoke with a marked Devonian burr. This was a virtually totally white world in which I was raised. I well remember as a fifteen-year-old schoolboy trainspotter sneaking without permission into Feltham steam engine sheds in west London. Climbing over an ash pile at a discreet distance away from the foreman's office, I suddenly came upon a black laborer in railway overalls snoozing in the sun. I stopped dead in my tracks for a few seconds. Then with elaborate care I tiptoed as quietly as I could through the clinker to flee this entirely unexpected, alien, and indeed frightening black man. Why the fear? Because I was trespassing there, yes. But also because I had hardly ever seen any "negro" before—as far as I am aware there weren't any then among Margate's 50,000 inhabitants. He might be dangerous.

This was July 1962. July 1962 was also the month when, after prolonged and sometimes highly emotional debate, the Commonwealth Immigrants Act was put into effect, banning most further black entry into the United Kingdom. Coincident with my starting school in the early 1950s, then, had been the beginnings of considerable black influx to Britain. That is, at the selfsame time I had been going to de facto all-white schools, British authorities had been bringing into my all-white universe black people such as those in this book. Coincident with my entering the academic high school in 1958, the Notting Hill white riots had occurred: a benchmark in the history of British race relations. And then, coincident with my moving in summer 1962 into the upper school—in other words, the decision having been made to prepare me for university entrance—came the ending of the free flow, by right, of Barbadians to Britain. They interpreted this as a clear indication that they were not welcome. The immigration laws of Britain, their transatlantic country of destination, dealt with them in ways very different from the way immigration laws, a decade later, dealt with me: they made me feel welcome indeed in my first transatlantic country of destination, Canada.

The year 1962 was also the year we got our first television set. This acquisition nourished curiosity about current international affairs and brought a degree of awareness—albeit not grounded in any experience of my own—that not all the actors on the world stage were white like me. Nevertheless, "race" was evidently something that happened mainly elsewhere. By 1962, vaguely recalled fusses over "Sharpeville" and over our prime minister's "Winds of Change" speech in South Africa had died down. By 1962, the TV told us, where "race" really happened was in the United States. Over there in America were brutal armed police and savage-looking police dogs and high-pressure fire hoses and drawling Southern white sheriffs and the oratory of Governor George Wallace and of Reverend Martin Luther King. It was a real ongoing show, a real-life melodrama. It was America where these crassly "prejudiced" white people lived and where racial violence seemed to flare in the city streets.

Truly a different and distant world, the breadth of an ocean away. The TV message came over loud and clear, in the comments of pundits and in the manner of presentation, that in Britain such goings-on were of course inconceivable: we believed in Fair Play; we were not a violent people (save when greatly pushed, as those Germans had found to their cost); we gave everyone, on their merits, pretty well a fair crack of the whip; we were comfortably confident of our liberal fair-mindedness; unlike America, we fortunately had no history of plantation slavery in situ, very few blacks had ever been slaves in Britain; and anyway, the overall number of blacks now in Britain was small. Yet if we were truly so confident, as the media would reassuringly have had us believe, why was it at this very juncture that the Commonwealth Immigrants Act was imposed? This was not a question that would ever have crossed my fifteen-year-old mind.

At university from 1965 the mix of students broadened: a good number of Welshmen (no women in the college at that time), people from the Midlands and the North, a Scot or two, and someone from Belfast—to me almost as much a curiosity as the Maltese, or the schoolteacher "mature student" who was an altogether remarkable fifteen years older than the rest of us. There were also a few elite personages from Nigeria and Pakistan. But my milieu, although it now spoke with an accent different from that of East Kent, was still young, male, and white. A representative of it, in the person of a drunk boat club member late one evening, racially abused our Jamaican law don in the quadrangle. Apologies were made the next day, and nothing more was heard of the incident. My reaction was that this had been rather boorish bad form, but hardly of much significance.

I did not question the structuring of my white male world, I who was a member, an insider. Natural enough to let it go unchallenged; it was the "normal" world.

University over, I left Britain under the auspices of Voluntary Service Overseas, the British Peace Corps. They sent me for just one year to Burundi, but that one year became two, one place led to another, there were two more years in Africa, then came eleven years of uninterrupted residence in various parts of the United States. Finally, at the age of forty, I returned to live in Britain after nineteen years away. Perhaps I should not say "to Britain" but rather "to London." For living in London for the first time in my life now called into question all those monoethnic memories of my Margate youth. In its variety of peoples London felt almost like an American metropolis. It happened that it was in W.11 that we took a flat: Notting Hill, a quarter mile from where Joan Springer in 1958 had been surrounded near Ladbroke Grove Station. Within, I'd say, a one-half mile radius of our street, just casually walking around in September 1987, our first week there, I observed evidence of white and black British, Irish, Serbs, Portuguese, Greeks, Iranians, West Indians, black Africans, Lithuanians, Americans, Cypriots, Indians, Malaysians, Chinese, Pakistanis, and to my eye indeterminate North African or maybe Middle Eastern Muslims. No doubt there were other Europeans, Canadians, Australians, New Zealanders, and white South Africans nearby.

I asked myself, was London, or this part of it, always like this? How accustomed was London, or this part of it, to such "American" diversity? How atypical of Britain were these streets, dog-dirtied, damp, dismal, unprepossessing under grey skies, newspaper-strewn, littered with the grubby white-yellow styrofoam detritus of fast-food outlets, peopled with often down-in-the-mouth damp greyish figures of so many ethnic ancestries?

For many of the Barbadians, London *is* different from elsewhere in Britain. Some of them even went so far as to contrast their settled feelings about London with their uncertainties and insecurities when in other, less cosmopolitan parts of the country, as when, for example, on vacation. Much of England is, if not foreign, at least "other"; whereas London is, if not Barbados, at least "a home." And for most members of the British-raised generation (the Barbadians' children) with whom I spoke, London is unquestionably "home."

"Home"—at first sight so cozy, so comforting, so solid a word—is nevertheless an ambiguous matter for both the Barbadian Londoners and for me. As soon as they and I start to look closely at it, we find that our belongingness to England is problematic. They are dark ex-strangers (though raised in a colonial version of "English" culture) who are now settlers and whose children are native English. I am a white ex-native who is now by preference expatriate, now ever less English; my partner and my child are native-born Americans. Though coming at it from different angles, belongingness to England is for the Barbadian Londoners and for me something that cannot be simply taken for granted. Indeed, during my year's fieldwork in Britain I was forced, perhaps really for the first time, to confront this matter, because during that year I lost my original home.

In July 1988 the house in Margate that my parents had bought in 1939, which was the only house in which I had ever lived until I left to go away to college and then overseas, was sold. My father had died in April 1987. In September I flew over for the year's sojourn in London. For the previous nineteen years since leaving Britain, I could switch on to a sort of automatic pilot once I had landed at Heathrow, and buying just two rail tickets could rock down to Margate in three hours or so. Easy. I was arriving home, a place that was indubitably mine.

Now, however, it had been agreed that my widowed mother should go to live with my sister beyond the far side of London. We put the house on the market. I moved my mother out; my brother and sister paid their final visits and left. A few days later I, having slept the last night on a sheetless bed in a half-empty house, supervised the Monday morning moving crew, and then the house-clearers for auction. By midafternoon I walked out of the door, needless to lock it, leaving it to the new owners. There was still a place in England where my mother lived, yes. But no longer was there my home.

In moments like this few, surely, can sidestep contemplating the course of a life? The loss of home, especially when compounded by the prior loss of a father, compels a certain candor. The unexamined, assured perspective that I had comfortably held of my place in things lost some of its persuasiveness. As the train clattered back toward London, jumbled thoughts elbowed each other. The twin towers of ruined Reculver church, tall where the marshes met the North Sea, seemed particularly symbolic. They demarcated the end of the Isle of Thanet, on which Margate and Ramsgate are situated. The marshes, at whose far side the Norman ruins stood, were once a tidal channel cutting Thanet off from the Kentish mainland. Over the past centuries silting of the channel had rendered Thanet a mere peninsula. So as a child, my surrounding geography was well-defined in that I lived on a promontory. To the north and east, the North Sea, edged by white chalk cliffs. To the south, I could walk two or three miles up gentle slopes to the open skyline of Manston airfield, and there below me again stretched the sea, the English Channel; on particularly clear days— and there were not a few in that clean maritime air—you could just make out the cliffs of France. Only to the west, from this thumb-end of Kent that was Thanet, was there a continuous land surface stretching away across the marshes toward the indistinct Bell Harry tower of Canterbury cathedral, then on into the distance. In most weather, the farthest west you could see from Margate was to Reculver towers. That was the end of my home patch, the beginning of the wider world. To have passed Reculver now this final time, on July 18, 1988, had a Rubicon-like feel.

The taken-for-granted home had now become a container for some household of strangers to occupy. So had the Westerns just been like them, purchasers of a container for a shade less than fifty years, birds of passage who skimmed through Margate in just two generations? This I found difficult to swallow. For me Margate was where the universe began; I therefore had total unquestionable entitlement to it. It was my *omphalos;* nobody could have a claim on it superior to mine. But I began to think: Maybe some people do? At school there were family names that seemed to have been in East Kent from time immemorial: Sackett, Cobb, Chittenden, Fagg, Gore. Western, however, was self-evidently not a name originating in this easternmost extension of southern England.

I looked out the window of the speeding train and saw distant figures strolling on the raised sea wall, silhouetted against the sky. Summer visitors, I presumed. With the vast growth in private car ownership, that sea wall walk, near no railway station, was getting more and more crowded. I imagined myself out there, meeting them. I imagined them asking, "Are you from here?" "Why yes, I've walked these miles in so many weathers, often solitary. Sometimes I've strode here in the tremendous winter winds when there are no visitors like yourselves." Ah, I imply that my entitlement is thereby greater than theirs, almost, indeed, that they trespass. But they respond, "Why do you so presume?" "Because I was born here, here's my house." "Very well, but who lives here now? Do you? No. Do your people? No. So it's no longer yours, is it? You've chosen to leave it—we've chosen to come. So we all stand as equals now: visitors both."

An inquisition such as this I had never contemplated before. I knew my roots, my home place, no one could dispute them. But now I felt a novel unease about my authenticity as a belonger. Doubt had sidled in where before there was none.

Similar doubts had been visited upon the Barbadian Londoners, though to a much more unsettling degree. Those who had come as young people in the late fifties and early sixties had been raised in "the great schoolhouse of Empire." England, they had been taught, was home, and they partook of its reflected glory. "In geography I learned all the English rivers, and I knew all the towns on the railway line from King's Cross to Newcastle." They assumed they would be welcomed in this home, that they had some *entitlement* to it. In Robert Frost's line, "Home is the place where, when you have to go there, they have to take you in." One autumn evening in 1987 some Barbadians and I were discussing contemporary Canadian immigration policy and the prospects of a young family member gaining entry there. Canada was sticky, one said, "because Canada's taking who they want, we've no *right* to go there. But in our day, we were coming to England, we had the right, this was *home.*" And his smile was only partly wry. Or as a Jamaican said to me with a sardonic laugh, "Oh, the Barbadians think they're Englishmen of course!" And one Barbadian said totally unselfconsciously to me: "We're the nearest you can get to an Englishman in a black man." Yet on arrival these Barbadians met—and occasionally are still meeting—a cool rejection, a categorization as strangers, as an unwanted "problem," as people who cannot possibly be allowed to join our England; I mean, just *look* at them.

One Barbadian reaction, after the immediate shock and surprise, was to, as it were, clench the teeth and say, "Rubbish. I know I belong. I won't take this. I have a right to be here. I *am* British, I know it." Such would be my water-off-a-duck's-back reaction to the probing on the Reculver sea wall: "I know I belong. If you dismiss my claims, I dismiss your dismissal."

Suppose, however, that nearly all those I meet consistently and unblinkingly counter my view. They tell me I am now merely a visitor, with no particular entitlement to this place anymore. I continue to dismiss their misguided opinion. But I begin to wonder now, despite my brave assertions; do they have a point? How many times do they have to flatly contradict me before I start to lose my certainties? Five, ten, fifty? Because start to lose my certainties I shall, in face of such denial. And what then? Do I come to modify my claims, reluctantly accept my exclusion, in order to dull the disappointment? Is this how the Barbadian Londoners have reacted to the dusty answer they received when asking—and one or two of them told me they really did, open faces expecting open arms—"Don't we belong in old England?"

Please appreciate that there is no implication here that the Barbadian Londoners whom I met are a sort of walking wounded, bearing psychic stigmata of rejection by white natives every moment of the livelong day. But you might say some of them evidently wear scar tissue, even though those past wounds don't appear to me to be significantly cramping their humanity today. What is indisputable is that the Barbadians have willy-nilly been forced to deal with these questions and uncertainties about geographical belonging, questions I never thought to ask of myself before. Perhaps for me, in order then to do this work, they were misgivings worth experiencing. But again, although such misgivings may have permitted some greater empathy with the Barbadians' experiences in England, one should not make too much of it. For did any of my Thanetian compatriots, any Sackett or Cobb, actually accuse me of no longer belonging and invite me to leave Thanet, or England, forthwith? Of course not.

I had much affection for Thanet. I took it that in some deeply formative sense it was me and I it. But I knew also I had to move on, apprehending the irony that "to live one's life close to home was not to be alive at all." Yet Marshall Berman, whose words these are, in his selfsame essay also celebrates the home of his youth and rails against Robert Moses' Cross-Bronx Expressway that tore through the heart of the home neighborhood.[10] There's the paradox: one cares so unconditionally for one's home—on condition that one is not obliged to remain there. Irresolvable ambiguities such as this seem, indeed, to be near the center of modern experience. "Irresolvable" maybe; but one makes one's choice and votes with one's feet. I quit Margate.

Thus if, as I am, *choosing* to go, then the Sacketts and Cobbs cannot really deny me and wound me anyway. Their sway is only over that which I am voluntarily relinquishing, my point of departure. But what the Barbadians are being denied is not their point of departure, but instead their aim, their goal. Having arrived in London, a number of the interviewees were told "Why don't you leave?" to their faces. "Why don't you go home?" has been leveled publicly by persons like Enoch Powell[11] at the category of "New Commonwealth Immigrant" in general. Also, I am after all *imagining* the hurt I speculate I might feel in such a situation. This is not the same as a Barbadian having felt for real such emotional assaults. Thus, in November 1987 Clive and I are chatting away about this and that. I let drop that perhaps I can see Britain in a different perspective, because I am a sort of stranger now, although once from the United Kingdom.

> "Huh, you've been away nineteen years maybe, but I've been here twenty-four. And you say you don't belong, but you can be back here . . . how long is it?"
> "Two months."
> "Yes, and you belong more than I can."
> "No, I feel it inside, I don't really belong."
> "Okay, not belong then . . . but you're *welcome* here. *I* don't feel that."

This point can be taken a little further. Those among the white English who—formerly overtly, but usually more indirectly nowadays—wish to deny the Barbadians the right to their goal in England, also wish, as seen above, to oblige them to "return home" to the Caribbean. Not only are the Barbadian migrants being denied an England that through their colonial education they'd been persuaded was in some manner "home," but also some of them now sense that the Barbados to which they in this scenario are to be propelled is no longer their "home" either. It has changed, they have changed, maybe they don't belong there anymore.

Conversely, a number of them *do* believe Barbados is ever and always "home," and are acting on that belief. Austin and Marie Pilgrim, for example, will be retired back in Barbados by the time this book sees the light of day. Another Barbadian professional man, in midcareer, told me,

> I can pinpoint the moment when I tensed up when I got back to England [from an overseas trip]. A group of youths walked by, and something about them made me feel I should be watchful. . . . Hell, I don't need this. I'm obliged to think "race" here so much. I don't want my kids to have to fight it.

And he and his young family have returned now to Barbados.

Another West Indian man spoke in this way about not feeling welcome, about not feeling at ease:

> When I walked into a bar in Port of Spain I didn't feel self-conscious. In England I would've walked into any crowded situation like a pub or a club or something and I would always be hesitant. . . . You never know what's going to happen, you never know whether the person who you happen to stand next to, you know, is a rabid racist. That is at the back, and sometimes at the front of your mind, in *all* kinds of social situations, and always puts you on your back foot. You're never as confident as white people are, so you're never working on full, in fourth gear, as it were. . . . In Trinidad there's no problem: everybody's black.[12]

My knee-jerk liberal reaction to this is annoyance, tinged with faint guilt, at how poorly some of my fellow whites behave. There are, however, other reactions to such a tale, ones I had always dismissed as conservative and unworthily exclusionary, but now my Reculver musings had prompted a possible reappraisal. That is, is it not possible to argue that the Sacketts and Cobbs actually *do have* a claim superior to that of the Westerns and the West Indians? Because of the succession of such families in situ, the nurturing and shaping of *our* land, and *our* prospect out over it from the house in *our* name for generations? Are not the labors of *our* ancestors somehow capable of being summed, to make ours a superior claim to belongingness?

> It is we country lords who know the country
> And we know what the country needs.

> It is our country. We care for the country.
> We are the backbone of the nation.[13]

So, don't they almost have the right, if they wish, to make others—like the Trinidadian in the pub or me on the sea wall—feel lacking in entitlement? Don't the white English as a whole have the right to make immigrants feel they are of course not truly English, nor truly welcome?

I had never before appreciated the emotive power of such calls on atavism. I was indeed half-persuaded by them. How to rebut them? I remember a sustained passage in *The Country and the City*. Raymond Williams discourses on the ever-surfacing notion of a past Golden Age of British country life. He leads the reader gently but undeviatingly back from the present, back down the "escalator" into the past, to question whether there ever really was a settled Golden Age. Williams makes me try to think back through the history of his beloved Welsh border, to imagine instances of the acquisition of lands through profiting from or abetting another's ruin, or of abandonment of lands through improvidence, or through a resigned emigration, or through plague or famine, or of extortion or dispossession through violence during recurrent periods of civil unrest or—most basic, inevitably—through the immigrants' dispossession by conquest of the Celts.

> Must we go beyond the Black Death to the beginning of the Game Laws, or to the time of Magna Carta, when Innocent III writes: "the serf serves; terrified with threats, wearied by corvees, afflicted with blows, despoiled of his possessions?" Or shall we find the timeless rhythm in Domesday, when four men out of five are villeins, bordars, cotters or slaves? Or in a free Saxon world before what was later seen as the Norman rape and yoke? In a Celtic world, before the Saxons came up the rivers? In an Iberian world, before the Celts came, with their gilded barbarism? Where indeed shall we go, before the escalator stops?
> One answer, of course, is Eden . . . [14]

When the matter is framed in such terms, who can argue with Proudhon's "Property is theft"? No one anywhere can possess infinite moral foundations to any rights of property or belonging, be they in Britain or (to take some contentious current cases) in Kosovo or in Palestine . . . or in upstate New York. Where I am writing now, the deeds of the property that my house occupies go back to 1790. Nothing prior to that, because the prior occupiers of this tract—who would never have denoted themselves its "owners"—were the Onondaga Nation, central component of the Iroquois Confederacy. During the American War of Independence they perceived, understandably enough, their interest to lie with the

British government rather than with the expansionist, land-seeking colonists. They picked the losing side, their villages were destroyed by the American General Sullivan's expedition of 1779, their granaries and fields and orchards were laid waste, they retreated to Upper Canada. Today I myself am unarguably a beneficiary of *uti possidetis:* to the victor the spoils, the right of possession by conquest. And so in turn that may have been the case with the Onondaga; I don't know. Perhaps it is always the case. Are there *any* peoples "native" in situ from the very beginning?

It seems little more than simply the putting of a different gloss on Raymond Williams's insight to see his preceding passage in terms of belonging, of entitlement to place. There was never any Golden Age, nor was there ever any once-for-all determination of uncontested, settled belongingness. Far enough back, we are all immigrants. Ultimately, none of us can claim uncontested belongingness—just as, far enough forward, none of us can have and hold it forever.

There is another argument, upon less philosophical, less absolutist grounds, against the superior claims of landowning lineage, against the Sacketts and the Cobbs, and by extension, against the superior claims of the "native" white English. On their behalf, it is asserted solemnly that over a thousand years or so an island culture has been created in Britain, a culture of continuity, not to be tampered with. It is a completed work, it is as we the indigenes would have it. As the *Daily Telegraph,* long a vehicle for such sentiments, editorialized under the heading "Races Apart" on May 17, 1989, "In a nation with as specific a culture as ours, racial differences are bound to be pointed up." An interesting code word, "specific." It implies distinctively native, in contrast to those alien influences—as especially, visibly symbolized by the influx of darker-skinned, "racially different" peoples since World War II—that cannot possibly be accorded a place of equal honor or power in the national culture. It has been by emphasizing the "thousand years" theme that a New Racism (as Martin Barker's[15] dissection has termed it) is able to exclude from consideration as authentically British any recent cultural admixture.

Such assertions can, however, be eroded. First, many commentators have observed that so much of what we today tend to term "traditional" in British culture was formulated, if not in part invented, in the mid- and late Victorian period. This was a time when there was (*pace* Peter Fryer's *Staying Power*[16]) virtually no black presence in British life in Britain. Or perhaps one should say that there was virtually no *recognition* of a black presence in Britain. But the point remains that, during this formative period of what is contemporarily viewed as "traditional" British culture, blacks did not get a look in. However, the very fact that traditional British culture did not just "happen," but, as historians show us, that political, economic, and social interests were partly successful in molding it, means that we can mold it again, surely? Culture is plastic, malleable. So—if we deem it to be a worthy national enterprise—we can recreate a new *inclusive* British tradition.

There exist, then, makers and would-be makers of both white (the New Racism) and black British culture. One could hypothesize further: Are not native-born young British blacks now making in concert (sometimes literally) with native-born young British whites a new British culture, one that is not necessarily color-specific? Simply by their presence in places they have not previously inhabited, are blacks ceasing to be oddities and becoming, say, Londoners? Blacks have since the 1950s changed British culture and will continue so to do, ever more ubiquitous on TV screens or in Parliament or on professional soccer teams or as principal actors in the Royal Shakespeare Company or whatever.

Yet these immediately preceding sentences have a ring very similar to that of the liberal consensual views of the 1950s and 1960s Establishment, in whose political culture I was raised and to which I suppose I rather unquestioningly aspired. It was felt that with the passage of time blacks would gently become ever more accepted, ever more included, ever more (in the word of the day) *integrated.* There was no certainty within the Establishment about actually having to *do* anything in particular (except to limit black incoming numbers!), no special programs needed to be mandated; leave it to British good sense and tolerance: a hopeful and in part paternalistic attitude. One of the Barbadian interviewees had thought about these issues a great deal, and although acknowledging some attempt on the part of the British government at "positive" intervention, offered this critique:

> "Of course the government put in those race relations laws later in the 1960s, but you can't simply legislate a change of attitude. And they keep the CRE [the quango[17] Commission for Racial Equality] toothless. We're just going to have to convince this country that it's a multicultural one now. What we need is education, I mean *propaganda* . . . "
> I interject: "You mean, to value the variety?"
> "Yes . . . the battle is on the cultural front now . . . "

To recapitulate, I have tried to counter the claims of the long-established to superior Britishness. A first attempt at rebuttal used Raymond Williams's depiction of an ever-retreating horizon as one searches for that upon which one might erect the notion of any settled belongingness. That is, all cultural structures are built upon shifting sands; there are no unquestionable Britons. A second attempt at rebuttal attacked the notion of British culture as an unchanging, traditional, ancient given; there is no unquestionable unity called "Britishness." But there is still lingering doubt in me; enough remains of the undeviatingly conventional English upbringing I received to somehow ruefully respect the poise that apparently comes with lineage—rather as so many of the British respect, for some reason, their originally German royal family. Of one tier down from that aristocratic summit, Virginia Woolf wrote in *Mrs. Dalloway:*

> Lady Bruton raised the carnations, holding them rather stiffly with much the same attitude with which the General held the scroll in the picture behind her; she remained fixed, tranced. Which was she now, the General's great-granddaughter? great-great-granddaughter? Richard Dalloway asked himself. Sir Roderick, Sir Miles, Sir Talbot—that was it. It was remarkable how in that family the likeness persisted in the women. She should have been a general of dragoons herself. And Richard would have served under her, cheerfully; he had the greatest respect for her; he cherished these romantic views about well-set-up old women of pedigree, . . . He knew her country. He knew her people.[18]

Such sentiments still contribute a not insignificant current to British cultural thinking. For myself, raised in Margate, consider that a Zaket (= Sackett) is mentioned in the twelfth century at neighboring St. Peter's church. Do I not reluctantly acknowledge, just a little, that somehow those with many generations of living in Thanet behind them *do* have a greater claim on it than I? At the larger scale of Britain, I find myself comfortably familiar with the assertions of Nathan Glazer when he writes that the making of the British people was substantially complete by the twelfth century, and that the later limited additions of Flemings or Jews or Huguenots or Italians resulted in no marked transformation of the British into whom the arrivals merged. So Glazer invites us to "sympathize" with the Western Europeans in their wrestlings with a multicultural present of which they had no premonition:

> Should one expect the ancient countries of Western Europe— densely populated as they are, and with historic traditions that link them for many centuries with one ethnic group, of one language—to achieve any such simple solution to the questions of the legal status of peoples of very different race, religion, culture, and history? The Western European concept of *nation,* which has spread all too easily and without analysis to the rest of the world, implies a state with a homogeneous population, sharing a common history, a sense of common descent from revered ancestors, common institutions, generally a common language.

Much of European history has involved the effort, through war and rebellion, to forge such nation-states, bringing together into a single political entity the members of the common nation-family, expelling those who do not belong. How does such a nation-state accommodate to the permanent presence of large communities of people who share none of these commonalities?[19]

Glazer implies that we should not then be surprised—although he certainly does not condone—when the Western European nations prove difficult soil for darker-skinned immigrants. However, in the British case the arrival of Caribbean migrants does *not* raise the specter of any profound cultural conflict à la Glazer. To reiterate, one deals here with persons who have been raised in a quasi-British cultural milieu. So the concordance between cultural differences and racial (i.e., phenotypic) differences, which the previously cited *Daily Telegraph* editorial directly implied, is in fact vastly misleading if one is speaking of Afro-Caribbean people. And of all the formerly British Caribbean islands, none is more British than Barbados. Both Barbadians and non-Barbadian West Indians will tell you this, though likely with rather different imputations: the Barbadians with pride and satisfaction, the others with mirth and exasperation. "Bimshire" was the nickname a British planter long ago gave to Barbados, because it seemed in some ways so like just another English county. The name has stuck. Not without a certain wry humor, the publication that is reckoned probably the best literary "little magazine" in the English-speaking Caribbean, and that comes out of Bridgetown, Barbados, is named *Bim.* Said one successful businessman,

> "You must appreciate the Englishness of the Barbadian. That's why we can love the English despite the hassles. We are what we are."
> "But it was forced on you against your will originally," I said; "yet are you saying it *is* you now?"
> "Of course. . . . We're us. What do you want us to be? Spaniards? French? No. Why should we change? Nobody's going to force us to change again, oh no . . . "[20]

When I went to see each of the households for a final time in August 1988, I said the next time they would see me I hoped it would be with this book under my arm for them, in which some of their words would be printed. This was premature: I made a brief visit to London in May 1989 during which I was able to see some of them again, but the book was scarcely begun. The striking thing for me about this week-long stay, however, was that for the first time I paid no visit to Margate. I stayed at the house of my sister and mother. It was like treading water. I was within reach of shore, it seemed, but I couldn't stretch my feet down far enough to touch firm sand. Treading water was fine in a way. I felt adept at it, I was confident no "harm" would come to me. But there was no longer a bedrock foundation. It was a curious sensation.

It was, however, hardly a debilitating sensation. I would imagine that much more inimical to one's self-confidence, to one's equilibrium, is the sensation of a lack of *cultural* bedrock of one's own. As a close Barbadian friend confided, "John, you know, there's this whole Cultural Orphan thing." Or as a young black British woman interviewed on BBC radio in May 1988 said:

> Sometimes I fear for the future in this country. It's a cultural fu-
> ture that I fear for. It's to do with in order to survive people
> have to compromise, and, in that adapting, certain things are get-
> ting lost. In order to completely survive have they got to com-
> pletely get rid of everything that is West Indian?

Then, after pondering that, for a white English person, cultural roots can be looked back to for hundreds of years, she continued:

> [They have] a heritage that you're steeped in from the moment
> you're born. To be a black person of Afro-Caribbean descent in
> this country is totally different, so what you have are a whole
> group of people over here who are possibly busily trying to for-
> get the fact that they're Caribbean, I don't know . . . um . . .
> um . . . and happily trying to create this group called Black
> British, because their Caribbeanness is slavery, and who wants to
> remember that?[21]

Once again, however, I want no imputation here that British people of Afro-Caribbean provenance are thereby psychic walking wounded, immobilized by cultural confusion. There is resilience and sanity in the people I met. One keeps going, one deals with the world sometimes with stoicism, sometimes with humor. Austin Pilgrim, now risen to manager at one of central London's premier Underground stations, just gets on with his life—with humor and with occasional opportunities to turn the tables.

> I tell my son there're good and bad things about being black.
> The bad I've told you enough of: the insults, the exclusion from
> dances, the "go back to where you belong," the fights. The good
> is the fun you can have. I'm the manager of my Tube station, but
> when people come to complain they come into the office and
> look around and see my white lineman or inspector or whatever
> and always talk to *him*. So I'll just walk off fast down the plat-
> form and then I'll hear them behind me shouting "Hey!" and I'm

deaf you see [with a wide, wicked grin] and they'll have to run after me!

My choice above of the words "resilience and sanity" to characterize blacks whom I met does have its dangers, however. All the interviewees have been stressed by racism to some degree or other. "As a result," wrote Frank Springer,

> like chameleons they [Barbadians] easily conform and merge with any neighbourhood criteria that they happen to live in. This art of neighbourhood adaptability allows them to travel the avenue of survival by being so discreet and inconspicuous that no one is even aware that they exist. We Bajans wear our mask of affability well. We smile a lot, which is a remarkable quality to mask our true feelings,[22] and this complexity of our personality gives me a mild form of schizophrenia.

No, I have not been subjected by racism to the psychic pressures the interviewees have undergone. Do I, then, have any right to attempt cheerily to discount reports such as that which appeared on January 25, 1990, in the *Independent*?

> Recent studies suggest that the incidence of schizophrenia could be 16 times higher among second-generation Afro-Caribbeans than their white peers. [And at the conference in question] a consultant psychiatrist said, "If this research and the diagnoses are correct, the most likely explanation is the socio-economic disadvantage, racial harassment and disappointed expectations experienced by Afro-Caribbeans."

One walks an authorial tightrope here. On the one hand, there is a strong urge to align oneself with the rejection of what in the United States pioneering black folklorist Zora Neale Hurston termed "sad negro stories"[23]—a rejection paralleled, for example, by Salo Baron's disdain for that "lachrymose conception of Jewish history" that harps on diaspora, inquisition, pogrom, and holocaust.[24] There is it seems to me a strong strain of the lachrymose—along with the angry and the hurt—in the general British racial discourse: blacks as losers, blacks as problem. (I remember my first, and naïve, reaction was one of amazement when on a race-relations expert's bookshelves I spied the title *Positive Images of Black People,* being a catalog for, I think, a 1984–85 photographic exhibition in Birmingham.) Yes, I wish to counter such inherent presupposition, and my experience with the particular interviewees I met does counter it.

On the other hand, who can deny the facts of black disadvantage in contemporary Britain? And is there not the danger of romantically ennobling the victorious struggle that those I met must have had in order to achieve their present, apparently unrepresentative measure of relative success? "Sweet are the uses of adversity," indeed. With little exaggeration, one could say that these particular families seem almost to have achieved the "American dream" . . . but they've achieved it in England, where most inhabitants would not empathize with so odd a tale of immigrant strivings. Orville Alleyne, resident in Britain for twenty-six years, had some misgivings about the researcher I might prove to be, were I too inclined to find good in everything. "Why are you doing this work?" Orville asked me at our second meeting. I explained that the Barbadian element was chance, but that the "relatively successful" element was intended. He then questioned the wisdom of choosing this latter stratum from among British Afro-Caribbeans:

"You're worried that it's not the full picture?" I responded.
"Yes, I suppose, in a way."
"Too rosy?"
"*Yes,* that's it."
"But isn't there a negative stereotype of black people in England, and couldn't this serve as an antidote?"
"Yes," replied Orville. "But on the other hand it could be used by the Thatcherites to say, 'There, you see, there's nothing wrong that individual hard work can't get you over. Color makes no difference.' "
"*That's it!*" interjects Pauline.
"But I do agree," continues Orville, "that not enough's been done on it, or I haven't heard of it."
"And he's the reader, too," says Pauline.
"No," Orville went on in response to my query, " . . . er . . . I don't mind a white person doing it. But you can't *feel* it the way we do . . . "

As I conclude this introductory chapter, I would like to state my hope that my own autobiographical intrusion does not jar. Knowing that such authorial visibility may strike academic readers in particular as a little unusual, I wish to take a conciliatory stance toward them, but without being too apologetic for presenting my findings in this mode. This is an attempt at a responsible, living report about Barbadian people who inhabited various parts of London in the late 1980s, how they felt about it, about themselves, their families, their past, their future, their "home." Certainly I am involved with these persons, and it is I who am writing the report, so that's one reason why there's been quite a bit of me in this first chapter.

More importantly, however, I assert again that their experience is not some curious, freakish one, but one in which we all partake, myself included. The dissection of some of the features of my own life is meant to illustrate this point more vividly—I certainly did not embark upon this study with any navel-contemplating intent, but found the interviewees' lives, as it were, insisting upon some increased measure of self-awareness from me. It is true that many if not most British readers may not feel themselves immediately challenged by the cultural conflicts, complexities, and ambiguities experienced by the people of this study. For many if not most American or Canadian readers, however—given their countries' more recent and more multiethnic societal mix—the Barbadians are not particularly strange. And given what the future may well bring, the Barbadian Londoners may indeed turn out to be resoundingly normal. Going through a draft of this study as the proverbial "intelligent layman," an American friend of Italian-Alsatian ethnicity who is now rising high in the law, enthused with just a little hyperbole, "These Barbadians are the pioneers of the twenty-first century!"

Two
The Island Relinquished

. . . *We were English. Colonial, overseas and overseered English.*

Austin Clarke, *Growing Up Stupid Under the Union Jack*

By this study's very definition, all of the immigrant-generation interviewees, with the exception of one Jamaican-born wife, were native Barbadians. Their childhoods spanned the latter part of the 1930s and the 1940s. It was a period of economic depression, yet childhood memories are ever a pleasure to savor. Trevor Brathwaite evidently enjoyed reminiscing about his boyhood duties, although at the time they must have been onerous.

> We lived at St. Davids, in the country, in Christ Church parish. My father did gardening and butlering for an English gentleman, very rich, in Christ Church. He [father] would take our sheep out at four o'clock, graze them three or four miles away, then he'd wake me at six when he went off to work, I had to get 'em back before school at nine. If you were late to school, you got lashes. I was the oldest son, so I had to take the stock out to graze in the evening again—but I could play at the same time. I had to get grass for the sheep to eat at night, too.

Spare the rod and spoil the child was an injunction heeded. Audley Simmons considers that

> it's different then to nowadays. If my parents were out of the house in Barbados, my eldest brother was the gaffer. If I misbehaved, he'd tell my parents the instant they got in the door. They'd hit you first, then ask questions. These days you can't get

27

anything out of the kids, they stick together, won't tell. There's less discipline than there was.

School days are remembered vividly. Schooling was one of the foundation stones of the British Empire; here one learned to be content with and proud of one's colonial station. D'Arcy Holder recalls:

Barbados is a good island. Of course I'm proud of it. The first reason is our good education. I only got primary school but it was a *solid* base. I was surprised when I got here to find my education was better than some of the English people I worked with! I had thought all English people must be wonderfully educated. All our top people had been to England to get education, doctors, lawyers, teachers, politicians. When I was a child you'd pick anything up, a knife, a bowl: "Made in England" it'd say, nine times out of ten; one time, maybe Hong Kong. I thought, this must be a great place, this England. Must be a big powerful country, full of well-educated people. People six feet tall (most Bajans weren't that tall, least not in my day).

Or Frank Springer:

We were brought up on all that English literature, you know, Shakespeare, *As You Like It, Julius Caesar,* and *She Stoops to Conquer* and *The Rivals.* . . . and British radio too, we used to listen to "Much Binding in the Marsh," and Dick Bentley.

Audley Simmons again:

We were brought up so English. When we got here, I was amazed in the cinema at the end of the film, we were the only ones who stood still for the playing of "God Save the Queen." Everyone else was rushing for the exits!

Or, Jeff Bannister and I are philosophizing away about British society one summer evening in his Enfield home. Up comes the subject of class, and with it the British royal family. He observes:

"As long as they're up there, we'll have this class thing here in Britain."
I said, "My sister-in-law from America's just come here, her first ever trip outside the States. We took her to Windsor Castle. You know what she said? 'It makes you feel so poor!' "
"Yes, but at least they looked like you, if you were poor English. We were brought up on the royal family too, you know. But they were so far off, up there."
"Unattainable, you mean?"

"Yes."

"Because they were white?"

"Well, um, I don't think I actually consciously thought in those terms, but yes . . . that has to be it."

"There's an American singer called Bette Midler who once came out with the line that the Queen of England's the whitest woman in the world!"

Jeff Bannister roared his approval of that.

Barbados is conventionally referred to as the "most English" of the former British territories in the Caribbean. Originally inhabited by Arawaks, the Amerindian people had apparently abandoned the island by the time the Portuguese visited it in 1536. The Portuguese did not tarry, although it was they who gave the island the name that has stuck: Los Barbados, after the bearded fig trees growing there. Barbados remained uninhabited until 1627, when a British expedition actually settled the island. Despite the varying fortunes of war in the numerous subsequent conflicts in the Caribbean, Barbados was never seized or annexed by any of the other European colonial powers, and remained under the British flag without interruption until independence in November 1966.

Barbados was founded by white settlers growing cotton and tobacco on smallholdings, their numbers augmented by indentured servants. But within twenty years it became clear that greater profit might accrue from large-scale sugar cane monoculture, cultivated by imported West African slaves. In 1643 there had been over 37,000 white colonists, but only 6,000 blacks. A score of years later, white numbers fell to below 25,000—smallholding whites were more or less pushed out to other parts of the Caribbean and to the American colonies, and were among the founders of South Carolina—whereas there were 50,000 black slaves, a more than eightfold rise. The reduced number of whites, now more of a plantocracy, were nevertheless able to maintain local self-government through the House of Assembly that had been established in 1639 during the period of white smallholder settlement. Despite the shadow of slave insurrections (as in 1816), the coming of emancipation in the years 1834 to 1838 did not bring the fearfully anticipated collapse into chaos. A qualified franchise had been extended to free persons of color in 1831, and the plantocracy found itself having gradually to share power with a mulatto elite.

Not all whites, however, became as a matter of course either members or auxiliaries of a resource-holding plantocracy. Some of the former indentured servants remained impoverished and became almost a sort of depressed rural underclass, referred to slightingly by other Barbadians as "Red Legs" and alleged to possess all those morally degenerate character-

istics of feckless, shameless laziness attributed so widely throughout the
ex-colonial world to ex-slaves. Indeed, they were *worse* than the slaves,
because,

> the greatest part of them live in a state of complete idleness, and
> are usually ignorant and debauched to the last degree. . . . It is
> notorious that in many cases whole families of these "free
> whites" depend for their subsistence on the charity of the slaves.
> Yet, they are as proud as Lucifer himself, and in virtue of their
> freckled ditchwater faces consider themselves on a level with ev-
> ery gentleman in the island.[1]

Today some "Red Legs" still live in poverty in the eastern St. Joseph and
St. John parishes,[2] variously exciting fascination or providing employment for

> social anthropologists, historians, novelists, race relations experts,
> and culture-oriented tourists alike. They are seen as living empiri-
> cal evidence that in slave society, a white skin did not necessarily
> symbolize wealth, power, and status.[3]

Not *necessarily*, no. But the main current of island history and societal
development was nevertheless the more familiar postslavery one of white
privilege progressively yielding political power under pressure, while
striving to maintain a vastly extraproportionate economic and social
clout. Despite long-term tensions and a number of crises, Barbados was
able in this context to sustain self-government, unlike the other British
Caribbean territories (such as Jamaica) where the whites were proportion-
ately fewer, and which regressed to direct Colonial Office rule from London. With the passage of time, voting qualifications were lowered until in
1951 and 1963 universal adult franchise was achieved. Whatever the
myriad racial and economic injustices that this bland constitutional recitation of gradual enfranchisement masks—and even though civil unrest
erupted in 1876 and 1937—the fact remains that for the past 150 years an
island society that might prima facie seem to have enormous potential for
communal violence seems to have avoided it.

The Barbadians I met were very proud of this and took it for a mark
of their superiority and greater political maturity. The themes of loyalty
to the Crown (Barbadians were prominent in the police forces throughout
the British West Indies territories), steadiness in time of crisis, and
evolution-not-revolution were taught in the schools during the colonial
era—and thus to the interviewees: most were quite unembarrassed by the
honor they counted it to have been only and always under the Union Jack.
(It almost seems as though the Shavian label "John Bull's other island"

might just as well have been affixed to Barbados as to Ireland.) These conservative themes are still taught in an independent Barbados, albeit in modified form. Barbadian children learn of the wisdom, "character," stability, and moderation that are their island's claimed hallmarks, and are still instructed that, after the Westminster Parliament and the Bermuda House of Assembly, Barbados has the distinction of possessing the third oldest House of Assembly in the Commonwealth. D'Arcy Holder again:

> Barbados is good because politics have been democratic, not violent. . . . Oh, but we were brought up on the Empire. "Little England," they used to call us. You know about the telegram when the war started?
> [This is the telegram alleged to have been sent to Neville Chamberlain on September 3, 1939, by the Barbados legislature saying, "Stand firm, England; Barbados is behind you"! It's a grand story.]
> And I was taught all *three* verses of *God Save the King.*
> [I can vaguely recall bits of verse two, but D'Arcy recites all three, with a hint of mock gravitas.]
> And *Hearts of Oak,* ah yes, "tis to glory we steer."
> [Parody is intruding more evidently now, with Cockspur Five Star rum on the rocks rendering us ever more jocular.]
> And our Nelson in Trafalgar Square in Barbados is older than *this* one in Trafalgar Square in London!
> [I recall in 1985 meeting in Barbados an eminent local (black) historian. I asked, I hope not superciliously, for what reason did a statue of Nelson—whose daring naval deeds long preceded the abolition of slavery—still stand at the island's symbolic center? The historian replied as if it were obvious: "Why, he saved us from the French"! . . . One could only agree.]

Among other islanders Barbadians seem to have a reputation of being too acquiescent to white superiority, of being culpably inert in the face of the evidently still lingering colonial-era pyramid of social prestige. Jeff Bannister recounts how he was taken aback:

> "I'm not sure how these things take root, but d'you know I was talking about three years ago at a GPO [Post Office] evening course with a Jamaican woman—I mean, she's British, but of Jamaican parentage, I can't say if she was born there—and she says to me, 'Why are you Barbadians so downtrodden, why don't you stand up for yourselves?' 'What on earth do you mean?' And it seems she thinks we're all Uncle Toms and that in Barbados the whites are high—she knew we had whites in

Barbados—and the blacks are low and that's that. It was if we were like South Africa!"

"But the Yacht Club," said I.

"Well, that's just a leftover from the colonial past."

"Yes, but such leftovers aren't permitted in Cuba or Jamaica, are they? So why in Barbados?"

"But things *have* changed so much in the last thirty years, really."

Whatever the degree of truth in such allegations, a geographer could very quickly conceive of some spatial factors that might bear upon the supposedly quiescent ultra-Englishness of Barbadians. That Barbados was always English-held, that it never changed hands after 1627, is not only due to Spain considering it hardly worth notice in comparison to a Hispaniola, a Cuba, or, preeminently, a Mexico. It also surely must to some extent be due to its standing one hundred miles out alone in an Atlantic Ocean prowled by the British Navy. Out beyond the eastern edge of the Caribbean Sea as demarcated by the Antilles, it had no near neighbors, no proximate islands or territories to be held by a covetous rival power; it was no St. Lucia next to a Martinique, no Trinidad next to Venezuela. Again, demonstrably, the island's very geography inhibited successful slave uprisings. First, Barbados is not intervisible with any other island. There's no faint, beckoning promise that one could sail to somewhere free seen far away on the horizon—one might not even know in which direction to bolt. Second, fundamentally, Barbados is both small and relatively flat; it is no volcanic mountain thrusting precipitously up, with large tracts of forest cover remnant on unclearable, rugged terrain. Plantation-fleeing maroons would have fewer places to hide—just some gullies out of which they could eventually be flushed. This was a floating prison house. Today Barbados still has the statistical distinction of being the sovereign state in the world with the highest proportion of its territory in permanent cropland: 77 percent. Unlike the broken mountainous terrain of a much larger island like Jamaica, or even more unlike the Guianas abutting onto the open-ended forests of a contiguous continent, there were in Barbados relatively few successful escapes. The topography itself militated against the establishment of defensible, sustainable, autonomous maroon communities. I do not wish to seem to be supporting the canard of Barbadian quiescence—there were indeed violent slave revolts[4]—but these were episodic, whereas in Jamaica geography facilitated continuous, centuries-long *marronage.* In contrast to the image of Barbadian decorum, surely the oft-alluded-to stereotype of the feisty Jamaican cannot be unrelated to the geographical frame?

Frank Springer, for example, wrote to me of the comparisons he perceived.

> I personally have a strong admiration for the Jamaicans. I don't
> think that the Bajans compare favourably with them. Because
> they are a completely different breed of West Indians. While the
> Bajans remains socially and culturally ambivalent, the Jamaicans is
> out there in the English community waving their flag of cultural
> identity, by refusing to accept the fact that because something is
> deemed impossible, that they should not try it. They are arrogant
> and stubborn enough to rush in, trample on all the taboos with
> volatile aggression. And as a result they succeed admirably against
> all the odds.
>   I personally think that the Bajans who are living in England are
> too conservative to be interesting. . . . The Bajans has a com-
> pletely different set of values [from other West Indians], different
> dispositions, different interests and enthusiasms. They have this
> tendency to conduct their lives at a sophisticated distance by
> avoiding confrontations and controversies.

Let us now return to the interviewees' recollections of their colonial-
era school days. The pecking order in Barbadian schools at that period
was well known. "In my day," said Colin Jemmott, now a successful London travel agent, "the two top schools were Harrison's College, then the
Lodge. They were fee-paying. Whites and mulattos went there, and a
handful of blacks on scholarship." D'Arcy Holder mentioned also that
"rich English boys used to come to Barbados to go to public school,[5] for
whites only: Codrington School. No, not Codrington College, that's theo-
logical." Dotteen Bannister, to whom in August 1988 I had brought
around that morning's *Guardian,* was reading there in the Education
pages a white woman's, Jean Sargeant's, reminiscences of being sent to a
private girls' high school in Barbados. Dotteen observed:

> "Now if you could afford it then black girls could go. But
> hardly anyone did. In fact, we wouldn't think of doing it. I
> mean, even if we could, we didn't, you know what I mean? It
> was custom."
>   "You mean, it was like England in the old days, you 'knew
> your station'?"
>   "That's *exactly* what I mean."

Jean Sargeant herself wrote in the piece in question that the school

> was virtually for whites-only and even more closely modelled on
> traditional English boarding-school lines. Here the headmistress,
> newly arrived from England, even tried to introduce hockey.

. . . The education I received . . . distanced me from the West
Indies, making England, the "Mother Country," the cultural and
educational focus; a form of psychological absenteeism which
reflected the physical absenteeism of the English plantation
owners in earlier times. [Subsequently it has brought home to
me] . . . the Englishness of the education I knew many black
West Indians had been given during the colonial period.[6]

Frank Springer filled out the picture on another occasion:

Harrison's; the Lodge; and Codrington College for divinity. Then
Combermere. All were boys-only. The girls' top one was Queen's
College. Then Lynch started the Modern High School. It was
coeducational (all are now, since Errol Barrow's premiership).
Now these top schools, in colonial days, *had* to have British
headmasters. When the headmaster retired, I remember this, at
Combermere, there was a chap, Frank Collymore, who taught
English, he took over as *acting* headmaster for three years, before they could find another British chap, Major Noot, to take the
job. That was the way it was . . . unthinkable that anyone but a
white man could be head.

Collymore was a *white* Barbadian, which indicates that it was not necessarily, or only, skin color per se that was the barrier to the top job—but
colonial as opposed to British birth and upbringing. Collymore's case, as
another Combermere Old Boy said, illustrated "the belief that excellence
could only be obtained from outside Barbados."

The colonial order was all-pervasive. Of this, Audley Simmons—"Ah
yes, Audley, he's very political," observed a friend of his[7]—was well
aware: "Barbados was very color-conscious. But that's all over the world,
isn't it, with colonialism? It's less than it was in Barbados, but it's still there
under the surface; it'll always be there."

Colin Jemmott, after remarking upon the longtime strength of An-
glicanism in the Barbados of his upbringing, found it led him to a most
wide-ranging consideration of the ramifications of colonial society:

The church made the slaves docile. The English are clever. They
ran their empire by a confidence trick—this little place [England],
all those millions of people around the world! And Barbados is
flat, there's no forest for slaves to escape into, no maroons, so
education when it came, came to all. Everyone got a little, could
read and write.

Another thing about the colonial system. Suppose you adopt a
child. It learns your language, your habits, it looks to you only
for everything. You're the only culture it knows. That's us. We

forgot Africa. I learned Shakespeare at home: "Now, what news on the Rialto?—Why, yet it lives there unchecked, that Antonio hath a ship of rich lading wrecked on the narrow seas. . . . " That's from *The Merchant of Venice.* We were told England was the greatest country in the world. The French were stupid. The Germans cruel. The Japanese couldn't make anything—I mean invent. "British is best." And yet in the canefields the Bedford's axles would break and the American Fords just drove on by.

American qualifications were looked down on, they *had* to be British. Our first Governor-General Dr. Scott[8] had a degree from Howard University—you know that, it's a top university in America—and the English running the civil service in Barbados wouldn't accept him as a doctor, he had to go off to Edinburgh for a year.

We were given an *English* education and so it made us feel inferior, you felt a conflict in you all the time. We came here—like the adopted child—and to our surprise found you wouldn't accept us. We could get very depressed, with a "what are we?" and "who cares about us?" attitude. The only thing the world noticed us for was cricket; we *were* the best at that.

"Cricket's the national game!" enthused George Farley. Cricket assumes an enormously important role for most of the male (and a number of the female) Barbadians of the immigrant generation. As C. L. R. James has pointed out so marvelously in *Beyond a Boundary,* the cricket field—where this, the quintessentially English, game was played—was one place where the chance to best their white masters was given to athletically superlative but "socially desperate" black men. James also writes of one H. B. G. Austin, who "could point to West Indies cricket and say with . . . justification 'This is the house that I built.' . . . the man who has more than any other made West Indies cricket what it is." And who was Austin, this founder of West Indian cricket? A white Barbadian, "undoubtedly a big man in the West Indies. He was the son of a bishop of the West Indies, business tycoon, Senior Member for Bridgetown in the House of Representatives of Barbados, at one time chairman of the Barbados Board of Education, etc., etc."[9] He was later knighted.

Austin was also the captain of the West Indies cricket team, "the natural captain of the West Indies," wrote James, "as long as he chose to play. You took that for granted." Once he retired in the late 1920s, however, the West Indies captaincy *remaining* in white hands became a matter of much dispute. James is celebrated for the agitation he led to have the captaincy conferred upon the most capable player, whatever his race. The reservation of the captaincy for whites denied the outstanding Frank Worrell (himself a Combermere boy) the captaincy until 1960. Worrell, later knighted, was the captain of the 1963 West Indian tour to England. It was arguably one of the finest Test (i.e., international) series ever played . . . along with the West Indies' 1960–61 tour of Australia, which Worrell also captained.

I was a sports-keen teenager in 1963 and went to watch the West Indies play Kent at Canterbury. Prior to coming to London in 1987, of the nineteen years I'd been living abroad, seventeen were in countries where to all intents and purposes cricket was not played; my cricket lay dormant. Yet I was surprised how much I could recall of that 1963 tour, and with how much enthusiasm, once I found the Barbadian men wanted to talk cricket. Seven or eight of the eleven first-team players on the 1963 West Indian side were Barbadians. D'Arcy Holder took up that point.

> "Ah yes, Barbados is the best cricketing island, or was . . . Well, football's coming in now, there's that—but there are more *openings* now in Barbados: TV, business, or whatever. In those days it was only cricket for the ambitious youth. Look how Sobers came up."
>
> "What about Wes Hall—he's a senator now, isn't he?"
>
> "Yes, but now Hall is from a different class—he went to secondary school."

Wesley Hall was one of the most destructive fast bowlers ever to play, was on the 1963 tour, and is currently Minister of Tourism and Sport in Barbados. Garfield Sobers, also on the 1963 tour, was arguably the most gifted all-round player in the history of the game and, with felicitous symbolism, was knighted by Queen Elizabeth II on the Garrison Savannah adjoining Bridgetown, Barbados's capital, in 1976. Given Barbados's claimed preeminence in the game, it is also symbolic that the first full international Test Match between England and the West Indies held in the Caribbean was played at Bridgetown's Kensington Oval[10] in January 1930. A wonderfully atmospheric shot of the era is shown in Figure 1, showing Herman Griffith and Derek Sealy, both of Barbados, going out to bat for the West Indies. Sealy, at seventeen years and four months the youngest player ever to have appeared for the West Indies, scored a most creditable fifty-eight runs; the match was drawn.

The stratifications of a conservative colonial society did indeed find themselves expressed in the local Barbadian cricket scene, as Alan Maycock explained:

> There were sort of first-class and second-class cricket clubs in Barbados in those days. First class were ones which had the better facilities: the "Association" clubs. Some were whites-only: Wanderers,[11] and Pickwick. Others were mulatto: Carlton, and

Figure 1: Barbados, 1930. Griffith and Sealy go out to bat for the West Indies against England

YMPC [Young Men's Progressive Club]. Another mulatto club would let in a proportion of blacks only. Others were black, but upper-class kinds of blacks, people who'd been at secondary school, like Spartan. Then, Empire was not quite so high-class a black club.

The second-class clubs, the lower level of clubs were local village clubs more, without good pitches, unlike the Association clubs. They were the "League" clubs. They were the poor, the working men. Very occasionally someone'd make it up from this lower level to the upper, and it was from the upper that you'd get to the international standard . . . so people like Everton Weekes would come up. And someone saw Garfield Sobers's potential and got him into the Police team, a first-class club, as a bugler in the police band or something! Whereas Wes Hall was a secondary school boy, just behind me at Combermere.

However, pride in Barbados's collective cricketing prowess could with apparently little ado overcome racial or class chauvinism. Unprompted, when discussing the great controversy in the 1950s over the West Indian captaincy, D'Arcy Holder praised John Goddard as "a very fine player": Goddard was a white Barbadian who was also one of the last white captains of the West Indies. Mr. Holder, a black Barbadian, also found words of praise for Roy Marshall, a "sort-of off-white" Barbadian mulatto, who made the grade in English county cricket, playing for Hampshire. (I recalled seeing him play against Kent on a couple of occasions.)

The top positions in government—that of governor, the highest-level civil servant posts—were reserved for the British. The top positions in schools, and even in sports, were reserved for whites. So was the locally top position of Anglican parish priest; the vicar had a lot of sway over people's lives in those days. Asked whether her first name (unfamiliar to me) was a family name, Dotteen Bannister replied:

"No, it wasn't. The vicar gave it me. My parents wanted to call me Naudine, but the vicar said that sounded a bit heathen, so he baptized me Dotteen. There were some other Dotteens around."
"The vicar changed your name?!"
"Oh yes, it was accepted in those days."
"Was he Barbadian?"
"Oh, they were all English in those days! And anyway, my parents and any of my early school friends knew me as Naudine. Everybody in our village knew me by that."

There was no doubt as to which group was at the apex of the social pyramid. Alan Maycock characterizes their interaction with a black such as himself:

Hmm. In Barbados with the whites it was either that they were very colonial, very superior, down-their-noses sort of thing sometimes when you had to talk to them; or else most often you just went your own way—they their way, you yours: no problems.

To use a characteristic Barbadian adjective, the white people were "great," meaning not only eminent, but also dignified, or rather, on their dignity. Blacks were subordinate and comported themselves befittingly. White noblesse oblige was, naturally, widespread. Eulie Eastmond told me,

Mother used to work half-days as housekeeping help to the Carters, a plantation family. The lady said to mum, "I can get her a good housekeeping job, I can put in a word for her." And I said, "I don't want to be a housekeeper." And you know, kids weren't expected to speak up in those days. It embarrassed my mum.

Trevor Brathwaite recalls that as a lad he did gardening

for an English lady. Her husband was the captain of a schooner running from Barbados to Guiana and back, would bring up rice and pineapples, they'd give some to the servants. They had a big house at St. Lawrence, it's been turned into a guest house now. She taught me how to ride a bike, she let me ride round and round on the verandah of the house.

Trevor's wife Beverly, who's now lived with him in west London for over thirty years, recalls that as a young girl she went to be a nanny for various white people.

The last one was an English lady, her husband worked in a bank, she told me a lot about England, to bring warm things, I wrote to them back and forth for a few years when I got here, then it fell away.

And Austin Pilgrim remembers:

"I was doing electricals for Saville, one of those very rich English people. One of the 'Big Six,' we called them in those days."
"A white Barbadian, like the Goddards?" I asked.
"Oh no, the Goddards came up from, well, almost slaves: the

poor, the Red Legs, the Ecky-Beckies." Austin grinned at my star-
tled ignorance of this last uncomplimentary nickname.

"No, these were *Englishmen*. Anyway, he comes up to me and
says, 'D'you know who runs this country, young man?' I was
naïve, so I gave what I thought was the simple answer, the right
answer: 'The government, sir.' 'No,' he said, '*we* run the country,
the six of us.'

"And his wife, oh, she was an utter snob, nose in the air. 'Im-
pignant,' we'd call it—now *there's* a Barbadian adjective for you!
Our firm was doing some rewiring in their big house and had
sent Walcott to do it. 'No,' she shouted, 'I'm not having anyone
so black in my house! Give me another workman.' So they sent
me in. 'He's the whitest we have,' said my boss.''

It goes without saying that black people were lower in the hierarchy.
A Barbadian who had been in Britain twenty-seven years, with whom I
was chatting over a pub lunch, let slip something I assume he'd learned
early on in life: "I mean, as a black I keep to my place." Ernestine Farley,
however, commenting enthusiastically on the changes she sees when she
goes back to Barbados on visits, told me, "Even the people have changed,
they're even employing black people in the banks. People stand up for
themselves now, they're not scared to speak out." And D'Arcy Holder
laughs, saying,

In Barbados there was segregation, we kept separate from whites.
I thought they spoke in a more superior manner than we did until, once I'd been living here, I went back to Barbados and I
heard them and I said "My God, they sound the same!" And I
laughed, too, when I went into our Tourist Bureau, in Kensington High Street it used to be, and a white person behind the desk
opened his mouth and said, "Can I help *yaw?*"—in the broadest
Bajan accent!

In an interstitial position were those people of mixed racial ancestry.
In fact, probably a high proportion of the entire Barbadian population had
some degree of admixture. In Britain they simply looked dark, but in Barbados there was great sensitivity to shades of color. Dotteen Bannister
remarked, "When I left home I was colored; when I got here I was black.
Most of us looked upon ourselves as colored . . . you had to be *dark*
to be called black." There were, however, certain persons whose racially
mixed ancestry was immediately evident, of whom Colin Jemmott spoke:

I'll tell you a thing, another result of slavery: the brownskins. In
the colonial system there'd always be slots, in the banks or whatever, for them, the English made sure of that. I remember at

secondary school they never worked hard, even if they did poorly they knew there'd be openings, whereas we black boys really studied hard.

Alan Maycock and I were discussing how much remained of the colonial racial hierarchy. I brought to his attention *Touch the Happy Isles* by Quentin Crewe,[12] which had just been published, and in which Crewe opined that Barbados was still very racialist, to the extent that it actually had a *Black* Businessmen's Association. Couldn't they simply have a Barbadian one? Alan observed:

> "There's some of it [racialism] left. The whites seem to have got the control of most of the large businesses in Barbados, they're not in plantation land any more."
> "Well, there's no money in that now."
> "No, that's it."
> "But do they intermarry with black Bajans?"
> "Very little. Sometimes you'll get a black who's gone abroad and got his qualifications and comes back with a white wife, American or Canadian, say." (As was the case, I found out later, of his wife's brother.) "But there's not so much of *local* whites marrying *local* blacks, though maybe they'll marry down a little, with the fairer-skinned, what we used to call mulattos.
> "I remember it used to be much worse. When I left school I might have fancied a job in a bank. *Oh* no! You'd leave school and see chaps who'd left a couple of years previously working there. Your qualifications would clearly be superior to theirs but they'd got in because of their fair skin; and you could only have straight, or wavy, hair. That was how it was. It's all changed completely now."

A number of households I worked with had some interracial admixture in their recent family history. One man's father was a white rum-shop owner in Holetown. Father had never married mother, also a rum-shop operator, but he had acknowledged their son. Another man had a white grandfather:

> He was a Scot named Webster. He was the manager of an estate. As a boy I saw him from time to time. He fell in love with my grandmother though they didn't marry, my father was born to them, he was fair. Now my father had six children: three fair ones, and three dark ones—like me.

When they were asked about their families, racial ancestry was one of the topics interviewees brought up. Another was their parents' occupations, and a third was their and their parents' home parish, clearly felt to

work. . . . Eventually he got into the Post Office, that was a
steady job.

Then there's another elder sister, she started off as a servant in
Barbados, then she went to America at age eighteen in the early
fifties, to be a maid. We had an aunt in New York, most of my
mother's family had gone to the States. But she didn't get on
with my aunt, she became a nurse's aid, moved out, then a cash-
ier at the A & P supermarket, now she does per diem nursing
over there. She went when I was thirteen. She sent money back,
some was used for paying for me to go to private high school. So
then there's me. And then my younger sister. She's gone to
America too. She had seven kids, they were raised mostly with
my mum in Barbados, but then they gradually all went over
there . . .

All of the interviewees except one were, at the time of their own impending departure, personally acquainted with someone who'd previously left
Barbados; even the exception knew of people who'd left. Emigration was
part of the accepted scene, what Bonham Richardson has termed a
"migration ethos." So when they began to ponder the big move away, it
was not in any way a strikingly innovative course of action, although, yes,
for the individual, it meant taking one's courage in both hands. Two persons left in 1956, five in 1957, one in 1958, three in 1960, five in 1961,
four in 1962, and one each in 1963, 1965, and 1966. Only one couple was
already married in Barbados: first the father came; then four years later the
mother and the youngest child; then, later again, all four other children
at once. Two other couples had an understanding that once both had arrived as single persons in Britain, they would set up house together, and
they did. In two other couples the women said they were affianced to the
men they're now married to when they left for Britain. But the men, asked
previously in separate interviews, had not mentioned this: "We were single," they'd replied! All except two men have subsequently married Barbadian partners in Britain (one remains unmarried; one married a Jamaican
woman).

Of the dozen men, nine had been formally recruited by London Transport, as had two of the ten Barbadian women. Of the three remaining
men, one sat the exam in Barbados, passed it, but was told he'd have to
wait until a suitable slot opened in Britain; so he signed up instead as a National Health Service worker because he was impatient to get to Britain,
and later, three and one-half years after arrival, he did join London Transport. Another man came under his own auspices, and has already recounted how he found a job with British Railways at its Cricklewood de-
pot. And the final man, who also came under his own auspices, had

already done three years with the long-established American agricultural labor scheme, driving tractors, planting, and harvesting citrus and vegetables in Florida:

> I didn't want to do laborious work in England. I'd had enough of that in Florida, all day in the fields. They were all the rest rough country boys, from St. Andrew and the like. They worked hard, extra, to make more money. But I just filled my quota, I paced myself. Contract life wasn't great. They used to shout and roar and get noisy and play cards. Not I.

After these experiences, Edward Pilgrim was eager to get to Britain.

In *Race and Labour in London Transport,* Dennis Brooks has described the recruitment scheme in comprehensive detail.[14] What follows is my précis of his definitive account. To start the scheme off in 1956, London Transport sent a recruiter and a medical officer to Barbados; seventy stationmen, fifty conductors, and twenty women conductors were recruited. Thereafter recruit selection and medical examinations were done there by local officials. For the recruit the most important single consideration was the interest-free loan the Barbados government made to cover the cost of the fare to London. Over 90 percent of recruits took advantage of this provision. The recruit had to find two guarantors for the repayment of the loan. Both had to remain on the island after the recruit's departure, and one of them had to own real estate. They tended to be relatives of the recruit, and the loan was repayable in monthly installments over a period of two years.

The first step in the recruitment procedure was the calling of applicants for a preliminary test in "simple arithmetic." The 60 percent who passed this were then given a talk on British conditions and advised that, although on arrival they'd probably regret they'd ever made the trip, after a month or so they'd settle in quite happily. The next step, only initiated in 1959, was an evening class emphasizing written and spoken English. (Many of the jobs, such as that of bus conductor, were to involve continual face-to-face contact with the London public.) The class teacher then recommended which applicants should be accepted. Recruits also had to complete the same test papers that London Transport recruits in Britain had to do; Brooks reports that the Barbadian failure rate was "very low." Then came an interview with a senior Barbadian Labour Department official; once again the failure rate was "low." Finally came the X-ray and general medical examinations.

Ten of the dozen men, then, and two of the ten women[15] had voluntarily submitted themselves to this somewhat demanding selection procedure. On being asked why they quit their native island, the interviewees gave reasons that were varied but that were nevertheless not inconsistent with each other. The most common response, with twelve mentions (from twenty-three persons) was the desire for a better job, in the clear sense of greater financial reward, a higher material standard of living. Audley Simmons told me,

> For work for a start. I wanted *regular* work; and to improve myself generally. I was in Grenada when John [his elder brother] left for England. Grenada was an opportunity to travel. I went with a friend to open a garage; we lasted about eight months!
> It was in most people's blood in Barbados to travel, it's a small place, there was no opportunity for young people in my day.
> You got to get out, get off to America, everybody's dream. Only time anybody thought about England was a doctor or a lawyer. If it was the money, it was America. But America closed down, and England opened up. There was a mad rush. It was fashionable in those days. People threw in good jobs, like a teacher or a policeman . . .

Audley's reference to "America closing down" alludes to the situation obtaining in the United States once the McCarran-Walter Act of 1952 had reconfirmed the immigration quota system operating since 1921 and 1924, and had made settling in the United States even less available to West Indians. The postwar Labour government in Britain, in contrast, had enacted an inclusive Nationality Act giving wide rights of settlement in the United Kingdom to such as West Indians. Such rights were removed again by the British after 1962, while in the United States, by contrast again, the quota system was abandoned after 1965, liberalizing West Indian immigration. Thus for fifteen years or so a "window of opportunity" existed for West Indians to settle in Britain, at the same time as such opportunity was denied them in America. The immigrant-generation interviewees in this book are some of those who seized this opportunity.

If the just-mentioned dozen persons were frank about leaving in search of jobs and material rewards, almost as many stressed nonmaterial rewards. These ten persons spoke in terms of "adventure/curiosity/see the world/taste of freedom/grass is greener on the far side of the hill" . . . in other words, youth attempting to escape the confines of the little island. Marie Pilgrim, the very acme of respectability, said she left

> because of my family situation. My father died when I was eight, mother married my stepfather, I never felt he really cared for me, we were brought up strict, I wanted to get away, a taste of freedom. In those days, especially if you were a girl, you weren't expected to think for yourself. You had to be in at such and such a

time: "Where've you been?" "Who've you been with?" all the
time. I didn't even tell my mother I was going [she had access to
funds from her dead father's family]. I thought, I'll get away. And
you know, when I got here I didn't do half of the things I'd
promised myself. I really wanted to run wild, but then, it didn't
seem so exciting anymore. I was a little scared too, in the big
city. England was the first place where I could think for myself.
No, I'm really grateful I came here . . . .

The next most common theme (six responses) was that of wishing to
improve oneself, perhaps expressly to gain qualifications, perhaps conveyed by the term ambition. Nothing was said directly here about financial or material considerations, in contrast to the first response above.
Alan Maycock revealed his reading of the situation thus:

"Ambition. The fellas above me [in the colonial civil service]
were just a couple of years older than me and I thought it'd be
slow progress for me—even if I got any. So I came on the LT. I
had no intention of staying with them, and that's what happened:
I came in August '61, worked on the buses, I'd left LT by May
'62, I got a job in local government." He rose high in the Greater
London Council.
"So," I punned, grinning, "you used LT as a *vehicle?!*"
(Both guffaw.)
"Ah well, the Transport was okay. But it's the same day after
day. If you're the kind of person who can put up with that,
that's fine for you; it's secure. But it wasn't for me."

Next most common (five mentions, all women) was emigrating in order
to join one's partner already in London. Four other people said that it was,
simply, "the thing to do" to go to England in those days. Two of the
women were young enough to have come because they were "sent for
by [their] parents" already established in England. One man said he had
quit Barbados for London in order to "help the kids to a better future"
(he already had three young children when he left). And one woman,
quite unexpectedly, said that she had come to England for her high school
summer holidays to visit relatives, had liked it, and thus had returned to
settle.

The eminent sociologist Robert Nisbet once pronounced that in his
view the four fundamental ideologies ubiquitously fighting a rearguard action over the past century and a half have been those of community, moral
authority, hierarchy, and the sacred. The little island on which the Barbadian migrants were raised forty or more years ago well illustrates the force
of those ideologies then: the village community; family and school dis-

cipline; the local network of relatives; the inculcation of one's place in the empire and in the local hierarchy of color;[16] the clout wielded by the Anglican church. These Barbadians, as we shall see particularly in chapters 9 and 10, now marvel at the changes in their island of origin and in themselves. The old values are questioned, if not destroyed. How did this come about? Let us now in the next chapter follow these twenty-two young Barbadians as they leave for London, and as the process of change thereby slips into gear. The average age of the dozen men was at that juncture twenty-three years nine months; that of the ten young women, twenty-four years precisely. What experiences befell them at these ages, as they crossed the Atlantic Ocean to the Mother Country, as they embarked upon a passage to England?

Three
The Island Attained: Newcomers to England

I remember in those days Wolf Mankowitz[1] *used to live in Barbados, had a gardener and a servant, and a chauffeur, we used to see him around a lot. Then I came to England and there in Ladbroke Grove one morning I see Wolf Mankowitz* doing his own shopping. *I just couldn't believe it!*

Frank Springer

It was always the youngsters, the Teddy Boys. They hated seeing black fellas with white girls.

Joan Springer

The structure of this chapter is straightforward and chronological. Accounts of the adventure and exigencies of the journey itself are followed by some most vivid recollections of arrival on English shores. Then, the section on early impressions of life in London reveals the remarkable and sometimes rather disconcerting mix of familiarity and oddness that those raised in "Little England" at first felt in the Mother Country. Matters became more than disconcerting for those of the interviewees who were caught in the antiblack riots in Notting Hill in 1958. Their experiences, which conclude the chapter, serve to throw into relief certain characteristics of the British that may have been rather overlooked until then. As Raveau[2] commented sagely, "Minorities constitute an excellent means of studying the very things which bring them into being: the societies in whose midst they exist."

Journey and Arrival

Everyone had a story or two to tell about their first impressions of Britain and early days in London. For many of them, the date of arrival was itself precisely remembered as one of the most significant in their lives. Tony Gill was one of the two men who had not been recruited for a job prior to arrival in Britain:

" 'I'll give myself five years in England,' " I thought (I was in my early twenties). 'Five years.' Anyway, I saved. Bought a boat ticket from a travel agent. The boat never showed up on time. So the agent arranged for us to go by air instead."

"That was good, then, to go by air?"

"No, I was a bit disappointed. I wanted to see the other islands, you know. The boat went round the islands a bit. Barbados is so flat, but *they've* got mountains. Also I heard [a very large grin] that good times were had on those boats!

"It was May 31, 1960. We were late taking off, a four-engine propellor plane, pretty full, first we went to Bermuda. We hung about there at the airport. On to Gander. It was *cold*. They gave us mugs of tea. On to Shannon. It was very rough up-and-down flying. A lady along the row from me looked terribly ill. When we landed in Shannon an ambulance came rushing out first and they took her off on a stretcher.

"Then they drove us in a coach to Dublin. That was nice. Saw countryside, green fields, a river twisting to and fro alongside the road." Mr. Gill gets very enthused, gestures with his hands the curves of the river. "We didn't have any *real* rivers in Barbados.

"We stopped at a pub for lunch. We were all treated to Guinness. Got a boat at Dublin to Holyhead. There was a young Irishman, Jim Kelleher, he bought me a Guinness. I gave him a taste of my rum (I came with just one suitcase). We got a steam train, to Crewe—how busy it was with all the trains!—we chatted all the way to Euston. He was coming to work in London. We felt very friendly . . . but we lost contact.

"We'd been going more than two and a half days. We all had addresses in our hands. One of the girls was married to a bloke, she came over here to be with him—no, they had no kids—and she couldn't find him! Well, there were four of us, all chums from Barbados, nobody to meet us. Got a taxi, all of us up in the same direction, the Edgware Road, but he charged each of us full fare, although some went only as far as Cricklewood. I went on to Hendon, a furnished room, a St. Kitts man owned the house . . . "

The earliest of all the arrivals was Frank Springer, who made his own way to pick up a job with the National Health Service at a southwest suburban London hospital:

We left on February 3, 1956. It took eight days to get to Gibraltar, then two days to Barcelona. Then we got the train from Barcelona to Paris. Then a coach from Paris to Calais. Across the Channel to Dover, got a train to Victoria. Nobody met me. So I found the train down to Epsom. It was cold. I arrived at the hospital at ten at night. There were two guys there I knew from home. We talked all night, and I got to bed at three in the morning. At nine I got a knock up: "Are you coming to work?" And I started work *that day*.

The next earliest of all the newcomers, recruited by London Transport, was John Simmons. He flew, arriving on July 30, 1956, but he recalled that some of his friends had already gone to Britain via "the Italian boats, the *Sirienta* to Genoa. There was another Italian boat too, I can't remember its name." The Italian line offered cheap passage to Europe, the disadvantage being, of course, that you did not disembark in Britain.

Some of these reminiscences of thirty or so years ago must naturally enough have become more highly colored with the passage of the years. But the woe that the interviewees today swear they felt then—over the drab greyness, the dampness, the *cold*—is attested to in a contemporary account by that most sentient of observers, Sheila Patterson, who had made it her business to be

at Folkestone on a bleak February afternoon in 1956. It was one of those days when the sea and sky were a menacing grey, the wind cut to the bone, and the rain was almost sleet. The Channel boat had docked two hours late after a rough passage, and its few ordinary passengers had come ashore and settled with relief on the waiting train. On board, some six hundred West Indians of both sexes and all ages waited in apathetic misery for someone to tell them what to do. Some leaned over the rail or against the windows, staring with unbelief at the unimaginable prospect outside; others, overcome with *mal-de-mer,* lay back with their eyes shut. Almost all wore sandals or light shoes, straw hats, and pastel-coloured summer clothes, now stained and crumpled after three days of train and sea travel from Genoa. Several had wound towels round their necks or heads, or had put on two or more jackets, in a vain effort to keep out the dank chill.

This dejected mass of humanity was finally moved down the gangways into the waiting train. The train had no restaurant-car, but most of the migrants had only a pound or two in cash. They had either spent their meagre capital *en route,* or locked it into their trunks—these, it now emerged, had not accompanied them from Genoa and would not arrive for several days. A few of the men brought out rum bottles and a certain animation developed in their vicinity. But the majority of the migrants remained frozen in apathy or apprehension.[3]

To obviate the hardships of arriving so vulnerable in a strange land, the Colonial Office set up a reception system, with liaison officers and the like, to ease the West Indian recruits into the day-to-day business of coping with Britain. Thinking back, Alan Maycock gives them some credit.

"I must say it was well organized by LT. There was pocket-money [he smiles at the school-days term] for me in pounds when I arrived. They were there at Gatwick with a coach to meet us. There was a liaison officer specially to help us settle in. He was on the coach, I recognized him. He taught me as a boy at Combermere. Palmer. So he'd come over and now here he was having taken on British airs—you know, tweed jacket, pipe, even his accent was a bit different! So he lectured us about how if we behaved quietly and properly here, we'd fit in alright. And we just sat back and smirked [at his airs and graces]. But it was a helpful thing all the same, trying to tell us what to expect. He knew something from real experience about this place; we knew nothing *real* . . . only all the stuff in our heads from the colonial schooling we'd had.

"It was August 1961 that I flew into Gatwick. The first things I noticed? The grey weather, it was raining, maybe it was in the fifties or even the low sixties . . . but it felt like the thirties. It'd been in the eighties in Barbados. We'd come via New York. We were just in the transit lounge for half an hour. Some people on the plane had family and friends in New York who'd come out to Idlewild—that was its name then—to see them. But they could only wave to them upstairs, through the glass. . . . Yes, we arrived with light clothes and suits, only. Oh, we felt cold.

"Another thing I noticed straight away in the car-park at Gatwick: all the cars were so small and so old. Austin 5s and Austin 7s. And that was the time of the Morris Minors too."

"But you're not going to tell me that all the cars in Barbados were big and new?"

"No, but we would always see some examples of the new cars as soon as they were out: the new Consul with big tail fins, for example."

"And so you thought everyone in England would have them?"

"I suppose so. The English in Barbados were the colonial government types, they had those cars; I didn't expect to see so many *other* kinds of English here."

"You mean, people who couldn't afford new cars?"

"That's it. I remember, one of my mates came rushing into my room soon after we got here and said 'Maycock, there's a *white* man outside sweeping the streets!'

"The coach drove us up to London, through Redhill. I was looking out of the window all the time to see some black people: I didn't see any. The coach took us round dropping us at places to stay. We all had addresses to go to. They'd worked it out so

Figure 3: The *Hubert* (Courtesy D. Peate, Booth Steamship Company, Liverpool.)

we'd be within striking distance of the LT garage we were going
to work at. One at Bromley, one at Catford, mine was at West
Norwood. So I got dropped with two other fellas at 190 Kirkdale
Road in Sydenham."

Four and one-half years earlier Trevor Brathwaite, Audley Simmons,
and Charles Eastmond had all come over on the *Hubert* to Liverpool (Figure 3). During the journey these three London Transport recruits became
good friends; they still are. Mr. Eastmond's recollection is that the journey
ended up taking seventeen days:

 I was seasick for the first couple of days. Then I got used to it.
 And the weather wasn't bad until we got to off . . . ah
 . . . that place that's always rough? ["the Bay of Biscay?"] Yes,
 that's the name. And then it got very foggy, so we hung about a
 lot. It was a slow end to the journey. I think they must have run
 out of food—they were only giving us cups of Bovril at the end.
 And it got very cold. I said to one of the ship's officers, "It's
 cold." "Oh no," he said, "this is *mild.*" Now that was a new
 word to me. I'd heard, and I'd been, hot or cold. But never mild!
   As we'd been recruited by LT, we were met at Liverpool. It
 was February 4, 1957.[4] Then down to London, to Shouldham
 Street near Marylebone. It was set up by Collins the liaison man.
 You know [fingers grasping money gesture]. Audley got out of

there very quickly, I stayed longer. It was run by a lady, a West Indian lady, but it wasn't hers. It belong to Hurley, a Jamaican, we never saw him, he didn't live there, he and Collins were in with each other.

Mr. Eastmond was not alone in making these allegations about "Collins." Another suspected incidence of irregular financial dealings concerned Trevor Brathwaite's fiancée, Beverly Browne, who came over to join him, on the *Hubert* again, at the end of the year:

"We left Barbados on November 26, and arrived at Liverpool on December 9, 1957. It was lovely. I was such a good sailor! I didn't know I could be, despite it being rough in the Bay of Biscay. I knew a lot of people on the boat, and I'd met Dora at the recruitment center." (They are still friends also. Dora today lives in Reading, forty miles west of London.)

"It was all done through the Barbados government, I was to go to London Transport, but that crafty man sent me to British Railways instead."

"What crafty man?"

"One of those liaison chaps got to her first," chimed in her husband, who had gone up to Liverpool to meet the boat, "and said, 'There's a job waiting for you on BR.' You know, a little behind-the-back unofficial commission. And they [BR] gave her a job in the canteen at Basingstoke."

"That's right," Beverly assented, "that's where I had to go."

The last day-of-arrival vignette presented here is this rather poignant tale told by Austin Pilgrim, who has subsequently risen very high in London Transport:

I was met here on my first day, May 1, 1960, by my sister, at Waterloo Station. She was already here, working at St. Tom's[5] as a laboratory aide. I'd never been on a train before. I saw all these lovely fields on the journey. Then when we got into London I'd never seen so many *chimneys*. And I couldn't come to terms with the fact that one person's house was joined to another and another. . . .

She took me home to her room, in Camberwell. We [recruits] had no idea what we were going to meet here. LT wasn't straight with us. They gave us a book to read on the British way of life. I studied it hard; I was bright, I wanted to improve myself. But it was the polite middle-class English, that's what I thought all England was. I'd never met *poor* English people; they were so ignorant.

Anyway, we went to my sister's. We sat and chatted. I said,

"Can I see the rest of the house?" "This is it," she said! I couldn't believe it. I saw there were other rooms. But other people lived in them! I almost went right back home—but I hadn't the money. We had a nice house of our own, of course, near Bridgetown. [Austin gets up and returns with a photo of a sturdy masonry house with a curved pillared verandah—a solid-looking house, painted a once bright but now fading turquoise green.]

So anyway, I'd been told to be up and ready at 7:30 the next morning, prompt. And I was. And the bus was there. They took us off to get our uniforms at the store. Oh, a *very* cold lady gives me some 36-inch waist trousers from the store! ["And you were 30-inch?"] 29. [He was a bodybuilder—as were, noteworthily, fully half of the male immigrants: physical fitness enthusiasts.] So the trousers don't fit. "Use a belt," she says. "Have you got a belt then, please?" "No—but here's a piece of string." *I* didn't leave Barbados to come and wear trousers tied up with string!!

The day's work was at Lambeth. When five o'clock came, I didn't know where Camberwell was. I asked someone [English] at work, he said he didn't know. Very quick. Too quick—I didn't believe him. I asked someone else. He said take the number 12 bus. I did, asked the conductor, she said yes, this is right. I asked her to tell me where to get off. We got there, she shouted it out twice, but I couldn't understand her accent yet, so I sat up there. She comes up soon after: "I thought you wanted Camberwell?" We'd gone right past! She let me off, I found a policeman, he walked with me home. When I got home to my sister that evening, I *cried*.

First Impressions

Once arrived in London, the interviewees started to learn the ropes. As their first weeks lengthened into their first months, some strong impressions of England and the English formed in their minds. Marie Pilgrim worked as a state registered nurse (SRN) at Mount Vernon Hospital in Northwood, Middlesex, a northwest suburb of London.

It was very dull in a way. Northwood was a typical residential area, a little village, a little shoe shop, a little Sainsbury's. People just stopped and stared at you as if you just landed from Mars.

I got some unfriendliness from the patients. Then, now I think about it, it wasn't just color though. The old people were unwanted, out of hospital. No one'd pick 'em up to take 'em home, didn't want 'em. They were too much trouble. So *this* was how the English were? Not in Barbados, we all were used to relatives helping out, looking after the old.

Asked directly in the interview to tell me his first reactions to life in Britain, Trevor Brathwaite employed an uncompromising adjective:

> It was very shocking. All grey and dull, smoke and soot on the buildings. Only nowadays do you see colours. Oh, the winters! The fogs! One evening I came home from work and I went into the wrong house![6] It was only when I got inside and went up to the landing that I realized it wasn't ours, because there was washing hanging up there, and no one did that in our house. You couldn't see across the street.

John Simmons concurred: "The houses were very plain and drab, they weren't decorated. Everyone seemed to wear dark clothes, winter and summer." And Jeff Bannister agreed too: "St. Paul's was black in those days. These are very odd people, I thought, they paint their buildings *black*. Well, I wasn't to know it was soot, was I?"

Frank Springer really pulled out the stops, penning a seventeen-page letter to me about that period of his life:

> I can remember vividly in my teens that most of my friends wanted to go to America. I always had this desire to go to England, "the omnipotent Mother Country." The land of my great heroes like Sir Walter Raleigh, Lord Nelson, Robin Hood, Sherlock Holmes, The Saint, Sexton Blake, D. H. Lawrence, Charles Dickens, Shakespeare, G. B. Shaw.
>
> England to me was the land of wit, intelligence and the sophistication of Noël Coward.
>
> Little did I know that fact and fiction were two different ball games. The England that I encountered was more Dickensian. They were nothing romantic about the cold chilling winds, the dense fog, and the endless row of ugly building with a conformity of chimney stacks continuously belching out black smoke. None of this endeared me to the rather charmless country that I first encountered.

Orville Alleyne was eager to tell me his predominant early impressions of Britain. He arrived as a recruit in late May 1961.

> Two things I noticed immediately. One, the weather. It was so cold. The first winter I froze. "Oh, you're above the kitchen, the heat will rise," the landlady said. Bah! There were three of us in the room, we were very fit, used to lift weights, so we survived.
>
> The other thing was that all white people looked alike to me. I had to concentrate very hard to remember at the garage who I'd been talking to the day before, what their hair was like, or their ears.

Now my lodgings were arranged by LT. I was unemployed after I left school and I hated it. We were met by the Barbados liaison officer, it all worked right. I was put in lodgings near the Kingston bus garage—I was a driver. It [the lodgings] was a very nice place. We had a West African, two Indian boys studying for the law, and a South African, as well as us. ["A white South African?"] Oh yes. He was sitting at breakfast one morning with me and he said, "You know, in my country I wouldn't be doing this." As if he was doing me a favor! I raised my voice to him rather. "But you're different," he said. "Our blacks are so docile, they can't think for themselves." "Not surprising if they've been kicked around the way you've done it to them," I said.

Oh yes, my landlady was so English, so proper. I said we had come over on the plane. "O," she said, "an *aero*plane"! The English *are* funny.

Joan Maxwell, today Joan Springer, found them less funny:

"English people are very, very aloof. I said 'Good morning' at the doctor's surgery, they just looked up, looked at me, and put their heads back down. I felt awful.[7] And I even had one person once move up out of a seat next to you in the train, and sit further away. And that was a bad one: 'Sorry, no blacks allowed,' when you're looking for a flat.

"Mind you, some were nice ones. There was a cab driver who went round and round to find me the address of my relative, he went out of his way.

"It was the elderly people that were really the snobbish ones."

"Was it that they were brought up that way probably, in a different era?" I submitted.

"Yes, they must've been brought up to feel superior. A young West Indian man I knew went with a friend at work, a girl, to her mother's for tea. (No, they weren't boyfriend and girlfriend.) Everyone had a chair. Except him, he got a stool. Why? *So his tail could hang over.*"

There were also less jarring early experiences and impressions. Jeff Bannister reminisces, "I used to walk along Tooting Broadway, that was where my first impressions formed. Well, it reminded me of Speightstown: the commercial buildings looking like warehouses, the big buildings, the Victorian terraces. . . . " His wife Dotteen also found reassurance in that "it all looked so familiar—we'd done so much English history and all. Looking at the houses coming along on the train, they didn't look strange." Sandra Gill was "fascinated by the variety of flowers, they were really pretty, the greenery and lawns in the parks, St. James' Park, Hyde

Park. When we were first here we used to go to them and to the museums and to the places of interest on Sundays."

And Charles Eastmond had some words of gratitude for the British:

At first I couldn't find my way around a lot—I always got lost. People were happy to show you where to go, they would *walk* with you. It's different now, you approach someone, they think you're trying to rob 'em.

I remember a man who helped me once. I was over by King's Cross, lost. He walked me all the way from there to the Maryle-bone Road and to Shouldham Street [his lodgings]. Another day I woke up late, I missed my 7:15 bus to work, I was standing there in my uniform, waiting there, looking worried. A taxi driver came along: "Where're you going?" "To work. I missed my bus. I'm a bus conductor." "I can see that. Now, where's your work?" "Willesden bus garage." He took me there, free, from Paddington Green. "It's on me, mate."

Likewise, Amelia Simmons:

I came at the end of January 1962 but my first full winter was 1962–63—you remember that one? It was so cold that I was get-ting on a bus and I couldn't move my fingers to get my fare out of my pocket. I just stood there with my fingers bent. I was *cry-ing* with the cold. "That's all right, luv," the conductor said, and let me go without paying.

Beverly Brathwaite, too, had some good memories of her earliest em-ployment experiences in 1957–58, despite the freezing weather at the time of her December arrival:

It was nice when I saw the snow . . . but I had West Indian shoes on my feet, West Indian clothes, oh, it was cold, it was snowing all the time the first three days after we arrived in Lon-don. They sent us to a BR "school," making teas and stuff. It was supposed to be two or three weeks; it took me three days. Me and Dora, we knew about money, making change, so soon they sent us to Basingstoke, to work in the station restaurant. (I remember the snow at the start in Basingstoke, too.) We stayed at the hostel, the rooms were quite good, we each had our own, there was a clean bathroom and toilets. There was a German girl, one from Italy, we were the only two coloreds, an Irish one, lots of English. They were very nice, they always wanted to take me with them, after Dora left, so I wouldn't be on my own. They took me into pubs (not accustomed to that, I wasn't). Everyone was buying me drinks that first time. Everybody was sending me drinks; there was a whole pile of 'em on the table, we left 'em there when I left.

They had me in the local newspaper. I was serving men—in their bowler hats, you know—changing trains early in the morning on their way to work. I gave them their breakfast of eggs and bacon. They brought me flowers, they sent flowers up to my room when I got ill, with bronchial pneumonia. And the chocolates! All my friends came and ate them. I didn't mind. The doctor and the housekeeper really bullied me and coddled me to get well again. They were so nice.

Mrs. Brathwaite's eyes lit up moistly as she recounted these last events. She was visibly touched.

In total contrast to the wholesome tenor of the foregoing, listen to one man's tale of country boys come to the fleshpots of the big city. The narrator, recalling events of thirty years ago, evidently relished telling this particular story. There was verve in his manner, and clearly there is a degree of embellishment, plus telescoping of time, but I am in no doubt that the basic sordidness-cum-pathos is true. This person, whom I did find to be a generally likeable man, injected on more than one occasion into our various conversations a certain lubricious tone. This tale is, however, leavened by a rather zany, Pythonesque raciness: a sort of black farce.

You can imagine how we wanted a girl. Now along Notting Hill Gate-Bayswater, by the park, there used to be hundreds of prostitutes. So a group of us went to one and it was into the bushes there in Hyde Park. Ten bob a time.[8] I always got to go last because I was the smallest, a slight little guy. So each took their turn and it was my turn and in I went to the middle of the bushes and she put out her hand and took the ten bob and just then there was police whistles and she jumped up and everyone started running in all directions so I ran like hell and that was that!

The next night we tried again. As Hyde Park hadn't worked out, "I've heard Clapham Common's the place," said one of the boys. So off we went, found a woman, it was evening, they went first, me last again, this time there are police car headlights just as it's my turn to have my fun. Everyone scarpers,[9] I didn't know what to do, I just stood there in the lights. The police asked, "And what are you doing here?" "Just taking a walk, sir." They took me into the car: "Where do you live?" "Mitcham." They took me straight to the station and bought me a ticket and saw me onto the train and sent me straight down there.

So the next time we tried Piccadilly. A man saw us there, a black man, and said, "Boys, you'd like to meet some nice girls?"

So we followed him upstairs to a club and there were three nice-looking women sitting there and he says to us, "Buy yourselves a drink." So we do, and then we have another, and another, and then we turn around, thinking it's about time now, and the girls have gone. "Hey, where are they?" "What do you mean?" he shouted, very angrily. "This is a reputable club. How dare you!" And he's got these two great muscular fellas there, and they're glaring at us and moving in on us and yes, we ran down those stairs and out. When we got to Victoria Station we'd missed the last train back, and we had to sit there all night on a seat in the cold and got the first train down in the morning. And of course we felt like fools so we told the guys back there at the place, "What a great night out!" and "What we didn't do with those women, all night long!" And all these fantasies. And, of course . . . they believed us.

So the next time we tried Brixton, in this house in Somerley-ton Road. And the place was busy and it was my turn and I went in . . . ["Was this an Englishwoman?" I interjected.] Oh yes, an English woman, a white woman—and I've never forgotten her words, never will, I gave her the money and she said straight to my face, "Listen, don't fuck about. I've got customers waiting." And you know, I couldn't do it. [He taps the side of his head gently with his finger.] Yes, I didn't *want* it anymore. So I went out and all my friends said, "Hey, that was quick!" and they grinned and I grinned and gave a thumbs-up sign and they thought I was fine. . . .

I was here a year before I got any sex. A *year.*

A less vividly painted account of the sometimes unsuccessful hunt for recreation was given by Alan Maycock:

I remember when I lived in Clapham [1963] there was a pub, on the corner of Silver and Wandsworth Road, that wouldn't serve blacks at all There was another which wouldn't allow them in the saloon bar.[10] So we all went to this one down on Lavender Hill, the publican didn't mind, so his was always full, always busy, he was raking in the money as opposed to those other places. I knew people who'd go to the public bar of the other pub just to make a point, to force him to serve us. I really don't think there's any point in doing that, I mean, my money's my own, why should I spend it where it's not really wanted, why should I give it away to someone like that?

It sometimes happens that a certain pub's track record of refusal to serve blacks is long remembered. A particular symbolism inheres in the burning to the ground of The George on Brixton's "Front Line" during the disturbances of April 1981. Lord Scarman's report on the Brixton riots referred to long-standing allegations of racial discrimination at this establishment. The allegations were well founded; revenge was had.

Violent Rejection

The reaction in the collective public mind in Britain today to the words "riots" and "blacks" is always to recall the civil unrest of the 1980s: Brixton, Toxteth, Broadwater Farm. Blacks are perceived as perpetrators. But in the memory of the migrant-generation interviewees, there was a time of shock when *whites* were the perpetrators of gratuitous antiblack violence. Occasional passing reference has already been made to these events at summer's end in 1958. Occurring in inner west London, they are always denoted the Notting Hill riots.

During that summer Beverly Brathwaite was lodged in her hostel in Basingstoke, but she would be continually visiting her husband, who was then rooming in Shepherd's Bush in a property owned by Peter Rachman (of whom more later). She describes the months before the outbreak of antiblack violence:

> A lot of people used to pass silly remarks when you pass, they'd call you names, not straight to your face. I felt scared—but I never got any trouble from the Teddy Boys,[11] I was lucky. They used to beat up colored boys and girls.

The phenomenon of the Teddy Boys and of their role in the 1958 disturbances has been ably and fully documented in Edward Pilkington's recent *Beyond the Mother Country: West Indians and the Notting Hill White Riots.* The first major incident occurred on Saturday night, August 23, when, after some drinks in a pub, a group of nine white youths—armed with chains, a car starting-handle, and the like—crammed into a car and went "nigger hunting" around Shepherd's Bush and Notting Hill. They picked on any solitary West Indian they could see; three ended up in the hospital for several weeks. Thereafter tensions in the area increased. By the following weekend large groups of young whites roamed about looking for black people to beat up; and later they attacked the police as well. Pilkington states flatly that on Monday, September 1, "Notting Hill experienced some of the worst rioting that Britain has seen this century."[12] The following two nights saw serious disturbances too.

In understanding the riots, one should first note the general context of English mistrust of "foreigners," all the more marked concerning dark-skinned "others" after so many years of imperial supremacy. To this one may add the particular context of the changing social geography of these tracts of northern Kensington and west Paddington. (Strictly speaking, "Notting Hill" is a misdesignation.) That is, the Colville area especially (see Figure 6, chapter 4) was becoming, along with Brixton south of the River Thames, one of the two principal reception areas for Afro-Caribbean migrants to London. There was a considerable, rapid, and inescapably *visible* influx of West Indians into Colville's down-market rooming houses. Abutting Colville to the west was the area known as Notting Dale, and here the matter of social class enters in. Although it would be unjust to issue some blanket remark about "working-class whites" as being the protagonists of the riots—the attackers were after all persons of only a certain age and gender: young males—they did come mainly from the particular neighborhood of Notting Dale. Pilkington asserts that although there is a lack of hard evidence to adduce, "it appears that the rioters were acting with the blessing of the majority of Notting Dale's white community. . . . The vast majority . . . maintained a complicit silence."[13] Notting Dale was a poor white neighborhood: introspective, disdainful of established authority, feeling itself ignored or demeaned by outsiders—a recipe for frustrated, defensive aggressiveness. The parallel with Charlestown in Boston, as portrayed in J. Anthony Lukas's *Common Ground,* is striking.[14]

Notting Dale felt itself at risk—and it was easy to misidentify the source of its problems to be the black immigrants. Many of the Colville properties were slums, no doubt about it. Prostitutes operated from some of them. There was also no doubt that marijuana could be obtained thereabouts: "Oho, you live in Notting Hill!" exclaimed Austin Pilgrim the first time we talked,

> Powis Square. *Oh* yes, we went to a party over that way with some friends when we were first here. There were loads of people. We were downstairs, dancing. All of a sudden: "Stay where you are!" The police. They come down, they start strong-arming people out, up the stairs. Lots of hubbub. It was drugs, you see. They were looking for cannabis. And there *was* some there, you could smell it. But I didn't know what it was, I never saw it before.
>
> They start heaving me out. I see an inspector. So I'm *so-o* polite: "Why are they pushing me around, inspector?" "You know." "No sir," I said, "We just came here to a party." I was very polite. "Where are you lads from?" "Camberwell. We haven't been here before." He looks us over: "Okay," he says, "You can go. But don't come here again. You don't belong here."
>
> The five of us got a taxi, and drove away quick. One of us

climbed in on the floor where the taxi driver couldn't see, we only paid for four!

Many of the properties that saw such shenanigans were owned by the infamous slumlord, Peter Rachman, the chicanery of whose barely legal complex property deals and the sometimes innovative brutality of whose strong-arm enforcement tactics gave rise to a new word in the English lexicon: "Rachmanism." He also consorted with Mandy Rice-Davies and with Christine Keeler, the two *filles de joie* who rocked the Macmillan government in the Profumo scandal of 1962.

John Simmons lived in 1958 at number 10, Powis Terrace:

> This was the bad one. The place wasn't so bad, it was Rachman's henchman, Edwards, a Nigerian. The people sharing the second floor were the problem. There was no central heating, the electricity was too expensive, they had a bunker full of coal up there: filthy! There were prostitutes at number 4, we all knew that; at number 1 too.
>
> On our floor we were Barbadians (and Audley stayed with me for a while), St. Lucians, and a Trinidadian. We used paraffin for heat. Edwards the henchman was on the ground floor. He wanted to control my floor, the first floor, as well as his. Trouble with his water taps, he claimed. "I'll have to come up and use your bathroom," he said. We said no. He gave me notice to quit. I went to the Hammersmith rent tribunal, the rent was £3.
>
> Rachman, to my surprise, turns out to be my landlord. He sent a message to come to his office over off Westbourne Grove. It was in a basement, there were no henchmen in the room, but one showed me in. Rachman was smooth-faced and—I think I'm remembering it right—strong-looking. He wore dark glasses, there was some animal-skin rug or maybe it was a covering on his desk. He was very polite, he doesn't want no problems. He offers me a self-contained flat for £3 in Notting Hill, in a nicer part, if I'll drop the case. But I thought, yeah, but you'll shove me out again two or three months later. I withdrew the case and moved out, away, to Balham.

Then I asked John Simmons what he saw of the riots, and he replied, no, he never actually saw "the troubles"; he was working nights and was still in training "down at Putney. And I was doing weightlifting then, I had a great body." The implication here was that only a fool would have laid a hand on him. And I could see why, when his wife showed me a black-and-white photo of him back then, in swim trunks on the beach. His physique was pretty awesome. His nickname is still "Big John."

Immediately opposite John Simmons lived Ivan Weekes, whose memories of that time have honed a certain perspective on British society. He reflects:

I'm not the first to run Britain down. Compared with Barbados this country has offered people a better life. But I'll tell you this: I have no illusions about living here. When you saw the Teddy Boys—I lived at number 9, Powis Terrace, one of Rachman's houses in his empire except we didn't know it, it was from there that I saw the nightly riots—when you saw the Teddy Boys, you knew who your enemies were. Nowadays you don't know who is. It's so subtle. England ran a colonial empire, they're the best people in the world at diplomacy. They can hit you without you seeing where the blow is coming from. The young black people [today, 1988] get so frustrated, they don't know what to do. You don't know who to punch. You're in a padded cell. I tell you, terrible violence will come here. I'm very pessimistic, if there's not open justice and equal opportunities.

Weekes, a Barbadian, had also been previously interviewed by Edward Pilkington, from whose book I now quote:

At the same time as whites were descending on Notting Hill to join in the affray, black people were doing likewise. Ivan Weekes remembers that Jamaicans showed particular solidarity. "They were the champions. They came over from Brixton, night by night, to help their brothers in Notting Hill. If they didn't have friends in the area they had relatives. The Jamaicans bore the brunt of the fight in Notting Hill—they fought back fiercely."[15]

A message that is clearly being broadcast here is that interisland rivalries were buried when white hostility was staring one in the face. Frank Crichlow, a Trinidadian by birth, insisted likewise to me that the Notting Hill riots had catalyzed the sentiment for *black* solidarity, and he wanted to know why on earth I should be concentrating only on Barbadians. (In 1969 Crichlow founded in Notting Hill the Mangrove Caribbean restaurant, which provided a focus for the black community for two decades. Crichlow remains one of the major figures in local black politics.)

Charles Eastmond recalls:

I wasn't living in Notting Hill during the riots, but I had friends at number 9, Powis Terrace, so I went down there quite a lot. I had friends who were in Colville Terrace . . . and . . . well . . . I had a girlfriend in Colville Terrace, I used to go down there after work, I was on the late shift, after midnight I'd get there. All along Ladbroke Grove, and to the right in Elgin Crescent, I saw all these cameras and newspaper people hanging around. I just walked by and walked into the house, they said something had been happening earlier.

Frank Springer, however, was less fortunate in his timing, and wrote:

I lived in Cornwall Crescent, which was the centre of the racial riots. I was chased by a gang of bottle-throwing thugs who was after my scalp. . . . Mosley and his blackshirts were preaching negrophobia, and their doctrine of organised antagonism against black people was frightening.[16] Those years were painful, it was a terrifying ride to the edge of darkness, having to endure all the friction.

Beverly Brathwaite, after recalling details of that time of unpleasantness, paused, and then added philosophically:

It'd be pretty enough the same as any other country. It's how you make it. You've got to make the best of it, if you leave one country and go to another.

It is pertinent, however, that Britain wasn't "any other country." It was the Mother Country—especially for Barbadians. Britain also prided itself, sometimes preeningly, on its "fair-mindedness" and "tolerance." Furthermore, in an era when its real power in the world was slipping, Britain attempted to make up for it by a claimed "moral leadership," especially vis-à-vis its leadership of the Commonwealth, as the nonwhite colonies of the erstwhile empire gained political independence. So the outbreak of native white violence against colonial blacks was an enormous political embarrassment. Wholly predictably, the beleaguered whites of southern Africa could not resist commenting on the incidence of racial violence in a Britain that had theretofore been admonishing and cajoling them toward according blacks greater political participation. The *Bulawayo Chronicle* of Southern Rhodesia wrote, under "The Case of the Biter Bit," "Now that the people of Britain have to focus on something nearer home, perhaps they will realise there is more to the colour problem than just colour. No sensible person will gain any satisfaction from signs that the colour problem is now erupting in Britain." Well no, of course not. Nor could such uncharitable sentiments ever be suspected in South Africa, where Cape Town's Afrikaner *Die Burger* hoped that the riots would engender in Britain "a humble desire for true knowledge." Orval Faubus—governor of Arkansas, battling the U.S. federal government at precisely this time over his refusal to racially integrate the Little Rock schools—also could not resist comment on parallels with Britain.

During the riots, West Indians barricaded themselves in strength inside certain rooming houses, the better to resist the roaming groups of whites outside. Trevor Brathwaite remembered his experiences in an intriguing vignette:

> We were inside a house, lots of us. There was a large bunch of Teddy Boys outside. We got ourselves stuff to defend ourselves with; I got a broom and broke off the head and it made a strong stick. A policeman saw me looking out the door with it. "That's an offensive weapon," he said. I looked at him as if to say, "Come on! What are we supposed to do?" "Hmm," he said, "let's take a look at these bricks. . . . " They were lying about in piles by the door, waiting to be used for building. He smiled slightly, the policeman did, yes. Get it?
>   He was good, that policeman . . . not an offensive weapon!

At the same time as this particular policeman was showing such tact and discretion—and the balance of references to the police in the early years is definitely and ungrudgingly on the positive side—the Springers were being ill served by other police officers. Recall in the quotation in chapter 1 how their police escort left them and then they had, in Joan's words, "to run for their lives." It was thought-provoking, on the occasion of the 1988 Notting Hill carnival, to go and talk with Joan at Westbourne Park station (my own stop), where she was working on special duty as a ticket inspector. The crowds thronged up the stairs past her. In the noisy street outside one could hardly move for the press of bodies, which vastly outnumbered the visible police presence, and in which white and black apparently mingled indiscriminately. She in her black uniform that sunny late August afternoon was just one Tube stop, and thirty years to the day, away from the harrowing moment in the 1958 riot when "I was never so scared in all my life."

Four
A Roof Over My Head . . .

I mean, the greatest problem for all of us was accommodation.

Alan Maycock

For the dozen households there has been a transition culminating in all of them now owning their own houses. For a couple this had been but a recent achievement, managed through Margaret Thatcher's sell-off of council (i.e., public) housing. However, all claimed home ownership to have been a long-standing goal of theirs, and that Barbadians always wanted to *own* their property. Also, of the eight applicable cases among the absent adult children interviewed, six were purchasing their own homes today. It is worth remembering that these households are not representative of all households of Barbadian or of West Indian origin in London. In 1982, for example, 59 percent of West Indian households in London rented council housing, whereas only one of the dozen was in council housing at that time. These dozen are economically above the average: homeowners, a number of them hold highly remunerative jobs (though others' jobs are less so). The very manner in which I met them implies some degree of self-selection; these were not a random set.

Chronologically, their first type of accommodation was the government hostel. Only recruits, of course, were provided with this; in this instance, the two earliest-arrived men, and five of the women (who came somewhat later). The sequence moves on to living in private quarters: furnished rooms in multioccupancy dwellings. It was in such accommodations that later male recruits were placed. Then, learning the ropes of the housing situation for themselves, they began to move out with an eye to better lodgings, still often only to a room, but sooner or later to a flat. It is at this juncture, as they left the cocoon of official quarters, that the Barbadians were directly exposed to the racialism and slumlords of the London housing market. Therefore a brief geographical description of residential segregation in London is here inserted for background. It was also at this juncture that, typically, their female partners would join them. The men frequently said they had wanted to have some reasonably acceptable accommodation set up before their partners' arrival. Later these sentiments were even more strongly expressed by both male and female when, with marriage, the matter of bringing up British-born children or bringing over Barbadian-born children arose; housing had to provide the right milieu for childrearing. In the hunt for an acceptable neighborhood in which to rent or buy a house, the matter of racial discrimination again obtrudes—but the tribulations of this last transition to home ownership are left until chapter 6.

Official Housing

The earliest arrival of all was Frank Springer, whose first accommodation was a room on a ward of a psychiatric hospital. It was clean; it was warm; he was a student nurse, so his expectations were not high. It was, after all, temporary accommodation; he wasn't going to live his whole life in such an institutional, style-cramping manner, and there were two other Bajans there with him, so they could keep one another company.

John Simmons, on the other hand, arriving in Britain as a London Transport recruit on July 30, 1956, had much less bland institutional accommodation waiting for him. He was sent to a former poor-law workhouse, the Swaffield Road hostel in Wandsworth (Figure 4). "The High Commission put us in there. We didn't know what we was going to get, we assumed that if it was government it would be okay." But this dank brick Victorian pile (now demolished) was designed almost like a prison; there was a central hall, used for dining, and a geometric semicircle of bare-brick, sector-shaped cubicles arrayed around it on one side. Attached to each tiny cubicle was an even tinier "disused stone-breaking cell" according to the 1952 suveyor's plan (Figure 5). "What was it like?" I asked John. This amiably easygoing man's first reply was a masterpiece of understatement: "Average." Then Mr. Simmons warmed to his topic:

> "Ooh, the cubicles! I wasn't in the cubicles—they were more like cells. Some of our chaps were put in there and they came right over to the warden's office and said no thanks! They refused to stay there. So I think most of the cubicles stayed empty.
> "I was in the annex. It was newer, a lower building, to the left

Figure 4: Swaffield Road Hostel, Wandsworth: front view. John Simmons was lodged in the building at extreme left. The cubicles were to the rear, right. (Courtesy London Borough of Wandsworth.)

as you came in. Like a dormitory: open plan. No curtains. Like a barracks, all the beds lined up. And we used the communal dining hall there, too."

"Pretty private, huh?"

"Oh no, no privacy!" Mr. Simmons laughed. "So, we'd never stay in the place—'d go off to Ladbroke Grove visiting friends. . . . Well, it was a roof over my head."

The first of the five women who were lodged in official hostels upon their arrival was Beverly Brathwaite. She was reasonably content with her British Railways accommodation—each had her "own room, there was a clean bathroom and toilets," and as we have heard she liked her fellow inmates at Basingstoke—but the great disadvantage was the terrible loneliness of being away from her husband so early in their marriage (he was living in Shepherd's Bush). The other four women came to work for the National Health Service, three of them between July 1960 and October 1963 when J. Enoch Powell was Minister of Health. The one nurse who arrived a little after Powell's tenure was Dotteen Bannister—Dotteen Worrell she was then—and the National Health Service assigned her to the Herts and Essex Hospital in Bishop's Stortford. She commented that her accommodation was "all right," that they all had separate rooms; but ev-

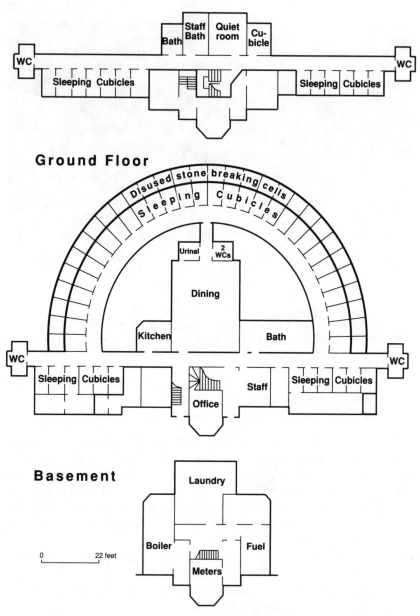

Figure 5: Swaffield Road Hostel, Wandsworth: floor plan (Courtesy London Borough of Wandsworth.)

ery day off she had, she didn't hang about the nurses' home, but went off to Bedford where her mother and stepfather were then working (they have since returned to Barbados). Incidentally, one realized how long ago in one sense this was, when Dotteen Bannister told me her day-trips to Bedford from Bishop's Stortford were made by train, via Cambridge. This was prior to Dr. Beeching's Axe—the track is lifted and built over now.[1]

The highly structured organization of the nurses' home, its strata and its regulations—"It's not like that now, I don't think, is it?"—made an impression on Dotteen.

> It got better as you got more senior; you got more freedom as it went on. First it was Training School House, then First Year House, and so on. You got locked in at night, you got two late passes a week. Hah! But that system didn't work. We got let in by knocking on the windows of whoever lived downstairs near the door. If you went and woke up the sister-in-charge to be let in you got your name taken and got disciplined.
>
> Then you got to the Third Year House, you was in with the staff nurses and sisters. And in third year you got a front door key. . . .
>
> Being locked in like that! It was . . . *Victorian.*

Another of the female interviewees—no acquaintance of Dotteen—had also, three years earlier, been assigned to that very hospital. That two out of only ten female London Barbadian interviewees went there leads one to think that there must have been some kind of institutionalized conduit, a "Barbadian connection," to the Herts and Essex. She said,

> Yes, there were a number of Barbadians there. It was quite friendly. There was a very friendly English lady who used to give us all Sunday lunch, Nurse Clarke. She'd teach us knitting and things. But it was my first time away from home; I used to cry every night the first weeks.
>
> The food was awful, we used to take it in turns, six of us, whoever's day off it was'd go and buy rice and chicken. I thought potatoes were awful . . . but I gradually got used to it. Otherwise we'd go and get tinned spaghetti and smoked bacon knuckles.
>
> The other nurses were very friendly. We each had our own bedroom, shared a bath, each block had a kitchen, there was always a bottle of milk and a loaf of bread there each morning if any nurse needed to make toast or a snack. It was pretty good, there was heating, a maid to clean the room, you had your own radio and bedside lamp.
>
> I didn't realize how nice it was till I left.

She became pregnant and went to live with the child's father, now her husband, an LT recruit who was then living in a back room on the ground floor of a house in Kensal Rise: "It was very poky, very cramped. We just had a bed (and then we had to add a cot for Sandra), a little sink, we shared the toilet. . . . But that was natural at that time; we've moved on since then."

Marie Pilgrim was at Northwood Nurses' Home.

> Oh, but it was very like school. We had these ex-armed forces "Home Sisters": sign in, sign out—very regimented. It was a big house, we shared rooms. In the second year, we got moved down to the hospital, into army huts. Sister kept the SRNs and the SENs[2] separate; it was so . . . rigid. The pay was poor, the food was awful. And the nurses' home was a good mile from the hospital. In the winter of '62–'63 the bus didn't get through. We had to walk in snow up to our shins. It was so cold. I think if I could've walked on water I'd've gone home that time!

There were possibilities. At Margate that winter, I remember ice floes, drifting down the Thames estuary, packed solid for a half a mile out. Nearby, at shallow Pegwell Bay, the press reported that the sea *froze*. Marie continues:

> We were only five black nurses out of say two hundred. But there was no animosity. But there *was* pilfering of underwear. I couldn't believe that English girls would wear another's clothes—especially *under*wear!
>
> Oh, we had fun, doing all the things we weren't supposed to do. We'd take the bolt out of the door if we were staying out late in London.

Pauline Hoyte—now Pauline Alleyne—relishes the pranks and japes of those days too. She was at Hillingdon Nurses' Home.

> We had good times, I broke the rules, I was a bit wild, I was. I'd hide my cape in the bushes, then walk in to work looking all proper at 7:30 A.M. We'd stay out after 10:30 at night, climb in through the window, then throw the cape out of the window for the next nurse who might need it.

The Pauline Alleyne of today still cuts a vivid figure. Her vividness must have been much the greater thirty years ago in a buttoned-down suburban English nurses' home in midwinter:

> It was always hot in there; they had wonderful heating. So it was winter. I was walking down the corridor in a bright dress—

green, yellow, and red—and it was low-cut, and flounced out from the waist, you know the style in those days. Oh, I had a good figure. I got told off. "Dress correctly," I was told. "Put a cardigan on over that." I was made to feel small.

(Matron, who is not amused, stalks off muttering to herself, "Fancy her dressing like that! The baggage! She'll come to no good end!")

Officially Arranged Accommodation

So many black people were brought in by London Transport—by 1958 there were over 8,000 working on the buses or the Tube, although not all of them actual recruits—that hostel accommodation was totally insufficient. Also LT wished to distribute its recruits to precisely those workpoints where they were needed—this was one of the great advantages of overseas recruits, that in the absence of local knowledge and therefore of intra-London preferences, they went compliantly where they were sent. The workpoints, such as bus garages, were widely distributed throughout Greater London, and there was not necessarily any hostel nearby. Thus LT arranged for room rental in privately owned accommodation, and it was to such addresses as 8 Shouldham Street, off the Edgware Road, that recruits such as Charles Eastmond and Audley Simmons were delivered in February 1957. Contended Charles:

I was paying three guineas[3] for my little room and supposedly getting food but I never got any. So I talked to all the boys—they were having the problem too—and said, "Look, if we all refuse to pay our rent, they'll have to listen to us." So they agreed and of course when the time came they backed out on me, left me on my own when I confronted the woman. "I'm not paying," I said. But she was clever and took my things, my blanket and my suitcase, and locked 'em up and said, "You can't have 'em back until you do." So I was really angry; I rushed out into the street, not knowing what to do. No idea. Just to get out. I turned up towards Marylebone, and saw a policeman in the street. Now we'd been told on our training that if ever you're in trouble, ask a policeman. So I told him the story and he said, "Hmm, there's not much I can do, this is a civil complaint, you can come down to the station and we've got a form there and you can fill it up. . . . "
    He thought a little and said, "I know your place, it's across the road isn't it? Well . . . you know, sometimes if people just see us coming. . . . " And when we got there and the woman saw him with me, the effect was immediate. She gave me my stuff

straight away. I walked out of there, had no idea where I was going, went off to Willesden Garage where I was working, met a
workmate. Told him my story. He said I could stay in his room
in Dollis Hill as long as I needed, and soon enough someone else
in the house moved out and I got a room. The accommodation
was really difficult in those days.

I asked Audley, what was the Shouldham Street place like? He chuckled:

Drab . . . pretty austere. The accommodation was disappoint-
ing, horrific really. It was supposed to have been sorted out by
the liaison officers, Collins (he was Scottish) and Sanderson (a
Trinidadian). But it was pretty rough. Bunk beds. I lived on the
top floor, the fifth. Getting up early in the morning was the
thing—in February! It was dark, wet, and cold, there was no central heating. Oh no, not for us. That's for you [he addresses me
jocularly]: for Americans, for softies! We had a geyser for hot water, and electric fires.

Alan Maycock is a man of erudition and a tremendous, engaging in-
formant. In his recollection: "The LT liaison man sort of gave us to understand that we're easing you in, we think you should move out to a place
of your own as soon as possible, so we can move others in." And then,
choosing his words carefully, Alan wondered aloud,

"There was some question about how we ended up in the particular LT housing we did. Sometimes it wasn't up to expectations, but especially we wondered what our own liaison people
had to do with it. Ah . . . I don't mean they were taking a cut
financially, but there *might*'ve been something in it for them
when we got diverted to particular addresses.

"Mine was a very big house, owned by a woman from St. Lucia, she lived there with her French boyfriend. A surprise, it was,
when she said, 'This is your room.' A room no bigger [he looks
around, and behind, in his semispacious office in County Hall]
than this. For all three of us. Three single beds. There was a
cooker along the corridor we all used. Luckily a nice man who'd
been there a couple of years, a Bajan, said I could share his uten-
sils for cooking. LT organized it like that. You either paid rent to
include meals, or not included. Mine didn't. Well, I didn't know
where any restaurants were, did I? So he let me share his stove
and pans and we shared the buying of food.

"I think a couple of the rooms had cookers or hot plates in
them."

"How many people?" I asked.

"Well, there were" (he counts on his fingers) "ten downstairs;

and one two three four five six *seven* upstairs: *seventeen*. Most were West Indians, and one maybe two West African students. I was shocked. However poor you are in Barbados you always have a house, even if it's very little, and it'll be surrounded on all sides by a bit of land. . . .

"Oh yes, I remember, you'd put a shilling in the meter [for gas or electricity], and magically people would appear with their saucepans, ready to use *your* shilling after you'd finished. But I worked out a wheeze where you only put it in partly. It triggered, it started, I did mine. They started on theirs, then it'd give out. They'd already started, so they *had* to put a shilling in!"

On another occasion Althea Maycock (then Althea Adams, Alan's girl-friend) told me that the owners had their own kitchen set up in the base-ment, but other cookers were communal, one per floor. "It was a three-story house. On our floor we shared the cooker with one other family. We kept our food locked in our room in our food cupboard. I remember Alan chopping onions to get them out of the communal kitchen while he prepared to cook."

In response to the question, "What was bad about it?" Alan was brief: "No women." Althea was not to come over until nearly two years later: "We had an understanding," she said. They also had a daughter: "I wouldn't bring Elizabeth from home to live among those conditions," Althea said. Elizabeth only came when she was fifteen, stayed in Britain ten years, and returned to Barbados, apparently permanently. This be-tokens no familial disaffection whatsoever; they visit across the Atlantic with each other quite regularly, and indeed I met Elizabeth at the May-cocks' in London. There is a much younger daughter, Susan, who was born and raised in Britain, where she has always lived.

On another occasion Alan was in a storytelling mood, and the topic was women.

"It was odd staying in a place like that—it was all men. A few chaps managed to get girls in."

"The landlady didn't mind?"

"Ah, you paid her a little bit extra to look the other way. I remember a couple of incidents. The chaps were so tense about it, so insecure, that one chap, he and this girl had been going out a bit and sometimes she stayed the night, he went off to work the next morning for the 5:30 shift on the buses. So he'd be get-ting home about two. *He locked her in the room and took the key!* He was that scared of the rest of us." I start smiling in antici-pation. "You've got it! At nine o'clock we heard her banging on the door, to be let out to go to the toilet . . . !

"And another time, there was a chap, his girl would come round and they would be cooking in the kitchen and he'd forbidden her to talk to the other chaps in case she liked one of them more. Say he had better conversation or more class. One evening four of us were down in the room next to the kitchen and she comes out and we start chatting and he's there in the kitchen and comes out and orders her back in there: 'I thought I said you don't talk to them.' She ignores him. So he wants to act macho [he pronounces it "mash-oh"] you see, grabs her, I mean roughly, and pulls her in. She grabs a kettle and splashes him with hot water and she's reaching for a knife and looking for some salt to get in her other hand. . . . "

"Bit of the old melodrama," I put in, somewhat disbelievingly.

"No, really. It was very nasty. But . . . we calmed them down."

Fending for Yourself

It was when they chose to leave officially provided accommodation (as some soon did) that the Barbadians met the full force of English racism as expressed in London housing conditions: limited choices as to what was open to them, limited choices as to where. Black settlers in any significant number were at that time novel, strange, to the vast majority of white Londoners. At the risk of falling victim to what Stuart Hall and Erroll Lawrence have fairly termed a "profound historical forgetfulness" over the centuries-long black presence in Britain, I nevertheless marvel that it is *largely* during my own lifetime that my native land has begun to modify itself into some kind of multiracial society. That is, it is actually possible—in a London that today would be quite unimaginable without the presence of Afro-Caribbean people—to go and look at the metropolis's two main focuses of black settlement history, and to perceive how very recent they are. One focus of black memory and sentiment is Notting Hill, and 150 yards down my own St. Lukes Road it intersected with Tavistock Road, where less than forty years ago a Mrs. Fisher was apparently the first landlady in the area to accept black tenants. From this acorn has grown the extensive Afro-Caribbean community of west and northwest London. And, apart from one block where demolition has been followed by the erection of sheltered accommodation for the aged plus a moderately sized complement of low-rise housing, the buildings on Tavistock Road are the same today.

South of the Thames lies the other, and contemporarily perhaps more high-profile focus: Brixton, associated particularly with Jamaicans in a way that north of the river is not. As Lambeth Council put it, with only a little hyperbole, "the man who discovered Brixton" lives yet in London: Baron Baker. And through the good offices of Edward Pilkington, I got to meet him. This slight Jamaican-born gentleman in his midsixties, hair incipiently white, and with a deceptively gentle, almost courtly manner— at least in the conversation he held with me—was living social history. It was he who, as a liaison man with the Colonial Office, got two Labour members of Parliament, Fenner Brockway and Marcus Lipton, to stand behind his plan of reopening the Clapham South deep air raid shelter as a reception area for the 492 West Indian passengers on the *Empire Windrush,* whose docking at Tilbury on June 22, 1948, is usually taken as datum line for modern black settlement in Britain. Brixton was only a mile away from the shelter and had the nearest Labour Exchange, on Somerleyton Road, to which the immigrants gravitated. Unlike the postwar situation in the West Indies, a lot of jobs were on offer in south London. The arrivals took them up and found they were able to settle in the vicinity. Forty years later Lambeth municipality and the *Guardian* hailed Baron Baker as the "Columbus of Brixton."[4]

A more chastening reminder of the recency of large-scale black residence in Britain is that we know exactly who was the first black person killed in racial violence in Britain in the modern settlement period. Kelso Cochrane, a carpenter from Antigua, was fatally attacked by six white men in Notting Hill on May 16, 1959; no assailants were ever charged. To live in America feels so different because of the depth of history of such interracial horrors. That is—leaving aside totally the matter of the white settlers' forcible dispossession of the native peoples—the record of black-white conflict in the United States is so long and so murky. There must be, surely, thousands of victims who have died anonymously in the waste of slavery or in the hysteria of lynching. It is almost as if such atrocities have simply been part of the landscape for a long time; one's mind cannot really grasp the enormity of it. But in London one can go to Kensal Green cemetery, adjoining Notting Hill to the north, and find Cochrane's grave. In the modern era, he was the first. That one can reach out toward and touch so recent a history, that one can say, *here* was a turning point or a moment of resonance and of symbolism, I find remarkable.

So it is that one can turn to Ruth Glass and Harold Pollins's *London's Newcomers* (1960), and find mapped there the very genesis of modern Afro-Caribbean settlement in London. Their survey, which seems to have been completed by the end of 1958 or early 1959, reveals the two main clusters in London at that time: Notting Hill (Figure 6) and Brixton-Stockwell (Figure 7). Glass and Pollins write:

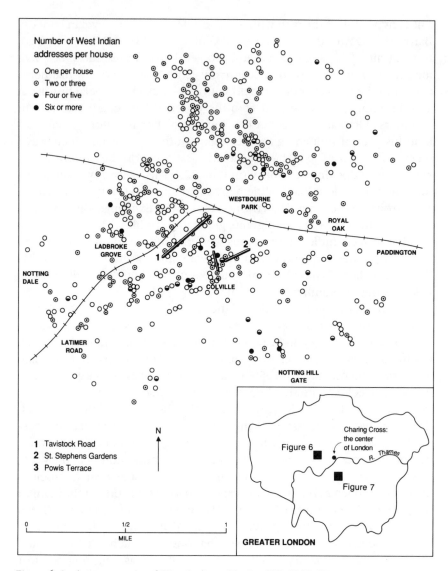

Figure 6: Settlement pattern of West Indians: Notting Hill, 1958–59

Migrants who come from the same territory in the Caribbean tend to live fairly near to one another in London. This is true especially of people from Barbados, from British Guiana and from Trinidad, the majority of whom are concentrated in the main areas of West Indian settlement north of the river. . . . Over 40

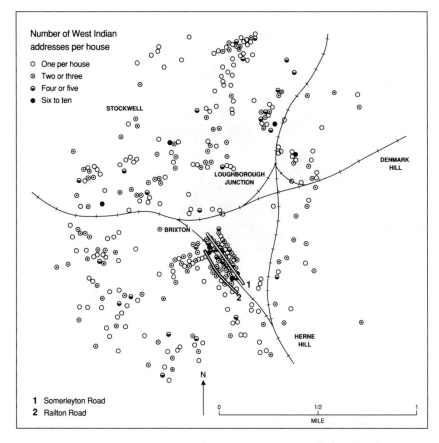

Figure 7: Settlement pattern of West Indians: Brixton-Stockwell, 1958–59

per cent of the migrants from Barbados . . . are clustered, moreover, in a particular district in the northern sector of London. . . . the West area [i.e., Notting Hill and vicinity]. The Jamaicans are in general more widely distributed than the migrants from other territories; but there is one cluster of them in South London, in the South-West area [i.e., Brixton-Stockwell].[5]

Some of the dots on these two carefully surveyed maps represent actual people whom I interviewed and whose words the reader has read or is to encounter.

The Barbadians did not end up so clustered either by chance, or by their own volition only. Birds of a feather may wish to flock together, but

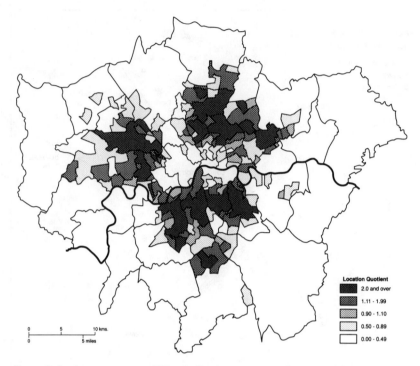

Figure 8: Settlement pattern of West Indian-born persons, Greater London, 1971
(Redrawn from Lee [1977], pp. 24, 77.)

more powerful factors were surely the economics of the housing market,
the changing nature of government intervention in housing stock provision, and the racially discriminatory practices of both white individuals
and institutions (whether willed or unwitting). Although becoming out-
dated, geographer Trevor Lee's *Race and Residence* (1977) is an astonishingly painstaking portrayal of the development of West Indian settlement
patterns in London up to the early 1970s. His key map (Figure 8) shows
how by 1971 the residential distribution of West Indian-born persons had
developed from the beginnings portrayed by Figures 6 and 7. In en-
deavoring to explain this pattern—whose black concentrations cannot by
any stretch of the imagination be termed "ghettos" in the North American
sense, except at the scale of one or two streets—Lee wrote:

> West Indians [experience] economic barriers shared by all low-
> paid workers, and irrational discriminatory behavior on the part
> of landlords and other agents in the housing market. The extent
> of this discrimination was clearly revealed by the 1967 PEP

[Political and Economic Planning] report. In a series of controlled tests in relation to private lettings, discrimination occurred in 75 per cent of the personal applications to landlords.[6]

And in a sketch written by A. G. Bennett in 1954—which seems to have become so widely retailed recently that in an interview one Barbadian man said to me, "Oh . . . you know . . . the 'neighbor' yarn"—one encounters the shamefacedness of racial discrimination:

> What is wrong is with what they style the "neighbor." . . . Since I came here I never met a single English person who had any color prejudice. Once, I walked the whole length of a street looking for a room, and everyone told me that he or she had no prejudice against colored people. It was the neighbor who was stupid. If we could only find the "neighbor" we could solve the entire problem.[7]

Such discriminatory attitudes were close to ubiquitous at that time,[8] but I do not wish here to offer them as "explanation" for the patterns of segregation. My goal is not to rehearse various theories of racial residential segregation, but merely to sketch the context in which the Barbadians came to occupy the kinds of housing in the kinds of localities that they did. The richly descriptive vignettes soon to follow are thereby not left to stand alone, but may be seen as part of the overall tapestry of the London of the time. It was only fifteen years after the destruction wreaked by the Blitz, and a buoyant economy played magnet for lower-skilled workers. There was an acute shortage of cheap furnished rentals. This is how the slumlord Perec "Peter" Rachman fits in. He was one of the relative few, after all, to offer accommodation (on his own terms) to West Indian people. This leads to a certain ambiguity, a certain reluctance on the part of West Indians to condemn him out of hand. Baron Baker said to Edward Pilkington: "Where else could you go? I don't feel he was a bad man even now."[9] Frank Springer feels just as prepared to defend Rachman: "I mean, we couldn't get accommodation, and he provided it."

Paging through old copies of the *Kensington News* ("Notting Hill" is loosely synonymous with northern Kensington), one with ease finds "to let" advertisements such as these:

> A large bed-sitting room. 2 divans. Newly decorated. Small cooker. H & C. Europeans only. References required. £3 10s weekly including cleaning. (February 5, 1958)

> Double room for two Englishmen. Breakfast and 6 pm dinner £2 18s 6d each. (September 1954)

Or "no color," or "no Irish," or "Colored, respectable businesspeople. References essential. Single: 50s; Double: 75s. Linen etc. Share bath" (September 5, 1958).

Rachman—and others—thrived in this milieu. The incoming West Indians had few choices. It was a landlord's market. The West Indians were prepared to pay what, for their limited means and for the quality of accommodation received, were very high prices. The properties Rachman bought up—he started buying in St. Stephen's Gardens in the Colville area in 1955—usually had "statutory tenants" in them, who had relative security of tenure along with a measure of rent control. Rachman of course wanted them out. Among various legal and extralegal ploys, including the threat of bully-boy violence, two were found to be particularly effective in ejecting the long-standing tenants: the introduction to adjacent apartments of prostitutes . . . or the introduction of blacks.

That the two should be so unthinkingly equated as threats by so many statutory tenants—one ad in the *Kensington News* in 1958 stipulated "*quiet* European tenants only" (my emphasis)—is quite an indictment of British racism:

> Colored people . . . were [for Rachman] welcome. Cheerful
> people, and given to much singing, to playing radiograms and to
> holding parties, they were not always appreciated as neighbors
> by the remaining statutory tenants in Rachman's houses. These
> started to move out, and what perhaps began naturally, Rachman
> began to exploit, seeing, perhaps, no point in paying controlled
> tenants to go if they could be persuaded to do so by other
> means.[10]

It was an official government report that could express itself in language such as this. The Milner Holland Committee had been charged with investigating housing in Greater London, and in its March 1965 report devoted an appendix to the consideration of, simply, "Rachman," from which the above is excerpted.

In most of these rooming areas, conditions generally ranged from the dingy down to the squalid and indeed unhealthy. Official statistics revealed that the Colville area experienced the greatest overcrowding in Britain, Glasgow excepted. Abner Cohen in 1982 went so far as to call it "the worst housing situation the country had ever seen."[11] Life was less than entrancing, especially when one considers the long hours of shift work that the interviewees were doing. The tales they told me, therefore, often are remembered "high spots," moments of animation in an otherwise rather dreary, pinched, day-to-day existence. They were in large measure hostage to the whims of the landlord. Of course, not all landlords were overbearing or difficult, but even so, the immigrant renters were always vulnerable. One man remembers the landlord telling him sharply, "Walk softly up there! That's our ceiling."

It is worthy of note that very many of those black persons (Afro-Caribbean or African) who could accumulate enough capital, and who were able to put a deposit down on a mortgage on a house, then profitably letted part of it as accommodation to *other* blacks at high, market rentals. Black tenants came rapidly and disproportionately to have black landlords. It is also worthy of note that the black immigrants were ineligible for public housing for some time after arrival because, with the housing shortage, there was a significant waiting list for council houses and one first had to be a resident of the local municipality in question in order to get on the waiting list. Ipso facto, newly immigrated West Indians disqualified themselves: a classic example of regulations framed with socially progressive aims (i.e., equality of treatment: wait your turn) having unanticipated socially regressive (i.e., racially discriminatory) effects.

Austin Pilgrim remembers his experience of the open housing market was of letting a basement room in Camberwell from a black landlord, a Jamaican. "He harassed us. He overcharged us. He didn't allow radio or TV. Only 25-watt lightbulbs were allowed. They were too weak to read in. I'd rather stay away." Then Austin moved to Brixton. This place was "far better," although it had no bath—he had to go to the Camberwell Public Baths.

> "It was cleaner, freer, you could have visitors. A Jamaican ran it. He was a gentleman. No harassment. But he overcharged: six of us at £5 a week. *He* rented from the Council on short-term rent at—what?—£1 a week? Then he dropped it to £3 10s a week if we said we'd sign a form saying we were only charged £1. Officials had come round checking on him. We signed.
>
> "Then we moved to Flaxmore Road, Camberwell. It was where we married."
>
> "What was good about it?"
>
> "It was a big room. We had a Blue Spot radiogram. Everyone was getting one; we couldn't afford a TV. You could get Windward Islands radio on it from Grenada. The news from the Caribbean used to make our day."
>
> "What was bad about it?"
>
> Austin's response, for a man of generally self-possessed demeanor, was vehement. "It was awful. They were always fighting. Pig-ignorant. *Jamaicans.*" (Austin does seem rather to have it in for the Jamaicans sometimes. The way he spoke the word on this occasion was as if to convey, "What more need I say?")

"They said we should all be 'family.' We never used to mix, they didn't like that. We were there one year, '63–'64.

"Then we moved to another Jamaican place in Herne Hill. '64 to '67. All the rest were Jamaicans. Again, they wanted to talk about everything in a big meeting, every Sunday."

"A pow-wow?"

"Exactly. That's not our style. . . . And oh, the colors of the carpets! Oh God, the furniture of other people! Eventually they [the landlord and his wife] said, 'You get new furnishings, you buy them, we'll pay you back.' She didn't. And *he* went off to the place in Sydenham I'd got 'em from with one of the pieces one day when I was out, and tried to get the deposit back for himself! But they knew me there, so it didn't work.

"And they used to nick our food: flour, and spices. They cheated on the hot water. Downstairs it was like a Jamaican club: parties, noisy. We'd go away for the weekends, she hated us for that. We wouldn't let Nigel play downstairs with her kids or in her house. We'd take him to the park and exercise him to tire him out so he'd just come home and sleep—so they'd have *no* grounds for complaint. They would sit on the stairs and listen to our conversation. They would open my pots to see what was cooking. They didn't want any white people in the house.

"When we were accumulating furniture for our home he brought people in to show them how well *he* looked after me, giving them the impression it was his! (You see, I later talked to people who'd been prospective renters and found that out.) And his wife came to Marie one day and said, 'The rent's gone up to £5 10s.' I asked him why, and he said, 'No, it hasn't.' So what was she up to?

"We finally found a house [to buy]. I took a deep breath as I walked away from that place: FREEDOM!"

Trevor Brathwaite remembers his first experience of the open housing market was of letting a room off Shepherd's Bush Green, from 1957 to 1959, from a white landlord: Rachman.

The house had no facilities, not even hot water.[12] The water was so cold I used to get a little cigarette tin—they held fifty, didn't they?—and heat it up. Then they put in a geyser. I made a mistake. I couldn't light it right the first time, putting the match here and there, then PHUT!, it loosed the glass, and it fell *just* past my head. . . .

We had some problems there. One bloke that came with us refused to pay his rent, things got so bad. There was a bit of a scuffle when his [Rachman's] henchmen, white guys, came round. They threw his stuff out the door. The man in charge was Mr.

Grew. Not English. Don't know how you spell it, no. His wife
was Irish. Oh, it was cold. Later they did install some little gas
fires. Put in meters. But they used to adjust them to cheat us.

Beverly Brathwaite after some effort got a transfer from Basingstoke to
London's Liverpool Street Station, in order to live with her husband.
What was this room like that she moved into?

Lord have mercy! It was in the basement. Very damp. It was near
to the road [no front yard], when the rain came, it ran down the
walls, through the windows. It was a terraced house, four storys
and a basement. Everyone in a room, cooking on the landing;
didn't like that. Two families on each floor, mostly Barbadians
and other West Indians. There was a bathroom and toilet on the
first and second floor only. We was lucky, we had our own lava-
tory. Gwen and her husband lived in the other room in the basement. She's a Bajan, she only had a gas-ring, so I'd let her cook
on Sunday, use the oven to bake something special. I ain't troub-
lin' she. . . ."[13]

Frank Springer's first place, once out of his room on the hospital ward,
was a room in a Rachman property in Cornwall Crescent, Notting Hill. It
was into this house that he ran (as Joan Springer has already related) in the
riots.

We came back late, we'd just got off the train at Ladbroke Grove.
I had no idea what was going on. There were millions of people
about. The police took us through the crowds [tells the same details as Joan] I ran all the way home. Up the steps, unlocked the
door, closed the door, all in one action, know what I mean? The
crowd was after me, they smashed the windows downstairs—the
prostitute's, not ours, she was English, we lived upstairs.

Audley Simmons stayed in a Rachman-owned property in Powis Terrace for five months in 1958–59. That he moved on so soon implies that
he may not have found it ideal, but today he can recall a number of positive features, if not of the property itself, at least of the neighborhood.

One plus was that you could go to the pub for a drink [many
other pubs—quite legally then—refused to serve blacks]. It was at
the corner of Portobello Road. And shopping, oh yes, the Portobello market. You could get some of the Caribbean food.
There was a little shop on the corner that was open on Sundays.
The Calypso Club was round the corner, in a basement in Ledbury Road. We'd drink and dance there. It's redeveloped now.

There was evidently a liveliness to Notting Hill. Even for Frank Springer, distance nowadays can lend a little enchantment: "Life in Ladbroke Grove was wonderfully sleazy," he reminisced.

Althea Maycock remembers a room she and Alan lived in for a year in 1965–66. In a most unintentionally revealing turn of phrase, this Barbadian said, "The landlord was Jamaican but he was very nice." The terraced house was

> in Lambeth. Well, maybe you'd call it Stockwell. The bad thing about it was the Africans, who weren't very clean. Especially when they went to the toilets. They called us slaves. They were from . . . Nigeria? Just "good morning" and "good evening" mostly, we never really mixed.

Charles Eastmond, not surprisingly after his experience in the Shouldham Street accommodation where the policeman so deftly helped him, enjoyed the "independence" of his room in Dollis Hill. The independence was relative, however:

> We all shared the kitchen—which was the same room as the bathroom! Never seen that before, or since! So you couldn't make breakfast in the morning if Grantley or his wife [the other roomers] were in there, so I'd have to dash to the canteen at the bus garage for a cup of tea. A man from Ghana owned it. We celebrated its independence[14] with him—oh, we had a party!

Edward Pilgrim gave me a similar account of his earliest, shared room, in a multioccupancy Camberwell house. He readily admitted that it was cramped and that other people used his money once he had put it in the meter, all the litany of complaints with which the reader has now become familiar. But Edward had a different perspective from all the rest, for he had done those years of agricultural laboring in Florida. His verdict on those grim London conditions? "After contract life, living like that was heaven."

Five

. . . And Bread on the Table: Employment

People from Barbados say about us who are living in Britain that it's just work, home, work. That we don't have any life, it's just go to work, come home, watch the telly, go to sleep.

Trevor Brathwaite

The previous chapter's report on the accommodation of Barbadians in their early years of settlement is clearly fairly typical of the London Afro-Caribbeans of that period in general. Similarly, the early experiences of the Barbadians in that other central arena of their British lives, the job, also appear to be not too removed from those of all London Afro-Caribbeans of that time. These early employment experiences are dealt with in this chapter. As the chapter proceeds, however, it becomes evident that these Barbadians, formerly pretty representative of a wider collectivity of Afro-Caribbeans, have with the passage of time become an above-average group. The responsibility and remuneration that come with the senior posts to which men like Tony Gill, Alan Maycock, and Austin Pilgrim have climbed sets these persons apart from most of their fellows who journeyed to London. On the other hand, others of the twelve may not surpass the average by much. But none is unemployed. None, conversely, is living a life of ease, and to none could a label like "tycoon" ever be affixed. So this is not a study of Barbadian magnates and their families, but rather, to use that woolliest of terms, of a nascent Barbadian middle class.[1]

Prior Employment in Barbados

Useful perspective is gained by first noting what employment the interviewees had prior to coming to Britain. In fact, six of the eleven women were either unemployed or not employed outside the home in anything they'd consider a career. One of the dozen men was unemployed also, and another six expressed some degree of dissatisfaction with the jobs they were then holding. For women in particular, the Barbados opportunity structure was highly constrained thirty years ago. Just two had gained their professional qualifications and held steady jobs before Britain. One was a nurse, although she had also gained business-skill qualifications by spending a year at a secretarial college in Montreal, financed by her aunt, her grandmother, and her parents who were already working in England. Another was a primary schoolteacher, who had in fact (having gone through three years of teacher training) given it up and become a secretary in the Barbados Ministry of Labour instead. Two more were typists, but the others did, as one put it, "little jobs here and there": serving in a shop, running errands, being a nanny. One was just completing school—not an elite academic high school, but one where "they trained me to be a seamstress, and to do typing. It was more like a finishing school for young ladies; they weren't training you to do a *job!*" Thus, in his memoir of 1940s Barbados, *Growing Up Stupid Under the Union Jack,* Austin Clarke recalls his awe of a "bright-bright-brightboy" who had won a scholarship to Harrison's College:

> My hero at the top of the hill went to Harrison College carrying big books in his blue English-made school bag. . . . his lunch would have consisted of bread with the edges trimmed, the trimmings to be saved for his sister, who was not bright-bright-bright and was not expected to be, and not given the chance.
>
> Boys got the best food and attention, and the least floggings, if they were high school boys. Girls were expected to be dressmakers, sugar and silent, spice and stupid, and wash the boys' clothes. So my hero's sister would have helped her mother with the needlework which sustained the family.[2]

Such was the milieu in which Joan Maxwell (later Joan Springer) left school at fifteen to work in a Bridgetown supermarket for six months. Then she went back home and "did nothing. I was the last one of the family, so I had to keep house for my mother." Then Joan went to Trinidad for two years and kept house for a white American oil-field family; while there she learned shorthand at evening classes. On her return to Barbados she found no job, and prior to being recruited by LT had been unemployed for eleven months. Another young woman had been doing evening classes, in typing and home economics, but then had to give that up to stay home and look after the baby whose father had left as an LT recruit. The final woman, Edith Fletcher (later Edith Simmons), lived at home on a

Jamaican smallholding with her mother, three brothers, and two sisters. She had done elementary school, and then her father, who had worked on plantations in Cuba and on farms in the United States and was now at a factory in Park Royal in northwest London, sent for a daughter to look after him. "He was away a lot, we weren't that close. It should've been the eldest sister, but she couldn't come because she fell pregnant. I was the second child—so it was me." To this day Edith resents the way she was called for like a piece of familial baggage: "It was barbarous. He should've been shot. To bring a fifteen-year-old girl from the country, to *this* [London]?"

The job situation for the dozen men was less strait than that for the women. Nevertheless, their options were still relatively few, and two-thirds of them were not happy with their employment. The other four of them do say they were reasonably content—two were trained electricians, one a butcher, and one a compositor—but clearly not so content as to be insensible to the blandishments of a job in London. Of the remaining eight men three held jobs in Barbados that could not really guarantee them a regular income. Of these, one had been an apprentice joiner and was now stevedoring; the other two were auto mechanics (one being Audley Simmons, who had tried to open a garage in Grenada that failed, but who clearly knows how to look after cars, for he drives a resplendent two-tone 1961 Austin Cambridge sedan around London!). Three other men saw no attractive prospects in continuing to be clerks, or, as one was, a handyman for a dry goods store. This last man, John Simmons, had in fact learned the coopering trade, but then the molasses company for which he worked changed over to bulk shipping, and he found himself to be a statistic of technological redundancy. Jeff Bannister, the eleventh of the twelve men, left school at nineteen with two A levels[3] (Latin and French) accorded by the British-based General Certificate of Education, and had been a payclerk for six months in a construction firm. The way he tells it, "it was a spur of the moment thing to come to the U.K. I'd never really thought of leaving Barbados. Three of us got to talking . . . and now one's in New York, one's in Canada, and I'm here!" The twelfth man had been unemployed for eighteen months, having been fired from his first job at the butcher's counter in a supermarket after (to hear him tell it) "horseplay" in front of an Englishman—who turned out to be a very proper parish priest and who proceeded to complain to the white Barbadian owner.

Jobs on "the Transport"

Given the way in which this whole study was set up, the preponderant employer was the transport industry. Nine of the dozen men were London Transport recruits, and a tenth joined LT after a few years in London. Two of the women were LT recruits. One of them, Beverly Brathwaite, was, as we have seen, told upon arrival that she'd been assigned to British Railways instead. This happened to one of the male LT recruits upon his arrival too, leaving eight men to be sent to various bus garages and Underground depots to begin as trainee bus conductors, bus drivers, and stationmen.

What impressions do they hold of these earlier months and years of their British employment history? Austin Pilgrim was the most negative. It was he who in chapter 3 told the story of being offered string with which to hold up the outsize trousers proffered as part of his LT uniform: "No! They lied to us. The *harshness* of personal interaction. . . . " Less stridently, a bus conductor said, "*I* never got any personal hostility, but what I did not quite anticipate was that you were more or less ignored by the majority of people you worked with." Another bus conductor, Charles Eastmond, thought for a long time before replying, almost as if he were searching for something positive to say; he eventually found it:

Well . . . hmm . . . the behavior of the people was really unique, it's fallen back a bit now. They never tried to get off the bus without paying then, you never used to get the cheating, people were very honest. And you know, even though in Barbados we had dollars and cents, we'd learnt pounds, shillings, and pence in school anyway—all the books had that in them! It was a bit strange to us over there. But when I got here, it helped.

George Farley gave a negative but good-humored reply:

I did three weeks at Chiswick, training to be a bus conductor. No, the money seemed less than I thought it'd be. The job was more complex, more difficult than it would've been in Barbados. There, bus fares were 10 cents, 20 cents, 30 cents. Here it was pounds, shillings, and pence, making change, passengers asking me for the names of streets, cafés, pubs, churches . . . all the way from East Ham to Ladbroke Grove or Acton, from Essex to Middlesex. The number 15. "You're the conductor and you should know." And I'm new from Barbados! Now *that*'s hard work.

And Trevor Brathwaite, who began as a bus conductor, said,

Well, you don't get the amount of racial jibes that you did then. People might *think* it . . . but no, you don't get the resentment from the public anymore. I remember giving change, and the woman drew her hand away, she didn't want to run the risk of touching me. The change fell to the floor. I've had nothing like that for ten years now.

Trevor soon became a driver, a job with which he seems content.

Another recruit who became a driver told the story of waiting around to move off with his bus one day a score or more of years ago, and

> this old English lady looks at me very serious, and says, "Young man, you have a lot of responsibility driving. All these people's safety." I was proud of my job because of that, and me in *London* too! But now I feel a bit annoyed, because she was telling me—now I study on it[4]—that she didn't think black people should have the responsibility. That's the difference between the English and the Americans. The English never come right out and say things. They're so polite. Never "no" to your face. You just don't get the job. They're very clever.[5]

And Audley Simmons, who also soon became a driver, said that, frankly, he hadn't known what to expect of the job. "I enjoyed it for a time, it was quite interesting, meeting people and all that." And then he repeated, "I enjoyed it for a time. . . ."

Clearly, it palled. Recall Alan Maycock's verdict that "the Transport was okay, but it's the same day after day. If you're the kind of person who can put up with that, that's fine. . . . " For Trevor it apparently is; for Audley and Alan, less so. Yet Audley did it for twenty-nine years, eleven months, keeping at it until, as staff numbers were slimmed down in Margaret Thatcher-inspired parsimony, he took voluntary severance. Alan got out after just nine months.

Jeff Bannister met with a surprise upon his arrival; he was summarily transferred from the Tube to the buses:

> I'd been recruited to be a stationman, that's what I thought. I suppose I'd say they misled us in the sense that they said there were lots of jobs in LT over in England, they made it sound attractive, and then only after we'd been *selected*—and so we'd committed ourselves, you see?—did they say, well, you'll be a stationman and this is what the job entails and I thought, what, sweeping up?! [He with two A levels.]
>
> But then you see it didn't happen. I came in on a Thursday, next day to Chiswick, was told to go to LT headquarters at Griffith House, oh, they said, you're not yet twenty so you can't be a stationman, or some such stuff. So it's a bus conductor for you. So I had another medical—with a lady doctor, that was . . . unexpected!—and they sent me to Streatham Garage.

John Simmons got a bigger surprise: a different employer! Believing himself to be a London Transport recruit, he found on his arrival one late summer's day in 1956 that he had been assigned to British Railways instead:

"I was directed to BR at Staines for the very next morning. I went down there and was put to work in the parcels office. The next day was a Bank Holiday. I thought, we won't be working. So I went over to Ladbroke Grove to see some friends. But I was wrong! I should've been at work.

"Soon I got into the goods yard at Staines, in the shed, sorting stuff and that. There was a lot of freight in those days, and at Feltham too. Then after a year I moved to the Wimbledon goods yard. I was there under a year, and then I got into electric passenger stock shunting at Wimbledon Park. I put in for duties as a guard: three months' training. That's when the problems started [he laughs broadly, without ill-feeling]. The other workers said, 'We don't want colored guards on this Region. We'll strike.' They wouldn't let us in to Feltham yard or Nine Elms goods yard to learn. There was just two of us. We went to Southern Region night school at Clapham Junction. Halfway through the training I went to see the guvnor, told him, 'I don't want to go on with this; I'm giving up.' The guvnor said, 'You mustn't, you've passed the exams, you're a union member, the union's behind you, they'll have to back down.'

"So I kept going. I got it, I did it. They backed down. I was made a guard. I never had any *personal* unpleasantness, but it was a hassle. But I got on alright with 'em, I got a mutual feeling for 'em.[6]

"I moved up from Link 3 to Link 2, with seniority. I wanted main line work and went to Clapham Junction, to Link 4: I liked that job. Then I did parcels trains out of Waterloo, that starts at 3 or 4 A.M. When I left in 1974 I was up to Link 2."

"So why did you leave the railway after all those years, and seniority too?"

"Well, it's the hours. You're on a roster. Whereas the job I got at Heathrow is more predictable hours. It was only very slightly higher wages, mind you. But it was also pretty near my house [Southall]. I didn't have an HGV[7] license at that time. I passed the HGV test in 1975; that put my wages up some more. And I learned forklifts, lifts off aircraft, jetways. Now I'm a team leader of a baggage-handling and aircraft-loading section. I'm the supervisor of my group.

"I'd like to retire in the next year or two."

Beverly Brathwaite had the same experience on arrival as John Simmons. Her reason for applying for recruitment was straightforward: to be with her man. Trevor Brathwaite had already gone to Britain to work for LT in February 1957. She was then still Beverly Browne; they already had three children. She has the habit of referring to Trevor as "Mr. Brathwaite":

> I said to myself, "I mustn't stay on my own. I'll only see Mr. Brathwaite on holidays, he be gone for years maybe, meet someone else, might fall in love. I already have my kids, I don't want to mess 'em up: I must go to England."

So she did, leaving the children in the care of Trevor's mother. One of the advantages of being recruited by LT—apart from the obvious one of getting her to England on an assisted passage—was that, by definition, LT could only employ her somewhere in London, that is, near Trevor: the object of the exercise. And then, imagine her consternation as she disembarked from the *Hubert* at Liverpool that December day in 1957 and they said, "You're going to work for British Railways instead; we've a job for you in the canteen at Basingstoke" (about forty miles southwest of London).

> We were the only two colored girls there, though there were two chaps who used to work down there sometimes. . . . I was so *lonely*. He [Trevor] used to come down weekends. Eventually I asked for a transfer to London. Nothing happened. Two other people asked; they got it quickly. Eventually I asked my supervisor. "It takes time," she said. A bit later I asked again. I got myself upset, I was so lonely. "Oh dear," she said, "I'll come clean. Your request has been sitting here on my desk all the time because I don't want to lose you. Please don't go."
>
> But I had to. I gave in my notice next morning. Got a transfer to London immediately, though they put me at Liverpool Street, the other end of town from Shepherd's Bush [where Trevor lived]. I served drinks in the station bar. I traveled on the Metropolitan Line every day. I didn't like the night work. Coming home at 11:30 on the Tube you'd get drunks, making remarks about coloreds. The guard used to have to represent[8] me. Then there was a not quite ten-minute walk home from the Tube station. Sometimes I was very scared coming home, in those days there were Teddy Boys . . .

Such were the reasons that she gave for her leaving BR's employ at the turn of 1962–63. It is worth giving a full account of her subsequent employment history; this woman has *worked*.

At the beginning of 1963 I did some months pressing in a laundry in Hammersmith. It was a ten-minute walk, but I got bronchial, I caught cold from crossing the park; the wind used to *whip* across there [this was the infamous winter of 1962–63].

Later in 1963 I worked for a few months at a little shirt factory around the corner: sewing buttons, pressing shirts, and folding them.

Later that year I went to Callard and Bowser [national-brand confectioners] at Acton, a friend suggested it. Just one bus, the number 105.

We'd moved to Southall [their present home] earlier in the year, it got too far to go all the way back in to Acton. So I worked at a food factory—jellies, cream, marzipan—over the bridge at Southall. I could walk. I did it for two and a half years, until late in 1965. Then I had words with the supervisor.

I moved to the Wolf rubber factory, making tires, along the Uxbridge Road, for one and a half years. They closed down. You got redundancy money after *two* years: that was bad luck! (My daughter Gloria came from Barbados to live with us then; but my other daughter Grace never came, she's always lived in Barbados, though she has visited.)

So I got a job in Ealing, a steel business. I was cutting tin, feeding sheets into machines, they'd come out as gadgets, I was using oil and grease and gloves all the time, I didn't like it. I only did it for two months [1967].

I'd made a friend at Wolf's from Grenada, when they closed she went to this industrial engraving place in Hayes. She told me about it. I worked there two years, and then got pregnant with Tommy. Now *that* was a surprise! (I was forty-one.) So I stayed home with him for nine months, and Trevor Jr. came over from Barbados [their elder son, then aged sixteen]. I did a bit of night work at Lyon's [café chain] in Greenford for about three months, but it was too exhausting, I was going crazy, I was breast-feeding Tommy.

Then I went back to the industrial engraving place. I leave here before 7:30, it's two buses, for an 8 o'clock start. I leave work at 5 P.M. back home maybe 5:45 or 6. I do drilling holes in metal, there's lots of dust, it gets on my chest. Don't we use masks? Well, er, we're told to . . .

Hopefully I'm retiring in January, at sixty. I'll have done a good twenty years with them, but there's no pension, and he's refused to make me redundant [i.e., implying a "golden handshake" severance payment]. No, he's not English, he's a Jew.
. . . It's a worry . . .

On January 7, 1989, Beverly retired with the gift of four weeks' pay. Not only had she held these grinding jobs, contributing to the payment of the mortgage and to the remittance of monies to help support aging Barbadian parents and parents-in-law; she had also been the pillar of her family, feeding and nurturing children, helping finance Trevor, Jr.'s, fee-paying high school education in Barbados so that, as he says, having been "taught by English teachers there, I speak the proper English. On the phone you can't tell I'm from the West Indies." Trevor, Jr., also made sure that I knew that, every evening once home from work, his mother would spend time helping young Tommy (now about to go to college) with his homework. Basically, this admirable woman has been wearing herself out. I felt a little chastened, sitting in their parlor after an evening meal that Beverly had prepared after work (this is in March 1988), listening to her recitation. She looked spent. Upon retirement she went off to Barbados to relax for four months, before returning to Trevor, Sr., who continues to drive the buses.

As opposed to the two previous cases of people who came over as LT recruits and ended up working for another public service, Frank Springer came to work for the National Health Service (NHS) but ended up working for LT. He came over to work on the wards at Epsom Psychiatric Hospital. He did it for two years and then chucked it in, worked as a porter and an odd-jobs-man in a restaurant in the City, found that unsatisfactory, then worked for the post office (GPO) as a temporary hand over the Christmas rush period (1959). He joined LT in February 1960, foregoing the offer of a permanent job with the GPO. After training at Chiswick, he was a station-man for just five or six weeks before going to White City where he trained to be a guard, which he did for five years. Then he became a motorman, i.e., a driver, for ten years; then a traveling ticket inspector for thirteen further years. Now he is no longer traveling, but is an inspector in an upstairs office supervising the issuance of court summonses for fare-dodging and the like. This steady rise up the ladder, based presumably on an ability to fulfill the demands of each successive job satisfactorily, has brought a degree of financial security yet little enchantment. Job satisfaction has been moderate: "It's a simple fact: I wanted a job. If you have to, you'll fit in to the environment." This is a man who "likes words, I'm good with them." He loves the theater, goes to the West End often, is in particular an enthusiast for Joan Littlewood's setup at Stratford in the East End.

> I would have dreamed of being in the theater. I'm just doing the LT job to keep bread on the table, I have no particular vocation for being on LT. Sometimes I feel I'm a frustrated man. My son—he's a go-getter—ridicules me for it: "Why don't you go to

evening classes?'' I tried a bit, but it's always shift work. The
wife's on shift work [with LT] too, so who watches the children?
"Rubbish," my son says, "Where there's a will there's a way."
He can study, with his baby on his other arm. So maybe he's
right; maybe it's me . . .

Now to the matter of financial security that Frank had assumed he had
amassed for himself through long years of uninterrupted service with London Transport. As part of Margaret Thatcher's shaking up of publicly
owned service bodies such as LT, there have been rumblings of reorgani-
zation, of a drive for cost effectiveness and profitability. These abstract
nouns sound all very well, but to most of the LT Barbadian recruits they
seem to represent another demeaning of what they were told (and in part
believed) was a great public service when they were granted an opportunity to be part of it, thirty years ago. As Austin Pilgrim said to me in January
1988,

> I suppose you could say I'm disillusioned. As station manager I
> was asked if I wanted to go for area manager, but I declined to
> be put forward. My job gets me down, LT's gone down, and
> with all these staff cuts to save money just to make profits . . . !
> LT's now being run by those two doctors[9]—chaps like you with
> university degrees. They don't know the railway, and that safety
> is the first thing.

(I should interject here that Mr. Pilgrim at that time was manager of an Underground station with a particularly grim reputation for muggings and
the like; a month previously a visitor to the United Kingdom had been
murdered there. Now, however, he has moved up to manager of one of
the Underground's flagship stations.)

It is not only the demeaning of LT that concerns Frank Springer, however. It is also the injection of uncertainty that comes with the attempt to
reshape LT in accordance with Margaret Thatcher's tenets. He and his fellow recruits have forged their way to the upper echelons of LT, but now:

> "You won't find one of us—well, maybe one—who doesn't
> really suspect that deep down this thing's racial. I mean, why
> does it happen *now,* now that we've got near to the top, that
> they change the rules, 'from seniority to suitability' as they say?"
> "What Americans call 'moving the goalposts.' "
> "Yes. We've worked our way up, put in our years, and now
> they want to abolish our grade [inspector] and retrain us and give
> us tests to pass, so they can fail us and get rid of us. LT is in a
> mess, it's all this profit stuff, that's all Thatcher and them care
> about. They've never worked at the lower levels, on the trains.

What about safety? What about the King's Cross disaster?[10]—
that's what happens when you cut staff too far, everybody
knows that. What about *us?* I don't like working for LT these
days at all.

"The union's had nothing to do with them at all. Looked at
the proposals, said no way will we negotiate on a basis like that.
But I don't think it's illegal for LT to behave this way now, with
her [Thatcher's] new union laws."

"So you mean there's a wave of black people of your generation getting to top levels when there were none before, so it's
aimed at you? But aren't there any black people coming up after
you, too?"

"Yes, it's aimed at us."

"But aren't there any young blacks at lower levels in LT now,
coming up?"

"No, not many. People don't like working underground, or
shift work. . . . Well, there are *some,* but it's young Asians[11]
you see now. Sitting in the ticket collectors' boxes at the
stations. . . . "

Whether Frank's allegations contain considerable truth or whether they
are misleading half-truths is perhaps not so important as their indication
that Frank and most of the others are today disaffected to some degree.
Frank particularly had something he wanted to "get off his chest" to my
apparently sympathetic ears. Certainly his sense of beleaguerment-with-a-
racial-twist loses no credibility when regarded in the light of the 1984
findings of the Policy Studies Institute, that "only in specific areas of the
service sector have blacks obtained non-manual jobs in the same proportion as whites. For West Indians, these are the employers that recruited
blacks during the earlier period of immigration, that is to say the health
service and the transport services."[12] Now, even in these fields, these
positive exceptions, it could easily appear to a skeptical black (or white)
observer that racial disadvantage is somehow being consciously fur-
thered.

Nor did it take George Farley long to warm to his topic. After twenty-
three and one-half years at Upton Park bus garage, he retired in 1985. In
the asperity of the upcoming quote from him we hear reiterated some of
the themes upon which his fellow workers have already touched: the decline in public behavior and with it a decline in job satisfaction, especially
if one's personal security comes to be at risk. George now works not quite
full-time as a security guard and is actively considering a return to Barbados. Aged sixty, he is the oldest of the interviewees:

It's a rotten job these days being a bus conductor. I'm glad I'm
out of it. I was recruited and told I'd be getting £9 10s a week
and when I got here it wasn't worth at all as much as I thought it
was. I think LT misled me. I was on the number 15 bus for thirteen years. It terminates out here at East Ham, so out here's my
garage. It's only a mile and a half from here [his house in Can-
ning Town]. These last years we were getting some bad passengers. I've had a lot of bad experiences, a lot of abuse. From
black people too; there are some bloody awful black people.

I used to drive to work. Before I went in in the morning I'd
take a long pee. Then into my car, and I'd get there ten minutes
later, and I wanted to go again. I thought I was getting old very
suddenly, that I couldn't control it. But the doctor checked me
and said he couldn't find anything wrong but it went on for two
months and so I went to him again and he said it's got to be my
nerves. And it was. So I'm glad I'm off the buses now.

Oh yes, I've been abused. I remember there was one Scot who
was very abusive and refused to pay more than 20p for a 50p
ride. So I stopped the bus to put him off. I was polite. He tried
to butt me. As he came forward I punched him really hard,
slashed his cheek. [George is still a big strong man, with great
hands. In Barbados he was a butcher, and when younger used to
lift weights.] Blood came out, he was screaming he was going to
knife me, my driver called for the police . . .

Trevor Brathwaite has worked even longer on the buses than George
Farley. It was in March 1988 after that evening meal that Beverly Brathwaite had prepared for us that my wife and I sat back and listened to her
account of the jobs she'd done. Then her husband talked about his thirty-
two years at Hanwell bus garage. Was he the longest-serving worker
there? No, there was a man from Grenada "who I found when I got there"
in 1957, so Trevor was second most senior:

"The prestige of working for LT has gone down. And the
roads are so much fuller. Sunday turns were easy then. You got
paid more, had to keep to the same timings but there was less
traffic: very nice. Now with privatization they're trying to save
money. So you get fewer Sundays, and there's this split-shift
thing. You come on at six, you work till ten, on at two, work till
six. You come home in the middle, but as soon as you get to
rest, the alarm clock gets you up again. Awful."

"Because of the rush hour?"

"Yes. I get one [a split shift] every six or seven weeks or so.[13]
That's all—they rotate. They pay you for the hours you're off in
the middle, too. So it's like time-and-a-half. But it's so tiring.

"I remember the fog made a great impression on me. Never seen anything like it. When it was really bad they used to put out flares for the buses where to turn in. No good looking ahead much, just down, trying to follow the white line. Can you imagine being a driver in such conditions! Once or twice it was even so thick we had a man walking in front of us with a flare, like a sort of big candle, to park [within the garage precincts]. It was so dirty: smoke and fog—smog."

"Even the trains were throwing it out, such a lot," put in Beverly.

"They cleaned it up with clean air zones—now, there's one improvement for an LT bus driver since those days!

"At the very start I was a conductor. I used to hate going upstairs in those days, especially in the winter. Nearly everyone was smoking.[14] Maybe they thought it'd help to keep them warm. All the windows were closed and it was a filthy smoky place. I couldn't wait to get down to my platform again and have the fresh air blowing past me. There's much less smoking now.

"There are other improvements. Buses are easier to drive now; it's the power steering. On the old RTs you *really* had to heave the wheel [he does a vigorous mime, like someone hauling in a rope onto a quayside capstan]. But the traffic's worse. And the people are worse. They litter the buses now—all this McDonald's rubbish, and drink cans rolling around the floor every time you turn a corner.

"And the pay seems really to have only stayed about the same, what with the rise in the cost of living. Well, no . . . we *are* better off."

This somewhat unenthusiastic admission from Trevor, that he and his wife *had* materially improved their lives by coming to work for LT, was backed up by Joan Springer. When asked would she do the same again—i.e., come as an LT recruit—she said with conviction, "Yes. I don't regret a minute of it." Yet she had that frightening experience in the Notting Hill riots, and at the end of the quotation that follows we sense her awareness of the lack of cachet of her LT employment. But then again, this cheerful (though pained with arthritis), genuine woman has a solid sense of perspective, and is glad LT recruited her after eleven months of demoralizing unemployment in Barbados:

I worked four years at Paddington (Bakerloo Line) as a stationwoman: sweeping, "Mind the gap," and all that. I was two years at Trafalgar Square. Then they sent me as a relief ticket collector on the barriers, all over the system. When I had the kids, the hours are more flexible as a stationwoman. That's the better job

to have 'cos you can nip off an hour earlier; somebody'll cover
for you. If you're on the barriers you can't do it.

So I worked part-time while I brought up the kids, then about
1979 I became full-time again, a ticket collector. Then in 1985 I
became a ticket inspector. We travel on trains, we do "blitzes"
on particular stations [a group of inspectors descend unheralded
on a station, cover all exits, and check for fare dodgers]. We've
done one on Westbourne Park [I'd said to her that was "my" sta-
tion], that's a tough place.

Was the LT job what I expected? Well, we weren't exactly
told the full details. I didn't expect all that sweeping and cleaning. I thought people were looking down on me. Sometimes
you'd get a "can't you find something better to do?" look from
your own people.

Austin Pilgrim concludes this section on LT employment with a few
more notes from the Underground. The theme of vulnerability to personal violence that arose with George Farley is more prominent here.
Once again, some of it springs from loutish drunks or roughs:

A couple of years ago some young black men ran through
without paying. [The manager's office, with one-way tinted glass,
sits by the ticket barriers in the station foyer.] "Come back
here," I shouted.

"Hey, you're a black like us, don't stop us."

"Listen, if you're in here without a ticket you're trespassing. If
anything happens to you there's no compensation. You've got to
pay, it's for your own good."

"We don't have to pay, we're black."

"You want to be treated like everyone else, right? Right! Suppose we all did like you then? We'd get no money from fares.
Then there'd be no trains. And then where would you be? Pay
up. We all pay for this train."

For not a few of the immigrant generation, Austin included, an emblematic villain is the Rastafarian. In the tale that follows, the man was
quite likely just a rough young black with dreadlocks; the young Rasta
couple I met (daughter and son-in-law to an LT recruit) were gentle and
charming to me. But that day at Austin Pilgrim's Northern Line station:

There was this Rasta with a six-inch flick knife, beating up his
woman friend. Pushing her up against the wall, I thought she was
going to get killed. Just at the top there. He'd pushed her
through the barrier without a ticket. I called out, tried to stop
them getting down to the platform. My number two phoned the
police. I explained why they had to have a ticket [at length, kill-

ing time]. He was crazy. He'd have killed her, I believe. The police came. They disarmed him. They were very good.

What's worse is that some interpersonal violence is routine and premeditated. I refer to the muggings at Austin's former Tube station:

> We've also had closed-circuit TV monitors installed in the last few years. That helps with muggers. We had three of them down on the platform, they operate when there are crowds. One bumps a lady, the handbag is snatched, the other two guys are walking in the other direction with a big bag, they get the handbag passed to them and pop it in.
>
> I go down and invite them to leave the station, nicely. [This rather officious, schoolmasterish sweet-reasonableness, this formality-with-a-potential-to-become-rapidly-tough, seems to be Austin's modus operandi with problem cases.] Eventually things get nasty. It turns violent. They go for me. I hit one very hard, the other two run away. The police have been alerted in the meantime. And the third guy runs the wrong way. The police come and we catch him. And they got another. "We know these fellas," say the police, "they're from a family of nine down in Brixton, they're all ruffians." They got eighteen months. Two had just come out of prison six months.[15]

Jobs with the National Health Service (NHS)

I have devoted such a lot of space to the experiences of the LT workers because it is they who constituted, as recruits of over a quarter century ago, the main peg from which I have hung this study of some Barbadian Londoners. The two other male workers (one on the railways, one in the NHS) I met through them. The female workers, their spouses, I mostly met through them. As we've already heard from the two women who were themselves LT recruits, there are nine others at whose job experiences we should now look. All have worked outside of the home in Britain, seven of them for the NHS at one time or another. The other two have worked in a clerical capacity for public bodies: one for British Railways; one for the Greater London Council and now for the London Fire Brigade. Clearly, then, after LT, the NHS has been the next greatest employer of the immigrant generation in London—a predictable and representative finding.

Edward Pilgrim is Austin's elder brother. He has a different perspective from everybody else I interviewed in the migrant generation, because he'd been on the farm labor scheme in America first.

"The U.S. was too rough. I liked the pace of life when I got to England. I said to myself, I could stay here for a while.

"I'd been walking the streets for six weeks or so [he was twenty-six; this was in 1961], when my sister, who's in the NHS, got a contact at St. George's. There was a job going as a stores assistant. The storeman was one for the easy life. He had his little operation at St. George's and he knew I wouldn't rock the boat. I fitted the bill, I didn't know too much, he taught me all I knew, no prejudice with him. He was a boozer. And he was a secret type. I think he was married to a rich woman. . . . "

"And now *you* run the little operation?" [He grins in reply.]

"It's a nice number now. I can sort of make up my own hours. I can close up and go off to do a bit of food shopping. And I go to lunch with the boys at the pub."

He was also able to make time for me on every occasion that I came around to see him during the working day. So he seemed content. But hadn't there been low spots?

Oh yes. But . . . you mustn't give in. You've got to stick at it, keep your head down.[16] That's why we're still here. But I'll agree, it's your personality too. Some *did* give up. Charlie's brother came over here for the Transport, stuck it for three days, and then gave it up, went off to Charlie's in Wales and found some job there with him. I don't know if they're still over here now.

Edward was not one for whom the job was an enjoyable end in itself, a fulfilling career. It's perfectly evident that he has for his own reasons demanded less of himself and less reward from his employment. His interests lie elsewhere than in a job:

Thank God we had cricket. It made me valued. The hospital was run very *autocratically* in those days. Some of those big administrators knew who I was and helped me—even paid me to play [for the hospital team] sometimes. Even then, a few of them [i.e., his English teammates: young doctors and the like] were not nice. We'd go off and play another hospital or college, eleven men on the field together, trying to win, drinking cups of tea in the pavilion together, on the coach together there and back . . . and then you'd meet them on the Monday, crossing the hospital quadrangle, and they wouldn't recognize you, they'd look straight past you.

The National Health Service has been the largest employer of the women of the migrant generation. Seven have worked in the NHS, four as state registered nurses (SRNs), one of whom started as a state enrolled nurse (SEN—a less advanced qualification). Another worked as an SEN, one as a nursing assistant, and one as a cook.

To put the upcoming job histories of these women in perspective, it is necessary to bear in mind that in nearly all of the families the male partner came to Britain first. The men got themselves recruited and none of them came over to Britain to join family or spouses. Only five of the women were recruited, whereas a partially overlapping five came over specifically in order to join spouses or fiancés already in Britain, plus another two to join their parents at the latter's bidding. The women, then, were as a group not making single-minded career moves in coming to London. The tenor of the times then (both in England and especially in Barbados), the expectations that Barbadian men held of them, and I suspect the expectations they held for themselves, all militated against the women achieving economic independence in a career outside the home. That is, all of the women have had children, and it is indubitably upon the women that the major responsibility for raising these children and creating a home has fallen. Their employment and their financial role has thus been supportive. To none of these women has the privilege of an uninterrupted career in one field been granted. None of these women has enjoyed steady professional advancement in a domain she has been able to make her own. To none of the SRNs, for example, has it fallen to stay with the job and rise to nursing sister or to a position of authority such as (as it then was) matron.

Pauline Alleyne has had the closest approximation to a straightforward career, but even her success in the nursing field was interrupted for a few years by being an agency telephonist. And she feels aggrieved at the way she claims she was misled on her first arrival.

> We flew in late. Off we go to Hillingdon. I'm still hurt about it, because I came as a "student" and no one told me that "trainee" was different. Matron gave me a green form. I signed it. It was the SEN form. I think it was a con. I signed it, I didn't know. But I saw it through [1961 to 1963]. I didn't want to go and stay with my mother in Nottingham because I didn't like her Jehovah's Witness husband.

Then she did an SRN at Redhill General Hospital, from 1963 to 1965, bore a daughter, brought her son aged seven over from Barbados, worked at a number of other hospitals and at a Cheshire Home,[17] and specialized in psychiatric nursing.

> "I was running a health center and this big white woman came in to ask for improvements in something and just glanced at me

behind my table. Then she goes and talks, loud and fast, at the little white fella who was my assistant at that time. 'Talk to her,' he said. But she just carried on and on at him. He was a sort of recovering patient. He got all nervous and started shaking. I was so angry I got up and walked away. Eventually she was brought over to me."

"No apologies? Wasn't she embarrassed?"

"No. I was so *furious*. . . . But I answered her questions, I controlled myself."

"You're a Bajan."

"Yes," she laughs, catching my dig at her. "Now a *Jamaican* would've let rip!"

Pauline, whose own marriage has not been all plain sailing, evidently has an empathetic manner with those whom she helps in her present work:

"What I do now is really interesting. I'm a private psychiatric outpatient nurse in Walton-on-Thames. They're all so rich down there."

"Isn't it a stressful job?"

"Yes, but not so bad. And you know, ah, they don't see me as any threat. I'm a black woman, they can't imagine *ever* meeting me socially as an equal, so they tell me all kinds of things."

"You mean, confessionals? And things sexual?"

"Oh *yes!* It all spills out. It's a relief to them. It would be different in Brixton or Tulse Hill, with our own people. *They* wouldn't confide in me."

Ernestine Farley has also worked virtually continuously since coming to Britain, but what with raising five children, her jobs have not been graduated steps up a career ladder. Instead, she has been a nursing assistant doing night duty for the past twenty-three years, in both general hospitals and mental hospitals. She is fifty-four. Why didn't she do an SEN or SRN?

Once you start training for qualifications, your money cut right down. And he [her husband] didn't encourage me. And there's no point now [because she is getting on in years].

Nursing has gone right down now. Nurses half-do things now, they're so low-paid. They don't help patients like family now[18] like they used to. [Then she adds brightly:] I enjoyed nursing, y'know.

She has other work interests, which she pursues at home. She is a famed producer of cakes, for birthdays and weddings and friends:

I was taught before I left home. People here have got used to me
doing it, so I can't get out of it now! I make a couple of pounds
at it. Oh, I really get into it, when I get down to it. I get lots of
compliments.

As she tells me this, you can see that this is something her self-image is
bound up with. And yes, indeed, she really exudes pride at her achieve-
ments.

Ernestine was one of the minority of women whom I met *before* meeting their spouses, being directed to her by her good friend Amelia Simmons. Amelia's employment history has elements similar to both Ernestine's and Beverly Brathwaite's: waitressing in a Lyon's tea-shop, working
in a factory (suitcases, in this instance) near to home, then working as a
nursing assistant, graduating to SEN, at a nearby hospital. One of the times
I talked with Amelia was soon after she retired during the summer of 1988.

I was very lucky with this retirement. I'm not old enough. But all
this lifting has hurt my back, and then once lately gave me a her-
nia too. So I couldn't work on the geriatric wards—they're at
least half the wards in my hospital—you're always lifting them,
old people fall out of bed. . . .
    So I got early retirement on medical grounds. I keep my pen-
sion and everything.

Another worker in hospitals, Marie Pilgrim, soon gave up being an SRN
after marrying Austin, and ended up for over twenty years in the records
section of a large multinational corporation, to whose offices she com-
muted in central London. The money earned helped to send their son
Nigel as a day boy to a well-known London public school. But the job did
not enthrall. When I met the Pilgrims in May of 1989 she told me of her
retirement.

I stopped work four months ago and I haven't been on a train
since! I've no wish to go into Town[19] like that anymore. My
replacement went on holiday and they phoned to ask me to fill
in and I said oh no. . . . I'm so glad I did.

The Pilgrims are very great friends of the Gill family, also Barbadian
migrants. Although one family lives in north London and one in south, the
logistical difficulties do not inhibit the frequent commuting back and
forth. One of the supports that enabled Marie to continue to work was the
fact that her son Nigel was looked after on a regular basis by Sandra Gill.
In order to do this, and to raise her own three children, Sandra in 1964
gave up her typist's post at the BR Cricklewood steam locomotive sheds
after four years, and has worked in her home ever since. There is, I as-

sume, some quid pro quo here for the Gills—but I do not know what it might be. I did not feel I could directly ask—"So, what do *they* do for *you?*"—if it was not volunteered. But the family symbiosis is evident: Marie Pilgrim told me, with a smile,

> As soon as Nigel comes home from college, he's not here a day before he's off up to the Gills. It's a second home to him. He and Derek [the Gills' eldest son, of comparable age] are like brothers. Well, they were brought up together, weren't they? And they even *look* alike—well, Nigel's just a little stockier . . .

The above accounts are not meant to imply that the men take no role in housekeeping, that they spend no time nurturing their children. But they do spend less time than the women. And it is the women's job trajectories that get interrupted with child-bearing. Dotteen Bannister, an SRN, married Jeff (the youngest of all the male recruits) in 1968, and did midwifery at an inner London hospital. But she did only the first six months of the course,

> "because Colin was on the way. I realized I'd never finish the other half, so I went and worked in the post office as a clerical officer for those months until just after Colin was born. Then we had another, Andrew. So I looked after the two of them. I worked three evenings a week, 5 to 9 P.M., at the Enfield War Memorial Hospital [they live in Enfield]. Those evenings Jeff'd come in from work and, bang! I'd go out!
>
> That was from 1972 to 1980. Since 1980 I've been attached to a family doctor practice. It's a new thing, it's been going maybe ten years: you've got six doctors and three "practice sisters." I go three days a week, I do part-days: mornings or evenings. I like this job.

Another woman's story, partaking of elements of a number of the foregoing accounts, had a novel twist: she had spent a year working illegally in New York City. She had a sister established there; her sister paid her fare over; she got herself a social security number, made "good money, in childcare work," and took her ten-year-old daughter with her. Her son, who was two years younger, stayed in Britain with his father. Then her husband "brought me back from there." This happened in the mid-1970s. Since then she has been continuously employed full-time in NHS-related social work in the locality. She feels the job she is doing is a useful one: "Awful things can happen to people. I help people who need help."

The one person whose employment experience has not been touched on by any of the foregoing narratives is Tony Gill. In Barbados he was Austin Pilgrim's immediate superior, and when Gill left for Britain in 1960, it provided a spur to Pilgrim to get to Britain later that same year as an LT recruit. Gill, however, did it on his own, like Edward Pilgrim and like the majority of Afro-Caribbeans in London who came in once the recruiting schemes had slowed. This apparently self-contained man, one rapidly learns, is someone who, like Pilgrim, knows how to do his job well; he gets things right. Unlike Pilgrim—they are each other's closest friends, "he knows what I'm thinking before I even have to say it"—he has no reservations about telling me that he likes his job, at least in the main. Of the three men, Pilgrim, Maycock, and Gill, who have done particularly well, Gill is the one who has risen the highest, as any outside observer eyeing their career trajectories would confirm. There is a strong stamp of steady confidence and *competence* about this man, now in his midfifties. Starting off at an elementary level, demonstrating ability and reliability, he then landed a leadership position. Observe his deft footwork, to obviate possible racial friction with those who were passed over for the post he won. Observe his awareness of the potential for accusations of his foreignness, and how diplomacy is called for.

"I wanted to see things: mountains, rivers, *trains*. (We had a train in Barbados, you know, but I came along a little too late to see it!) I wanted to see how other people in the world lived, the different habits. . . . I was making good money as an electrician for General Electric, I could've stayed, but I had dreams of travel. Five years, I thought.

"So I got the job at Cricklewood sheds, and the electricals were so simple on the carriages they assigned me to. This first job was a waste of time; nothing to it, boring at times. I did it for nearly ten years. Then, as you move up, it gets more interesting. . . .

"Now, in those days it was still steam-hauled carriages."

"Oh yes, I used to go trainspotting the steam engines at Cricklewood and Neasden and Kentish Town," I said.

"Yes, when my wife came from Barbados a few months later, came to marry me, she got a job in the office at the steam sheds across the lines, very handy. Then the DMUs[20] came in and they sent me off to Derby on a course (and to Crewe and to York on other occasions) and I got the hang of it. But there was one thing though in the diesel ignition system, a glow-plug. . . . Got a bit of paper?"

I dig into my briefcase and come out with one.

"Now, see this. . . . " And he draws me a diagram, spontaneously, of a battery unit or whatever for the lighting on the train. This, I say to myself, is a man who is involved in his job. A long account follows of his jobs on the way up. And then:

"A Grade D post went vacant at Hornsey, with a retirement. All four Cs there applied, all four were interviewed, and I was chosen. (This is more than ten years ago now.) There were some very bad feelings about me getting it, a black over three whites: 'It's our country, not his.' I've always known I had to be extra careful because of that. I don't open my mouth too much, I make sure I've got my facts absolutely straight before I do. I *never* let myself lose my tongue.

"So as soon as I was settled into my Grade D, I made sure I did things absolutely right—and made sure my superiors knew I did it dead right too! So I had *their* support. Then, once that was done, I made sure my staff, those under me, knew I was absolutely fair, though I could be tough too." In response to my interjected question, he tells me there are ninety staff, about 50 to 60 percent black.

"So I did that. So the three who were passed over, who wanted to make trouble for me, couldn't; I'd isolated them. People are different, you know. Some you know it won't work with [i.e., friendly relations], like them; others you find you can go to the pub with; but there're a lot fewer who you can go to parties with.

"Anyway, I've gone up another grade since then. I'm in charge of all rolling stock between King's Cross and Letchworth [about thirty-five miles out of London]. I was offered a move up again about four years ago but we would've had to have moved away. I declined. Well, with the kids getting their education and the house all set up, we've modernized it. . . . If you want the grass to grow then the horse'll have to starve."

"Excuse me?"

"Meaning, you can't have everything; one thing or the other."

Even though Tony Gill had to find his own job upon arrival, he had a better hand with which to play than had Edith Simmons. It was she who was brought at her father's demand from rural Jamaica to London. She was thrown in at the deep end, struggled, and eventually did more than just survive.

> I went to work as a shop assistant at John Barnes on the Finchley Road. I had no idea. What were these dinner- and tea-breaks? What was this someone always telling you what to do?

Later she worked as a cook in Willesden General Hospital, and later in a local authority-run nursery. Life now seems easier, the children are raised, the mortgage is under control:

"Other people looking at us would say we're middle class, and I can see why. But I'm definitely working class: I've worked all my life. And what they see's just *things*. I feel working class. Just things, money, don't make you middle class."

"Some would say they do in America," say I.

"Well, that's America for you!"

Six
Making It: From Flat Rental to Home Ownership

Ladbroke Grove was not a place to bring up children.

John Simmons

As the Barbadians continued to work steadily, advancing in their jobs, they found they could afford better housing. In this chapter we hear from them about their moves up out of slumlike conditions to acceptable apartments. Then they talk about their searches for a home to buy; some encountered difficulties and discrimination, some did not. They tell of the vagaries of home ownership—all are now home owners—and of their satisfactions or dissatisfactions with the neighborhoods they have bought into. They finally discuss their expectations of what neighbors should be . . . and indeed *who* neighbors should be. The ethnicity of those among whom one resides is of some concern: Are they Barbadians, other Afro-Caribbeans, whites, or Asians?

A Sketch of London-wide Patterns

It is useful to try to first put the housing experiences of the dozen Barbadian households into some kind of metropolitan context. It's not as if they were interviewed by me on the moon. On the other hand, the degree to which they fit into overall Afro-Caribbean settlement patterns in London and certainly the degree to which they illustrate various theories of racial residential segregation are not at all my primary concerns in this work. In the subtitle, "sketch" implies both brevity and a certain roughness, indefinition. Indeed so. There are all kinds of logical problems, such as those

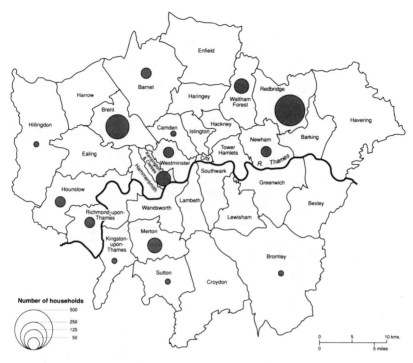

Figure 9: Overrepresentation of Barbados-born persons among West Indian-born persons, Greater London, 1971

of comparability of data over time, in the first few pages that follow. In addition, not only is the sample tiny, but it was not chosen for its overall representativeness either. Nevertheless, the attempt to compare the various distribution maps does, I believe, leave the reader with a serviceable sense of the overall London context, of the social geographical backdrop to the experiences recounted.

If today we could estimate that about 5 percent of those who live in the former Greater London Council (GLC) area are West Indian, then in turn about 10 percent of those are Barbadian: 1 in 200 Greater Londoners. A return glance at Trevor Lee's Figure 8 (chapter 4) is a basic step toward a perspective on the interviewees' various addresses through the years. But Figure 8 illustrates the 1971 pattern of the *general* West Indian-born population in Greater London. Figure 9, based on data provided by Ceri Peach, helps to give a more precise background. It shows where in that year the *particular* Barbados-born population was overrepresented with respect to all West Indian-born people. That is, Barbadians then making

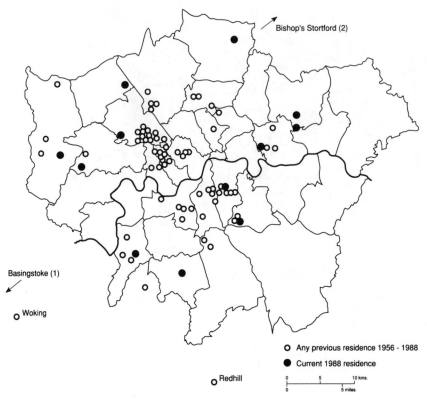

Figure 10: Location of residences of the twelve Barbadian Londoner households, 1956–88

up 10.73 percent of the West Indian-born total, one would expect that for every 1,000 West Indians living in, let us say, the borough of Greenwich, 107 of them would be Barbadians. If there were more Barbadians than that per thousand, they would show up as a positive deviation on Figure 9, the size of their dot being proportional to the magnitude of their over-representation in the particular borough. Thus we see that the London borough of Redbridge at that time had the largest positive deviation, followed by the borough of Brent, and then Waltham Forest, Kensington and Chelsea, and Merton.

With this information in mind, now look at Figure 10, wherein some confirmatory regularities can be made out in the pattern of the residential histories of each of the dozen immigrant Barbadian households studied in this book. The most evident concentration of the interviewees' housing over the thirty-two-year period of their presence in Britain (1956 to 1988) has been in inner west/northwest London: Shepherd's Bush-Notting Hill-Willesden-Harlesden. This dovetails satisfyingly with the information presented about Barbadians by other researchers. Glass and Pollins (Figure 6) had found a strong early concentration of Barbadians in Notting Hill-Paddington in the late 1950s. The borough of Brent, which includes Willesden and Harlesden, was found by Peach (Figure 9) to have in 1971 the second largest overrepresentation of Barbadians; the adjoining borough of Kensington and Chelsea, which includes Notting Hill, the fourth largest. The next greatest concentration of addresses of interviewees, with half as many mentions, has been in inner south London: Brixton-Stockwell-Camberwell. This also meshes with the previous work of Glass and Pollins (Figure 7) and of Lee (Figure 8).

In plotting Figure 10, I made no attempt, as I might fairly have done, to accord greater weight to those dots denoting long as opposed to short stays. A sojourn of a week at an address (there was one such case) is depicted here in the same manner as one of fifteen years. Not surprisingly, the frequency of changes of residence declines rapidly after the early years of room rental. Despite its glossing over such pertinent information, this unsophisticated map does indicate a clear trend of dispersal outward from the inner city. How typical is the pattern of dispersal evidenced by this particular group of Barbadians, compared with London Afro-Caribbeans in general? Figure 11 presents the pattern of residence of West Indian-born heads of households in London according to the last census, in 1981. The contrast between the 1988 residence of the dozen Barbadian households and that of this general London West Indian population is striking. It is closer to being the *inverse* than to being the same. Unless widespread black suburbanization had taken wing in London in those intervening seven years—which seems truly unlikely—then these Barbadians appear to be a most untypical set.

Lambeth had in 1981 the greatest number of West Indians of any borough in Greater London; none of the Barbadian set lives there. Hackney in 1981 had in Greater London the greatest proportion (15.1 percent) of its population belonging to the West Indian group; none of the set lives there. Brent had the second highest number of West Indian-born heads of households (Hackney was third in total numbers), and one of the set does indeed live in Brent. Then, in order, come Haringey (none), Lewisham (one), Wandsworth (none), and Southwark (one). Whereas the outer suburban boroughs of Harrow, Hillingdon, Kingston-upon-Thames, and Sutton, all with small or very small 1981 West Indian populations, have one each of my sample; the comparable borough of Redbridge has two. Also noteworthily, Figure 11 shows few West Indians in the easternmost

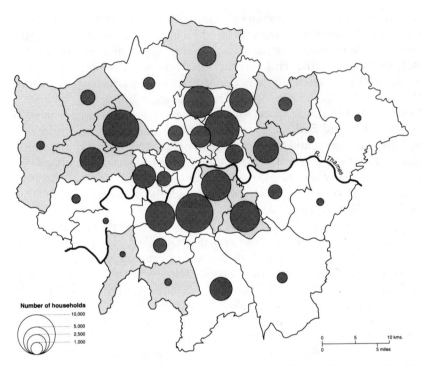

Figure 11: Settlement pattern of West Indian-born heads of household, Greater London, 1981

boroughs of Havering, Barking, Bexley, and Bromley; nor did any of the set live there. (In order to facilitate visual comparison, in Figure 11 the GLC borough of destination for each of the dozen Barbadian trajectories has been lightly stippled.)

I interviewed only twelve households, whereas there are thirty-three London boroughs, so there are obviously going to be empty spaces. Two of these empty spaces are the boroughs of Greenwich and Croydon, where significant numbers of blacks live (Figure 11). None of the interviewees themselves may have lived there in 1987–88, but one household had lived in Croydon from 1971 to 1982, and three other households had children living in either Croydon or Greenwich. In sum, given that there do have to be empty spaces when mapping the dozen households in GLC boroughs, *where* the empty spaces are is instructive.

Some empty spaces are in places where there are lots of blacks: Lambeth is the most striking example. In 1981 just over two-thirds of all West

Indian households in London lived in "inner" boroughs such as Lambeth; only three of the twelve Barbadian households did. In economic class terms most of the twelve could afford to live farther out. It is perhaps also worth noting that Lambeth is south of the river, whereas two-thirds of my Barbadians-only sample live north of it—a distribution that goes back to the years of immigration, as Glass and Pollins noted then. Other empty spaces are where there are precious few blacks at all: Bexley. But I would strongly suspect that such blacks as are now moving into the Bexleys of the metropolis are going to be very like most of the people who constituted my sample: blacks who could afford to do so if they wished.

From Flats to Houses

In general terms, we are, to begin with, returning to the 1960s. Times were not easy, and, as we have seen in chapter 4, accommodation for many was not of the best. One of the interviewees actually tried giving up on Britain and lived in the United States for a year. Two more households today say they came close to returning to Barbados (one of the men spent five months back there). However, these dozen households did eventually start clambering up the ladder. As we have seen in chapter 5, one gets a sense of how much *work* was put in, doing overtime and putting some money aside. While saving for the down payment and then for the monthly mortgage repayments, while taking inexpensive vacations if any at all, the interviewees were also remitting a portion of their earnings back to Barbados: twenty out of twenty-three said they, in their first years in Britain, had sent significant amounts home. Yet they got themselves into better housing, and eventually saved enough to buy.

Early experiences of apartment life mirrored much that has already been told about rooming. Tony Gill and Sandra Yearwood (they were not yet married), for example, went flat-hunting in Hendon in 1962.

> We would look in the papers and in the shops. We had some difficulties. I remember going to one house after work, the lights were on, and as soon as I rang the bell they went off. They were looking at us. No one ever answered the door. Funny, isn't it?

Trevor and Beverly Brathwaite had a flat from 1960 to 1963 in Coningham Road, Shepherd's Bush. Beverly asserted,

> The furniture was in terrible condition. It was run by a Polish couple. It was the wife, she used to make the colored people pay a lot of money, £4. The Irish downstairs were only paying 15s (they had a dog—what a mess!).

For many of the interviewees, however, as they learned their way around London, and as they continued to have a steady income, life in rental accommodations began to look up. Jeff Bannister recalls an acceptable apartment he shared with a Barbadian friend from 1964 to 1966:

> Bentley and I got a flat at Manor House, the top floor of a modern two-story building. It was owned by a Jamaican couple; they had no kids. It was pleasant, the neighborhood was okay, it was clean. It was a convenient spot: the pub, the greengrocer, the Tube, the buses. It was *very* convenient for work (I was at St. Martin's-le-Grand). The landlord didn't bother us. We'd have a talk and a drink together—though his wife was a bit fiery. I stayed there till Bentley got married in '66. He stayed, she [Gloria, Bentley's fiancée] came, I left.

As the Barbadians learned the ropes, they came to realize that a good landlord-tenant relationship was a boon. When one landlord moved, he took his tenant, Charles Eastmond, with him, much to Charles's satisfaction:

> "The owner was Barbadian. He and his wife and only child lived downstairs. He gambled on the horses then. Sometimes I went with him."
> "You always liked the horses?"
> Charles grinned. "It was the landlord that encouraged me to do it! Sometimes I lost. Then I didn't have to pay up the rent straight away. That was okay with him. And sometimes I won. Sometimes he and his wife raved—and I got pulled into it. His wife hated him gambling. They'd have Friday night fights, before his day for going out gambling, Saturday.
> "Anyway, he sold up and took us with him to a bigger house: King's Road, Willesden. It was a terraced house. Eulie came and we got married, we had the top flat. It was ideal really. We shared the kitchen with a law student (he was very good), we had our own bathroom. It was only a bit over five minutes' walk to my work [at Willesden bus garage]. We were there from 1963 to 1967. We started really saving. Then Eulie got pregnant and stopped working at the hospital. We were looking to move. . . ."

Joan Maxwell had a basement flat off Warwick Avenue, owned by Rachman. She had been there two years when Frank Springer came to live with her in 1961.

> There were other people on the upper floors; they were all black people. But we never saw them hardly. We, and them, were do-

ing shift work. The basement was always dark and cold. You had to keep the lights on all day. Our little boy was born there—that's why we had to get out of there.

Thus, typically, as the chapter's epigraph indicates and as Charles Eastmond and Joan Maxwell explain, the establishment of a permanent union or the arrival of children precipitated the search for a property to buy. Frank continues the story Joan began above:

We started looking. We'd just got married. I was a motorman at White City. I had a friend at work, a Bajan. He said, "You should buy a house. Look over my way [South Woodford]. Houses are cheap over this way." He left a note the next day, saying come over to Ilford way. There were very few black people out here then [1965]. We got the brochures, we kept going through the process, and then, being black, it'd fall through. But he kept on keeping me informed. We even got one in Wanstead—a nice area—but then at the last minute the chap said no, his neighbors didn't want no blacks. I got so frustrated. Then we got this finally. It'd been standing empty, there was long grass in the garden. The first night in, the fuses blew, the wiring was so old.

Joan fills in the picture:

Derek was eighteen months when we moved in here [1966]. I saw this house and liked it: £4,200. There's only £443 to go now on the mortgage! It feels very good now, this house. . . . Our energy, our love, our labor, has gone into this one, *this* is our home.

It is quite evident that Joan is really content and house-proud in what has become a most comfortable home. One of her children also remarked, with amused tolerance, on her love for her back garden: "Whenever I pop round mum's got some new flower coming up that I've never seen before!"

Now back to Charles and Eulie Eastmond, newly married and with Eulie pregnant. Of the dozen households they were the second, after the Springers the previous year, to move as home owners into the GLC borough of Redbridge. The deal was closed ten years to the month after Charles had arrived on the *Hubert*. Their experience—at least as retailed to me—was far less stressful than the Springers'. Charles recounts:

I was walking along Willesden High Road, I saw a friend from home (he'd worked at the Oistins Press there with me). He was living in Scarborough in Canada by then, but here he was, over here in Willesden visiting. He was with a friend. He [this second man] says, "I live over Ilford now, the houses are much cheaper." "But how do you do it?" I asked. He told me the GLC were giving mortgages.[1] So we filled up the form the next day, and sent it off.

Well, they called me for interview. "Do you have £500 saved?" I said yes, even though we had only 300—because I'd just been spending a lot for clothes for the baby and everything. "All right," they said, "go and find a house, and get back to us." Our friend went and looked around, found an estate agent's [realtor] on Cranbrook Road, and got stuff on a number of houses. We found a nice place. Saw the owner, he said okay. We went back to the GLC and took it from there. The Smiths left the fittings and the furniture. They were building a bungalow to re-tire to in Devon. This was in February [1967]. "Can you wait to move in till September?" they asked. We said yes. And we did. I did all the overtime I could do—and so we got the deposit.

And Eulie explains to me in conclusion:

It was all English here. There was one black family next door, and one at the end of the [long] street; and two on Ilford Lane. Now there are a lot more Asians here, but it's still not too bad an area.

The Eastmonds were not the only ones to have had a relatively un-stressful time of house-hunting. The Bannisters, for example, married on September 7, 1968. Jeff told me that in the spring of 1969 they started looking, and had moved into their first (and present) house on September 4, 1969. Trevor and Beverly Brathwaite, on the other hand, had a less for-tunate time of it. Trevor told me,

We were always thinking about bringing the children over here. But you need a real home, not a flat. So Audley [his great friend, ever since on board the *Hubert* in early 1957] said, "Let's get to-gether and buy a place." So we did—but we got taken in by a con man, that Jamaican, he was a false estate agent. We lost our money: £200 [this was 1962].[2] So, we had to try again, to strug-gle and struggle and save to get a deposit.[3] We wanted to stay in Shepherd's Bush—we still had a lot of friends around there then—but it was too expensive.

Beverly takes up the story:

I went to an agent looking for houses around Shepherd's Bush Green, but there weren't any. I had a Barbadian friend at work,

at Callard and Bowser's. "You could get a house in Greenford,"
she said. "Where's that? I don't know it." So she took me on a
bus there, to an agent there, he showed me pictures. I fell in love
with this house in Southall. I didn't know where it was! So I
found out, came and saw it. He [Trevor] couldn't—he was working on shift. "Do you like it?" he said. "Yes," I said. "Well then,
let's buy it," he said. And then he came out and saw it and said
yes. So we bought it. Oh, we so wanted the children to
come . . .

They acquired the house in 1963. One child was brought over in 1966,
another in 1970. A third never came. A fourth was born to them in the
house.

Audley Simmons also lost £200 in the con man debacle, but had
bounced back enough by the end of the year (1962) to have pooled
resources with another friend, Everett Johnson, to buy a place very close
to Notting Hill.

I bought a house with a mate—he's back in Barbados now. It was
a smallish terraced house in North Kensington: Brewster Gardens.
There were just another couple of blacks in the street at that
time, that's all. It was good because you were at your own place.
You had to pay a mortgage now, but you had more space. It was
nice to be your own landlord. If you come back and you've left
your light on all night, nobody's going to tell you off. If you
want you can have a party there. Edith and me got married there
in 1962. It was okay round there.

Tony and Sandra Gill went the route of being landlords in their first
property (as did a couple of others among the interviewees). This fact appeared to be the reason for an interesting maneuver on Tony's part during
a long, animated, free-flowing conversation I had with him in January
1988.

My first place in Britain was in Hendon, a furnished room. A St.
Kitt's man owned the house. We paid very high rent. It was
mainly West Indians, and some Africans. They didn't like us.
They called us . . . well . . . slaves. He [the landlord] was ex-
ploiting us, a black man making money out of black men.

At this point in his narrative Tony visibly checked himself and assumed
an altogether less righteously indignant tone:

Mind you, he was giving us somewhere to stay. But he was easily
covering his mortgage, charging each of us £2 10s a week for the

room, and probably paying £16 a month for the mortgage. He lived there too.

I don't blame him, though. He owned it, so, naturally, it's his right to want to pay off the mortgage.

Some time later in the conversation, at least part of the reason for Tony's reining in his ire at exploitative fellow black landlords became clear:

Then we did buy this place in Colindale. It was our first step up the ladder. We rented out rooms. First my two brothers and a cousin came to live with us; they paid rent. Then others came. I never exploited them. I mean, I made money, but I kept it up well, and they all eventually moved out to get their own places and we keep in touch today. So I wasn't a bad landlord, was I?

When a little over two years later Sandra became pregnant with their first child, she and Tony sold the Colindale property and were done with being landlords. Said she: "We needed more room, more privacy. We went through the estate agents, it took four or five shots to find this place." The previous owners were Guyanese who were reemigrating to Canada. The Gills have stayed in their well-set Canon's Park semidetached home ever since (1965).

Alan and Althea Maycock, their second baby arriving (and their first child living in Barbados), wanted to get out of their Stockwell rented accommodation. The Maycocks bought a terraced house in Norbury in 1971, "good for Susan to grow up in, suburban, a nice neighborhood. Some natives are friendly," quipped Alan of his English neighbors there, "We still keep up with them." And then in 1982, for reasons that echo stereotypic metropolitan American middle-class concerns, the Maycocks moved again. Alan told me:

Croydon [the GLC borough in which Norbury lies] were messing with the schools. Susan had just started secondary school. I was in the PTA; I could see the schools were going to go down. One of my fellow workers at County Hall was retiring and going off to live in Canada. We agreed to buy his place at Wimbledon. But it fell through because Norbury took too long to sell. Then another colleague of mine, a Guyanese friend living in Tolworth, suggested we look in that area. Still we couldn't sell Norbury. But we were getting to know this part of London. We were looking at the listings the estate agents had down here. All of a sudden we got *two* firm offers on our Norbury place. This one [their present Surbiton house] was available, we liked it around here, the schools were better, so here we are!

In a separate interview three months later, Althea offered exactly the same rationale as had Alan for their move: a superior school district. Susan is now at college in northern England.

It is probably fair to infer that one of the reasons for the resoundingly comfortable ordinariness of the Maycocks' house change in 1982 has been the enactment in 1968 and in 1976 of laws against racial discrimination in housing. Austin and Marie Pilgrim did not have their full protection when they went house-hunting toward the end of the 1960s. Before Austin was able to exult "FREEDOM!" they had to go through some emotionally and physically costly experiences. The great part of the story as told here is in Austin's words, but on two separate later occasions Marie, in Austin's absence, confirmed the gist. Itching to escape an unhappy rental situation, with Nigel a toddler and Marie pregnant again, Austin recalled,

> It was a tough business. My wife and I would go off searching
> separately off work [as with the Brathwaites, shifts didn't mesh].
> She found a place through the estate agent and went to see the
> lady who was selling and Marie liked her. The lady said, "Bring
> back your husband." So I came along too, and it was a good
> place, a lot of garden and all the grass trimmed just so, the same
> height everywhere [holds up his thumb and index finger to show
> an inch or more]. And she said, "Yes, I'll sell to you, you're such
> a nice young couple. I know you'll look after it." But then the
> estate agent, Kahn,[4] said no. His partner said yes. "No," he said,
> "We can't have blacks living in *that* area, it might drive prices
> down." He refused, point-blank. We were very upset. My wife
> had a miscarriage.

Of this time, Marie has told me, "I'd lost all my confidence, I'd lost a baby, we had such a hard time hunting for a house. I wanted to go home." This is not a casually retailed sob story. During my brief return visit to London in May 1989 Marie informed me that it was a *six-month* miscarriage: a major trauma for a couple. That she has had three midterm miscarriages altogether does not in any way mitigate the fact that the stress of unsuccessful house-hunting precipitated one of them.

I frankly found the episode of the two real estate agents discussing race and housing prices *in front of Austin* rather difficult to credit. I later asked Alan Maycock about such an occurrence. "Perfectly believable," he wrote in response, "You must realise that little account was taken of black people's feelings then." Much later, on a visit to London in May 1990, I had the temerity to raise the matter with Austin and Marie again.

> "Yes, he said it in front of me. I could see his partner wasn't
> too pleased. We weren't people in those days, you know. They'd
> talk about you as if you're not there."

I insisted, this was really so?

"Oh John, *John!* You can't understand how horrible it was! I hadn't *done* anything. Why would they treat another person so?"

His voice choked. He actually sobbed for a second or two. And then he regained his composure: "Look, you're a professor. I'd be a fool to tell lies to you, you could see through them. Tell me, *why should I lie to you?*"

"I'm sorry," was all I could say, and punched Austin lightly on the shoulder as we sat next to each other on the sofa in order, I hoped, to indicate however awkwardly some degree of receptivity.

After the Kahn episode, Marie and Austin continued their search. He told me of two more places that tantalized but then fell through. Austin then decided not to let Marie know of his further searching, and eventually he came across

a policeman who was selling up to emigrate to Australia. He was very nice. We got on very well. He was asking £6,000. This was 1969–1970. How much is it worth now? *Oooh!*

We agreed on the price. I said nothing to her, so that after all the disappointments I could pleasantly surprise my wife. So things slowly take their course, and then one evening the chap turns up at my door! My wife doesn't know who on earth he is. "Why are you here?" I ask him. "Well, I haven't heard from you, I wanted to make sure it was still all right." "Look," I said, "I gave you my word, so that's it."

They successfully closed on this place, and live there still. Marie said, "I never knew about it till the letter came saying we could move in. What a release! I can't tell you . . ."

I have become friends with the Pilgrims over the three years or more we've known each other, and am now becoming accustomed to some of Austin's idiosyncrasies. For example, on a couple of occasions during our first conversations I would exclaim, "I don't believe it!" in the almost phatic sense of "No!" or "Go on!" He, however, was three-quarters ready to jump up out of his seat to show me the document or whatever to prove that I should believe it, and him: there's a certain righteousness about the man. But the distress provoked by my pressuring him on the Kahn episode left me chastened. I feel some sort of bond to Austin Pilgrim now. Already, after only my first, afternoon-long conversation with him, he offered me a big firm onion to take home with me; he is a prize-winning vegetable gardener. "Oh, you were *honored!*" said Marie on a subsequent occasion, "He must've liked you!"

Not a few of the Barbadians are keen flower and vegetable gardeners,

*"We're sorry to bother you, but Dorothy and I are rather concerned as to
whether or not you will be rioting this summer?"*

Figure 12: *Punch* cartoon, July 28, 1982

a predilection that sits very well with the English. Along with the Pilgrims', the Maycocks' back garden in particular is a horticultural triumph.
Living near very few other blacks, in well-set white suburbia, these
middle-class Barbadian couples are light-years away from any stereotypic
British popular media representations of metropolitan blacks, as this cartoon from 1982 wittily underlines (Figure 12).

One smiles. Austin, however, on one occasion felt the indignation of
almost precisely the cameo portrayed by the cartoon:

"Lots of our friends now are white—like all our neighbors.
They were cool at first, but now we've been here over eighteen
years, we're among the old-establisheds. We go to each other's
parties. There was a lady up the road who never talked to me.

Eventually I met her, years later, at one of the parties. I got her to talk. She'd been convinced I was semisavage, that I must have come from a grass-roofed hut. I nipped back here and got a picture of my parents' home. Took it over and showed her. You should've seen the relief on her face!"

"No embarrassment?" I asked.

"No. . . . Well, after that it was fine. Oh, people can be so *ignorant!*"

The Farleys' story is different from all of the others recounted so far: they bought their own council house. In the late 1960s they were renting a large bed-sitting-room when they brought over their children from Barbados and put themselves down for council accommodation. George recalled,

> We had about a two years' wait. Then they offered us number 12, Gage Road. It was very old. Some dogs was living there. The windows was boarded up. "It's all we have to offer," they said.
>
> Well, it was the right size, and we were living *at ourselves.* If we wanted to have the kids with us, we had to accept what accommodation they had. It did have three bedrooms and a box room.

Ernestine assented: "It wasn't the best but it was having your own place. It was very damp, it was freezing, very run-down, the toilet was outside. But we tried to make the best of it." "I did it up nice," claimed George, "I spent my own money, couldn't get it back from the council. You'd have to pester them to repair a window."

Gage Road no longer exists on the street map of London; it was totally cleared. George tells that "we didn't have to ask [to move into their present house]; they demolished the previous one." Ernestine was delighted: "Oh yes, I love it. The kids loved it. Moving into a new house, we're the only people [to have lived in it]. There were no repairs needed, no need to call them in." Having been rehoused in 1976, things fell into place "like a fairy story," as Ernestine put it. George took severance from his longtime job on the buses in 1985. A year and a half later he used some of this gratuity to buy their own council house in the Margaret Thatcher-induced sell-off program: "*And* we got a big discount from renting from the council for so long. We bought it only two years ago for £29,500. It was valued last month at £73,000—it's with all this Docklands[5] development and the new airport and all." Understandably, both of them are hugely pleased. George sums up:

> Fortune has smiled on me financially, just now I'm getting old. The value of this place has gone up and up. Well, you can't sell

in less than three years, otherwise they take 40 percent of the profits. So of course I'm going to sit here until that's done. And then I'll go!

The Present Neighborhood, the Ideal Neighbors?

The Farleys' contentment is mirrored by the reactions of the other immigrant-generation interviewees to the milieus into which they have bought. When George says that he'll go, meaning "home to Barbados," he is not casting aspersions on his London house or neighborhood; he likes his neighbors, he likes his house. But as with a considerable proportion of the immigrant interviewees—and this will be the focus of chapter 12—Barbados is still for George the goal and the touchstone. Thus another interviewee said happily of her present neighborhood, "It's the closest you could get to Barbados!" As a whole, the interviewees seem well pleased with their homes and their areas.

If such was the measure of satisfaction in general, upon what particular aspects of life in the neighborhood was it based? The largest single response volunteered, with eleven mentions, was that the area was convenient for shopping, schools, or public transport; a further four said that it was specifically convenient for work (only one felt it was inconvenient). The next most important topic to the interviewees, judging from their free responses, was the high quality of their neighbors. Next came some negatives: road traffic and parking difficulties (such as the lack of a garage) were mentioned eight times; dirty streets, five. Conversely, a different five approved of the quiet or the "country atmosphere" where they lived; and a partially overlapping five said how much they were able to enjoy gardening at their current home. Four said of the home itself that it was comfortable, that "it suits us"—but plenty more did not say so specifically, although one could clearly sense they felt it.

Back to neighbors, where once again I sensed that most of those who did not choose to specifically mention their neighbors are nevertheless in general satisfied with them. Tony Gill was positive; his neighbors are "friendly. We've English on one side, Indians on the other. They're fine." And, pointing to a photo prominently displayed on the mantelshelf of an elderly (white) English couple, he said, "They [our former neighbors here] were great. We keep in touch. We used to give them the key to the house when we went away."

I asked Dotteen Bannister, "What's good about this area?" She replied,

Neighbors. Hah, we've got a little Hilda Ogden[6] nearby, she knows everything! Even though people move, we seem to get good new neighbors. I know everyone on the street, and the children've got their friends, nice friends on the street. There are five or six of Colin's friends [he's now eighteen], they all started school with him the same day, he's the only black kid. . . . It's nice. It's one of the reasons we've stayed here [in Enfield, for nineteen years].

When asked what qualities they would ideally seek in neighbors, the most commonly desired characteristic was friendliness, with eleven mentions. Edith Simmons made a twelfth, but she put it backward—she was happy enough that they were not *un*friendly:

When we were first here they weren't unpleasant to us, as the first blacks. That's important. We were the first blacks at this end of the [long] street, near the park: the up-market end [a small, wry smile].

Then she expressed what eight other interviewees said they would look for in neighbors, that "people don't stand and talk anymore, they're too busy. But—that's okay." That is, the second most desired characteristic is that, yes, neighbors should evidence a certain friendliness, but that they should also definitely observe a certain distance. Edward Pilgrim said,

One wants privacy. When first away in England from Barbados you miss, at the beginning, people saying hello, good morning. But after years and years of it you get used to it. In London, that's how it is. I don't see my neighbors much. They're Asians, very quiet. That's fine by me.

Pauline Alleyne said:

I'm very private. I want no gossip. I'd like friendliness without going over the top, running in for this and that. I'd want loyalty, I'd help out, but I won't butt in.

Joan Springer talked all around the topic of neighbors, both ideal and actual, and in so doing seems to sum up the views and experiences of many interviewees:

Well, if I was going on holiday, I'd like them to keep an eye on the house each morning and evening. If next door she was sick, that I could knock and say, "Shall I go and shop for you?" If I was ill, that I could bang on the wall for help. Not living out of one another's pockets, but approachable.

I have no problem with the neighbors here. I just go my way and keep to myself: I'm reserved. I don't have a lot of *friends* in the gap,[7] but I've got a couple around Ilford. I've got a nice new neighbor from Wales, very friendly. There are the Indians next door—not much communication with them. And there're a couple of Jamaicans, not exactly friends, we don't visit their house, but if I haven't seem 'em for a month or so I might pop across to their front door just to say hello.

Only two people openly criticized their neighbors, and only one, of the twenty-two applicable cases, actually volunteered that it might be nice to have Barbadian or West Indian neighbors. In addition to this one person, Orville Alleyne let something slip too. He had been asked, "What's bad about living in this area?" "No disadvantages," he replied, "I feel a bit conspicuous, though." I was not quite sure what he was getting at. Two questions later, after the free-response one asking about ideal qualities of neighbors, I asked (as of everyone), "Would having Barbadian neighbors make a difference? Or Caribbean ones?" Orville replied: "No, it doesn't worry me at all, living in a white community." I suspect that in some measure it does.

But if one, as it were, challenges the interviewees with that direct question—Would you want Barbadian neighbors?—then their response is unambiguous. Of twenty-two, ten give an untrammeled "no." The most extreme response of all of these was John Simmons's:

"No. I think it'd be worse."
I showed surprise.
"They'd take it for granted they could borrow tools. No, nor with West Indians in general either. West Indians abroad are different—they impose on each other."
"Is that because they might feel beleaguered, need support?"
"Hmm. Well, maybe it's *because* they're abroad. . . . I'd like to live in a place with all different people, that's my ideal."[8]

Another nine respondents to the Barbadian neighbor question said "not really" or "not necessarily," and the remaining four were even less forthcoming, being totally noncommittal. So no one expressed a clear wish to be among their supposed "own people."

Is there some sense here of the interviewees feeling they perhaps "ought" to reply in a certain way, especially as their questioner was white? Or are these people nonracial democrats? A few quotations from their responses can throw light upon this matter. Alan Maycock:

Do I want Barbadian neighbors? The question is more, what sort of people are they? One might have an affinity if they were Bajans, but not necessarily.

Audley Simmons:

> Not really, could be a minus for all you could tell. (If I had
> Trevor [Brathwaite] it'd be a plus.)

Beverly Brathwaite:

> Not really. But sometimes I think it'd be nice—but then again,
> wouldn't they be running in the house too much?

Ernestine Farley:

> Mm, well, it depends. Yes . . . *no,* they might cling on to you
> too much. . . . Not now, we get to mix now.

Charles Eastmond:

> No, not really, no. . . . It's funny really, we've Jamaicans on
> one side, and Bajans on the other—and we talk to the Jamaicans
> more!

A number of themes emerge. The interviewees insist that they would
judge people worthy of their friendship on their individual merits, not on
their ethnic affiliation. (Yet, as we shall see in chapter 7, for most of the
interviewees, most of their close friends happen to be Barbadians.) There
is also a wish for independence and privacy, a worry that fellow islanders
or fellow West Indians might "cling" too much. The interviewees perhaps feel that they are surviving satisfactorily in this mainly white world
without support from fellow blacks; but they may suspect that other
blacks are not so successful or so confident. There is also an idealistic
strain of the "people are people" variety, a liberal integrationist theme. As
Joan Springer mused,

> We West Indians still have a long way to go to integration. . . .
> If only they [the whites] could just get to know you and get to
> realize you're just a person. This skin color's not important;
> we're all the same as people.

Unfortunately this is not the whole of the story. No one directly said
to me that they minded having whites as neighbors, and only one indicated he might prefer having Barbadians or Caribbean people as neighbors. A nakedly cynical observation might be, however, that although the
majority of the interviewees might be integrationists in the direction they
consider "up," they might not be so in the direction they consider
"down"—i.e., toward the Asians. Eight of the interviewees let anti-Asian
sentiments of various kinds be known; perhaps others felt this way too,
but sensed that it might be unworthy to reveal such sentiments to me.

This chapter has been concerned with housing, so I shall here confine this final discussion to one concerning Asians only as neighbors, and not in other potentially contentious roles as, for example, in business matters (about which remarks were indeed passed to me by a number of Barbadians). If in the British popular image Brixton and Notting Hill are associated with Afro-Caribbean people, then one of the places unquestionably associated with Asians is Southall. Beverly and Trevor Brathwaite have lived here for twenty-six years, predating the major Asian influx: "A white town went down to an Indian town," said Beverly. On my route to their house in May 1989, I passed the Sikh Gurdwara; then the travel agents whose most prominent front-window advertisement was the genial statue of the pudgy Air India rajah; then the surgery of the Drs. Mukherjee, and then next to it the mélange of spicy and fruity aromas emanating from the Asian corner greengrocery, then the bills stuck on the wall advertising the upcoming antidowry conference, and then there was the beturbaned school crossing guard. If ever there was a prima facie recipe for ethnic friction or hostility, an unthinking observer might prejudge the Brathwaites' situation to be it. But that is not the way they have reacted: ambivalence, yes; at first, a bemused unfamiliarity, yes; but not hostility. Trevor:

> It was all whites in this road when we moved in twenty-five years ago. Now it's all Asians [this said without any visible rancor]. They keep their places up. There were all kinds of greens and blues when they were moving in, but now it looks all right.

Beverly:

> When we were first here, it was a nice little English town, Marks and Spencers and all that. Now there're all these new greengrocers and saris up the road.

Trevor:

> What's it like to live in this area? It's all right, I've never had any bother yet. I'm always reading in the papers that the Indians are forming gangs. But the youths that grow up here, just like everywhere else, have different outlooks on life: good and bad. One was shot in the leg recently. But there's never been any problem with the people immediately around us. . . . The Indians ask me if I'm selling (now it's the off-license[9] man). Oh, the tins and bottles in the road because of his darned off-license! Oooh, the traffic!

Beverly:

> It's all right here. People don't interfere with you, don't insult you. The Indians are very good neighbors, they will look out for

the house when we're not here. This house is worth a lot. We've had lots of offers on this house, because it's on a corner *and* it has a garage [in an area of row/terraced houses]. Mr. Brathwaite wouldn't leave here if you kill him, you'd have to put a time bomb on he!

The neighbors are all right. The little gifts over the garden fence have grown [in number]; the postman leaves us parcels for each other; and I have a nice Indian friend at work. Oh, and I like watching their processions.

Trevor:

Very nice neighbors are Indians. I sweep up leaves and dog dirt from the pavement [sidewalk], and so do they. They keep the shop. They give us things from it, like mangos. . . . But sometimes I feel a bit like a fish out of water here now . . .

Oh, and because we're on the corner, I'm always picking tins and food out of the garden [a lovingly tended front rose garden]. My daughter saw an Indian lady and her two children sitting on our wall eating, and when they'd finished, they threw the bottle in. "You wouldn't do that in *your* garden," said my daughter. "Well," they said, "you're on the corner, aren't you?"!

To sum up his feelings, however, Trevor said:

The ideal neighbor?—just like these people: friendly; considerate; they ask after you. The children have been asking, "Where's Mrs. Brathwaite?" (She's been away on holiday.)

One Tuesday I was having lunch with the Brathwaites and there was a knock at the door. "Oh, that'll be Beverly's friend," said Trevor. And it was: the Indian lady from the greengrocer's two doors away. "She's coming to use the toilet because their shop doesn't have one." This was clearly routine, betokening trusting neighborliness.

However, Audley Simmons has had a similar neighborhood turnover experience and is less sanguine about it.

When I first came here [Alperton] it was quite nice actually. Now it's more busy, there're more cars, people've taken out their front walls and paved over their front gardens to make drive-ins. When we came [1966] there were two other West Indians, and no Asians. Now it's *very* Asian: I'd say 80 to 20, Asians to everyone else. There were no Asian shops down the road then, no Asian take-outs [fast food]. It was very nice, very quiet on Sundays. It's a bloody market now. They come down on the weekends from Bradford and Leicester in coaches to shop. Lorries block our road.

> So . . . I'm stuck among Asians. Maybe I feel like leaving, but
> no, I'll live among them . . .

There seems to be among the interviewees as a whole a somewhat un-
easy oscillation between anti-Asian suspicions and a contrary impulse toward fair-minded, democratic coexistence with them, as with all. Eulie
Eastmond, who perhaps because she is a social worker and deals with "all
sorts and conditions of men," seems to have a more inclusivist attitude
than many. She responds to the question, "Would having Barbadian
neighbors make a difference? Or Caribbean ones?"

> At the start, yes. But any race now, even Asians. Color is nothing,
> it doesn't matter, we've become multiethnic now. I've worked all
> the time with white people now, I've got used to them, it
> doesn't matter. I've worked with whites, Africans, Cypriots. . . .
> It's personality, not race.

This chapter's structure, like that of other narrative chapters in this book,
was fashioned in such a way as to let the Barbadians first talk around the
general topic (in this case their later housing experiences). Then, whatever
general themes were implicated in their accounts could be drawn out and
placed before the reader. In this way the Barbadians, rather than the author, are the first to tell the reader what's important.

One couple's account of their housing history can serve as a coda to
this chapter, illustrating many of the themes already drawn out. John and
Amelia Simmons will make reference to the search for improved housing
being precipitated by the arrival of children; to the sense of freedom from
landlord supervision once one owns a home; to the positive neighborhood attributes of convenience to facilities and of good neighbors; to the
importance of the quality of local schools; to perceiving living among
whites as a positive, but living among Asians (the Simmonses were in fact
the most virulent Barbadian family in this regard) as a negative; and to the
lack (or at least ignorance) of any race-related complications in their attempts to purchase. Also note their forward planning for their retirement
home in Barbados, and, finally, that their Hillingdon house was evaluated
differently by husband and wife. He loved it: the location, the generous-
sized garden. She was less happy: its inaccessibility for a woman without
a car who goes out to work, its small kitchen.

John:

> We left because we needed more accommodation, the kids were
> coming over. We found a flat on St. Mark's Place [Notting Hill]:
> unfurnished; started from scratch. The kids came: Pamela straight

away in 1963, the boys in '64, from their mother's mother's house in Barbados.

We were there till 1968. It was self-contained, it was good, you could do what you liked, no problem. Shopping was great: Portobello market. The Tube station was near; very convenient. But ever since then I've never been able to get near a station! *But* . . . Ladbroke Grove was not a place to bring up children. Nothing actually happened to them, like drugs or violence, but you were always wondering if it was going to. We wasn't so happy with the schools. We said, "We have to get our own place." So we bought in Southall.

We were there on Coniston Road from 1968 to 1979. A terraced house, three bedrooms, two down, nice garden 'n everything. We really liked this property. A nice old English lady was next door. She decided to move away to her daughter's in the Midlands. An Indian moved in. Oh God. The English lady had a beautiful garden. Within three months cars were driven over the lawn, there were old cars rusting, they chopped down the fruit trees. We went home to Barbados for a holiday, came back . . . Indians on the other side! Another Indian came across the street. My workmate, a Barbadian across the street, sold up and left for Northolt . . . an Indian bought it. We used to leave each other parking spaces in front of our houses, but they had no understanding, they were parking in front of our house, perfectly legal, but no *courtesy.* We moved. Sold to an Indian. Prices were rocketing; we sold well.

We moved to Cassiobury Road in Hillingdon. There from 1979 to 1984. It was superb. Nice house, semidetached, nice garden. I made a beautiful garden, with a lawn and vegetables and all, out of the bush. The people was great, it reminded me of living in a country area, everyone knew everyone in that street, right up in that corner everyone was helpful. We was the only black people on that street. I'm still in love with that place. One problem: it was a fifteen-minute walk to a bus stop, and if the car wasn't working and the wife had to walk . . .

Amelia takes up the story:

It was so far from the shops and the bus, I was scared in the dark under the trees early on those winter mornings. And it was icy; I *hate* walking on the ice. If you'd had a hard day at work and John wasn't able to pick me up, then the bus journey was tiring, the extra time; and *then* the walk. . . .

The kitchen was too small, too. But we liked the neighbors. It was comfortable. It had a big lovely garden: John's pride and joy.

He put lots of effort into it. It was like a jungle when he started. The neighbors said they'd never seen it so good. . . .

Then we moved to here [Hayes]. We moved down-market, in order to realize capital, to start building our house in St. Philip [Barbados]. It's nearly finished there now. This place [Hayes] has less garden, less hassle. We chose to do it, so we mustn't complain now.

John concludes it:

We didn't need a big property, the kids were gone, we were going home soon. We started looking around. The real estate chap sent me to a place near here that had no garage. I saw this one instead. It had a little swimming pool and a big garage, not a big property, we don't need it. We were here within six months, no trouble.

Thus for the Simmonses their accommodation history in Britain comes to an end. Although on one occasion John said he would hope to be back in Barbados "in six months," and on a later occasion "by the end of the year" (1988), in May 1991 they were still in Hayes. Nevertheless, it was utterly evident they were, in Amelia's words, "marking time" until they returned home.

Seven
Valued People, Valued Places

I love England really, as a place to go. If you take a lot of the people out of it, it's a lovely place.

Edith Simmons

This chapter looks, in part geographically, at the varied lineaments of the social life of the immigrants. The bonds they feel, both to people and to places, reflect their birth in Barbados but their living in London. For most of them, nearly all their adult *working* lives have been spent in London; for all except three (the Farleys, Dotteen Bannister) more years of their *entire* lives have actually so far been spent in the metropolis than in Barbados. If on the one hand the expectation might be that the remembered years of childhood and youth in Barbados could have a visceral grasp on the emotions of the interviewees, on the other hand one might expect that the accumulation in London of the years of making their way in "the real world," of their working lives, of their raising families of their own in properties of their own, has engendered some sense of spatial rootedness in Britain. They'll have a sense of belonging to both Barbados and London, and of being bonded to both fellow Barbadians and fellow Londoners. The precise form of this admixture will of course vary from individual to individual, in response to their different personalities and experiences.

It is straightforward enough to ask someone about people they value: immediate family, special relatives, good friends. The answers are provided, can be totted up, and offer solid information of the kind that fills the first portion of this chapter. To inquire about valued places is altogether more problematic. So simply framed a direct question as "Are there any places you like/don't like around London/Britain, and why?"

seems to be more than a little flat, almost guaranteed to miss subtleties. Yet this is in good part the basis of the second half of the chapter—although it is augmented by more indirectly gathered information volunteered during the course of long conversations. Not surprisingly, the second part of the chapter, I warn the reader, is somewhat inconclusive. That doesn't mean it's worthless. The very fact of confusion—one person answered a question as to whether there were places "important" for blacks in London or Britain with "I'm no good at geography, so I don't know"!—tells something of interest. As a social-cum-cultural geographer eagerly looking for symbolism in "place," I had hoped to uncover some, to their minds, redolently "black" locales in London, if not perhaps in Britain. But even going at the issue head-on, by bringing up the great Afro-Caribbean festival of the Notting Hill carnival, did not reveal any such commitment to any "own" ethnically specific places among these interviewees. Some even took the opportunity to decry such a notion. As a whole, what this selection of individuals quite understandably wants is a pleasant house, amenable neighbors, an attractive garden, some disposable income, solitude should they so wish: the good, the quiet, and apparently the nonracial life.

Valued People: Social Bonds

It seems fair to expect that for most people, among the very strongest bonds in their social worlds would be those to their parents and to their children. For the immigrant generation, nearly all the former (if still living) are in Barbados, nearly all the latter in Britain. So as always for the migrants, places toward which affection is directed and to which loyalty is owed lie on both sides of the Atlantic Ocean.

The bond with parents in Barbados was for many years not only an emotional tie but also an economic one. Twenty of twenty-three interviewees had remitted money home to their parents or parent (and some to other family members there) for a considerable number of years after their arrival in Britain. Today fewer do so: their parents have died; their small children who were being looked after in Barbados have now joined them in Britain; both living standards and government welfare programs for the aged have improved appreciably in Barbados too, so there seems less need to send money. Today, seven said they still regularly remitted funds; ten said they did not; and six said yes and no, it depends what you mean: "Occasionally to my dad: presents," or "Not money so much now, as a barrel of goodies[1] at Christmas, you know." Half of the interviewees still had at least one of their parents alive in Barbados. (Edith Simmons, the one non-Barbadian, said her mother had gone back whereas her father remained in London: "She retired and went back to Jamaica. My father refused to go. He likes his betting-shop and his *draught* Guinness.")

For the interviewees this is very much the time of life when they have to anticipate losing their parents: Orville Alleyne lost his father during the time I was getting to know him. Others try to travel as often as possible back to Barbados, in order to see "the old folks." The interviewees' relative economic security gives them the ability to fly back—and how jet-age air travel has facilitated crossing the Atlantic for them! Or they try to bring their parents to Britain for a visit, sometimes for an extended stay: I met one octogenarian Barbadian lady who was enjoying a six-month sojourn in her son and daughter-in-law's suburban home. (Her request to the British immigration authorities for an extension of stay was turned down.)

As for the interviewees' children, only two live in Barbados (one never came to Britain; one came aged fifteen, stayed ten or eleven years, then went back). A third, a young man born in London but possessing a Barbadian passport, seems to be able to sojourn in both places alternately. By the summer of 1988 he had been back and forth three times, and his father said he would be back in London next year; apparently there was no trouble with immigration regulations. By contrast to these mere three, sixteen adult children have left home and are living in the London metropolitan region (I interviewed nine of them). Another grown child was with the Royal Air Force, first in Germany and now in Lincolnshire. Another, whom I interviewed, was at college in northern England. Yet another (whom I also interviewed) was starting a job in Liverpool after finishing a college degree, also in northern England. There were a further eight children still living at home with their parents, one of these children having in addition her infant son with her. In sum, for the migrants the ligatures to Barbados through their parents are, in the nature of things, inescapably lessening with the passage of the years; whereas the ligatures with their almost wholly London-based children are constant. In fact, they are increasing, with the arrival of that joy of one's mature years, grandchildren. Six of the twelve migrant-generation households already have London grandchildren.

Finally, I also asked about any relatives who might be "specially important," such as, for example, an aunt who might have helped raise the children in Barbados once the parents had emigrated to London. Twelve such relatives were mentioned in Barbados and six specified around the London metropolitan area. Three were said to be in New York City (one specifically pinpointed Brooklyn), two in Canada, one in Boston (Massachusetts), one in Bermuda, and one in another part of England. So putting parents, children, and "special relatives" together ends up giving an almost evenly balanced Atlantic-spanning spread.

Moving from ties of kinship to those of friendship with persons unrelated by blood, we meet once again a transatlantic distribution. However, the emphasis is preponderantly on the London side: only six mentions of "close friends" in Barbados (one of these a returnee from London), but for metropolitan London, ninety-one (I am afraid some of these may be double counts, husband and wife making separate mentions of the same friend). Other locuses within Britain were Reading (two), Birmingham (two), Bristol, Cambridge, and Hinckley. Canada was mentioned twice (one was a former resident of London), the United States and Saudi Arabia once each.

One should be wary of assuming that the over one hundred mentions of places other than Barbados (itself gaining a paltry six) implies some resplendently cosmopolitan set of close friends. I was careful to ask in the next three questions about how they had come to know these friends, and whether any of them were Barbadians or West Indians. To the first of these three questions, 35 (of the total of 108 close friends) had been met first in Barbados, mainly as school friends or friends from "the same gap" or neighborhood or village, plus a few had met at work in Barbados (e.g., Tony Gill and Austin Pilgrim). Eight mentions of "close friends" referred to persons first encountered on the boat coming over (e.g., Charles Eastmond and Audley Simmons specified each other), and one to a person met on the emigrants' airplane. Seven mentions were, through my oversight, unspecified as to locus of first meeting. All these mentions combined were still outnumbered by the "met them here in London" category—of which there were fifty-seven instances.

By far the most significant occasion of meeting in London was the workplace. "Friends of friends"/"at parties"/"around" came a poor second. Among yet other occasions of meeting, a particularly interesting instance was that of the woman who was decidedly approving of the social side to her night-school class in cake decoration (she showed me some of her creations, the most delicate sugar flowers):

> It gets people together. We'd never meet otherwise. No, we'd never . . . except that we all have this one thing really in common. People from other islands; English too. Everyone gets together and encourages each other, we exchange phone numbers. [She was very enthusiastic.] And especially, Brent subsidized it. You got it for £15 and it should've cost £50. And *now,* of course, they're cutting down on 'em.[2]

Did these fifty-seven instances of London meetings represent, however, a random selection of Londoners, that is, a preponderance of persons of English origin together with a cosmopolitan scattering? Indeed no.
To the question, "Are any of them Barbadians, or from families of Barbadian origin?" twenty mentions were unfortunately imprecise: "most"
(six), plus fourteen for "some." Only nine friends first met in London
were specified as white English; there was one Spaniard, one Irish person,
and one Pakistani . . . but fifty-six mentions for Barbadians.[3] The
follow-up question established whether, if not Barbadians, were the persons mentioned other West Indians? They were. In addition to the just
noted twelve non-Barbadian friends first met in London (nine English,
plus three others), there were at least twenty-six mentions of other Caribbean people: at least eight Jamaicans,[4] eight Trinidadians, three Guyanese,
two each from Grenada and St. Vincent, and one each from St. Lucia,
Dominica, and Montserrat. For the migrant generation in London, unsurprisingly, it has seemed easier to establish that relaxedness with former
strangers, that affinity of temperament or of interests that is close friendship, with those whose regional provenance is the same. To achieve such
closeness with the white natives has seemed more difficult. Furthermore,
three of the nine British were the friends of a woman who said they were
"in mixed marriages. But I met them through the Barbadian partner." To
reiterate, the racial specificity is clear: at least fifty-six Barbadians, plus at
least twenty-six other West Indians . . . but only nine white British.[5]

It is clear that the great majority of close friends were met in London,
at the workplace. This is where friendships with the white British were
to be most likely made. But in our open-ended conversations, spontaneous recollections indicated why there'd only been a limited blossoming.
Trevor Brathwaite, over thirty years at the same bus garage, tells me in
1988,

> I feel I'm not really accepted still. Everything's all right, but in
> the canteen I notice all the Europeans [i.e., whites] sit together,
> you can't go and join 'em. Sometimes if we're making up a bil-
> liards game, something like that, then we mix . . . but not just
> to sit and talk.

His good friend Audley Simmons, who came over with him on the
Hubert, had a number of thoughts about the qualities of the British working people whom he first encountered in February 1957:

> When I came to England I couldn't believe how ignorant the
> working class was. I mean, not just that "where's your tail?" kind
> of stuff; you mustn't let that bother you. But I'll tell you, one of
> them said, "Where are you from?" and I said, "Barbados," and

he said, "In Jamaica?"! Some were so stupid: when I started as a bus conductor, they couldn't make change.

In fact, I hardly ever got into any business over color. It's there, my friends assure me it's there. But in my experience, no. I keep away from those things, I don't hassle. I'd have to agree that in that regard things have got better a bit. But then again, at the start the Englishman would go out of his way to help a colored person, to show compassion: "Oh yes, let a colored man have that job." But then we started moving up a bit, we became *rivals* for the same job. . . .

Audley's earlier comments were reiterated with great vehemence by Frank Springer. He wrote virulently:

I was appalled at their rather compressed range of intelligence and how insular they were about the West Indies. They used to drive me insane with their stupid utterances about going back to the trees where I come from, and a whole lot of other bullshit that is too absurd to recall. In those days I was young and I read a lot, and my brains were hyperactive with a lot of irrelevant facts about the world, and to be surrounded by such a bunch of absurd and ambiguous assholes, just simply blew my mind.

Audley, however, observed that there was also a positive side to the British workplace into which he had been introduced.

In Britain I found that at work people covered for you. If you didn't know what was going on, when the foreman wasn't look-ing they'd show you, help you out. [A long example ensues about a bus synchromesh gearbox.] In Barbados it was very different. There was no unionization there. Each person was on a different wage: what the boss wanted to pay you. Never tell any-one else what you were earning. You had to be watchful. Why should they help you to make more money [which might leave less to go to them]?

On another occasion Audley made a telling observation about the work ethic he knew to be inculcated into himself (and virtually all the other Bar-badians I met), but which did not seem to be present among many of his English workmates:

In Barbados we were brought up that you had to make some-thing of yourself, you couldn't show your face back there [having left] otherwise. We're different from the English working class. They're not interested in bettering themselves. They just want food and steady wages. If I started as a worker I'd want my child to work hard at school and become a teacher, and *his* child to be a professional, a lawyer or a doctor.

I noted that Audley's comments were mirrored by Sam King, a Jamaican who came over on the *Empire Windrush* and ended up as mayor of Southwark. He was interviewed in the *Daily Telegraph* on the fortieth anniversary of the ship's arrival: "For every third of the English people who are unreasonable to us, there is another third who will go out of their way to help you. The other third couldn't care less one way or the other as long as their football team plays on Saturday and they can get beer in the pub."[6]

The differences between the Barbadian immigrants and (many of) their British workmates begin to add up: differences of background, of experience, of place of origin, of motivation and values, and of color. No wonder there aren't very many close friends who are British. And even if the racial variable is removed, these Barbadians still clearly prefer fellow Barbadians over other West Indians. Nor is it as if they knew most of their close London friends from home, which would explain a Barbadian preponderance. No, a far larger number of Barbadian close friends were met in London than those who had been known already from the home island: fifty-six to thirty-five (plus nine on the journey). These Barbadians stick together . . . partly no doubt through the strength of shared Barbadian pride, or, if you will, chauvinism, a force encountered on more than one occasion in this book.

Geographical Bonds

Another angle on this same theme—that when choice exists, Barbados or Barbadians get chosen—can be introduced here. Given that vacationing is discretionary spending, to where does one choose to spend one's money traveling? The conspicuous number of replies "to Barbados" straightforwardly indicates a continuing wish to see parents and other family, plus (to a much lesser extent) friends. But for some also, surely, keeping in touch with the old island fulfills the same perhaps subconscious role that choosing so many of one's London friends from among fellow Barbadians also in part fulfills: a reassuring affirmation of place-based identity.

It is evident that visiting Barbados has been a significant preoccupation since coming to Britain. To afford such trips has been one of the goals behind the long, steady hours of work conscientiously put in. *All* of the migrant-generation interviewees (including Jamaican Edith Simmons), and all except one of their eleven London children interviewed, have visited Barbados at least once. Full-scale family vacations have been much rarer around Britain (for example, to Devon or the Lake District) or to Europe. The norm has instead been more the cheaper day-trips or weekend outings to the seaside or to amusement parks (for example, to Margate). They require less prior organization, and they are nothing like as expensive. This last facet was, naturally enough, important in the years before the migrants became financially secure—an exalted status a few might still balk at according themselves even now. And for fifteen or twenty years ago, when their children were small and their salaries less bolstered by seniority, replies were like "a week at Butlin's in Bognor Regis with the kids," or "a week at Salvation Army camp" or "at holiday camps with the kids: at Pwllheli, Dymchurch, Brixham, and a place in South Wales—I've completely forgotten its name now."

Barbados dominated all other vacation destinations. Figures give a misleading impression of precision,[7] but they'll be provided because their drift is so evident. The total for Barbados exceeds by a small margin all of the other destinations summed together, with at least 103 mentions. When one thinks how far it is from London, and that it is certainly not a down-market vacation destination, and then also bears in mind at what wage level the interviewees entered the British labor force, this becomes an impressive figure. Typically, the first visit back could be up to a decade after first arriving in Britain. In one man's case it was seventeen years. When he finally went, he went for six weeks—and by boat, because he does not like to fly; *that* upped the expense. The ultimate case was that of another man who was on his twentieth year in Britain before he went back; that, however, was not only because of an inability to afford the trip, but also a matter of pride, of not wanting to show his face in Barbados unless he felt he had first achieved enough in London. Conversely, the rise in real income that the interviewees have enjoyed more recently, and the fall in real terms of the cost of flying to Barbados, have increased the island's accessibility to them. The extreme case is that of John and Amelia Simmons. He says he has been back "at least twenty times"—and then one recalls that he has been working for British Airways for fifteen years and thus he and his wife get preferential rates.

The impossibility of totaling up all the day-trips within southeast England—all one can say is "many"—leaves Britain in third place (seventeen mentions) for vacations, after the United States, with thirty-four. Nearly all these latter, where specified, were to New York City; Boston got a handful of mentions, Atlanta and Miami one each. For Britain, as well as the unknown number of visits to the coasts of Sussex, Kent, and Essex, the seventeen destinations are predictable: Devon (four), North Wales (four), Cornwall (three), then other such holiday spots. (One destination

was, I thought, very unpredictable: Northern Ireland.) Two interviewees
specifically averred they would not dream of vacationing in Britain.
Trevor Brathwaite—whom I feel I know quite well, for he is the uncle of
the Barbadian graduate student who came to Syracuse University, and
thus is the first of all the interviewees I met, in June 1986—ruminated:

> You can never be *sure*. You always feel you're different. Why
> spend so much money in order to be told you're not wanted?
> So, you go home, where you're welcome.
>   Though I do know things may've changed. A few months
> back a Barbadian chap I know, married to an Englishwoman,
> they went off to Spain. He told me you couldn't've had a better
> holiday. There were quite a lot of black people there, too.

Austin Pilgrim gave an utterly different reason: "I wouldn't *think* about
a holiday in Britain. The sun never shines. Fifty degrees and it's 'summer'!
Oh no! I live for a bit of warmth." To this there was at least one contradictory voice, that of Pauline Alleyne: "I've been to Penzance a number of
times. I love it down there. It reminds me a little bit of home, what with
the sea and it's warm. . . . "
    After Barbados, the United States, and Britain, comes Canada, with
twelve mentions; then France, with nine (plus at least five day-trips, at
least three of them to Calais specifically for shopping); then Spain, with
six; various other West Indian islands,[8] totaling five; Italy, four; and then
a spread of mainly European destinations, including Greece, the Canary
Islands, Tunisia, and perhaps most exotic, Kenya. At least some of the interviewees are financially (and by inclination) able to participate in the
great growth in overseas vacation travel enjoyed by the average British citizen in the last decade or more, the British citizen who shares Austin Pilgrim's just-mentioned evaluation of English summer weather, and thus
who prefers the Costa del Sol to Blackpool or Bournemouth. Joan
Springer told me she participates (without Frank, who sometimes goes to
Barbados on his own) in "once-a-year group holidays, organized by a
ticket inspector at work. It's just our own club. Last year it was Tunisia.
This year we've chosen Spain. I've already paid my £75 deposit." Ernestine Farley has a particular friend with whom she makes shopping sorties
across the Channel "nearly every other weekend: she and me have been
to Calais lots of times, to Dunkirk, and Brussels." Sandra and Tony Gill
have enjoyed vacations in Spain, Italy, and France. Most of these non-
Barbadian destinations outside of Britain are quite recent indulgences,
however. Over the thirty years since their arrival, the evidence on such
vacations as have been had points clearly to thrifty holidays within Brit-

ain, but priority given to getting back to Barbados. As a corollary to this, all sixteen persons whom I asked[9] said yes, people from Barbados had come to London to stay with them. This was clearly considered a normal thing; in three of these eight households such a visit was occurring while I was getting to know them.

Some Social Activities

Human geographers have, along with other social scientists, frequently studied "activity patterns": where people habitually go to meet relatives or friends, to shop, to visit the doctor, to worship, to go to school, and so on. Having pursued such inquiry fruitfully before—in a small bayou-country city south of New Orleans in 1971, and in South Africa in the late 1970s—I tried it again in London. It didn't work. That is, in talking with whites and blacks in Houma, Louisiana, and with so-called Coloured people in Cape Town, the activity webs I mapped across the city seemed to further inquiry into the role of "race" in structuring social life. The geographical patterns themselves afforded clear insights into, or provided evident confirmation of, or excited questionings about, the interrelation between skin color and social organization.

But having assiduously plotted out the information from the current households onto base-maps of London, I find no particular insights leaping out at me as I enjoin myself to "think geographically" in inspecting them. London is vaster—six times the size of Cape Town, one hundred and fifty times the size of Houma—and by that fact alone, vastly more complex. It is also immensely older; it is also far more cosmopolitan; it is protean. In London, too, at least some lines are drawn subtly and ambiguously. Many are evanescent, writ on water. Susan Smith has courageously and rather ambitiously asked whether there is "a geography of English racism";[10] it does not seem to me likely that new answers will be furnished to her question just by doing this kind of straightforward mapping of the elements of people's daily lives, at least not those of this very small minority of Greater London's population that is comfortably-off Barbadian. One has to dig much more deeply, as indeed Smith has subsequently done in her 1989 *The Politics of "Race" and Residence.*[11] Matters racial and spatial seem much less cut and dried in contemporary London than they were in Houma and in Cape Town, where geographical segregation stood exposed camera-ready, as it were.[12]

Although no geographically triggered insights were on this occasion gained from merely mapping social activities, there were some interesting things to be learned from responses to questions about such matters as, for example, attendance at religious services. In Barbados, fifteen used to be churchgoers (all Anglicans, except for one Methodist and one Baptist), six were not (plus Edith Simmons, who did not attend in Jamaica), and one gave a noncommittal reply. By 1988 the position was almost precisely reversed: fourteen no, eight yes, and the same noncommittal man. Some of the factors involved in this reversal seem rather general in impact: the greater importance of organized Christian religion thirty to fifty years ago, especially in Barbados's staid colonial society, where the established Church of England was numerically dominant and state-sanctioned; the greater secularity of life in a religiously cosmopolitan London today. Perhaps today's greater economic security has diminished the appeal of organized religion—does affluence blunt for some the desire for religious consolation? Perhaps greater individualism or general sophistication—a decline in automatic deference to powers temporal and spiritual—is involved? Dotteen Bannister explains:

> My religion isn't of particular importance to me, not now . . . but I used to be a Sunday School teacher! Well, it was expected then [in Barbados]. Everybody went to church. . . . Dear me, I couldn't let my gran know that [of Dotteen's partial apostasy]! Well, the kids do go to church every Sunday, and Colin's in the Boys' Brigade.[13]

If the above observations could have been made by many a well-churched white English person of Dotteen's generation, certain other of the interviewees made remarks that are more specific to black Caribbean immigrants. One man mentioned how disappointed he was upon his arrival in England at the lack of brio in the congregation's singing. And Trevor Brathwaite said, "We didn't meet a warm reception when we got here—you must've heard that? That's why they've sheared off to form these black churches: Pentecostal and Baptist." On a later occasion, his wife Beverly said,

> In Shepherd's Bush the C of E was High Church.[14] The majority of white people didn't want us in their churches when we came here. Vicars like to see you, but they say they're losing their congregation, so please desist. [Observing my expression of incredulity, Beverly continued:] Yes, John, that's what he said; he took me aside politely after church, about the third time I was there. *That's* why colored people started their own little churches.
> Then when we moved to Colne Gardens I couldn't go to church, I worked on Sundays, had a weekday off.

Beverly now goes every Sunday, sometimes twice, to the Salvation Army service. Orville Alleyne—a warily sensitive man who likes to keep his own counsel, and who earlier had spontaneously brought up the question of his sense of being "conspicuous"—surprised me with a vignette almost the opposite of Beverly's: "I used to go at first, for a year. But the C of E made too much of us! I felt uncomfortable. . . . " The end result was, however, the same: Orville, like Beverly, is no longer the practicing Anglican he was raised in Barbados to be.

Participation in sports has clearly played a large part in the lives of the interviewees. Trophies are common on their living-room mantelshelves, photos of their sports teams sometimes hang on the wall. The recruits were, indeed, selected in part by their physical fitness—six of the dozen men either active or former weightlifters, another one clearly a gifted cricketer, to judge from his still springy, athletic gait and the photos of his representing "the Trans*port*" (emphasis on the second syllable) in matches at Edgbaston (Birmingham) and in Yorkshire. Cricket has the advantage of permitting one to continue playing effectively as one ages. Two of the men still played regularly, another only gave it up a few years ago at age forty-nine. Committed participation in sports was clearly not expected of the women of this Barbadian generation, but nevertheless a number mentioned their pleasure in cricket: two specifically said they watched it on TV, another was the scorer[15] for her husband's team. It emerged that Ernestine Farley had been a gifted acrobat in her youth, and a number of the other women also said how much they loved dancing. Some still do, but for others it is a memory of younger days. Frank Springer observes his wife Joan with understanding:

> We still go to parties around London. She loved dancing. Now she has the arthritis. Sometimes I look over at her [sitting down] and I can see her shoulders going, she's moving her shoulders to the music, you know. She loved the music . . .

Joan recollected animatedly:

> There were lots of house parties when we first came here. There were those Blue Spot radio consoles. It was a way of meeting a lot of West Indians. You'd go from house to house at weekends . . .

These are memories of good times.

Working for large organizations permits the employee the use of their in-house sports centers to keep physically fit. Three of the women did so at facilities associated with their work, one specifically mentioning aerobics, another swimming. Another woman did keep-fit at a municipal gym;

one of the men mentioned he too attends such a gym, to lift weights. Two mentions (by men) were made of billiards/snooker (pool) at work, and one each (all men) of darts at work, of athletic meets, and of soccer: "I used to go to football at Upton Park to watch West Ham but I've stopped going with all the violence, the last five or six years."

Cricket, however, is preeminent. Eight of twelve men said they go to matches; a ninth regularly watches it on TV—"You can see better." One was a paid-up member of Surrey County Cricket Club and took me to The Oval to watch the West Indians versus England there in August 1988. Another man responded to "When and where do you go to play or watch sports?" with immediate and unbridled enthusiasm: "Lord's and The Oval: two places in England I'd like to take with me! [if I return to Barbados.] The hallowed turf of Lord's! [with only faint irony at what he knows to be a sporting cliché, whereas his wife groans hammily]. Ah, Sobers at Lord's! That fifth day at the Second Test: Cowdrey with the broken arm [in 1963]." Another couple—I presume this was mainly the husband's doing—had given their son the unusual name of Rohan, born at the peak of the career of Rohan Kanhai, a Trinidadian of South Asian ancestry famed for the ebullience of his batting for the West Indies team.[16]

On a couple of occasions I visited with the West Indian (and mainly Barbadian) workmates of Frank Springer at the Waterloo Underground offices. The first time—"Come and meet some friends and tell us what you're doing"—I got the semianticipated grilling: "Who are you? Why are you asking these questions? You're writing a book? Oho, you've been in South Africa! Prove to us you're not a spy," and so on. Returning a month later to the same faces, it seemed that my testing out may have been somewhat pro forma. Almost immediately, without any wary circling, the conversation ran to cricket. Having been out of touch with the minutiae of the game for so many years, I asked a question about the particularly complex law surrounding a batsman's dismissal for "leg before wicket." The result was Pythonesque. In this upstairs office, a senior LT inspector mimes the flight of the ball, drops down on one knee among the desks, holding an imaginary cricket bat *so . . .* "and it hits you on the pads and you're out." "Not necessarily," interjects another Barbadian, the most senior man in the office. "That was the way they tinkered with the law after the Valentine and Ramadhin business." And what, I ask, was that? (vaguely remembering Sonny Ramadhin as one of those childhood "nodule" names). I should have known better. Now we get a disquisition, with mimed illustrations, of how England's Peter May and Colin Cowdrey *thirty-one years earlier* had "padded up" to the West Indies' Ramadhin, one of the cleverest spin bowlers in the world at that time, and controversially destroyed his effectiveness by what some of the men claimed was gamesmanship; "not cricket," indeed. As I recall that Sunday morning in June 1988 now, I see it as bizarre, almost surreal.

Perhaps, also, cricket stars are more accessible and are—or were— much more high-profile on a small island where there are only a limited variety of distractions. As a child and a youth I never saw (except on the pitch at Canterbury or Dover) any cricket or other sports stars, never knew any, never knew anybody who knew any. Yet two of the interviewees had been at school with the world-renowned fast bowler Wes Hall, and one day at the Farleys' house it turned out that the quiet man sitting on the sofa, related by marriage to Ernestine Farley, was none other than the celebrated West Indian all-rounder Keith Boyce: "Cricket's gone down in Barbados. But we're putting a lot of effort into coaching, Wes Hall, Joel Garner, and me, coaching schoolboys, to get it up again." It was George Farley who, on a separate occasion, had said effervescently of Barbados that "cricket's the national game!"—yet he was one of the three of twelve migrant-generation men who made no mention of it when directly asked in the questionnaire about sports. Four of the men, and one woman, mentioned they were active members of cricket clubs; in addition, Edward Pilgrim was a member of two. His brother Austin claimed laughingly that "the wife has made me drop it." "Oh yes," she said, "otherwise he'd be away all weekend. I'd be a cricket widow!"

A final word on the importance of cricket to the male Barbadian Londoners can be left to Jeff Bannister, who proceeds to ruminate more widely:

> The cricket commentators on radio'll say "that's a very *West Indian* stroke."[17] Now, we've changed the game. It's not just English any more. . . . And *we* are what we are too—mainly English, but changed a bit. You accept it and that's fine and you get on with it. It's not a bad thing to be. England's a pretty civilized country.

For the men, cricket clubs were the most common voluntary associations belonged to; for the women, social clubs at work. Three men mentioned their trade unions; two spoke of the LT sports club; two, dominos clubs; and two, thrift clubs (one of which was titled, yes, the "Bimshire Club"). All other mentions of voluntary associations were single ones: for women, a keep-fit club, a holiday club at work, a mental health organization, and a nursing association; for men, the Freemasons, Kiwanis, a sickle-cell organization, and a book club.

Other recreational activities ranged from one woman's Open University to another man's betting-shop. For the women, the most common replies specified "a night out on the West End," whereas for men the most

mentioned hobby was gardening. There was little to surprise in the remaining less numerous mentions: do-it-yourself home improvements,
dancing, catering, or evening classes. Audley Simmons likes working on
cars, Tony Gill likes cooking, Joan Springer likes the VCR: "We don't
bother to go to the cinema any more."

Valued Places

There is one particular recreational event that symbolizes West Indian
(though not necessarily Barbadian) participation in the life of London: the
Notting Hill carnival. I purposed using it as a link between the first and second portions of this chapter because I anticipated it would stand both as
one element of West Indian social life and as a symbol of a valued "black"
place in the metropolis. Instead I found that as a whole the immigrant Barbadians viewed it with much ambivalence on both counts. The way in
which they express their ambivalence about the carnival itself is instructive, and so some quotations will be provided. Their doubts about Notting
Hill as a symbolic locale are also instructive; these latter fit in with the activity pattern findings discussed previously, wherein nothing illuminating
of a *particularly geographical* nature could be clearly adduced about race
and place in London's societal web. And lastly, their ambivalence about
the place Notting Hill is of a piece with these Barbadians' seeming lack of
ethnically specific rootedness to *any* places in London or in Britain—
something they will reveal in this chapter's final subsection.

Taking place over the end-of-summer August Bank Holiday, the Notting Hill carnival attracts hundreds of thousands of visitors: two days of
costumed street processions, parades of competing live bands, dancing to
music from stationary "sound system" loudspeakers of astounding rever-
berative power set up on the street corners, stalls offering a multitude of
ethnically specific (or otherwise) foods, and general revelry and frolic.
Celebrating its quarter century in 1990, the carnival's organizers hype it
as "Europe's largest street festival." It has also been bedeviled by street
crime and occasional civil disorder. Figure 13 shows the path the 1987
and 1988 carnivals took through Notting Hill. In this area lies much of the
space associated with the early London settlement of West Indians from
the 1950s onward, such as the "acorn" of Tavistock Road. Place names
already mentioned by interviewees abound here: Powis Terrace, Powis
Square, Ledbury Road, Colville Terrace, Elgin Crescent, Westbourne
Grove, Portobello Road, St. Mark's Place, Ladbroke Grove Tube station,
and Ladbroke Grove itself. It was here that the 1958 Notting Hill white
riots redefined British race relations. And just as these place-names are in-

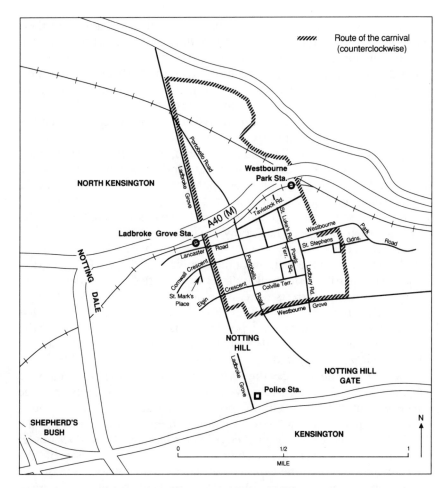

Figure 13: Route of the Notting Hill carnival, 1987 and 1988

delibly associated in the minds of the migrant generation with the 1958 Notting Hill riots, so has the Notting Hill carnival—since a considerable civil disturbance in 1976 a likely arena of confrontation between black youths and white police—become a symbol of a subsequent change in British racial discourse: the criminalization of black youth and the deterioration of relations with the police. Abner Cohen and Peter Jackson, among others, have penned academic studies on the political and cultural meanings and symbolisms of the Notting Hill carnival. Cohen, for instance, sees the carnival as a "ritual of rebellion," as a "contested cultural performance . . . uneasily poised between compliance and subversion."

The notion of carnival is Trinidadian rather than Barbadian. Furthermore, given the reasonably prosperous middle age that most of the Barbadian immigrants are now reaching, public street revelry is not for most of them the preferred mode of relaxation. Also, the Barbadian style is perhaps more buttoned-down than that of many other anglophone Caribbean territories. That the enthusiasm for the carnival among this group of Barbadians is somewhat lukewarm, therefore, should not come as a particular surprise. Of twenty-three replies, only five claimed they went "all the time," two "many times," plus one "sometimes." At the other pole, nine said "never" or "hardly ever." For the remainder, 1976 was a watershed. Three said they had gone a number of times until 1976, but had never been back since (Eulie Eastmond said she had actually been caught, peripherally, in the trouble). Others said they had gone often until 1976, but since then have been back only once or twice.

On August Bank Holiday Monday 1976, more than 250 people were injured as affrays in some sections of the carnival flared into a full-scale riot, aimed particularly at the police. Twenty-six officers were detained in hospital, sixty-eight arrests were made, looting occurred, several police cars were burned—and an enduring image of the Notting Hill carnival as dangerous, criminal-ridden, and possibly racially tense was coined by the popular media: "Ulster in Portobello Road" (*Daily Mail*); "Calypso Mobs" (*Daily Express*); and "savage hatred" (*Daily Mirror*) (all from August 31, 1976). The next day the *Daily Express* used some highly emotive language in commenting on the event. Did these "animal spirits" presage "race war in Britain"? Without police provocation, had not "young blacks" simply "run riot"? And "are police, then, to keep a 'low profile' in black areas of our own capital city?" Peter Jackson (1988) does not let the burden of this last sentence elude him; he correctly takes note of "the revealing contrast that the *Express* draws here in its juxtaposition of 'our own' (implicitly white) metropolis and the (implicitly hostile) 'black areas' within it."[18]

Such a conjuring up of some violently racially polarized metropolis, with carnival as a flash point, is light-years away from these Barbadians' reported experience. For those who had ever attended it, it seemed an occasion of apolitical pleasure. None had ever gone to the trouble of dressing up in "mas" costume (from "masquerade"), but four said they liked "jumping up" (dancing along behind a band whose music spontaneously appealed, as it moved down the street). "Yes," said Joan Springer, "jump up behind a band—the music get you going." By contrast, thirteen said no, they had not participated, just watched. Orville Alleyne said pensively: "I would have . . . but I never did. I just watched the floats go by. The music makes you feel good. It reminds you of home. I used to jump up behind the bands at home." (Did he? I wondered.) Frank Springer admitted, "No. An observer is what I like to be. I get musically involved, and there's the whole occasion, scenario, fantasy . . . but I'm too inhibited to jump into the crowd and enjoy it!" One of the never-beens said she abhorred crowds, but loved "watching on the telly. And after the carnival you can go to a concert in Town and see all the costumes." Tony Gill informed me, "Jumping up's not my cup of tea really." And Jeff Bannister's "ho-ho" in reply to my question expressed in two syllables the message, "C'mon, John, *me* do that?" But then he went right ahead and spelled it out: "It's an expression of joy, of abandon, isn't it? I have problems with expressing myself openly. I'm envious of people who can do that uninhibitedly." It would seem we have some in-bred residues of puritanism and of control here.

There was general agreement—among those to whom the carnival meant anything at all—that its positive aspects were the overall festive spectacle, the fun, the artistry of the costumes and floats, and the music (steel bands, soca, and calypso were specifically praised). Three opined that the carnival was a good thing because it promoted interracial harmony. Two others said it was a pleasant reminder of home, one spoke of its positive representation of West Indian culture for her British children, and three others talked of its educative aspects for the native white British—"to show them what fun it was," said one. Alan Maycock gave an insightful reply.

Of course, it was Trinidadian to begin with. But it's become a chance to show people a *positive* side of all us West Indians—as opposed to a certain section of the press, who're always nega-tive. That we're innovative: steel bands, et cetera. That we could organize something, that we had some creativity about us. That we're not just people who work on the buses and on the trains.

Given the opportunity to say what they felt to be detractions from the carnival, by far the largest number of replies (seventeen) brought up the issue of crime. "I was stolen from at Westbourne Park at carnival time," said Joan Springer.

I had my string-pull bag over my arm, there was a real crush at the station. "Watch out for your things," my friend had just said. I stood for a moment on the platform waiting for her to catch up with me, and in the crowd, pushing past, someone got their hand in there, I couldn't have pulled the string tight enough, and they took my purse.
No, it only had £5 in it, to buy a drink. But also my keys, *that* was annoying. Never felt anything or saw anyone. We went

down to Notting Hill police station later in the day to ask. You
would not *believe* the number of purses and bags there, tables
full. And there was mine; they'd thrown it away immediately into
the gutter, I got my keys back, it's only the money they want.

The second major cluster of negatives (nine) revolved around the civil
disturbance theme. The third cluster of negatives, with eight mentions,
was made up of complaints about the introduction of stationary sound-
system amplifiers, associated particularly with reggae music and its
Rastafarian, Jamaican provenance; or the complaint that the band could
not keep in motion along the street the way it should in a carnival. Jeff
Bannister:

> It's got distorted. Carnival, the Trinidadian idea, is movement
> through the streets at Mardi Gras. But the Jamaicans have altered
> it, they've plonked these dirty great damned sound systems at
> one place on the streets, and it's ruined carnival.

(In response to such criticisms, the 1988 organizers separated sound sys-
tems and the dance parties that would grow around them onto side
streets, and left the main route of the parade and bands free of such com-
petition.) Final complaints were that the event was disorganized (two),
that there was too much of a confining crush (three), and that the media
was biased against it (three). Frank Springer:

> Two days a year when the West Indians have the freedom of the
> city, to do what they want. But a small group destroys what
> we're working for, hurting us by unacceptable behavior, spoiling
> our image for the media . . . who are ready to paint us as
> villains.

After the 1976 carnival riot, and on a good number of occasions since,
there has been official and media talk of either confining the carnival to
a large stadium (that of nearby Chelsea soccer club has been mentioned),
or of banning it altogether. How germane is it that the carnival is presently
held in an "unsuitable" Notting Hill where, complained Edith Simmons,
who had once lived there, "there are too many people in too small a
space, the streets are too narrow once you're away from Ladbroke
Grove"? How important is Notting Hill in itself, that the very streets from
which white youths attempted violently to drive West Indians thirty years
ago are instead now totally appropriated for two days by a West Indian
cultural symbol? Outright, overt banning of the Notting Hill carnival
would clearly be perceived by many Afro-Caribbeans as a racially and politically oppressive act—even many of the rather conservative, "nonpolit-
ical" Barbadians felt this. Some more politically minded Afro-Caribbeans

claim, however, that overt banning will not be the method the authorities will employ. Instead, a wittingly fostered gentrification will quite simply try to price the Afro-Caribbean presence out of inner London via the property market mechanism. In the 1987 official carnival guide, Rosie Pearson addresses this concern vociferously.

> Notting Hill's Carnival, on the other hand, is a glorious aberration from England's staid normality, an opportunity for escapism and showmanship in a country not renowned for such qualities. As a result, it has remained a minority event, and has faced, in its time, opposition from residents, politicians and police. As property prices in the area continue to rise, many of the newly moved-in professionals would like to put a stop to the whole noisy thing. But they will not. After all, if the English weather has not stopped Carnival, what can a bit of gentrification do?[19]

A bit of gentrification can go a long way. The area of the carnival mostly falls within the northern end of the Royal Borough of Kensington and Chelsea, the richest of all the London boroughs. As Edward Pilkington's *Beyond the Mother Country* makes clear, there has long been a fundamental dualism in the borough, the rich south ruling a poorer, relatively neglected north.[20] As living space has come to be at more and more of a premium in London, so have the monied sought for residences ever further—and ever northward—from long-fashionable Kensington or Notting Hill Gate. As figure 12 has shown, the once preeminent north-of-the-river black focus of Notting Hill (as Brixton-Stockwell was the south-of-the-river focus) was by the 1981 census a mere sideshow: sixteen of the thirty-two other GLC boroughs had greater numbers of households whose head was Caribbean-born than had Kensington and Chelsea. There has been a related intercensal population decline in the borough, the greatest in all of London: 26.24 percent from 1971 to 1981.

To live on St. Lukes Road in 1987–88 was to feel the edge of a gentrification wave lapping at one's feet from the south. In that direction, less than one hundred yards away was Rachman's clutch of holdings on Powis Terrace where in the late 1950s, according to a 1987 Police Foundation report, 16 houses were divided into 140 lettings, occupied by 300 people, most of whom were black. No more emblematic address of the early black London of the modern period could be found. John and Audley Simmons lived in 1958 at number 10. Precisely thirty years later, here it is transformed up-market as "Hedgegate Court" (Figure 14). Powis Terrace, just one hundred yards long, runs into Powis Square. (At this corner, marvelously, stands the Asian-operated "My Beautiful Laundrette": Life imitates Art?) Here, in July 1988, for £73,000, one might acquire "a delightful

Figure 14: Powis Terrace renovated, a former Rachman slum rookery in Notting Hill

Figure 15: St. Lukes Road, Notting Hill, 1988

raised ground floor one-bedroomed flat offering superb accommodation for the first time buyer in the heart of fashionable Notting Hill Gate. Tel.: 01-221-3534." The geography's a bit off (we're a good half mile from Notting Hill Gate), but the price is right.

One April 1988 day I took from our flat window the photo that is Figure 15, a photo that seems almost didactically symbolic: a young black man carrying a guitar walks on past the "For sale; Open 7 days a week" signs. Formerly West Indian-tinctured Notting Hill is fading (I was surprised to be told that blacks were not even the major *minority* group in far north Kensington and Chelsea anymore; Moroccans, of all people, held that distinction). Consider the image of the water spider. The spider is real; it has mass, a body. As it pauses and then proceeds across the pond, it depresses the surface of the water. The footprints can be seen. But they are gone in an instant, the surface is smooth again. Was there ever a spider there?

So a few days later that April I went off to take photos of the past addresses of those interviewees whom I had so far met, all over London. Looking for footprints, as it were. It was instructive. First stop—just across Ladbroke Grove—St. Mark's Place. John Simmons lived here from 1963 to 1968. Outside stood a shiny Suzuki jeep with a Kensington and Chelsea resident's street parking permit. Across the street, a plumber's van, as renovations were being done. Inside the flat that had been the Simmonses', a grand piano. On to a second Simmons address: Brewster Gardens in nearby North Kensington. This had just been remodeled, with an added attic flat pushed up under a new mansard roof (thereby awkwardly breaking the pitched roof line of the terrace of which it was part). Two agencies were advertising these new apartments. Then to Grace's Road, Camberwell, where Austin Pilgrim had rented with at least fifteen other people from (alas) a Jamaican in 1961; the street was clean, the house neatly painted, a black child walked in its front door as if it was his . . . and directly outside a dumpster rented from Quick Skips awaited some (I presume) considerable work on the house.

Edward Pilgrim's old address from 1965 to 1967 was up the hill in Grove Hill Road, Camberwell. The house was in the process of being gutted, the inevitable skip (dumpster) was filled with ripped-out plaster and the like, the realtor's board was already up to advertise "another development of luxury apartments," each with "quality fitted kitchens, luxury bathrooms, central heating, fitted carpets, [and] entry phone system." And the little Peugeot outside announced self-effacingly across the top of its rear window "Vins des Côtes du Ventoux" (though I am not sure what that exactly has to do with it).

Alan Maycock's first address on Kirkdale Road in Sydenham had disappeared, demolished and replaced by sheltered accommodation for the

aged. Next door a considerable Victorian detached residence (I presume
pretty similar to what Maycock's had been, from what he and Althea had
told me of it) stood empty, gaunt, as the garden lawns and the driveway
were occupied by great tracked construction machines and Irish-accented
contractors; I could not tell if the house itself was to come down. John
Simmons's first London accommodation, the former poor house Wandsworth hostel, was totally gone, replaced by a medical complex. Even in
nearby modest Earlsfield Road, his second stop, the house to the immediate left of where he had lived had, yes, a skip at the curb. And now the
little newsagent's next door on the right bore the South Asian name P. N.
Patel, a name it surely didn't sport in John's day.

If, as it would seem, the interviewees have skimmed across the pond surface of at least some parts of London leaving little or no trace behind them,
do they themselves care? Are there, to them, any *valued* places in London,
where they would like to make some permanent mark, some tangible
difference, or to which they would feel they would owe allegiance or
wish to defend? Are there any places they would find it hard to do without
or, conversely, places they would be glad to see go, or at least, places from
which they would maintain their distance? These matters constitute the
final portion of this chapter.

"I like London," said Edward Pilgrim.

> It's a good place. There's movement, it's a bright place, with lots
> of happenings. There's a High Street[21] in every area, that's very
> convenient. I love Lord's and The Oval. And the river; I like to
> sit by the river at Richmond and have a drink.

Other persons specifically mentioned historic buildings such as cathe-
drals, others the beauty of the flowers and the trees in the central London
parks. Frank Springer said he used to be a real aficionado of Speaker's Corner: "Roy Sawh speaking on race, Lord Soper on religion, Fenner Brockway debating hanging . . . " Recreational spaces like Kew Gardens,
Hampton Court, Windsor, Hampstead Heath, and the Thameside prome-
nades in central London received mention, as did the theaters of the West
End, and the museums. All the other answers on liked places named
residential areas. The largest number of positive replies for any particular
locale were those twelve for one's own residential area. Only two out of
twenty-three were negative (with another three rather glumly tolerant of
London).

Asked directly whether there were any London locales they did *not*
like, four persons were not prepared to point any fingers at all. Joan
Springer said,

I don't go out and around that much. I can't criticize a place if I haven't stayed there any length of time, even Brixton. You can't just go for a couple of hours. I don't think it's fair to have an opinion just based on what I hear on TV and in the papers. That's wrong.

This combination of skepticism and fair-mindedness was shared on Brixton with four other respondents; two said the same of Balham ("I got it from the media, so is it really true?"), likewise one each of Peckham, Notting Hill, and Tooting.

Joan's phrase "even Brixton" was revealing. Far more respondents expressed negative opinion about Brixton than anywhere else (thirteen, plus the five who in naming it wondered about media-drawn information). To any Londoner, indeed to any Briton, Brixton's infamy is self-explanatory: the riots of 1981 and 1985. To most British people Brixton stands taken for granted as a symbol of the run-down, racially disaffected, high-unemployment inner city, where violent, unruly, youthful black predators roam the streets. But it also has some positive associations. Even though the Barbadian Londoners tend to view Brixton as Jamaican, Austin Pilgrim did not calumniate it. I suspect that is because he loves the Brixton food market, where fresh Caribbean (as well as Asian and British) foodstuffs are to be had; he walked me all through it with delight one day: "Brixton may be decadent, with Rastas and marijuana, but there's nothing you can't get in the market." Others praised Brixton's market too.

Far behind Brixton came other geographical designations. Five pointed generally to "the inner city" or "all the seedier areas," then four to Notting Hill (one of whom entered the caveat about media-furnished information). Harlesden, Stockwell, Hackney, and Broadwater Farm (this last is a large public housing estate in Tottenham where, during civil unrest in October 1985, a policeman was knifed to death) all received multiple mentions. Fourteen other "unliked" places were named, eleven of them in the inner city. One of the three outer exceptions was Southall, not unexpectedly the bugbear of John Simmons (as told at the end of chapter 6). There seems, once again, little to surprise one here. These established Barbadian respondents no longer frequented poorer inner-city areas so much, if at all. They were as dependent on information relayed by the media as were the rest of their fellow citizens, although they may have been a little more skeptical of the media's claims to veracity.

As opposed to "liked" or "not liked" places, the Barbadians were asked if there were any places "important" (the adjective intendedly vague) to them or to all Afro-Caribbeans. The question bemused many of

them—half of the interviewees simply answered "no"—but Alan Maycock for one agilely caught the drift of the question:

> I've never thought about it like that at all. . . . I can't think of
> any particular place where large numbers of Barbadians are con-
> gregated. . . .
> You get beyond thinking about Barbadians and Jamaicans and
> Trinidadians when you're all facing the same problems. So, "im-
> portant" could be seen in the sense of safety in numbers, espe-
> cially after the '58 riots. As time went by and as you felt more se-
> cure and *confident,* then you'd want to move away, from some
> who were the wrong type of West Indian: one doesn't necessar-
> ily like loud music!
> At that time people tended to go to work, come home and
> then they sat around looking at the TV or playing dominos. But
> if you wanted to go out, you could go to places like Brixton and
> Shepherd's Bush, for ladies, for example—we were bachelors,
> recall—for *all* kinds of ladies! And Brixton was "important"—
> what they've come to call the "Front Line"—in the sense that a
> chap could find a room, if you looked hard enough. You'd know
> somebody who knew somebody who knew somebody who.
> . . . Other parts of London would be difficult if not impossible.
> In that sense Brixton gave *stability.*
> Nowadays, we're scattered throughout London.

Alan's central thought here is perhaps the temporality of "importance."
Brixton mattered once, in the early colonization phase, for mutual Afro-
Caribbean support. Nowadays, in his case anyway, it is not so relevant.
John Simmons concurred:

> These days, 1988, not anymore. We've spread our wings and live
> out now [of inner London]. In the early sixties and late fifties it
> was more important to have Brixton and Notting Hill-Ladbroke
> Grove, because the people were there, and their clubs. But not
> anymore. West Indians've got conservative, they want to go out
> on a day off, to visit somewhere in the car with the family, and
> come home to the house again. . . . They're all moving out,
> looking for gardens and three bedrooms.

Dotteen Bannister said, "I can't think of any . . . unless you mean
people who like to live where there're a lot of people from Barbados or
the West Indies, Tottenham or something. Otherwise one place is just as
good as another." Four other respondents took this last sentiment further
and indeed made a virtue out of it: they expressed sentiments *against* any
particular place being associated with Barbadians. Joan Springer was one:

I don't know of any. Hmm. Like the Indians have places to go,
schools, community centers, we should have somewhere like
that. We should have more black representation [too]. But don't
get me wrong, this is a white community—it's a white majority
here in this country—so we must all learn multicultures. Everyone could get to understand one another better: prejudice is a lot
of ignorance, you see. I don't want a setup of all blacks on one
spot, or all-black schools. I want a *balance*.

Joan emphasizes here black cohesion but not black exclusivity; she is evidently against geographical exclusivity.

Marie Pilgrim moves us into the responses to a final question as to
whether important places for Barbadians or Afro-Caribbeans existed at the
broader scale of Britain: "There are high numbers in Bristol, Liverpool,
and Reading—but I don't know the significance of that. I do remember
being surprised once in York [where her son Nigel was at university],
however, how few West Indian people there were." Even more than in
the prior London question, there is a striking inability to point to *anywhere* that is "important" in the rest of Britain. Did I frame the question
wrongly? Is this something you cannot get at, just by amiably going
through a questionnaire? Or is there, for these particular Barbadian Londoners, nowhere in Britain that matters that much?

I tend to the latter interpretation. One woman said, more damningly
than I think she realized: "No, not really. . . . I love England really, as
a place to go. If you take a lot of the people out of it, it's a lovely place!"
More people said there was nowhere that's "important" than those who
actually designated any place as being "important." Reading got five such
mentions (for Barbadians *specifically*), Liverpool two (both persons allud-
ing to the long history of black dockland settlement there; another mentioned Cardiff, for similar reasons), and all other places only one each, including an anticipated one (which was delivered with a big grin): "The
Oval, you see all the Barbadians there."

Once again, a handful of interviewees took the opportunity to inveigh
against geographical segregation—and two of them have had their
claimed idealism, their integrationist views put to the test. Trevor Brathwaite, recall, lives in a now strikingly Asian-flavored Southall. Of places
important in Britain to Barbadian or Caribbean people, he responded,

I don't like that. Better to have people spread around. You
mustn't have this street all West Indians, or all anything. It's a
better community if we live among each other, mixed; we've all
got things to learn from each other.

His friend Audley Simmons, in south Wembley, makes similar points but ends on a much more enigmatic note:

> Other people'll think that Willesden or Brixton or Ladbroke Grove or Broadwater Farm . . . or Brent, because we have a black man in the town hall. I don't subscribe to that. I don't think that any one place is different from any other place. It's good that people should have the choice to live where they want to. So I'm stuck among Asians . . .

At the end of so lengthy and so information-packed a chapter, what does one gather from this dissection of the interviewees' social bonds, spatial bonds, and valued spaces? First, that, given their personal histories of migration, their emotional bonds are stretched across the Atlantic . . . but that the Atlantic is probably less of a factor than ever before. This because, simply, it is easier to cross it now; and because, until such time as they themselves actually do return to Barbados, ever more of their family bonds (children and grandchildren) are in London, ever fewer (aging parents) are in Barbados. Second, that it is to fellow Barbadians in London that they still mostly look for intimate social congress, for that reassurance of their personal worth that is close friendship; it is only fellow Barbadians, and to a lesser extent fellow West Indians, before whom they are prepared to appear vulnerable. But third, it seems that these days you do not have to be *geographically* close to close friends. These car-driving, mainly suburban Barbadians seem as a group very content with the comfortable residential areas into which they have forged, not without toil and for some not without stress. Their activity patterns are not focused upon zones of black residential concentration. Instead, these Barbadians are prepared to be members of a small minority among white neighbors, for, as they often rationalize it, this is a white country . . . and they have done all right in it. They did not come from Barbados thirty or so years ago assertively bearing aloft the banner of black solidarity or whatever. They came as individuals, for themselves (and perhaps for their immediate families, yes), individuals who wanted to get on in the world. And these particular ones have. So if in the early days force of circumstance (an agreeably bland term for white racism) led them to congregate in the Notting Hills and the Brixtons, the majority of them are no longer convinced of the contemporary utility of such congregation. Nor do the majority of them—viewing the world as the rest of us do through the lens of their own particular experience—see these locales or others like them as important for Barbadians or for Afro-Caribbean people in Britain today.

Eight
British-Raised: A Profile

It annoys me when white people here say, "Where are you from?" I of course say "London."

Nigel Pilgrim

Colin Simmons, son of Amelia and John, was aged twenty at the time. He was about to return to London from Seawell Airport after a Barbados vacation when he there met Carol, a seventeen-year-old young woman coming to London at her father's summons. Here she was, apprehensively traveling beyond the confines of her small home island for the first time, to a destination she did not know, and here was this good-looking young man who had been living in that destination for a dozen years. He tells it thus: "I helped her, built up her confidence. I liked the look of this . . . and jumped right in!"

Carol Pilgrim had been living in Barbados with her mother, Mary Barrow. Her father was Edward Pilgrim. After nearly nine years in Britain, he'd returned to Barbados on a visit in 1970.

> I saw my daughter. I liked her. I loved her. I wanted to do something for her, get her a good education in England. So I had to find accommodation suitable for her. I got a GLC mortgage . . .

Thus it was six years later that he brought her over to London, after she'd been out of school in Barbados for a year and a half. Carol was enrolled in a secretarial college in London. She found life in her father's house in Peckham "boring. I couldn't wait to get out. One of the first things he said to me was, 'Don't you *dare* get involved with any Jamaicans!'" Fortuitously, she'd already got involved with Colin. And in 1979, twenty-three-year-old Colin moved into a privately rented, roomy flat above a small shopping arcade in Addiscombe, part of Croydon in outer south London. It was found for him by his brother-in-law, who is white English and who also lives in Addiscombe. Carol moved in with Colin soon enough, a time of which they have very fond memories: "Freedom. Our own life."

They married, and after four years, with help from Colin's parents, they bought a small modern terraced house, in which they are now raising two toddlers. "It's nice," says Colin. "It's a step up, no doubt about it. Peaceful. Nice for the boys. Work's nearby, school's nearby, the neighbors are friendly." Carol isn't quite as pleased about the neighbors but observes all the same that

> it's convenient, close to mummy and daddy [i.e., Amelia and John]. But I don't feel really settled, I keep wanting to go back to Croydon, a nice conservative place! There's not much shopwise down this way, you have to go to Uxbridge and then that's limited.

What could be more prosaic than this account?

Carol and Colin's trajectory serves to introduce the eleven adult children who were interviewed from the twelve migrant families. (The Bannisters' children were not yet old enough to have left home.) However, although seemingly so conventional, Colin's and Carol's experiences are in some respects quite unlike all the other nine adult children. They are, for example, the only ones who say their goal is to return to Barbados. Not unrelated to this desire is their being the only couple in which each was the child of Barbadian immigrants, immigrants who themselves plan to return to Barbados (Amelia and John Simmons, Edward Pilgrim). The other three adult children who are married have spouses from Grenada (brought up in Britain since the age of five), from Jamaica, and from Ghana (both also British-raised). Another adult child has a stable gay relationship with a native Englishman.

Colin's and Carol's thoughts of return are also straightforwardly linked to their both being Barbados-born, but brought over to England as youngsters by parents already settled in London. They have, in other words, Barbadian childhood memories. Of the five who were sent for from Barbados, Carol is the most recently arrived (1976), the oldest upon her arrival, *and* the only one not to have attended any state schools in Britain. Colin arrived in 1964 aged eight, the other three in 1966 (Gordon Alleyne, aged seven), 1968 (Paula Farley, aged eleven), and 1970 (Trevor Brathwaite, Jr., aged sixteen). Carol was therefore the only one of this set of five (and thus of all the eleven) to have at the time of our meeting lived longer in Barbados than in Britain. The other six adult children, native Londoners, were, with an average age of twenty-four, somewhat younger than the Barbadian-born five. Having lived their entire lives in Britain, they do not see Barbados as a place to which to return; it's not home. All this serves to explain why Carol and Colin say their purpose is to get back to Barbados—although I do wonder how much they truly mean it (of which more in chapter 12).

The rest of this chapter is organized in a straightforward manner, the topics arranged in quasi-chronological fashion. That is, these young people report first on their school days, then on their employment experiences, then on housing, and then on their social lives, with, as in the previous chapter, a glance at the Notting Hill carnival and a concluding discussion on "valued places."

Education

Of the five Barbados-born—whose average age in 1988 was thirty-one years—only two volunteered anything on their Barbados school days, school days interrupted for four of the five by their parents calling them to London. Colin Simmons told me of his mother and father:

> They were able to build a financial base for themselves, which was the main reason for the migration from the Caribbean. It also led them to believe that they could give their own children a better education. It was true in my case. . . . See how carefully I've tried to express that, John. They believe that. Maybe I do. But I have a friend who'd strongly disagree that he ever got a better education by being brought here. And we're not happy with what Kevin's getting now in school—no spelling! no accountancy!![1]

Carol and Colin are evidently concerned with their children's education. Colin in particular, because of his own experiences, feels they should move to Barbados pretty soon if they are going to at all:

> It's crucial not to interrupt the kids' schooling. My education was broken three times. I came here [aged eight] after three years' schooling at home [in Barbados]. When we moved from Ladbroke Grove I was in secondary school. In fact, I was halfway through the year, when we moved to Southall. Sometimes I think I would've been better off to have stayed in Barbados.

Trevor Brathwaite, Jr., was the other who made any mention of Barbados schooling.

With the money my father made over here on the Transport, they sent me to Barbados College, that's a private school. A lot of my teachers there were old-style Englishmen, they taught me to speak without a Barbados accent. ["He sounds so different from his sister," his wife Catherine interjects.] So, I speak the proper English. On the phone people don't know I'm from the West Indies, they can't tell I'm black, and a lot are surprised when I arrive at the door of their office, put out my hand, and say, "Hello, I'm Mr. Brathwaite from AT & T."[2] I can see their brains whirling round as they take stock. Some, a few of them, seem a bit put out, but we get on with it. Now at the level I'm at—one of the accounts I'm with, for example, is our BBC account; that's very high-profile—it would be really . . . um . . . bad ["Uncool?" I suggest.] yes, uncool, for anyone to show racial surprise. Only once in three years was there any trouble, only one guy. He said, "I don't do business with black people." "I don't do business with white people," I said. And there I was sat opposite him. . . . "Well," I said, "Are we going to do this all day?" So we got down to business!

At thirty-four the oldest of the group, Trevor Brathwaite, Jr., impresses me. I get a sense of someone who's worked out who he is, isn't too unhappy with what he's found, and has confidence and ability with which to compete and to succeed. A number of the eleven younger people here seem, in the old American high school phrase, to be "the girl or boy most likely to . . . " Indeed Trevor, Jr., with years of private secondary schooling behind him in Barbados, came to his British high school at age sixteen and less than two years later graduated with an A level and as Head Boy—this latter an honor more or less a combination of class president and student council president. In the hierarchical world of an English school, to be appointed (not elected) Head Boy signals a real conferral of official approval.

One evening a long and animated conversation on schooling took place between Trevor, Grenadian-born Catherine, and myself. The emphasis that the GLC borough of Brent (into whose catchment they just fall) allegedly placed on "black" topics in education did not sit well with this couple. They were also against "special cases" (in their words) being made for blacks, analogous to U.S. affirmative action programs. We also discussed parents working outside the home (they both do). Catherine opines that it is difficult to be a satisfactory guide to children if both parents work; "they're latchkey kids, no discipline." Trevor, Jr., counters that

my parents have always both worked, but they were really good
parents, they told us the importance of school. . . . I'll say this
for my mother: after work each day she'd spend time for Tommy
[his younger brother] and his schoolwork.

But there's a generation of black kids who don't know if
they're coming or going, there's only the music—reggae—and
this easy grouping, black, because we all *look* black. No, the kids
have got to learn confidence and learn to live with themselves.
We're putting our kids in private school.

Trevor was not the only Head Boy from this group of six young men.
Quite remarkably, there were two more. Whence, I wondered, did their
acceptability to the powers-that-be spring? They were all three from
homes where, evidently, trouble was taken over the children's education
by "respectable" parents to whom the work ethic was second nature.
That elusive quality, *confidence,* had somehow been inculcated. Perhaps
related to social confidence is the kind of poise that comes from the good
fortune of athletic ability? Two of these three were athletes, which again
might in some measure have been a gift from their parents; their fathers
had in particular been physical fitness enthusiasts. And athletic and sports
ability was often an important criterion in the selection of Head Boys.

After another free-wheeling summer evening's conversation with
Trevor, Jr., and Catherine, I found myself wondering, on the empty Tube
going home that night, to what degree did Trevor's confident personality
stem from his having been raised in a black majority society (and in a fee-
paying school at that). He knows from his own experience that there are
places in the world where black people at least ostensibly run the show,
where one does not feel one may have to mentally genuflect to outnumbering whites above one. Indeed, he could in the last resort—though he
would not wish to—shake the dust from off his feet, and quit London for
Barbados if the English became too insufferable. I recalled, too, from
Burundi, the air of sheer superiority some of the Batutsi carried with
them—the Belgian colonialists had been a mere interruption in their
dominion over the country. I recalled also Abubakar, who drew admiring
and, I sensed, envious glances from the three black American students in
a graduate course I had taught the previous year—because as a young,
good-looking elite Hausa man from northern Nigeria, there was little in
this mainly white American world that could overawe *him.*

Racial context, however, can offer only a partial explanation. The ebul-
lient Gordon Alleyne had arrived in London at just seven years of age; he
too was made a Head Boy. Yet nearly all his educational experience had
been acquired in British schools where he was in a minority of one, sur-

rounded by an ocean of white faces. If racial context were all, he surely would have been browbeaten? He wasn't.

"Being brought up in Woking and Surbiton our family were the only blacks anybody had ever seen. So there wasn't racism against us, we were more . . . um . . . *exotic.* I remember falling and cutting myself in the playground at school and running to the biology teacher—'cos I thought she'd be the right one!—and I remember she was cleaning the cut and said, "Oh, it's pink under there too!" I mean, if *she* felt like that, what are the others going to be like?[3] People used to come up and peer at me sometimes, but it wasn't racism, it was curiosity."

"Well," I put in, "you could say that's a kind of racism in a way, treating you as a curiosity?"

"That's true."

"Mind you, I remember when I was first in Africa—and I was twenty-one, I'd been 'educated'—and I wanted to pat an African schoolboy on the head, just to see what it felt like![4] And it was soft, which I didn't expect."

"You thought it'd be wiry?"

"Yes . . . *so* . . . that curiosity wasn't malicious, I mean, I'm not sure whether that's 'racist'. . . . And I remember the first time one of the schoolboys blushed: he went sort of purple in the face. I'd never seen anything like it!"

"Yes, I remember once being really embarrassed, and my friend looked at me, and looked shocked, and said, 'My God! What's happened to you?'

"Once I got onto the school teams and athletics and everything and became a 'star,' any kind of bullying stopped. Then one day I was walking home and there was a group of five or six from the other high school nearby, the sin-bin, I mean, they were a really mindless sorry school. They were on the pavement [sidewalk]; I saw them way ahead. Now I'm like my mum, very willful. I could've crossed the road—instead, I walked through them. One of them spat. It landed by my feet. Didn't hit me. I stopped, looked at him, carried on. Next day, there they were again. And I wouldn't give in. Walked straight along, when I got into them, one spat again. This time it hit me. What d'you do? My father always said, 'Hit the biggest one,' I mean, they're going to get you anyway. So I did [big grin]. And of course I got done over.

"Well, next day at school it's all 'Wow! What happened to you?' I was a mess, and the athletics championships were coming up in a fortnight, so I had to heal. But on the way home, oh shit! There they were again. I'm so stubborn. Walked right up to them. The first blow was just falling, then all of a sudden it

seemed from everywhere people came running in, it was our
rugby team, they'd been tailing me secretly to see me home.
. . . And yes, did they teach those lads a lesson! They got *hammered* [even bigger grin]."

Gordon has a younger, London-born sister, Mary. Although it proved
impossible for me to meet her, her situation was a weight on her father's
mind. Orville Alleyne mused:

"We only half-belong, we're immigrants after all. But not our
children, they're from here. My daughter is very sensitive, she
hasn't dealt with it well. She's certainly got it in her to have gone
to university. It's not just self-confidence, she's . . . *lost direction.* She feels she has by right the same as everyone else here,
but she's not getting it, so she's resentful."
"So because it's unfair, she's giving up?"
"Yes. You've got it in a nutshell. Instead of fighting for it.
Sometimes you've got to accept things 'cos that's reality: it's unfair. But you try to change things. That's the only way.

With samples so small as these speculation is foolish, but one is led to
wonder about the significance of gender. *Are* school days for the comfortably off Afro-Caribbean British girls more stressful than for the boys? (Can
one even frame the question in those terms?) That is, three of six males
had been Head Boys, but none of the five females had been Head Girl.
Only one girl, Susan Maycock, had met with anything approaching conventional academic success. She is one of the three of the set of eleven
who gained at least one A level at school (the others being Trevor, Jr., and
Nigel Pilgrim). Five more persons had gained at least some O levels, by the
ages of sixteen or seventeen. The remaining two had left school by sixteen
years of age, the statutory minimum in Britain—but one of these, Max
Springer, has subsequently gained both O and A levels through his own
exertions, as we shall soon hear. (Carol Pilgrim, now Simmons, did all her
schooling in Barbados, where she gained no O or A levels.)
Derek Gill, who has lived all his life until recently in Canon's Park, a
far northwest suburb of London, clearly could have gained A levels but
chose not to. The reason emerges in the quotations below, but first he
talks of being, like Gordon Alleyne, in a conspicuous minority at his high
school:

It was bad in dad's time. But there's nothing like that now.
Just a few racial taunts at school, nothing. I'm the only Bajan
around here, and was the only one at my school. Hardly any
blacks. Some Asians, that was better for us, because the Asians
kept separate but we mucked in—so it was better on us. And in

turn it'll be better for my children. Nearly all my friends are
white. . . .

My parents took me to Barbados as a small kid. But they never
really sat me down and told me about Barbados, the history of
Barbados and things like that. I got interested in it of my own accord. I like history anyway. Harrow schools[5] were good. They
taught about the migrations. They taught all about modern history, not just the battles of Agincourt and Hastings and kings and
queens, but the Tolpuddle Martyrs[6] and the immigration in the
1950s. That's some of the stuff my father went through—you
know, people going off to work and another chap coming back
and getting into the same bunk to sleep.

Derek gave an open smile—clearly this was a great yarn, not something
to feel aggrieved about. After some success at O level, he decided to join
a large, high-tech, quasi-public corporation as an apprentice. In 1981, his
decision was taken precisely at the time of the worst unemployment
figures, the "unpleasant medicine" for three million that a monetarist
Thatcher government had decided was necessary to revive a "flabby"
British economy. Derek was choosing a prudent course; black youth unemployment was at an all-time high.

So, I joined Simms,[7] and I'm still with them. I thought I could
get A levels *and* get an income as well with the apprenticeship.
But I'd like to do evening classes, I think . . . though not quite
yet!

My job, exactly? It's . . . the assessment, control, and
management of design changes as affecting production: project
management. [And in response to my query] No, I've never felt
discrimination that was visible to me. In fact, I wonder if I've
ever been a "victim" of positive discrimination, I mean getting
more opportunities *because* you're black: good PR for the company. I'm the only black up at my level in my division.

This he says as we watch, in late June of 1988, a television report stating
that the Commission for Racial Equality has found racial disadvantage in
Britain to be very marked: blacks are twice as likely to be sent to prison,
or to be unemployed, or whatever. We watch. I gesticulate, without
words, the obvious question, are you really immune from that? He
ponders. "Yes, despite that." And then, "I'm not bothered about being
black or anything like that. I don't notice it."

The furthest from the stereotypic black school experience in London
must have been that of Nigel Pilgrim. He told me nothing of his school
days (but plenty about other matters, such as his strong positive feelings
about being a Londoner). Perhaps he was being modest—Head Boy of the

southwest suburban private school of high repute his parents saved to send him to. He has an easy and engaging confidence of manner, and let slip just one oblique acknowledgment of his school days: "The social skills I've learned are useful: a Londoner; public school. I know my style in the interview got me my present job, and the placement [on-the-job internship during his degree course] too." Not what England expects of a young black?

Successful businessman Colin Jemmott, reflecting that "English prejudice can be very subtle, especially these days," told the story of the (lack of) expectations of the north London high schools to which his son was allocated.

> [The first] . . . had a "non-academic" reputation with a very high proportion of blacks. I went to the chief education officer of the borough. He was a very RAF-looking[8] chap; very RAF manners too. "Look here," I said, "my son's no duffer. He deserves better." He listened—and my son was immediately put into a better school, no problem. They had *assumed* . . .
>
> But we [i.e., Mrs. Jemmott and I] were some of the very few who would've had the nerve to question their judgment.

Colin continued his tale, recounting how his son had decided he wanted to be a commercial airlines pilot. "The careers officer at school was helpful, but said, *'Impossible.'* There was justification for saying that, too." But Colin, as he tells it, expended a large amount of money—thousands of pounds—and saw his son successfully through all the lengthy and complex training, to land a career in his chosen field.

That others (white) have low expectations for one's own (black) educational achievement—and the belated transcendence of such expectations—is the nub of Max Springer's account too. "I left school at sixteen [1976] with four CSEs:[9] sociology, biology, English, and geography; I failed maths. The teaching was really bad. It was an antihomework school. The *culture* of the school was antihomework." Four weeks later I was talking with Max's mother, and Joan alleged,

> They told Max he was stupid at school. "Why don't you get on the banana boat and go back home?" one teacher said. Well, we went up there, and they apologized. But, with a teacher like that, why should the kid then respect you, and even bother to learn? . . . It's just *ignorance* coming out again.

Max also now observes of himself at that period, that "when I was at school I didn't put enough in. I mean, success breeds success." And then this man in his late twenties, who admonished his father Frank for being defeatist or at least overly discouraged by obstacles, tells a remarkable tale. His rampant, almost battle-hungry entrepreneurial spirit makes him seem close to a caricature of the transformation that observers such as Ralf Dahrendorf feel Margaret Thatcher has effected in British working people's values.[10] Here is a superachieving individualism par excellence:

> At first after school I was unemployed for eight or nine months, I had enough of that. Then for three or four years I was a kitchen hand at D. H. Evans, a big department store in the West End, and at others too, off and on. I hated it. It was awful.
>
> I thought, "I'll try evening classes." I tried O level chemistry and maths at Redbridge College. Got a B in chemistry, a D (that's a fail) in maths. So then I went full-time at West Ham College. I did five O levels, and I failed 'em all. I was doing a succession of manual jobs, like delivery jobs. I took two A levels and failed. Yet I felt intelligent. So, what was going on? I thought I must've been poorly trained *how* to take exams at school. I retook A level maths and passed it.
>
> Then I started reading about self-made millionaires, how did *they* do it? It's the mental attitude of the person, a certain kind of desire, a positive attitude. Hard work pays off. I wanted to do accounting O level, I decided I'd get an A grade . . . and I did! I started off this market research interviewing for a couple of companies, especially National Opinion Polls.

(And indeed, Max was the only interviewee who interviewed his interviewer! That is, after I had finished doing my questionnaire with him, he asked me if it was okay for him to do one of his quota on me. Thus was effected an immediate quid pro quo.)

> It was tough at first, people didn't want to know. "Right," I said, "I'm gonna *control* this job." After three weeks I got the hang of it, by six months I was the best in the company, out of hundreds. I just had to prove I could do something. But . . . what are the prospects? In interviewing itself there's not much; it doesn't lead anywhere. "I'll go to college and do business studies and finance. The Polytechnic of Central London," I said to myself. I got six distinctions, ten merits, and three passes! After one year. There's another one to go.
>
> I'm gonna win, man.

Max's account simultaneously mixes education with employment, thereby affording a neat lead into the next part of this chapter, the job experience of the British-raised.

Employment

Colleen Simmons, daughter of Audley and Edith, is Colin Simmons's cousin. She reflected on her parents' lives:

> "When I think about what they must have gone through, I think yes, they did achieve something with all that hard work. They came here to work, there was nothing for them there, they worked shifts and everything. So now they've got a house and it's okay. But here's us in our [council housing] flat, we try to buy but we can't do it. It's a very nice flat, we've got everything here, but . . . um . . . I feel as if all their work's gone round in a circle. Um, I mean . . . here we are near the bottom, after all their work of a generation."
>
> "Like running fast to stand still in the same place?" I suggest.
> "Yes."

Like her father, Colleen chose a Jamaican partner (although Ken Wright was raised in Britain). If indeed Colleen and Ken's material situation is, in her words, "near the bottom," then part of the reason has to be their staccato employment histories, plus the priority they give to the making and appreciating of reggae music. They are Rastafarians. She told me, "I used to organize a 2p-a-time sound system in the school hall at break, the headmaster let me do it. Then, after O levels, I was expelled, on my seventeenth birthday: I used to bunk school and go to the record shops in Harlesden."

In her first year out of school Colleen worked behind the counter at a big national-chain department store, then did a year as a trainee accounts clerk with another firm. For a while thereafter, in 1979, she was "not in work, out touring with a band." Then she worked four months as a clerk in a betting-shop, then fourteen months as a wages clerk for a car-hire firm. Then, in 1982, her and Ken's first child arrived, and soon another. She worked in the home, "with a bit of music" being done too. In December 1987, with Ken out of work, she worked at a West End agency, telephoning people up. Two months later she became a ledger clerk at a Willesden black music company, the job she presently holds. She also recounted that a little over a year previously, "We got in on a Youth Enterprise Scheme thing. If you put up £1,000—we each did, making £2,000—they'll pay you £40 a week too, for one year [i.e., matching it]. We made two records." How were sales? I asked. Both she and Ken gave embarrassed grins.

> Ken: "Well, we didn't sell too well. . . . [a sheepish laugh followed]. But we're putting another one out this October. No,

we don't have the government grant anymore, so I do the music
[with a synthesizer] Thursdays and Sundays and work another
three days a week."
   Colleen: "We've got to keep with the music, we've got to
keep it coming out, even if only one a year; people do ask me
for it, that's nice."
   Ken: "Did I tell you about my phone call?" (excitedly) "Yes,
last week a deejay from Liverpool phoned to ask us when our
next one's coming out, he wants to plug it for us!"
   Colleen: "We've got to keep the music coming out. Until it
breaks."

An hour or more later, and I'm leaving, and Ken asks, "Have you heard
our music? No? Well, I must give you a disc, I'll go and find one." He goes
off and rummages for an inordinately long time—as in thrice-underlined
humor in a TV sitcom—in a closet in the hallway. "Yes, this is our Youth
Enterprise one." Offstage rummaging continues, then "Here!" and he
hands a twelve-inch single to me: "Reggae Ray-day" is the catchy title. I
am genuinely surprised at this kindness, a little embarrassed by the gift.
I ask him to autograph it. He takes it and inscribes in the middle, "To John.
One love, Mahitema." ("That's my Rasta baptismal name.") He also signs
his name in Amharic. I leave the apartment building, down the staircase,
as if descending from the podium at my grammar school's Speech Day:
with a prize.

The Wrights are, of the eleven young people I met, the most unconventional in their employment histories. By contrast, Susan Maycock hardly
has an employment history at all. Just off to college, she's so far just done
the anticipated behind-the-sales-counter temporary jobs locally, and
some temporary clerking, plus working in a wine bar in nearby Kingston-
upon-Thames over the preceding Christmas season. Meg Eastmond eventually gave up on nursing and did a number of clerical/typing jobs until
she found her present rather satisfactory word-processing office post in
the East End. Carol Simmons's work has been in significant degree in the
home. She did "temp jobs, on and off, then I was home on the dole. Since
1981 I've been a nursing auxiliary at St. Cecilia's psychiatric hospital, part-
time. I do three evenings a week." On those days, when she leaves the
house in the late afternoon, Colin is able to look after the two little children, because, being self-employed, he can organize it that some of his
work's at home. He's been doing electronics assembly and sales for six
years, having previously done a three-year on-the-job training stint with
a large local company. Work seems to be an uncertain thing: he's on con-
tracts, from factory to factory; he's been trying to diversify away from the

west London suburbs, to Croydon (where they used to live); he's evidently having to expend a lot of energy. However, he must be keeping his head above water financially if he's been going for half a dozen years. But he did not say much about his work at all.

One thing he did say. I had asked him to compare his own work experience with that of his father's generation.

> "Workwise, yes, I've met racial confrontations. But I go round from place to place, and I'm self-employed, no boss, I've got more choice. If my father had said "Screw you," he'd lose his job. Not many others to go to in his time. But *I* got something they want, so . . . they have to behave."
> "Have you ever lost a contract, or halted a meeting, because of racial stuff?"
> "Almost, once. But they cooled it . . . "

Some of the older generation cast admiring and perhaps envious glances at these rather favored young British blacks with their greater range of choice. Marie Pilgrim said to me over lunch,

> There's a certain level above which it's very difficult for a black person to rise at Smith's.[11] I've sensed it. Yet I've stayed there twenty years. Some of the young people I've talked with there can't believe it. They're wonderful, these young people. If they don't like a job, they'll leave it for another, or even if they've got nothing to go to right away. They're very brave like that. I . . . I'm still a bit intimidated . . . um . . . This still isn't actually my country. Whereas Nigel was born here. He expects everything, just like anyone else. No favors, but it's all his by right. He can't be put off, you know, he's very determined.

The echoes are very strong here. Recall Orville Alleyne's diffidence, just like Marie's now, over "only half belonging" in Britain whereas his London-born daughter Mary expected equal treatment by right. Yet, as Orville perceived it, failing at first to receive equal treatment, Mary retreated. Whereas Nigel, with his confidence and his success at "public school," does the opposite. His determination to succeed at high job levels has been doubtless underwritten by his succession of part-time jobs while at university; he knows only too well what he *doesn't* want to do. He says of stints at a pizza parlor, as a security guard at one supermarket, and as a fetcher and carrier at another, that

> it's ill-paid; it's so *boring.* I can't understand why people do it. . . . Some of the lower-grade [white] people have a "how dare you do better than us?" attitude. They hate it. They're inse-

cure and surprised. Or they try to tell you about friends who *are* doing better than you. "Is he finding it hard?" ask the people across the road here[12] [of his engineering degree course]. They want my parents to say "yes."

Black people are usually easy to put down.

At the end of our conversation I asked Nigel whether he thought he would have been better off if his parents had stayed in Barbados. His reply was, "Not particularly," and, having been to Barbados twice recently, he drew a parallel with his cousin there, a young woman of his own age.

"She's going to find that there're a lot of young educated people who *have* to leave Barbados anyway, to go to England, but especially to the U.S.A., that's the place. But I do know she's had fewer hassles up to now than I have. Yet, it's true that I wouldn't fit in in Barbados. If I have to make my way somewhere, better do it here than there. . . .

"I wonder if I might be more confident if I was part of the majority. I'm slightly demoralised in some ways: cynical."

"I wouldn't say you're cynical. If you really were, you wouldn't be bothering to try, to do well."

"Ye-es . . . I'm doing well at the job . . . and I know I do have those social skills. . . . But there's the 'what am I?' thing. Black British? English? I'm not still completely comfortable about that. I know how poorer black people feel here, the self-doubt. If I get a big car with my good job, I know I'm going to get stopped. Or, will I be calling attention to myself if I'm dressed in a smart suit? It slowly but surely wears you down. Oh, I've got a lifetime of this!

"Maybe I'll just defend myself by being snobby—that these [racially discriminatory whites] are ignorant people, they don't think. They're merely 'the masses'. . . . And then I worry about that [i.e., the dishonor of adopting such an attitude toward less well-educated, 'ordinary' people]."

All very well, then, for one to ascribe "confidence" to some of these successful young people—but there are also some doubts under the skin.

Another one of these successful ones is Gordon Alleyne. Of him, his father Orville had said:

My son's twenty-seven, he was Head Boy at school, he's done very well. He works very hard, you'll be lucky to see him! He says he has to do that much extra because he's black, to stay on top. There's no doubt in his mind about that. Does he enjoy his job? Not so much now, but you've got to keep at it.

And indeed, upon subsequently meeting Gordon, it became very clear that his job was not something in which he delighted. He hardly talked about it at all, and instead let me know:

> The worst thing I ever experienced was being out of work for three months. And in *Woking* too! Going down to the DHSS[13] to sign on when all these other people are hurrying by to go to work in London.[14] It really made me depressed. I'll never let it happen again.

This may have indeed been a spur keeping Gordon at his demanding central London office job, with long hours and some responsibility, with monetary reward but—his father was correct—affording Gordon little satisfaction. When I revisited London in May 1989, Gordon had left this post, after eight years. Gordon's having stuck it out for so long at a job that did not enthrall seems to call into question Marie Pilgrim's assertion that "these wonderful young people, if they don't like a job, they'll leave it for another." So does Paula Farley's story.

Paula is also dissatisfied with her work. She too keeps at it. For she has her financial commitments, her voluntarily assumed responsibilities: her mortgages, her twelve-year-old daughter's private education. (Her daughter's father, St. Lucia-born but raised in Britain, lives elsewhere in London.) In an echo of the migrant generation—for many of whom the job first and foremost was "for putting bread on the table"—Paula strikes a bargain: she'll do without job satisfaction, but grasp the tangible monetary benefits and perquisites. One cannot expect her, in such circumstances, to adopt other than a somewhat acid tone:

> "I went into National Provincial when I left school, that's fourteen years ago. They don't like blacks, we don't get promoted, we get held at Grade C, people who came in with me are up at Grade G now. There're about seventy of us [blacks] on our floors, but you go and look at the good jobs, they're in the international section, and there are only two blacks in the whole nine floors up there."
>
> "Isn't there anyone you know well enough who came in at the same time as you, who was with you at the beginning, who could put in a word on your behalf?"
>
> "I know them; yes, we're friendly . . . but I don't *trust* them enough. I mean, if I told them how bitter I felt, they might go up to the supervisor and tell on me, you know? Then if I asked again, I'd get known as a troublemaker, and they could put me in not so nice a section, like records or something awful like that."
>
> "Isn't there a union? Aren't there any black union officers? I mean, if there really is discrimination they [the union] could do

something about it. The last thing the bank would want'd be bad
publicity of that kind."

"I'm in the union. But there's nobody black in it. No, I'm not
happy, they [at the bank] don't treat us fairly, but you can't do
much about it. You don't want to make too much fuss, you'll
hurt yourself."

"Why not leave?"

"Well, I've friends who left, they went to other banks and insurance companies in the City, and it's no better. There's no
point. Anyway, I know the ropes of this job. I can phone in un-
well when I like; I can take time off; and I do overtime, I get in
every day at 8 A.M. I mean, I'll take them for everything I can
get. . . .

"Yes, I get up at 6, get to work by 8. I do overtime. I come
home tired, see to Sharon and eat a meal, by then it's 10 or 11 at
night and I fall into bed."

You can see by her wry manner that she is implying, self-deprecatingly,
"and that's my daily routine in all its glory." For her—but most definitely
not for some of the others of this British-raised group—the world of work
looks almost like an updated version of that which her immigrant parents
had to experience.

To conclude this section, however, an utter contrast between the
generations: Trevor Brathwaite, Senior, thirty-one years on the buses;
Trevor Brathwaite, Junior, young man in a hurry. When I asked Trevor
Brathwaite, Jr., about his job history his reply was well thought out. With
precision he enumerated his one year in 1977 doing such and such, then
his two and a half years doing such and such, until he moved to a competing multinational, where he was the first black in the company's British
operations to be some particular type of financial analyst. Other job designations in succession, in 1982, 1984, 1985. Then in 1987 his capabilities
moved his supervisor to offer him some amicable advice: "Get into sales.
The big rewards are there."

Trevor relates: "You take a 50 per cent cut in salary, but there
are great commissions. It's taking a chance—as opposed to the
security that people of my father's generation looked for. I came
home and I said to the wife, 'What shall we do?' We agonized
about it, then decided to give it a go."

Catherine: "It's changed him. It's taken him eighteen months
to get into his stride."

Trevor again, an enthusiastic, confident Trevor: "I'd done all
five divisions of the company in two-thirds the normal time.
With good fortune and determination, I knew I could do it. And

I'd hate nine-to-five sitting behind a desk; I'm out selling in the field, marketing.''

Catherine: ''Afro-Caribbeans need self-confidence, and to be assertive—like him. One of our friends has a real chip on his shoulder about color. He's terrified of someone saying something to him because he's black.''

Trevor: ''The young here aren't in any doubt that this is where they belong. But many of them get intimidated about color: they give up job-hunting. . . .

''But no, I'm strongly in favor of changing the system from the inside. Confrontation only gives rise to harder opposition to blacks. I can see all the angles. I'll manipulate and massage the system. Like any problem I deal with in business, there are some parts that you can see you can change, so I go for them first and do it. *Then* I'll turn to the more complex ones and see what can be done. . . .

''For me the big thing is doing a job well. Color isn't part of it at all. If I do well, it's profit for the company, and it's reward for me. *And* I'm getting rewarded too.''

About two months later I again went round for an evening's conversation. Trevor informed me, ''Since I last saw you I've decided to study further and get a degree. In economics and management, at Harrow College at night.'' ''Isn't that,'' I queried, ''rather a tall order? It's a lot of work, you've three small children and a full-time job and your wife is starting her own beauty business?'' Trevor responded, ''I want it so I'll do it.'' And then, with a disarming grin, catching on to what he'd just said: ''Arrogant, aren't I!''

Housing

Thirty years on from their parents' often unenviable experiences, the younger generation are immeasurably better housed. Some of them seem to be almost unaware of their parents' travails. Others, like Derek Gill, see it all as a bit of a yarn. Yet others, such as Carol and Colin Simmons, are aware of the unquestionable improvement in conditions. ''Look,'' said Colin to me, ''how much shorter a time it took us to get a flat, and then a house of our own! My parents were able to help us.'' Naturally enough, even those of the younger generation who are cognizant of the change can't really appreciate its magnitude. Joan Springer talked of the long years of hard work and saving that it took to get up out of Rachman housing to a comfortable, modern home of one's own, and then observed matter-of-factly that for her children this meant next to nothing; the striven-for house was to them simply a place to start from. And six of the eleven younger generation interviewees were already home owners, young in years, when I met them in 1987–88.

Only one of these young people, Meg Eastmond, had lived in official accommodation of the kind so many of her parents' generation had. Meg stayed in a nurses' home at Southend Hospital for a year, but didn't like the unappealing combination of loneliness yet lack of privacy, gave up nursing, and returned home to find clerical work nearby. Three others have gone to official accommodation of a kind their parents never experienced: college residence halls. Nigel Pilgrim was one, and after graduation, immediately upon landing a job in Liverpool (as has one of his York University friends), is going in on a house purchase there with this friend and two others. That their son is becoming a home owner (if only a part-owner) in his early twenties must surely sometimes amaze Marie and Austin Pilgrim when they recall their own early twenties in Camberwell and Brixton slum properties.

Gordon Alleyne also lived in a college hostel in northeast England, his first time in that part of the world. He was worried there'd be nobody from London, with whom he'd have more in common: "North of Watford," he quipped. Instead, after his first year, he moved out to share a house with three other local students and found "the people were very genuine up there—much less duplicity than down here." Gordon was a wonderful raconteur, the possessor of a lively and articulate intelligence, who enthused to me at the end of our first meeting, "This is really interesting. You've made me think about things I've never thought about before—no, really. I'm grateful." Returning briefly after college to his parents' home then in Woking, Gordon presently made a life-style decision. He moved into London, first to Streatham, then to Clapham, into a London "where there's more space for me as a gay." He and his partner then landed a plum: caretaking, for a nominal rent in a charming area of privileged Chelsea, a small private block of old people's apartments. After a little over a year they broke up; so then he and some other gay friends rented a house in Camberwell; then to Clapham for a month in a friend's place, "a crash-pad," before he and his new partner, Kit, found a "cozy, warm" cottage in Putney.

> I lived with Kit for nearly three years, and I suppose that was beginning to become home . . . or was it? It would take a lot of investment of emotion for a place to become home.

Then Kit and he broke up. He moved back to Clapham, at a different address. He met his present partner, Ted, a medical doctor from Shropshire. After some while in Clapham, they moved to Earl's Court. Now (June

1988) they were looking at buying a large flat in Belsize Park together, Gordon thereby becoming the seventh of this group of eleven interviewees to own property.

> The gay scene in central London now is so insanely fast. Young gays come into London for the first time and just want to be picked up right away by some older man. But if you want to maintain a long-term relationship, you've got to move into the suburbs a bit for the quietness.

If this athletic former Head Boy went in an unconventional direction, so at first did another. Trevor Brathwaite, Jr., was, on leaving school, in no hurry to enter the middle-class world. Seemingly having no immediate interest in any career, this robust-looking young man trod water at home. "I'd go out at eleven, come home at five [in the morning]. I was into girls. Dad didn't think it was cool. 'Why don't you move out if you're going to behave like this?' he said. . . . So I did!" Trevor, Jr., lived in various rooms around Southall, rented from Asians; he lived with one woman for a year, "sowing wild oats"; then he lived in a council flat on a large estate: "right in the middle of the concrete jungle—where they'd hive off all the black people. Really depressing. The grey buildings." After a year of this he "went back to mum."

The present elements of his life then started to come together. In 1976 he met Catherine. A little later he became warden of a housing association block of flats in Ealing, and also started work as a trainee production manager with a large multinational company in Greenford. (He has stayed in the same field, but has as already noted changed multinationals since then on his way up.) Catherine and he set up house together. Their first child arrived in 1980, then a second.

> "We needed more space. We needed a garden. We spent a lot of time looking for houses, four months. We even went as far as Camberley. This one [a most substantial semidetached in Kingsbury] was owned by a Trinidadian-Jamaican couple. We moved in on January 12, 1984. The decision to own is the best decision we ever made. Thatcher's got the right idea!"[15]
>
> "Have you any plans to move in the next five years or so?"
>
> "Oh yes. We'll modernize and extend this one, then we'll move in a year and a half or so. Out to Hertfordshire. Or Buckinghamshire. We've already been let down a couple of times: Pinewood in Berkshire, Gerrard's Cross (my best friend lives at Denham). We would move out so as to have room for the kids, land around the house. And it's more prestigious, 'badge of success,' y'know. And to get out of the Brent catchment as well."

The conversation becomes most animated, and I become a part of it (such that my notes and recall of it here must have become less objective reportage than usual). Of trying to purchase a home in the leafier exurban areas to the northwest, Trevor recalls,

> "Yes, on one occasion we were really led along. The chap's mother told us he was really going to sell, to move down the road, they showed us around and everything. At the last minute they withdrew it from sale. 'That's too bad,' I thought. But did you see—"
>
> "Yes, I did," I leaped in, anticipating.
>
> " . . . that program just on the TV: 'Black and White'?[16] Ever since then I've started worrying if that's what's going on."
>
> "That's it *exactly,*" says Catherine, "second-guessing."
>
> "It's no good doing that, you'll end up immobilized," I put in.
>
> "Right," says Trevor. "You just keep trying."
>
> "And surely you guys can treat it as water off a duck's back now, you're doing so well you can beat that stuff?"
>
> Hearty approbation, and then Catherine says, "Yes, the difficulty's not for us now, it's for the kids. I don't know how we're going to teach them to cope with it without overdoing it, like I think Brent education does. They don't know anything about it yet—the eldest isn't eight yet—they've got to get the self-confidence to deal with it."

Thirty-two-year-old Paula Farley by contrast seems to have no sense of ever having been racially discriminated against in her house-hunting. Given her watchful nature, and the racially tinged suspicions she's already expressed about her relative lack of job advancement, I suspect she'd have been pretty sensitive to any discrimination against her in housing. But it never came up. Instead, a story of some achievement:

> I moved out of my parents' place in 1977, and moved into a ten-story council block in Stratford [relatively close by]. I suppose it was all right; the rent was cheap at first, got expensive later. The flat itself was okay. Once inside the front door, it was okay. But I didn't like the fact of the pub next door, all the swearing and carrying on. If you were going by when a drunk was coming out, it wasn't nice. I would worry, I'd be frightened, and my daughter was little. On the other hand, to be upstairs and safe and look down out of the window and see them fighting and drunk and . . . well, that was entertainment!
>
> In 1986 I moved to Manor Park. I got a two-bedroom flat in a house converted into two flats. A 1918 terrace house, the structure was fine, but it hadn't been well maintained by the previous owner: damp, garden overrun, poor décor, signs of woodworm.

I got everything seen to, I got all the workmen in straight away, cost me a couple of thousand. I got it beautiful.

Now I've sold it. I chose to move up. I made a good profit. I've a three-bedroom now, it's nice it's a house, not with somebody walking above my head. I went to the estate agent. Within two weeks I'd seen this one in East Ham. The décor was terrible, the paintwork was ten years old, the carpets were well-worn and filthy . . . but *I* see it as potential. It's a good location. It's a nice wide street. I like it 'cos it's next to a bus stop.

At first you say to yourself, "Good God, why did I do this?" Then you feel great afterwards, after you've done it up again with your own décor. It took six weeks' solid work to do it up [some of the family helped]. I bought it in February, if I sold it today [August 1988] I'd get £10,000 more. This is the best one so far. The neighbors have all come and said hello. They saw that the old people had moved out, they saw us moving in. It's brilliant, they made me feel safe, I don't have to come in and lock my door. . . . No, they're all whites, except one Jamaican family three doors away.

If Paula's slogging away at a job she doesn't much enjoy seems to echo the experience of many in the migrant generation, on the other hand her entrepreneurial buying and selling of property outside zones of black residential concentration seems more a symbol of a younger generation raised in Thatcherite times. Paula is delighted she can afford to send her daughter to a private school in Ilford, and seeing as the daughter comes home on her own from school—a "latchkey" child—Paula is also delighted to have been able to move into an area where the neighbors seem so good. As for the job,

I mean, I'll take them for everything I can get, I get every possible loan I can get. I bought one flat, now I'm buying a house just eighteen months later. I'm moving up the market, and I can get my mortgages easily through National Provincial.

The most unequivocally Thatcherite of the younger generation is the "wired," full-of-energy Max Springer. This would-be tycoon—whose parents rather ingeniously gave both their names to him, calling him after his mother's maiden name, Maxwell—moved out from his parents' home in Ilford in 1982 and went to live in a council flat in the Whitebeam Tower block, a few miles away in the GLC borough of Waltham Forest. He and his Ghanaian-born partner were already together. The place they were allotted "wasn't bad at all. The rooms were big, airy, the sun used to come through the big window. But the next-door neighbors were a bit slummy." In 1986 they shifted to West Green, into an Edwardian-era terraced house that the Haringey council had nicely converted into two flats, on a well-set, short street, pleasingly lined with mature trees. They bought the top flat from the council in the Thatcher-inspired sell-off program: "Yeah, it's quite good. We paid forty something thousand; now it's valued at £65,000. House prices are rising fast. It's like living in a bank. The neighborhood is satisfactory. Anything bad about it? They stole my car!" (There is only on-street parking.) This was in June 1988. He intended, he said, to move into an at least £100,000 house within two years. His sights are high. He mentioned Hampstead, not far to the west.

Max was not the only young homeowner to aspire to higher-status areas proximate to where one presently lived. Paula Farley in East Ham fancied Chadwell Heath. Nigel Pilgrim, raised in Upper Sydenham, his degree successfully completed, eyed Dulwich—but from afar at present, as he's starting his career and his property-owning life in Liverpool. Dulwich is a place much esteemed by his parents, who took me for a little drive through it in the Volvo one summer's evening. And Nigel enumerated Dulwich's charms:

> It's very attractive, very pleasant to live in. It's a southern equivalent of Hampstead. It's villagey, it's countrified, like Surrey or Sussex, with grass verges. It's got three public schools, an art gallery, a golf club, a riding school. There are small quaint shops. It's like a green island in south London. . . . If I wasn't to live in Dulwich, I'd live in Covent Garden.

Moving elsewhere is on ten of the eleven's agenda for sometime in the next five years—not surprisingly, given their life-cycle stage. The projected move was not necessarily in response to any perceived unpleasantness of the present neighborhood—eight out of ten[17] liked it, two said it was acceptable but boring—but more a realization either that their general life circumstances were likely to change, or that they might be able to gain financially by moving up-market. Only three of the eleven mentioned a non-London preferred destination. Only two, the young Simmonses, considered a (wholly predictable) non-British destination, but whereas Colin sounded definite with his "Barbados," Carol allowed room for maneuver: "Croydon in the immediate sense; Barbados in an ideal sense."

Colin's cousin Colleen is the only one of the eleven never to have seen Barbados, the one of the eleven who's taken a most un-Thatcherite and arguably the most unconventional path—Rastafarianism—and the one whose present housing most conforms, I'd suspect, to stereotypes held about contemporary black London. Colleen and Ken moved into their first home, an eleventh-floor council flat in Kilburn, in August 1980. They already had two babies. Apart from the view—"the sunsets in the summer were something else"—they really disliked the place.

Our life was all bound up with trying to get out, writing letters, seeing our MP. Our daughter's eczema was bad, with the dampness and dust in the building. That was how we got out—it gave us a medical priority. In May 1985 we moved to here [a top-floor apartment in a four-story block]. It's all right. There's good shopping. You can travel to anywhere in London from Kilburn. [She reels off a whole string of bus numbers; they don't have a car.] It's a good flat.

The only bad thing's the graffiti on the stairs. No, there's not too much crime at all here—well, there's quite a bit of vandalism. And there are squatters in this building. Some are okay, some are still here, the community association has rallied round to help 'em, which is right if they don't have a place to stay.
But . . . the ones we had messed up the place, left their rubbish outside, their kids were a trouble to ours. And you know, we do get the Travellers[18] around this spot every so often, and the rubbish *they* leave behind . . .

The next time I went to see the Wrights the new graffiti, replacing what had been cleaned off, were complained of again, and then Ken exclaimed,

"Oh, did we tell you about the firebomb? No? They got one thrown through their window, down below us. Eleven at night. It was dark. We heard a big bang. Looked out. Smoke had already got up to the top of the stairs. It's the smoke that's dangerous, isn't it? So we took the kids, got their shoes on, and rushed down outside."
"Did it gut the flat?"
"No, it caught their curtains alight immediately, that's why there was all the smoke, but by the time the fire brigade came—"
"How long?" I interjected.
"Oh, about . . . um . . . ten minutes—it was almost out, they'd controlled it themselves."
"What was it about? Hard drugs or something?"
"No, it's just an argument that's going on with another family close by."
"You know who they are, then?"
"Yes, people around here know who they are."
"Any arrests?"
"I don't know."
"But what's the argument about?"
"Oh, it's, uh, a nasty argument, um . . . you know, if you hit

me, then I'll hit you back. Revenge kind of thing." (This felt a bit evasive, not just simply vague. I let it go.)

"But if it's known who they are, and they're right here, couldn't it happen again?"

"That's *right!,*" agreed Ken emphatically. "It's going to happen again! This could be dangerous."

"I don't know," put in Colleen. "But one thing *is* wrong. There's only one set of stairs out in a fire, they should have some in the other direction too. That's the problem with living up high."

Social Bonds and Valued Places

In this last section these eleven young people evidence certain contrasts with their parents. First of all, the young's lives are London-centered, Barbados being of much less importance. Second, the young's lives are not so racially specific as those of their parents. There's more mixing with the native British; indeed, six of these eleven are themselves native British, of course. Third, the young are much better off materially than were their parents at the same stage of life. This emerges in a number of contexts: they have, for example, traveled widely. Fourth, there are marked changes in emphasis compared with their parents in religious observance (although their parents as we've seen have themselves fallen away since being in Britain) and in sports—especially cricket's decline. But the concluding consideration of "valued places" finds the eleven young to be much the same as their parents. The young are just as unconvinced that valued places exist and are just as lukewarm in their attitude to the Notting Hill carnival—although when pressed a number of them offered very insightful comments on it.

It elementarily follows from the way this study was set up that the parents of all of the British-raised are now living in London, with the exception of Carol Pilgrim's (now Simmons) mother who never married Carol's father Edward, and who never left Barbados. Six of the eleven, also, have British-born children of their own, living with them in London. Barbados's only strong showing is in "special relatives": six of seven mentioned are in Barbados—"granny who brought me up"—so it's mostly the Barbados-born young Londoners who mention them. For all eleven young persons taken together, 90 percent of their close friends live in London. The only mention of the Caribbean is St. Lucia, to where an Ilford high school friend has returned with her family.

As with the migrant generation, mapping the social networks of close friends, shopping, school, doctor's office, and so forth does not seem to spark particularly novel insights. That, for example, Susan Maycock has one of the most spatially restricted activity patterns does not surprise: she is the youngest of the interviewees; she is only now leaving home; she doesn't have a car of her own; her friends, all from high school, are nearby in Surbiton, Kingston-upon-Thames, and Thames Ditton. All except two of the interviewees' networks, when plotted, are largely within the particular sector of London they inhabit. The exceptions occur for straightforward reasons. Colleen Wright's Rastafarian faith leads her to "Rasta church" in Hackney, to "the music" in Brixton, and to the Brent Black Music Cooperative and her job in Harlesden and Willesden: respectively the northeast, southeast, and northwest sectors of London. Gordon Alleyne's contacts in London's gay society lead him to various inner London neighborhoods: Earl's Court, Denmark Hill, Covent Garden, Docklands.

With a group as young as this, school days still loom large as the source of friendships. Again, the exceptions are logical. The oldest of the group, Trevor Brathwaite, Jr., has no friends from Barbados school days whom he mentioned, for he left Barbados eighteen years ago when he was sixteen. His one close friend is instead from work, also a striver, an achiever, a young Welshman—and thereby also something of an outsider? Although one of Colleen's two close friends was met indirectly through school days contacts—a school friend's sister's best friend—the other one "sells me the herb. We smoke herb, maybe one or two spliffs a day, when we're reasoning, when we're reading on the Bible." And Gordon's chosen lifestyle has left school-days friends way behind; his present associates were met "socially around London." Apart from his partner from Shropshire, Gordon's specified three "close friends" are also white British. For the five Barbados-born subjects of this chapter (as was Gordon), there were only four white "close friends" mentioned, and three of these were Gordon's. The Barbadian-born five mentioned thirteen close friends, by comparison, who were of either Barbadian or West Indian provenance: a more than three-to-one black-white ratio.

For the six British-born, the black-white ratio shifts to exactly half and half. School, work, and socializing—e.g., "at the pub, friends of friends" —are all involved in this more nonracial pattern; but school days are the most frequent source. Edith Simmons observed of the younger generation,

> I really don't know if racism's better or worse now. I s'pose I
> think it's better. It's especially because of the children, they grow
> up in school together, they're used to different people now.
> That's why it's so bad in South Africa, because they don't let them
> mingle at all. I think there'll have to be some blood shed there.

Just to rub shoulders with persons of a different color who have been allocated to the same high school does not necessarily lead to lasting friendships—but it helps, most obviously because (as Edith understands) you'll never meet them anyway otherwise, you'll never even find out whether they would be desirable as friends. Nevertheless, after going through Greenford secondary school with its racially mixed student body, Colin Simmons enumerates only blacks as close friends: "five or six guys I grew up with in teenage days, they live around Hayes, Northolt, and Greenford. Three are Barbadians, one from Jamaica, one Grenada, one St. Vincent."[19] The mention of other islands made me wonder whether the Barbados-born might tend to be more inclined to have specifically Barbadian friends than the London-born, who'd have friends indifferently from all over the Caribbean. There was no evidence to support this hypothesis, however, from the tiny sample.

For Derek Gill the option of Barbadian-ancestry friends at high school did not exist, for he states he was the only Bajan in his school: Canon's Park was different from Greenford in that regard. His job circumstances— he works out at Hemel Hempstead—are similar to his school days: he's the only black at his level. All of his friends, except Nigel Pilgrim, are white. At the age of twenty-three he is already something of a cosmopolite: "I've been to Barbados lots of times. I've been to lots of places: the U.S.A., Toronto, Montreal. I organized a skiing trip for twelve of us from work to the Italian Alps." He doesn't bother to mention the race of his skiing chums—it's not germane. I think it's fair to assume they're all (or nearly all) whites. For Nigel Pilgrim it is the same story. Derek is his only close black friend. Two other friends, both white Lancastrians, were met at York University; his other three close friends he met at his public school at the southwest edge of London. His girlfriend at the time of the interviews was white. Thus when, for example, he goes to the Notting Hill carnival—"I've made a point of going, each of the last six years now"—he does not actively participate in it. "I wouldn't mind jumping up, but those I go with are watchers, it's the spectacle they like. They're mainly white people. They feel hassled by the crowd, they wouldn't want to jump into the mob."

If one great change from my own school days in Britain a quarter century or more ago has been the mixing of the races—i.e., that there are now other races with whom to mix—another has been the mixing of the sexes. The results are predictable. The government's publication *Social Trends,* as reported by the *Economist* (January 16, 1988), revealed that "over a quarter of West Indian and Guyanese men and women under 30 who are attached live with white partners." Two of the eleven interviewees of this chapter had siblings who were married to whites, another interviewee now had a white aunt, and Gordon's partner was white also. On the other hand, far more marriages or live-in relationships were with black partners: one with an African, but the others with persons of immediate Afro-Caribbean ancestry—Jamaicans, Guyanese, and Grenadians as much as Barbadians.

There is another great change from my own school days, which were also the time of arrival of the migrant generation. For myself in those years, as for the parents of the eleven young black Londoners, overseas vacations were a luxury confined to mainly the upper strata of British society. Now, however, all except one of the eleven (Colleen Wright) have visited Barbados more than once. In fact, the average for the ten is 4.2 times—for a group whose average age is under twenty-eight years! Nine of the eleven have already visited the United States, and three Canada also. Furthermore, in part because of British school vacation parties, and in part because of the ever-increasing ease of taking Continental holidays (during the decade or whatever since they left their parents' home), this group has traversed Europe with a familiarity that their parents never achieved. While Gordon may be particularly privileged, with his "we go to this lovely farmhouse in the Dordogne at least once a year," and likewise Derek with his ski trips, eight of the eleven have vacationed in Europe, from Spain to Ireland to Switzerland. They also have fewer qualms about vacationing in England—for the majority of them, after all, it is their native land! So, although they've all except one been to Barbados a number of times, it is also quite correct to say that the preeminence Barbados clearly enjoyed as a vacation destination for the parents is not the case for their children.

In the midst of this plenty, there are a few examples of straitened circumstances. Colleen has for years not been on anything more than a weekend away. And although Carol Simmons has been back to Barbados twice and to Germany once (visiting her RAF brother-in-law), she gave me a "don't be daft" look when I asked her about vacations: "No holidays around England. We're always *saving*, John!" With a mortgage, two toddlers, and a self-employed husband whose income is not guaranteed, the luxury of a good vacation has to wait. Yet they did have a Parisian honeymoon.

Contrasts with their parents emerge in other domains. Only three are presently churchgoers (one Anglican, one Baptist, one Rastafarian), and one is a Church of England "waverer"; the other seven stated that no, their religion was not of particular importance to them, and only two of these said it previously had been. One was Trevor Brathwaite, Jr., who said it had been important while he was being raised in Barbados in the Church of England. Trevor, in Barbados till he was sixteen, was also the only one of the six males who now actually played cricket and on occasion actually could sound like his father's generation: "We threw it back at them [the English]; we bested them." Only one other—Nigel Pilgrim, whose father Austin and uncle Edward were both talented players and still are great fans of the game—actually volunteered anything relating to cricket at all. If cricket in particular has lost its glory for this generation, then sports as a whole have declined somewhat too. Part of this may reflect the fact that their recruited (and selected for healthiness?) fathers, in particular, were sports and physical fitness enthusiasts: a skewed sample against which to measure "decline." For sports *were* mentioned by the young . . . but less emphatically. Colin Simmons is a keen soccer player, others do a bit of swimming, squash, badminton; some go to watch the tennis at Wimbledon (Meg Eastmond), or take ballet class (Gordon Alleyne).

As for clubs or organizations other than sporting, five belonged to none; Max Springer was emphatic: "I don't mix with them things. Most are controlled by communists and stuff." Not unrelated sentiments (but expressed more temperately) from Nigel Pilgrim, just graduated: "I was a member of Student Community Action. We worked as volunteers with disadvantaged children. It was *practical*. It wasn't concerned with anything like political theories." Further recreational activities range from keep-fit to calligraphy, from ornithology and photography to evening cookery classes and dancing. Max told me, "I used to do a lot of clubs, all over London. Since I've gone to college I've cut it all out. My major recreation now is reading books on self-improvement."

And in conclusion, we arrive at the matter of alleged "valued places." As I did with their parents, I tried running the symbolism of Notting Hill with its carnival past them. How do the British-raised evaluate it? Well, like their parents, the answer is "so-so." They mention the same pluses and minuses. Only three have been three times or more . . . but everyone's been at least once. It is interesting to observe the correspondence between parents and their children on this matter. Parents, for example, who claimed they went "all the time" have a son who's been "the last six times"—i.e., since he has been a quasi-independent adult. The Maycocks used to go until the 1976 unrest; since then they have been more circumspect. Their daughter Susan is circumspect too; she's been twice, but feels, "I'm not sure if I liked it or not. I remember thinking it wasn't what it was cracked up to be." Ten of the eleven British-raised clearly have attitudes on the carnival concordant with those of their parents. The only exception is Meg Eastmond, whose parents go "almost every year," whereas she replies she "went twice as a child. There were lots of crowds—didn't like that." She is a retiring and, in her mother's words, "passive and dependent" young woman. As opposed to her lively brother, the carnival is not for her. Of those who do attend, they are split equally between those who participate and jump up (but wear no "mas"), and those who do not, e.g., Susan Maycock, who thought the whole idea was, well, just a little infra dig; but "it happened that we had people visiting from Barbados, so of course they had to see carnival—it's on dad's Tour of London" (delivered with the sweetest of irony).

Some representative comments, the first from Nigel Pilgrim:

> The media coverage. The expectation of violence. There are probably a number of politicians who are hoping there'll be a riot so they can ban it, don't want black people running in the streets in great numbers. . . . It's such a handy focus to pin the crime image on to.

Colleen Wright:

> The few spoil it for the many. Again they're trying to ban it. But the majority of black people think it's important, it's our contribution to the culture of England.

Colin Simmons:

> I liked it when it used to be a *carnival* [implying movement]. It's too tightly controlled now, because of the violent eruption in '76. I was right there. I think there was a mugging, the kid ran off into the crowd, the police waded in to get him, the crowd reacted. That's how it started. The police had been violating people's enjoyment in their youth clubs—they were a big thing in those days—there'd been raids, people let their feelings run. They wanted to get back at the police. The police with dustbin lids, trying to defend themselves. Oh, they were *defeated!*
>
> In the city everybody understood the business. But back in Feltham in the suburbs, it's a different world, they'd seen it on the news, they were asking me all about it. They'd worked with me for three years, and now all of a sudden one morning they were looking at me and were asking, "Are *you* one of them?"

Gordon Alleyne has the last word:

> I must say to you that I tend not to see things in terms of sociology or politics—it's just that I'm dancing and a little drunk. [But then a little later this is belied by the following observations:] I dislike the way it's used as a political football if there's any violence: "Gangs of youths marauding the streets." It's geared to putting a group of people down who are trying to create something that could be quite wonderful. And if there's no violence,

the TV is patronizing: "They've had a happy day." Isn't it surprising? "These people" have organized something! I *hate* that phrase: "these people."

Did these eleven young persons attach any affective value to Notting Hill itself or to any other particular places? Only Colin Simmons talked of Notting Hill, recalling fond memories of childhood haunts: "St. Mark's Place. My first four years in England, the house I came to. Those places are so precious to me, the first school I went to, the first roads I walked on." Colleen Wright spoke similarly: "I took my two kids, seven and five, back to Wembley"—she grins ironically but happily at the lack of status resonant in the toponym—"and showed them where I grew up and the streets around, where me and my friends played, and my school. Oh yes, Wembley's home."

Four people praised London as an entity, an ensemble, mentioning the theaters, the West End, the restaurants, the vivacity and variety, and "the traditional stuff: Buckingham Palace. When you're in New York," said Derek Gill patriotically, "you think back about London as a whole." Other particular London locales viewed positively were in the main very predictable, being favored residential or recreational areas: St. John's Wood; Dulwich; Highgate Village; "down by the river in Kingston, that's lovely."

When considering places *not* liked in London, the most-mentioned zone, by fully nine of the eleven, was the inner northwest area (Harlesden, Neasden, "the Stonebridge Estate: rough elements there"). Trevor Brathwaite, Jr. mused about this zone:

> "Why haven't we had—by some quirk of fate?—a heavy disturbance in the NW. 10 area? These are heavily populated black areas . . . but not because they're black, but because they're run-down and depressing, unbelievably depressing. No big shops anymore, even Marks and Spencer's has moved out, just little corner shops, and some of *them* are empty.
>
> "I don't go there visiting, but I drive through sometimes on work on a short cut. There are black men on the street corners, hanging around. If I jump out of my big white car to get something, he [one of the men] and I exchange glances, and I sense that he thinks I'm with him, that I understand, because I'm black too. But I don't. If he knew what I'm thinking, he'd call me . . . [searches for the right term; is the pause because it's difficult, or because it's abusive and he doesn't want to say it out loud?] *English.* "
>
> "You mean, black outside, white within?"

"Yes."

"Black Americans used to call them 'Oreos,' after a biscuit [cookie]," I explain.

"Same thing here: Maltesers [chocolate-coated, whitish-centered candies]," says Catherine.

"I'm not sure," continues Trevor, Jr., "if I'm supposed to feel he's my brother, or something? I really think differently. I drive through it and look around as a black person—yet I'm a complete stranger."

Trevor, Jr.'s is clearly a "top-down" view of within-black social strata. He takes it that the black man on the corner in Harlesden can only be perceiving him, Trevor, to be a brother. But Trevor may be wrong. Given the way I set up this study, "bottom-up" sensibilities on intra-black status strata are absent. By chance, however, a view from beneath—although certainly not from "bottom"—was granted me one day at the London School of Economics. A Barbadian-born man about my age, a friend of one of the interviewees, coincidentally worked there in a skilled manual capacity. He came round to see me in my office, inquisitive and I sense suspicious about what I was up to. Carl and I got chatting:

I get feeling down here sometimes. I see all these young people who are going to make so much money. I'm rubbing shoulders with them, but I'm just a maintenance man, I'm not going anywhere. The black ones treat me as though I wasn't there—no extra consideration because I'm black or anything.

Our conversation ranged widely. Carl had been a Black Power sympathizer fifteen years previously; we talked of young British blacks moving up into the moneyed middle class—"forgetting their people," he said—and of how even some of the Black Panthers had changed their spots: Eldridge Cleaver's preaching of Christianity, Bobby Seale's entrepreneurship with "Righteous Barbecue". . . .

The only other widely disliked London locality was Brixton. Five pointed to it, although Colin Simmons's mention was tempered: "Brixton was a bad name, we were scared of it. Always associated with Jamaicans. Mind you, when I grew older I wanted to go down there, on the Tube, and see what was going on." There *is* a certain ambiguity over Brixton. It was the most mentioned (but by only four out of eleven) London place deemed "important" by the younger generation for Barbadian or for Caribbean people. Two of the four talked of the importance of Brixton's market (as did two of that of Shepherd's Bush), and Susan Maycock said, " . . . but I'm not sure why I'm mentioning Brixton except for the fact that a lot of black people live there." Nigel Pilgrim said The Oval cricket ground in adjacent Kennington was important, but otherwise, the largest response of all among this set was that, no, in London, nowhere was particularly important for black people. Gordon Alleyne, especially, developed on this: "Not particularly, no. *For me,* no. I can live anywhere. Maybe for others, but me, I don't have to be surrounded by Caribbean people. I'm me." Gordon's gay identity is to his mind more important than any black identity; he emphatically does not want to be *obliged* to be black (as we shall hear in chapter 11).

As to whether there were places in Britain important for blacks, be they Barbadians or West Indians in general, eight of the eleven gave a definite "no." A number were quite puzzled by the question, as their parents had been, and I didn't help with clues. "Never really thought about it," said Colleen Wright. Her cousin Colin Simmons was the only one of the younger generation to specifically speak out *against* ethnically specific important places:

> Personally, I don't tend to think places should be set aside for particular people . . . though there's Southall for the Asians; there's a link there. . . . [And speaking of where he had once lived] I despise Southall now, the way it's developed has changed it so. I'm not . . . er . . . *compatible* with it now.

In holding such views Colin is repeating almost verbatim his father John Simmons's sentiments. To reiterate, it was noteworthy, though hardly surprising, that so often when a rather singular point of view was expressed, the only other person of the more than thirty interviewees also to hold it was a spouse, or a parent or child.

As one of those three persons who thought there were places in Britain of value to blacks, Max Springer couldn't articulate exactly why they were important, but he was getting at the same point Susan Maycock has made about Brixton: the reassurance of a black presence. (Over half of Britain's Afro-Caribbeans live in Greater London.)

> There are a lot of black people in London, so anywhere you are in London, they're not far away. I wouldn't like to live in Cornwall or the Lake District because there're no black people there, I couldn't live there. . . . Probably Liverpool and Birmingham and stuff are important too, 'cos that's where they [black people] are; all the major conurbations.

Nigel Pilgrim used the question to go off on his own train of thought.

> No. West Indians in the U.K. don't have a tight-knit community as such. Not a structured or disciplined society. We don't have

any elders who everyone listens to. It's seen in the wildness of some of the young people, they feel no responsibility for others.

Each town with black people has its own sort of center, those communities are tightly knit, like Moss Side in Manchester. I met a black guy up there who said, "If you're not from Moss Side you're not black!" Whereas in London we can choose to forget the black community if we wish, and go out and live in the suburbs and the greenery, and commute.

Trevor Brathwaite, Jr., gives a wholly representative reply to conclude this matter. To the question, "Any important places?" he shook his head quizzically: "No-oh." A pause, then:

I know no historical information on a particular place being associated with them. My father maybe might know where the Barbadian feet first touched dry land. . . . But I don't know where you could find a group of ten Barbadians together.

Nine
The Island Reconsidered

> *In Barbados these days we don't say let's go to the rum-shop and have a few drinks. Oh no, I'm in my car, let's go to the Hilton and sit by the pool!*
>
> John Simmons

The migrant generation have, we have seen, maintained links with the old island. The British-raised have developed such links as they grew up. Respectively, what do the migrants and their children think of Barbados now? Their opinions stem from their own numerous visits to Barbados, from news brought by those who come from the island to visit them in London, and from the frequent telephone calls to the Caribbean. There's also plenty of second-hand information to be picked up either from mailed copies of the *Barbados Advocate* or the *Nation,* or from the London Caribbean-oriented newspapers.

How It Has Changed: The Migrants' Perceptions

Nearly all were decided in their opinion that the home island had advanced materially: the increase in amount of housing; the improvement of housing quality; the further development of roads; the spread throughout the island of such facilities as piped running water and grid electricity. Should they compare their island with the company of newly independent countries that it joined in the midsixties, Barbadians may fairly be excused some pride in their achievement: a non-oil-producing state whose per capita gross national product rose to U.S. $5,140 in 1986—marginally higher than *Ireland* in that year—plus an unsullied record of peaceful changes of democratic government. Marie Pilgrim said, "Oh, it's more af-

194

fluent. In some ways we [in London] are behind them there. Barbados can never be called a Third World country." (Austin bellowed from the kitchen: "We shall be First World. All we need is a bit of industry!") Dotteen Bannister remarked, "People have found it easier to buy land, so the housing's better—no more chattel houses[1] these days. Everything is better. Even to the point, I've heard," she adds with a twinkle in her eye, "that the Barbados government's got a *submarine!*"

Beverly Brathwaite gave a pretty typical reply.

> Oh, it's changed a great deal. Barbados seem just like America now, with the shopping and the changed names and buildings and roads with the big vehicles on them. People have changed a very lot: prosperity, luxuries, houses, they're living very nicely out there. Everyone is too great to work on the land now [i.e., to grow sugar cane]. Where they're getting the money from I don't know.

Eulie Eastmond thought she could see that

> attitudes have changed, because others that've come out, have now gone back. Ones who've just stayed are very narrow-minded: if people are Rastas, or if they've been in prison, or living together unmarried, that's never forgotten. They're still very narrow-minded.

Austin Pilgrim was one of five who perceived, as did Eulie, a greater general sophistication than in years gone by: "The island's on the up and up. It has always been stable, and now children are far better educated. Barbadians are traveling more than ever." "Why's that so important?" The tone of his response indicated that I really should have known the reason without asking: "It's educational, it takes away the small-island mentality." Six others felt that education had improved in quality and availability: "We've a university now."

Others felt that the leap in material affluence had not been an unalloyed blessing. Pauline Alleyne asserted that "the village community's gone, it's very much every man for himself now," and Audley Simmons felt "the standard of living in Barbados has gone up quite a bit. But people are so materially oriented there, it's like America. They worship material things. There's such competitiveness." Frank Springer's feeling was that

> the friendliness is still there, but it's lessening. In the new tenantries [housing developments] you're getting that isolated middle-class environment. People come home from work and start cooking . . . and that's all. The wife works too. Women work now,

they've got their cars, women have emancipated, they're not economically dependent on men anymore.

A few felt that crime was definitely on the increase in Barbados, and that
morals were in decline. And a couple of other people mentioned the rise
in the cost of living in Barbados; one of them averred that on his last visit,
to his astonishment, he had found things "no cheaper than in London,"
and blamed it on the high prices that the kind of tourist to which Barbados
caters is prepared to pay.

Tourism's rise, and agriculture's—basically sugar cane's—simultaneous
decline are the great changes in Barbados's economic life. Althea Maycock
said,

> Sugar's gone down. Sugar factories have closed. Young people
> don't want to work on the land anymore, even if they'd be un-
> employed otherwise. They have to bring in people from other is-
> lands now, like St. Vincent.

Barbadians prefer tourism-related jobs: four respondents spoke of greater
job opportunities in this sector for black people on the island (three link-
ing it implicitly to the fact of blacks now holding the reins of political
power).

Barbados—in part, I suspect, because of its greater distance from North
America than, say, Jamaica or the Virgin Islands, and similarly, its greater
distance from Britain than Spain or Greece—is definitely an up-market
tourist destination: an Eastbourne to a Margate. It is marketed as such in
Britain, and inevitably certain stereotypes, or perhaps presuppositions,
are conjured up. For example, in London in February 1988 a trendily
chatty piece by Jeffrey Bernard appeared in *Midweek*. His admirably
ravaged, world-weary *bon vivant* face gazed out from the photo apparently taken at some bar; there was a cigarette in one hand, a glass in the
other. Ruminating on the impending loss of his "West End attic," he la-
ments his departure

> when my friend and landlord's lease runs out. If we all have to
> leave, that is. Depending on the financial situation the only alter-
> natives I can see are beachcombing in Barbados and taking an
> overdose of sugar cane, or moving into the Muthaiga Club[2] and
> becoming the resident bore.
>   Meanwhile, my Maltese man from the Coach and Horses [a
> pub] has done an excellent job putting up bookshelves for
> me. . . . [3]

One catches on, I trust, to the social stratum involved here; Barbados
is a very middle-class tourist destination. Also published, not coinciden-

tally, in the miserable London midwinter, a big *Observer* (January 31, 1988) story was headlined "Sunburnt Piece of England," where "the British way of life thrives in a tropical climate." Nigel Hawkes wrote,

> The Honourable Wesley Hall, now the Minister of Tourism and Sport . . . emphasises that Barbados is an "affordable and safe" destination for tourists.
>
> Affordable, of course, is a relative term. . . . By booking 21 days ahead and travelling economy, the price comes down to £425 return.[4] According to Wes Hall, British Airways traffic to Barbados is up by 81 per cent this winter.
>
> There is a cheaper way of doing it. Airtours, a company based in Manchester, has started running flights to Barbados of £299 return, a sensationally low figure which has many on the island worried. They fear that low-cost tourists will spend little on the island—"They even travel by bus," said one rather grand lady to me with a curl of the lip—and that Barbados will suffer all the effects of mass tourism without any real financial benefit.

A number of the interviewees had heard the news of the inception of cheap flights and viewed their home island's apprehension with slightly ironical embarrassment. Certainly the stereotypical Lancastrian[5] proletarian might find the preferred, decorous Barbados touristic style a little unfamiliar. I found in the free newspaper the *Visitor* for July 29 to August 11, 1985, for example, "presented as a public service by the Barbados Board of Tourism," a cartoon sequence admonishing that *"Humidity* is not an excuse for NUDITY." A bikini-clad young woman, attracting admiring glances, strolls by a clothes store:

> Oh what a glorious figure!
> Oh what a succulent peach!
> But please don't wiggle it all around town
> Save it for the beach!

After two more such jingles, we are informed, "Most Bajans are not Snobbish or Stuffy, but we do think there's a time and a place for everything. So let's keep the Bikinis on the beach and dress appropriately for shopping, business, or church." Amen. No Jamaican north-coast "Hedonism" camps here.

The Barbadian government itself was responsible for the above self-characterization. One of the London Barbadians smirked when I showed him the cartoon, for he, and virtually all the other adoptive Londoners, saw themselves now as more sophisticated venturers who had transcended their blinkered small-island vision. Audley Simmons:

When I went back after seventeen years I saw some schoolmates who'd done well there, even a little better than me. But after I'd get talking to them, then I thought, "My God, I've *learned* so much!" They're still in the easygoing little island way. I was so . . . naïve when I came here. [He laughed out loud.] I knew *nothing.*

This flattering self-perception was, however, occasionally belied by the Barbadian chauvinism that revealed itself in them. If the English have presuppositions about Barbados (partly fed by Barbados officialdom itself), then also the Barbadians in turn hold presuppositions about the people of the other Commonwealth Caribbean territories. There have been allusions to this in a number of places in the text so far; the sense that "small-islanders are country cousins—we provided their teachers and priests and police in the old days" or that "Trinidadians are mercurial, we're historically prior (and thereby superior) to them because we peopled Trinidad and Guyana significantly, *and* they're mixed in with Indians down there too. And Jamaicans are, well . . . Jamaicans!" The reader cannot have overlooked, for example, that Austin Pilgrim is a not infrequent Jamaica-basher. The following tale is one of cold comfort being offered someone who, his ego bruised, took Austin to be a fellow black in time of need, but instead found him to be a superior-seeming Barbadian. Austin relates:

When I first started working in the allotment [garden] I'd ask [English] people how do you get tomatoes to grow big and how do you get the beans right, and they'd just say they didn't know. In the end one man helped me and I put my mind to it and got it right. There was an old English fella—he's very old now, he can hardly move, don't see him so much now—who was a real old bigot. He used to come over as I was working and say, "Why don't you go back to where you belong?" He did it for years. Then a second black chap came out this way, a Jamaican, you know what they're like, noisy and friendly. So he goes over saying hello to everyone and to the old man. He gets abused of course, comes rushing over to me and says, "He's a racist, he told me to 'eff off, nigger.' " I looked at him very calm and said, "Well, what do you expect if you go pushing yourself on people?"

Again, Orville Alleyne surprised me one evening too by the moral he chose to draw from an incident of which I was informing him. Pauline had just told me what a great reader her husband was. I delved into my briefcase and came out with a recently purchased copy of Ken Pryce's *Endless*

Pressure; "D'you want to borrow it?" Then I mentioned that Pryce, a Jamaican, had landed the post of sociology professor at the University of the West Indies; but also, that I had been told he had recently been found floating dead in the harbor in Kingston, Jamaica. The point I was trying to make—we were in the middle of a conversation about the whys and the wherefores of my questionnaire—was that social research to my mind had never seemed a calling one would be likely to be *killed* for! Orville drew a totally different moral: "Yardies.[6] . . . But there, Jamaica's very violent, they're always shooting people. I'm not putting us too high, but that wouldn't've happened in Barbados."

Tony Gill's consciousness of Barbadian superiority did not demand any active put-down of other Caribbean territories; it simply, calmly, pervaded his manner—Barbados had been the hub.

> "My wife's grandparents lived in Guiana. Her mother was brought up there, came to Barbados as a girl, never went back to Guiana. No, my wife, nor me, never went back there either. Her grandfather on her mother's side was a teacher, and his brother was the sanitary chief of Queenstown."
>
> "I bet you they were Barbadian in origin?"
>
> "Oh yes. Barbadians *settled* Guiana. Trinidad too. There are Barbadians all over the Caribbean, especially teachers. We had good education in Barbados."
>
> "Police too."
>
> "That's right," said Tony proudly, clearly glad that I had known that.

Migrant-generation Barbados chauvinism is a real, and in part unconstructive, force. English traveler Quentin Crewe did not like it (he is writing of 1986 or so):

> I was not sorry to go. The island was the most English we had seen and although the people, for the most part, were far better off than those on other islands, it distressed me that so many of our worst traits had survived so vigourously. The colour bar, the pomposity of asking people to wear dinner-jackets [tuxedos] for Christmas[7] and what they call Old Year's Night, the general philistinism.
>
> It is a smug and snobbish island . . . so pi[8] an island.

Gladstone Codrington is a middle-aged London Barbadian who has risen very high in British official circles. He was decided in his opinions of Barbadian society.

> You know what they mean when they say it's "too small," these people of yours who are thinking about whether to go back? It's

that Barbados hasn't changed, it's still a colonial mentality. It's still the same old big families, even though the white rulers have gone. You can go back there, they'll greet you in the street, but they'll *never* invite you to their houses. To them, I'm just a pushy young chap who's done well over here. *Barbados is a more conservative society than England.* That's why [he gives a semisly, semirueful grin] we get on so well over here.

One Saturday afternoon the Eastmonds told me the following story. He, by the way, says he has no thought of returning to Barbados, whereas she said she would like to. They both contributed to the telling of this tale, so it is simpler not to differentiate between them in setting it down here:

"We were talking to a lady just yesterday who's come back. Well, *she* had a story! She and her husband sold their house here and went back to Barbados and she got a job in Jenkins's [big store] on the main street in town as a shop assistant. They're very slow down there, and she . . . well . . . she showed them up. She was always going up to the shoppers, 'Can I help you?'—you know, the way they do here. Well, the other workers resented her English ways, she was too eager to help. The English and American tourists liked her style, of course, she got far more sales than anybody else and they're paid on commission so she got a lot more money than the others. . . . And they pay people who're back from England more than local people anyway.[9]

"So, at the end of the day at 5:30 she walks out of the shop. And someone had put an article in her bag without her knowing. And of course they'd tipped off the security man, so he says, 'Can I search your bag?' and he finds this. Shoplifting. The manager's called. He doesn't believe it. But they call the police and they come and take her down to the police station and search her, even under her wig, and charge her."

"But they found nothing else?"

"No."

"But they pressed charges? I mean, what about the manager . . . ?"

"The manager didn't believe it, but he didn't back her up either and say 'drop the charges' because he thought it would have alienated a lot of his other workers. . . .

"Now she got very upset and nervous about it all so she went round with a friend to the British High Commission to make sure she could get back into England, to get her passport stamped up-to-date, and the police found out and said, 'Why did you go and get a reentry stamp for England? You were going to jump the country, weren't you?' "

"So it looked more like she really was guilty?"

"Yes. But she said it was just a renewal, to make quite sure she had it. Luckily she got a good lawyer, and she was found not guilty. And the manager came up to her afterwards and said, 'I *knew* you wasn't guilty.' "

"But the publicity!"

"Yes, it was in the paper, it's a small place, everyone knows, it gets around so fast, you can't keep anything secret."

"And the finger had been pointed at her anyway, even if she was found not guilty."

"Exactly right. People said, '*She's* the one who got off.' . . . So, she was so upset she came straight back to England, she's staying with a friend of ours here."

"Didn't you say she had a husband?"

"Aha, now *there's* something! Yes, he worked as a storeman at the same place."

"So he stayed?"

"*Wait.* I'll tell you. Three weeks later they sacked *him.* Here [London] it doesn't matter where your wife or husband works, people don't know, they don't care. But back there it's different. . . . So they sold up their place in Barbados and they're both back here and she says she's never going back again."

Whether this is the whole truth and nothing but the truth I'm not able to say, but the main lineaments seem to look pretty true to human nature: the mix of envy and vulnerability as motive for the local staff; the pusillanimity of the manager who chooses what appears to be the path of least resistance; the stress and humiliation suffered by the revenant. These themes will resurface from time to time in the next section, being the migrants' response to the question, "Would you consider going back to Barbados to stay?"

To Return?

The use of the verb "consider" made it easy for the interviewees to say "yes," but they did so with varying degrees of decisiveness. Only two out of twenty-two gave a flat "no," and another said not at the present time. Four others seemed to be in a complete quandary; they really couldn't answer the question. They comprise two couples: the Alleynes and the Springers. Interviewed in the absence of his wife, Frank Springer said,

I'm in a dilemma, a *serious* dilemma. I want to go, no doubt about it. I'm just an old teenager, I want to go back and enjoy the beach and the water. My wife wants to stay here to watch her grandchildren grow. So I guess I'll have to stay. And, if I had to go home, I know I'd miss the theater, the culture, the cinema, the shows. . . .

And Joan Springer, who exuded house-proudness, or rather house-fondness in Ilford, said, "I'd really miss England, I've lived here so long I really like it here. My children, my grandchildren are here. And my parents aren't there."

A person who had some doubts about returning, Tony Gill pondered his answer:

If you go back from here for the first time, you see the sun and the palms and the progress, you think, "Wow!" You must beware of getting a rush of blood to the head.[10] But if you go back quite often like us, more gradually, then you can be clearer about it. I won't go back at this stage. When I retire, I don't know. Most of my friends live in England or Canada or the States—or they're dead—we've been away so long. I'm not obsessed with "I'm a Barbadian."

Yes, and I've known people who've tried going back . . . and some come back here again! Once you've lived abroad you can't go back. You get bored pretty soon, once you've gone to the beach in the sun day after day. If I had enough money I'd live there, but in order to go and travel a lot from there, like a base. I wouldn't go back to shut myself in.

Mind you . . . I suppose if I was *absolutely* broke, it'd be better to be in Barbados than here. You could always find yourself something to eat there: fish, breadfruit. It's not commercialized like here . . . er, I mean, people still *give* people things at home. Better to be a beggar in your own country than in another man's country.

Colin Jemmott has done numerous business deals to facilitate successful Barbadian Londoners setting themselves up again in Barbados upon retirement. Pointing to the island's bland provinciality, he relates,

I went back to sniff out Barbados myself. My wife says she'd miss London's amenities, she goes to the theater let's say nine or ten times a year—I bet you didn't think black people go to the theater?!—and she says there's no excitement to living in Barbados. There's nothing to get you angry like in the *Sun!*—just the *Barbados Advocate.* It's not so alive. It's funny; you get used to having the annoyances.

Another Barbadian Londoner was less than happy when I informed him that a fellow immigrant was able to view the *Sun* as merely a purveyor of pin-pricking buffoonery.

> But so many of our people read that damned paper. Don't they think? Don't they realize that the negative view of black people bit by bit affects them, and gives them a . . . a negative self-image? . . . You know, crime and all that?

And Audley Simmons was sourly dismissive: *"Some* call it a newspaper. [Pause] I mean, the *Sun."*

(The *Sun* is Rupert Murdoch's right-of-center London tabloid, famed equally for its "Page Three Girl"—each day a photo of an unclad young woman of ample proportions is there—and for the irresponsibility of its sensationalist reporting. The latter manages to offend nearly everyone sooner or later. My favorite during the 1987–88 year was in response to the Church of England synod deciding that practicing male homosexual priests should not be banned: "Pulpit Poofs Can Stay."

Black people as a group are often calumniated. If the racial element can be combined with bashing a "Loony Left" GLC local government, so much the better. Thus, a story headlined "Freebie Trip for Blacks but White Kids Must Pay" was eventually taken up by the watchdog [but then toothless] Press Council, which in October 1987 deemed that the article was "loosely written and inaccurate, and carried a headline which was provocative and potentially racially divisive." The matter in question was the Brent Council's scheme to organize an exchange trip to Cuba. There was in practical terms little recourse to be had in such a case. And the damage was done.)

This digression on the *Sun* serves to point up, perhaps rather glaringly, the pervasive racism in England that the migrants might fairly assume they could escape by returning to Barbados. What a breath of fresh air, to go home! But it isn't that simple, it doesn't always work out that way. The already-told tale of the Eastmonds' acquaintances serves as a cautionary precursor to the following accounts of those who've tried going back. "Going back to do what?" is a central question. To retire, or to find work? The latter has until recently been the focus of the migrants' thoughts. Now, however, the passage of the years brings the reality of retirement closer. Chronologically it makes good sense to first report about attempts to return for work, and then to move on to reports about retirement.

None of the interviewees had really tried going back in order to work (one was scouting things out for a few months, inconclusively), and none has yet as I write gone back to retire. They know people who have, however. Dotteen Bannister reported,

Yes, they like it. They went back, got jobs, got right into things, after fifteen years here. Mum and dad too, after twenty-five years. He didn't want to go back but he eventually fitted in and likes it now. He'd lost touch with all his friends. He didn't like writing letters, so he never did write. But now he's got all his friends again, living a lazy luxurious life.

By many accounts, the first people referred to who "got jobs" were very fortunate. There was an awareness that there weren't many job opportunities in Barbados, that it might be all right if you retired with money and "went in at the top" (in Eulie Eastmond's phrase), but otherwise, it could well be a struggle. Frank Springer told a cautionary tale:

"Some achieved when they went back. Some got disillusioned back there. You spend your money. You get no job or income there. You just eventually run your savings dry. Then what? Back to England. I had a friend who went back to try to start a fish business there. He thought England was hostile and cold. But his fish business failed. He picked up a job in Bridgetown, and his fellow workers there said, 'Imagine you in England all them years and you can't buy yourself a car.' They kept on throwing it at him, that he was a no-hoper. He came back; he couldn't take it.

"You can't live in Barbados on nostalgia. You need money. Take me. I'm too old for the job market. 'What've you got to offer?' they'd ask. The skills I learned here I can't use there directly."

"You mean the Underground, running a railway?"

"Yes. You need qualifications on paper you can take with you, that they'll accept, what's that word?"

"Credentials?"

"*That*'s what I mean. . . . And you left too long ago. You're no longer part of the community, unless you're lucky enough to have kept up contacts . . . "

Many answers balanced pro and con. Trevor Brathwaite, asked how people he knew had found it, told me,

Some went home, and came back soon. Some went home and stayed. A woman we know went back and found they were better off in Barbados than here, they'd improved more, she lived in very poor surroundings here in London, she'd left to improve herself, but. . . . She hardly knew how to face it [the shame, when she got back to Barbados].

Alan Maycock replied:

Mixed. Once you've lived here, you get into the habit. Despite my saying Barbados has got more sophisticated, you can go back and open your mouth and they say, "O, where have you been away?" And how *inefficient* the Bajans are, and how *unwilling* to serve you. They don't queue, there's just a mad rush for the bus.

So you have to adapt back there. I've heard stories of people who can't settle back in, but most seem okay. It's a question of one's approach: be adaptable.

Amelia Simmons reported varied experiences also:

Most are very happy, but there's one set [of friends] who've never been happy back there—but they haven't come back here either (though their children are here). They went back on holi- day, fell in love with the place,[11] but he can't find a job he really likes. He's a motor mechanic, those under him there are very slow, don't-carish, y'know. He found it difficult to control them. . . . They *are* so slow back there. "You must slow down," said a friend, we were getting some building materials for the house [their retirement home], they took ages. Well of course, we only had two weeks there to get it done in."

That his and Amelia's decision to go back has been made and is being acted upon (as we saw at the end of chapter 6) did not blind John Simmons to the difficulties that others attempting a return might meet.

For those who were still working [and who wanted to continue to work in Barbados], it's been rough. . . . Ah well . . . we've discussed this so much. They go back. Then two or three years, and they're back here. You cannot live the life you live in Eng- land in the Caribbean. You run through your capital, build your- self a home, take a car down. Friends and hangers-on desert you when the money runs out. Barbados is expensive, you need in- come coming in. You've got to feed the kids. One man I know said it got to the point that he could buy the children eggs for breakfast but couldn't afford the bacon anymore. That's when it got to him . . . and he felt he had to come back.

But for us, it's different. We'll be retired, living off a pension. No overheads. Sell here, buy there. We'll live quite happily. We don't want to make an enormous splash.

By contrast, a number agreed with the earlier comment that to retire to Barbados obliged one to go back in at the top. "You've got to be able to *afford* to," said Edward Pilgrim.

"So, as the Brits say, if you won the pools?"[12]
"Oh yes, a nice house with steps down to my beach, go swimming any time. But that's dreaming, isn't it? So I don't study it. . . . I could [he grins] fly to the U.S. and U.K. and see those places on holidays. That'd be the ideal life: jetting over here for an extended stay when I felt like it."

There are such people. Colin Jemmott deals with them, "the very successful Bajans. They're building holiday homes there, they spend two or three months in the winter there, but keep established here." Not only some of the migrant generation, but also some of the British-raised aspire to such a privileged Atlantic-spanning style.

Charles Eastmond's friend isn't quite in this jet-set league, but all the same, things sound acceptable:

Another one retired and lives off his U.K. pension with a very middle-class life-style, he's quite happy, he visits the U.S. and Canada too. But he likes getting the *Mirror* and the *Telegraph* posted from me.
One friend went back to retire through ill-health, his arthritis improved considerably there. He says, "If I wasn't ill, I'd still be in England!"

Two other people, both women, mentioned their arthritis and how Barbados's climate might alleviate it. Three people specifically mentioned that returnees had loved having warm sunny weather again.

Some knew of people who had chosen not to retire to the Caribbean, in part because Britain did have its attractions. There was Edith Simmons's Jamaican father who allegedly loved his *draught* Guinness, for example! And Trevor Brathwaite talked of a friend:

Another friend of mine says he's worked all his life here, he can get good social security, pension, improvement loans as an OAP[13] for his flat. The welfare state's much better here than in Barbados.

If all of the households I met at least have the resources to be considering the matter of return, Ivan Weekes reminded me that they are the fortunate ones among Britain's Afro-Caribbean population. For many of the latter would retire in Britain not because of its attractions, but because they would have no choice:

Our people learned to survive, it's true, but many stayed not because they wanted to, but because they were financially trapped. A lot of my friends now have gone to America; some retired back to Barbados. My roots are in Barbados—it's the natural thing to return there when you retire, but some people won't be able to, they'll be trapped here. There's the matter of pensions, and how much you'll actually get, and how it would be paid directly to you in Jamaica or wherever, and whether it would be index-linked[14] here or . . . because my work is concerned with race relations, I'm in the process of consulting with the relevant government departments on all this now.

What complications there may presently be for remitting which particular pensions to the Caribbean I do not know. John Simmons (as we have seen) was clearly certain there would be no problems with his. Ivan Weekes, however, has here happened upon the much-discussed matter of "the Myth of Return." That is, if one asks whether people would consider returning, nearly all of them say yes. If the question is framed with greater definition, however—"Are you going to move in the next five years?"— those who say "yes" among the Barbadians with whom I talked are outnumbered by the combined total of "no" and "don't know." This doesn't necessarily imply that the myth *is* a myth, however. Half of them are still more than five years away from their anticipated retirement date. Also, all of them are now owners of London property. Were they to sell, they *would* have the capability to go back to their island of origin . . . if they really wished to. It's not just pie in the sky; myth could become reality for them.

In sum, then, a leaning toward Barbados. But an inclination not without a considered evaluation, by some, of the old island's shortcomings. Nor without a realization that they too have changed, as well as Barbados. Nor without a weighing of the practical difficulties involved. All of them express some degree of ambiguity, even, as we have seen, John and Amelia Simmons, who have indeed already made the choice to return and are acting upon it.

The last word in this section belongs to the Alleynes: the ambiguity they express rises almost to the point of confusion. Will they move in the next five years? He: no; she: yes, within London somewhere. Will they consider returning to Barbados to stay? He: yes; she: no. Yet in another discussion that occurred one evening a couple of months earlier, it was he who had put in a good word for Britain, whereas it was she who felt the stress melt away on getting back to black Barbados. Although in the subsequent conversation she was to praise England's Penzance as a holiday venue, on this earlier occasion she claimed that "we usually go home for holidays. He'd like to take more here, I always don't want to." I prompt and pry for greater explicitness, and Pauline responds:

"Yes, you might not get a welcome in some country hotel. You can never tell what they're thinking, going some place

where blacks are few. When I get back to Barbados, it all drops
away, it's like a load off my forehead. I can't say what it is,
maybe it's because everyone's black there . . . I don't know.
. . . And yet, when I come back here, it's not as if as soon as I
put my foot back on England I feel anything bad. I don't feel any
bad at all."

"This country's not so bad," offers Orville. "I say that to my
black friends when they're sounding off. Lots of worse places
around. Just because Africa's run by black people. . . . We'd
still be foreigners there."

"And so, will you stay?" I ask.

"Yes, I think we'll retire here," Orville says.

They glance at each other. A touch of wryness at the familiarity of the
same old issue. It's clearly been discussed—and it doesn't look like an easy
decision.

The Younger Generation's Evaluation

The young's situation was different from that of their parents, in that most
of them had no memories of the Barbados of many years ago. So one
couldn't in mechanical fashion ask exactly the same questions: "How has
Barbados changed?" is inapt. However, impressions that are capable of
comparison to those of their parents can be gathered by asking, for example, what have their parents told them of the former Barbados? For the
minority of the young born in Barbados, what do they recall? As vaca-
tioners there more recently, what do they discern, and what have other
returned acquaintances reported to them? And, to what degree do the
British-raised have any interest in Barbados—would any of them consider
settling there?

Colin Simmons was the second youngest on arrival in Britain, aged
eight. He and Carol, both Barbados-born, are, as we have seen, of all the
British-raised perhaps the most positively inclined toward the island. So,
had he been taught about Barbados? Colin replied,

No need to, because I knew where I'd just come from! We have
made a point of getting Kevin—he's four and a half—to relate to
it. People from there come to visit, and then they go back. He
asks where they are. We tell him, "in *Barbados.*" And he's been
there. It means something to him.

On a later occasion Carol said:

He went at age two and a half. Yet he can remember his grandmother, one special auntie, and the gap where we lived. . . .

We're going to ensure they don't forget Barbados as a part of them—although *this* [London] is what they know as home.

Colin and Carol's attempts at implanting an awareness of Barbados in their children stands in utter contrast to their parents' generation. The young report that their parents had been desultory, to a greater or lesser degree, in attempting to imprint any Barbadian consciousness. Max Springer: "We never approached it in any sort of structured way, just . . . it just turned up in conversation sometimes. . . . They told me it was pretty poor but that they had had a great time as kids, even though things was hard." Nigel Pilgrim indicated that it was he who was the initiator: "Only because I ask questions and my dad tells me. My parents have let me discover what I want to know. Dad never tried to force anything down my throat." "In the eighteen years I've been here," Trevor Brathwaite, Jr., remarked, "my father's probably talked [about Barbados] three times!"

These laissez-faire attitudes of their parents were viewed by nearly all the young as posing no problem, as being neither a good nor a bad thing particularly. Gordon Alleyne's sharp intellect wanted to pursue the theme further, however.

It wasn't as if they were trying to re-create the culture here. We went back on holidays, but it wasn't as if a point was being made. All this national cultural identity stuff . . . I'm not ashamed of it or anything, but . . . I'm not into it. It's *used,* and *I* am used . . . a further divisive measure, by black people to keep themselves black—and by whites, who want to keep us separate. What is the point of keeping a tradition if it's a *bad* tradition?[15] The music, the more cerebral things, yes, may be worth preserving—but not other things, like some of our foods, just for the sake of it.

I think those black student political types are doing a great disservice. And I see Black Sections in the Labour party as divisive.[16]

Catherine Brathwaite, Trevor, Jr.'s, wife, sees things similarly. "She's Grenadian," said Trevor. "No, I'm English," she countered crisply, "I came here aged five and a half." And then, up comes the topic of Brent schooling and its attention to cultural identities. She said,

Our kids are English. These are their roots here, in this house. This is all they know. At school Jeremy came back very upset one day because they said he was "Caribbean"! Well, we eventually went up, and saw the teacher, and hammered it out. The child is English. That is what he must be told. *We* are Caribbean, yes.[17] Not him. All this here [she gestures around the substantial house] is their foundation, if anything were to happen to us.

Such issues, confronted by second-generation families such as the Simmonses or the Brathwaites in educating their third-generation children, seem only to have really exercised one of the first-generation couples: the Maycocks. Susan was the only second-generation young person who felt that her parents had actively *taught* her about their island of origin.

> We *do* have chats about stuff, and they've told me what it was like when they were growing up. There are always people here from Barbados and they're always talking about the olden days. . . . Everybody has a nickname!

That her parents have seen to it that Susan is aware of her Barbados connection is all of a piece with other actions of theirs. The Maycocks place great value on education; members of the PTA, they moved out of the GLC borough of Croydon because they were dissatisfied with its schools. Althea Maycock was, of the migrant generation, one of the more certain that she would like to return to Barbados—after all, her other child, her grown daughter Elizabeth, is back living there. Alan Maycock was convinced that the history of Barbados and of the Barbadian migration to London was in itself something worth focusing on, and thus was immensely supportive to me in my work. "I have always believed," he wrote to me across the Atlantic, "that the experience of Barbadians working in the transport industry was worthy of academic investigation." Fittingly, it was in *his* fine back flower garden in Surbiton one wonderful late May afternoon in 1989 that we sat in lawn chairs and from his Barbados telephone directory chose the pseudonyms for the subjects of this study: "Oh, we should have a Codrington. *Must* have a Springer." "I like the name Maycock," I said—little knowing at that moment that I was going to confer it upon him.

It was curious that the one member of the younger generation who has no firsthand experience of Barbados, Colleen Wright, is simultaneously sister to the only British-born person from this sample of households (her younger brother Jimmy) who is currently living in Barbados. Audley Simmons remarked upon his youngest child's currently rather *dolce far niente* existence (I had just asked whether Jimmy was there because, among other things, Barbados was black-ruled):

> No, he doesn't talk about it, I don't think he's political. He likes it there because he doesn't have to pay rent at his cousin's! He's nineteen—been there about a year now. So, everything he makes

is his to spend. He can only work ten hours a week if he likes.
Here [at Audley and Edith's home in Wembley], if he's earning,
then he pays rent.

And of course, it's a little island and he's from the big city and
he's something special and the girls. . . . And the sun and the
weather; he loves being in his frayed shorts . . .

Whereas his elder sister in her council flat in Kilburn has not been on a
real vacation for some years.

The ten who have visited the island on average four times (although
some visits were when they were still very small) have had opportunity
enough to observe it. Their responses are overwhelmingly positive. For
most of them Barbados is, at its simplest, a superb vacation spot. "Beautiful, it was like paradise," said Paula Farley. The responses of a minority
mingled elements of the positive and the negative: "The old island's
thrived," glowed Trevor, Jr. "Ah, but he was going demented when they
closed at twelve noon on Saturday!" Catherine countered. There were
only three negative responses, all that Barbados was "too small." Susan
Maycock, every inch the young Londoner, gave one of the mixed
responses.

I liked it. It was hot. I liked being with the family. Here, there's
only us [laughs]. Over there, there's everybody: aunts and uncles.
It was a bit small, everyone lives near everyone else. People always live in the same place, that annoys me, it was all right for a
holiday, but . . . it was a bit small. As I said, everyone lives
near everyone else.

I liked the holidayfied bits, beaches and hotels, but there *are*
places there that've been spoilt by the tourist industry. . . .

They still think it's a big effort to go from one end of the island to the other, and it's only twenty-one miles!

In addition, she reported of some friends who had recently been there
that "they liked it as a holiday, but it's all behind in music; a bit *slow.*"
Nigel Pilgrim, another young Londoner par excellence, revealed,

Last time was in '82. At first I didn't like it, away from home,
from friends, getting bitten by mosquitoes. Then at the end I
didn't want to leave!

So, when pleasurably reflecting on the topic of Barbados, any specifics at
arm's length, nearly all of the young talk in generally positive terms of
their ancestral island. Just one partly negative voice was that of Max
Springer, who after enthusing about a vacation that was "great. I couldn't
believe how great it was. I expected much more poverty," then slipped

into his entrepreneur's persona and dismissed Barbados with, "But it's too small for the sort of businesses I want to get into." And the one person who was by far the least enthusiastic was the only one who hadn't been there, Colleen Wright: "Well, maybe I wouldn't mind visiting—if I could get in. It's not easy if you're a Rasta. Take Dominica,[18] for example."

The notion of actually *living* in Barbados was an altogether different matter. The eleven gave highly variant responses. Only three of them gave a "yes" with any certainty: Colin and Carol Simmons, and (slightly to my surprise) Trevor, Jr., who nevertheless immediately added, "but not in the next five years." All three were born in Barbados and left at the ages of eight, seventeen, and sixteen respectively. Then, five responded non-committally, and the last three, symmetrically, were a definite "no." These last "nos" were consistent with previous observations of theirs that I've been quoting here, and the reader could likely make a good guess at who the three were: Max Springer, Susan Maycock, and Colleen Wright—all Londoners born and bred.

Max's dedicatedly materialist view of the way the world works obtained once more:

> No—because it's a place that you've gotta have money first, *then* you can go there.
> But there are places where there are better opportunities. England's getting better, but America's the place. It's the best place for business on earth. When I was there, on the East Coast, New York down to Florida, I could see, "Yeah, this is the place for entrepreneurs." You just couldn't escape it.

Susan Maycock, fresh off to college and full of the joys of spring, certainly wasn't going to parlay London life for a little Caribbean island. "No. I think mum and dad may well go back there. Not me. It can be my holiday home—or one of them! *Dahling!!*" This last, delivered in a stagey grande-dame drawl, had us both laughing. I loved her for her self-aware impudence.

Nigel Pilgrim was uncertain, picking his way through his response's ambiguities:

> In the long-term future, maybe. I wouldn't [want to] be young there. Maybe [very tentative] to retire? . . . That's so far ahead! . . . My parents are going to live there, to build a house. I do expect it of them to build a "Nigel's room," and I'd look upon it as a second home. . . . I might get bored. Perhaps I'd get restless if I stayed, I'd sound and feel different. You can imagine how I've had that "Where're you from?" stuff here. Well, people *there* would ask, "Where're you from?" . . . and, here we go

again! Yet, I wouldn't be immediately spottable. I'd be part of
the majority there . . . until I opened my mouth. But, then
again, in London one isn't spottable, not so much, as one is outside London . . .

It may also be significant that when I asked eleven young British-raised
blacks if they wanted to live in their ancestral Barbados, four of them then
spontaneously mentioned the possibility of the United States. Derek Gill
told me,

> I'd like to give America a try, but it's difficult to get in. If I stay
> with the company, I could get a job secondment, it'd be on the
> cards, a number of people from my department have done it,
> we've got links to Tennessee and Connecticut. That's the way to
> do it.
>   Nigel and I thought about starting up a business in Barbados,
> there must be opportunities there? We could get a loan from a
> bank, we thought of importing second-hand cars, but the duties
> were too high, the idea died a quick death, it fell through.
>   Ideally I'd like to live in Barbados and spend a couple of
> months or so each year in London. I'd use Barbados as a pad—
> it'd probably be too quiet at times—and go off to visit the States
> or London. You'd need lots of money. . . . And you might find
> after four or five months that you'd done everything, you'd get a
> bit bored with the place . . .

His rumination trailed off into silence. So maybe Barbados-as-pad wasn't
such a good idea after all. It's notable, nevertheless, that Derek's first-
glance "dream setup" is exactly the same as that of the rich with whom
Colin Jemmott has had dealings.

Trevor, Jr., was caught somewhere in the middle too; maybe there
wasn't a perfect answer? One obvious complication is that Catherine is
Grenadian-born; going to Barbados wouldn't be going home for her, especially given Barbadian island chauvinism. Trevor, Jr., was aware of
other complications too. He tied his response as to whether he'd return
to live in Barbados to the next move the family was contemplating, beyond the boundaries of Brent and the GLC, into Buckinghamshire:

> We want to get away from this big London black community.
> We don't want the kids to feel the pressures of *having* to be
> black. It's no good saying we or they don't fit, out in these white
> suburbs. There are difficulties everywhere. In Barbados, for ex-
> ample, there's this mix of resentment versus admiration [of black
> returnees]: "They know more than us, because they've come
> from England."[19]

Trevor, Jr., is certainly impatient with the shortcomings he perceives in the Caribbean style. Listen to the way he uses the adjective "West Indian" to mean unsophisticated and inefficient, as one July evening in 1988 he sounds off at me:

"I think that the radio lets us down. I mean, you've listened to this black London radio program? It's been going for over twenty years and it's so unprofessional. You'd've thought that by now the presenters would've got some more polish. It's so . . . *West Indian.* Only West Indians will listen to it, I think. I mean, I'd want people like *you* to listen to it, because they'd want to, they'd learn something that's well presented.

"And our newspapers! I don't read the West Indian press anymore. It's pitched at just too low a level. I wasn't learning anything from it. First, years ago, I used to read the *World;* then the *Voice* or the *Caribbean Times.* And I was just getting frustrated. It was always so negative, I mean, seven pages of negative stories of failure, or rape, or murder. And then there'd be seven pages of music. And then another bunch on black fashion. And there'd be a lot of racism there too." Unsure of his meaning, I ask about this last. "Well, you know, 'It happened to me because I was black.'

" . . . West Indians have no *organization.* We went to the Capital Park Hotel,[20] to a beauty contest:[21] £50 a plate. Charity contribution. And you get a bit of old lettuce and some dry chicken . . . and then you wait half an hour for the next course!

" . . . Some of the TV programs we've had here are *idiotic.* Of course Alf Garnett[22] in "Till Death Us Do Part"; but that "Love Thy Neighbour" program too. The white guy making monkey noises in the jungle, all that stuff."

"It's demeaning to white as well as black, I think."

"Of course it is. And it's not funny either. It's so . . . *facile* . . . I get so impatient with the picture one gets of blacks here. And I don't just mean in those 'comedies.' "

"Blacks come across as losers, you mean?"

"Yes, but I don't only mean that. I mean, *where are they?* There's not enough black TV presenters. There's Moira Stewart—if she *is* black, I suppose she is.[23] On ITV I must admit that Trevor Macdonald has done well. He's from Trinidad. But there's only one young chap they've got reporting now on the TV news, economic affairs I think it is. . . . The media's important, and we don't do well enough in it."

Trevor, Jr.'s, frustrations, amiably enough vented to me, indicate his awareness that the Caribbean would likely not be an ideal place for someone like him. His achieving nature seeks success in the wider world. He would be out of place in Barbados, at least for a while until he moderated his ways. He anticipates difficulties whether there or in London; he feels the racist irritations in Britain. But the rewards he is beginning to garner and of whose continuance he seems confident are to be found in Britain; he thinks he can deal with the drawbacks. Not that I truly know him and Catherine well, but I'll wager they'll not go back to Barbados.

All of the other interviewees, of whichever generation, also experience such crosscurrents. Many of the respondents do not feel the conflicts as acutely—or perhaps, did not give expression to them in my presence so revealingly—as does Trevor, Jr., (who, I might add, seems to be bearing up pretty well under the strain). But the conflicts are there. Barbados changes, one changes. Britain changes too—and, nearly all of the interviewees feel, for the better. They say racism is in retreat, as we shall see in the next chapter. Where then is the best bet, all things considered?

Ten
England Reconsidered

*I've had hardly any racial problems here of any kind that I've
noticed. I've just been called a "black bastard" maybe two or
three times. Well, that's nothing to blame England with . . .
I'd have been called worse things if I'd stayed in Barbados,
far worse, oh yes!*

Jeff Bannister

"The weather changed," Amelia Simmons replied. I was totally taken
aback. "How has Britain changed since you came here?" I had asked. My
face must have betrayed my consternation at her reply. If there is just one
day-to-day drag on the feet of the immigrants, it is the ashen lack of bright-
ness of London weather. Away for nineteen years, I had forgotten; they,
from their sparkling island, have never been able to. Then Amelia started
chuckling. I saw the joke being played on me, and we laughed.

Seven months later, in the *New York Times Magazine,* the joke was
played out at greater length in an imaginative tour de force. An excerpt
from Salman Rushdie's *Satanic Verses* was printed, in which one was invited to imagine London tropicalized:

> Gibreel Farishta floating on his cloud formed the opinion that the
> moral fuzziness of the English was meteorologically induced.
> "When the day is not warmer than the night," he reasoned,
> "when the light is not brighter than the dark, when the land is
> not drier than the sea, then clearly a people will lose the power
> to make distinctions. . . . City," he cried, and his voice rolled
> over the metropolis like thunder, "I am going to tropicalise
> you."
>   Gibreel enumerated the benefits of the proposed metamorpho-
> sis of London into a tropical city: increased moral definition, in-
> stitution of a national siesta, development of vivid and expansive
> patterns of behaviour among the populace, higher-quality popular

216

music, . . . better cricketers; . . . No more British reserve;
hot-water bottles to be banished forever, replaced in the foetid
nights by the making of slow and odorous love. Emergence of
new social values: friends to commence dropping in on one another without making appointments, closure of old folks' homes,
emphasis on the extended family. Spicier food. . . . [1]

Some of the interviewees feel that, to a more moderate degree, something of the kind has indeed happened . . . and that they are in part the
agents of such change. Alan Maycock:

"What the English don't realize is that we've *improved* some
things here, we've brought change."
"I'd say food," I responded, "they've woken up a bit since I
was a kid. But . . . isn't that the Common Market?" (I was al-
luding to the closer ties with a culturally varied Continental
Europe.)
"Yes, but they eat rice now, they didn't before. *We* did that.
There used to be no brown rice, just rice for rice puddings. It
was an art to make it edible for our dishes, very soft rice it was.
The Brits are more fashionable now. We came wearing bright
colors; *they* didn't think it was the thing to do. They've become
more informal: then it was Mr. X, Mrs. X; now it's Christian
names. Eating habits've changed. Chinese and Indian have become 'staple foods,' as it were."

Tony Gill concurred.

Attitudes of people have changed. The English have become
more cosmopolitan and open, which is much better. Take all
these Asians. All the vegetables that are available [from Asian
greengroceries; he runs off a list of exotic vegetables and fruits].
You can get everything you want now in Burnt Oak [a local
neighborhood shopping center]. It's been a benefit to English
people as well.

Austin Pilgrim:

There are fewer "grey" people in bowler hats, you know? Now
they've changed, they've woken up, they're more fashion-
conscious. I used to have this mental image of the Englishman,
dowdy in his demob suit.[2]

And George Farley was certain that Britain had changed

a *lot*. Every house was painted ashes color: *grey*. On British TV
they complained about us with our bright colors, especially the
Pakistanis. And now they're [the white English] brightening up.

Entirely logically, it was members of the migrant generation who really took note of such change. The young have grown up with it, and only one of them, Nigel Pilgrim, mentioned it at all:

> Mind you, the British are loosening up. Perhaps with European and American influences. They show their emotions on TV game shows. And I'm sure that's why so many people like Ian Botham[3] and admire him, as opposed to that old-style proper style of Ted Dexter.

Has Racism Changed?

So how *has* Britain changed, according to the interviewees? The reply was totally theirs to structure: no hints, no promptings. By far the most common topic that sprang spontaneously to mind—mentioned by three-quarters of the immigrant generation and by two-thirds of the British-raised—was the topic of racism. And of these, all the British-raised and two-thirds of the immigrants felt that things had *improved:* that racism was still there, yes, but that it was not so blatant (and therefore not so immediately personally hurtful) anymore, that those white British who espoused it kept it under wraps more than in the old days. I am not at all sure what I expected from these answers beforehand, and I am aware that those I interviewed are a "successful" sample of black Londoners who may not be typical, but this finding helps me continue to feel hopeful, to feel that we are not talking unmitigated societal tragedy here. Alan Maycock considered that "England has done very well over these last thirty years in a way. You think of all the trouble, the violence America has, and they've been trying for three to four hundred years."

Nigel Pilgrim mused, speaking as both a young black (aged twenty-four) and as an Englishman (for the latter he did consider himself, "just about"):

> "I can see it from both sides of the fence. I might say England's a richer country than the West Indies, but as long as we've got poor people here [England], you just can't expect to be able to say to half a million people, especially black people, to come over and get some of the good stuff. But that doesn't mean they weren't treated poorly. It wasn't right . . . but I can see why they [the English] did it. People don't give up power like that. People aren't like that.
>
> "There was a lot of ignorance around then too. Did white people believe they needed to *know* about black society? Unthinkable!"
>
> "You mean," I asked, "they assumed there couldn't be any value in it, culturally?"

"Of course not."

"Is there less of that now?"

"Well, whites are not comfortable with us. They don't feel guilty though, not like American whites do over slavery. (Nigel has visited America.)

"Now, in York there were few blacks. I said that to you, that it was like going back twenty years. I was something to look at and to be treated slightly different. Whereas in London people just tramp over you, it doesn't matter who you are. . . .

"The main difference is that black people are now part of the community. So the question has become not 'Can we stay?', but 'What role are we going to play?' . . . It's easier for us than for the Asians: we mix better, speak the same language."

Dotteen Bannister was sure things had improved:

"One of the first times I went to the greengrocer here [Enfield], people were waiting about to see me, to see what would happen. I was in the shop, I came out, a woman was staring at Colin in the pram [baby carriage]. She was so intent on him she didn't see I'd come back, at first. She said to me, 'But he looks so clean, I don't know what people are goin' on about'!

"And for instance, when I first moved here, no one spoke to me. There was a man at the corner out in the garden, he did say, 'Good morning,' and his wife said, 'What the hell are you doing?' to him. After a few weeks, that lady wouldn't stop talking to me! Another one came and knocked on the door and said she was prepared to talk with me, even if the others weren't."

"That was very grand of her," I said sarcastically.

"Yes, it was *very* nice of her," said Dotteen, in a sincere reply. I felt more than a little like a mean-spirited smart aleck; I was being made to realize that maybe it *did* take some courage on the part of that white Englishwoman to proffer neighborliness back in those days. Dotteen continued: "She and Barbara [Dotteen's daughter, born in Enfield] became very good friends; she's very old now. . . .

"All that's gone on this street now."

Eulie Eastmond was positive too.

I can only speak for London—I don't know about "Britain." Attitudes *have* changed. Now we're accepted quite easily, at least superficially. None of that touch-your-hair stuff like in the early days. I don't think there're many places that'd openly snub you now. You can walk in and get a loan from a bank manager, no problem. Certainly I think that any black person who *really* wants to get ahead in London can do it now. You can see blacks at higher positions: doctor, headmaster, managerial positions.

Joan Springer knew that advances had occurred, but that there was still a long way to go:

> Britain's changed a lot. People are getting on better [materially], take me for example," (she chuckles at her own presumption) "I've come a long way, and West Indians in general too. But we West Indians still have a long way to go to integration, we're light-years away. You can hear it in the way they talk, I feel it in the streets, and the way they look at you. . . . The whites think of you as inferior, and it hurts. . . . It just don't seem as though it [integration] is going to happen—it's sad, very sad.

Colin Jemmott wanted the record quite straight on these delicate, controversial matters:

> Now I must say this. Black people are not innocent either. They're hurt . . . they're prejudiced . . . um . . . I want to choose my words if you're taking this down. . . . Some black people are not even capable of giving the white man the benefit of the doubt. We get it wrong sometimes, I've seen it.

Trevor Brathwaite, Jr., said: "The racial mimicry, the novelty factor has gone. We haven't seen the rivers of blood[4] that Enoch Powell said." Catherine Brathwaite interjected, "We're the bullies now."

Catherine here implies at least partial agreement with the widespread contemporary stereotype of criminality pinned on British black youth. One of them, Nigel Pilgrim, observed with a dash of humor that

> a lot of people assume young blacks are criminals or something. Eight times out of ten the last seat filled on the bus is the one next to me. So I travel lounging out, you get to enjoy it, it's quite handy!
>
> My dad [Nigel gives a big laugh] and his friend used to do the same thing in the trains in the old days when they were all compartments. One would sit next to the window, one would spread himself next to the door. They could usually keep the whole thing for themselves!

If a Pilgrim from each generation offers instances of white circumspection and fearful avoidance of blacks, then by contrast nearly all of the migrant generation have vignettes to retail of small acts of immense kindness and understanding shown to them by native English a quarter century or more ago. Unfortunately, today, Charles Eastmond claimed, you go to ask the way from a white person on the streets of London and they think you're going to rob them.

This last sentence is perhaps a trifle exaggerated, but even so, something very serious has happened here. Taken-for-granted images have been refashioned; of the Afro-Caribbeans on the one hand, of the "London bobby" on the other. Some regressive cultural alchemy has been worked: blacks have become criminalized; and the police—almost without exception white persons[5]—are more often seen nowadays as corrupt or inept bully-boys. It is not just the moral panic of the London tabloid-inspired "mugging" scare of the 1970s, nor the violence of the Brixton and other riots of the 1980s, nor the turnover of the black generations; it is also social changes that have little to do with racial matters—like the policing of the 1984 coalminers' strike—that have dissolved forever the Jack Warner image of an amiable, comfy, dependable "Dixon of Dock Green."[6] But the alchemy is felt with particular sting where skin color seems to be involved. As Stuart Hall, who has discussed such matters with great insight, writes,

> At one time . . . the black population was specifically identified by public authorities in this society as being astonishingly law-abiding. It requires some social explanation as to how a particularly law-abiding population in the 1950s became a characteristically and stereotypically illegal and lawless population in the 1980s.[7]

The expectations young blacks and white police officers hold of each other evidently add volatility to their encounters. Joan Springer, the sweetest of women, surprised me with the vehemence with which she accused the police of using inappropriate force on certain occasions: "I've seen them on the Underground, when I've been on duty. They're really far too *rough* on some young blacks, they pick on 'em. I call them [the police] the Bovver Boys[8] in Blue!"

George Farley, perhaps with some embroidery, tells a more disturbing tale in which he, a bus conductor physically attacked by a drunk and truculent Scots passenger, finds himself then verbally attacked by the policeman called to deal with the incident:

> "We stopped the bus. A young copper soon turned up, I was at the top of the stairs, the Scot at the bottom shouting he was really going to get me, the copper shouts 'Get down the fucking stairs' to me. I couldn't believe it."
>
> "You were in uniform?"
>
> "Of course. . . . 'Get down the fucking stairs,' he yelled again. I was scared, I thought he was going to go for me, I put

my fists up ready. Then the passengers upstairs, a dozen or so of them, one shouts out, 'It wasn't the conductor, that fella was hassling him.' And the policeman didn't know I had all those witnesses upstairs, he couldn't see. And then the sergeant arrives and pulls the young policeman back a bit and then my driver, an Irish chap, tells the sergeant that I was being hassled and only doing my job. So they let the Scot go.''

"They let him go! No charge?''

"No. If he'd've been a black they'd've taken him down to the station and knocked out a few teeth. It was a good job the passengers took my side. Anyway, my garage manager phoned them up the next day and talked to the sergeant about the behavior of the young copper. The sergeant was quite rude. Then my manager told him he was a JP,[9] and the sergeant changed his tune and got much more polite.''

"Did you ever get an apology?''

"Oh no, you never get an apology. The police were only good on one occasion. It was a Pakistani woman. She was trying to pay less than full fare, pretended she couldn't speak English. I said, 'You got on at Piccadilly Circus, you paid me 10*p*, that gets you to Aldwych; now we've got to Ludgate Hill, you've got to pay more.' She called me a black bastard.''

"Not so very clever of her if she was pretending ignorance of English!''

"Right! . . . I went towards the stairs to go down to tell my driver, she followed me, I turned round and she hit me in the face with her shoe. We called the police. One came. *Then* she started speaking English. But the passengers represented[10] me, she got booked on a number of charges there and then on the bus, before we started again.''

Contemporary mistrust of the police contrasts in most cases with appreciative memories of years ago. Recall Charles Eastmond telling his tale of the Shouldham Street rent-strike attempt and how, when in trouble (1957), he went and found a policeman—who resolved the matter with aplomb, with class. Recall the sympathetic deftness of the policeman who in the 1958 Notting Hill white riots indicated to Trevor Brathwaite the possible uses of bricks.

Police-immigrant relations were not all rosy in those early days, however. Austin Pilgrim recalls:

Another time I was attacked by a dozen white guys after the pubs closed. They hit me, kicked me on the ground, I'm lying there thinking no, I'll fight, nothing to lose, so I knocked one down really properly, hit a second away really hard. The police came, held me, took me to the station, my face was bleeding. "Why did you hit those blokes?" I told them, "Self-defense." I don't think they ever arrested them. And the police let me go with a "Don't you *ever* hit a white man."

Twelve on one, I found myself thinking, even if the one is the only one sober. Hmm. Exaggeration? Then I glance at Austin today. He too was a weightlifter then, an athletic cricketer. His arm muscles and barrel chest still make themselves evident through his cotton shirt: a powerful physique. And when I met him at his door for the first time in January 1988 he was forty-eight; I met a smooth-faced man who at first glance appeared perhaps to be in his midthirties, and I was not sure if this was Austin Pilgrim . . . or his son Nigel. Yes, the story might be pretty true.

Austin today has dealings with the police in different circumstances. As manager of his Underground stations he has had to call on them for aid. Sometimes he portrays them as good professionals doing a tough job, on other occasions as racists. Sometimes they respond with solidarity toward a black Underground manager, sometimes with great if not insulting indifference. The ambiguity of the relationship—the uncertainty that such a pillar of middle-class Establishment values as Austin Pilgrim feels toward those who guard the civil peace on his and supposedly everyone's behalf—is disconcerting. He is never sure, he says, which way they are going to jump. But he's ready to give credit when, in his eyes, credit is due— as when the knife-wielding Rasta was efficiently disarmed (chapter 5), and on an occasion when a policeman was a co-hero.

This, Austin's most dramatic tale, was of (as the station announcers on the London Underground so blandly render it in explaining delays) "a person under the train"—that is, a suicide attempt.

She jumped. We called the police and the ambulance. I took charge, overriding the policeman who wanted to move the train. I know what to do—I've been trained. You short-circuit the live rails [i.e., turn off the current]. Then I climbed down under with the ambulance man. They have a special kind of stretcher, you can clip two halves together under a person without moving them. The policeman's right down under there too. The wheels had sliced the woman's neck right open, a great chunk of flesh had sort of folded out, just held by skin, you could see her vertebrae, the neck itself wasn't hit yet. I picked up the flesh and folded it back into place, as directed by the ambulance man, while he put a bandage around it to hold it. "Wow," said the policeman, "you've got guts." "*Now* we can move the train," I said. "Keep your head down and absolutely still else it'll slice your head open."

So we got out, and the policeman said admiringly I was quite a
guy and why don't you join the police force! And I said, "Man,
I'm too old now." And the woman survived—she'd just had a
big argument with her husband—and they gave me a public com-
mendation for bravery. Funny thing, I did the same thing back in
1969 and I heard *nothing.*

It was not shown to me then, but in May 1989 when I visited the Pilgrims
I noted, not placed at all prominently among the various framed plaques
on the wall, the Royal Humane Society's award, presented in 1984 by the
Hon. Mrs. Angus Ogilvy, that is, by Princess Alexandra, cousin to the
Queen.

Austin's experiences over thirty years range from rejection and insult
and brutal physical assault to the bestowal of honor from the highest official level. To attempt to encapsulate all this contradiction into a simple cal-
culus of whether English racism has become "better" or "worse" does
feel a trifle leaden-footed to me. All of the other interviewees have contradictory experiences in this domain too, in greatly varying degree. But
to talk of ambiguity and contradiction and to leave it at that also seems to
duck the question. Indeed, most of the interviewees themselves did come
down on one side or the other, without any prompting. And, to reiterate,
in toto three-quarters of those who referred to racism felt that things had
improved over the years.

Four people regretted they had to say (two firmly, two uncertainly) that
things had stayed the same. All of them were from the migrant generation.
Edith Simmons said,

When we came, the problems were with the job and where to
live. Then you get comfortable, settled. Then they change the
law, some MP makes some stupid speech, you can go out in the
street and feel the atmosphere. You don't know whether you're
here, there, or wherever.

Three other interviewees, all from the migrant generation, said apparently decidedly that racism was *worse* in Britain than when they had arrived. Charles Eastmond said the very converse of the majority view,
namely that "people are more *open* about racialism now, it's more rampant. . . . With the more ordinary English people on the bus, you hear
it there." And Frank Springer, of all the interviewees the longest resident
in Britain, expressed himself with marked acerbity:

I still think it's more racial than it was. It used to be curiosity and
wariness. Now it's indifference: you are not that *relevant.* England's got extremely rich under Thatcher, it makes people cocky,

arrogant. They got money, they'll tell you straight out they don't like you, that "you're not important to my life." They felt guilty about doing that before, they didn't come out with it.

Observe that all the nonpositive evaluations were from the migrant generation. The eight younger persons who chose to bring up racism were all of the opinion that things had improved. Some were more certain about it than others, however, and the ruminative reply Gordon Alleyne offers serves one last time to remind us what murky waters we plumb here.

Yes, Britain has changed since then, as far as black people are concerned, yes it has—but not nearly as much as some people'd like to think. . . . Those stories I told you about fights and bullying at school, was it racism? There was a very, very red-haired guy in my year too—he got it just as bad. So was it because you're just *different?* If people are in a bad mood with you they'll jump on anything that marks you off as different.

Gordon then told a school-days tale of which the burden was that still, today, he does not know whether race was involved in the unpleasantness; it was all so very ambiguous: "You can't *know* whether the hassle's anything to do with race or not." And a moment earlier in our conversation he had opined, "There's none so oppressed as those who feel themselves oppressed." Here is a minefield—"Did it happen to me *because* I'm black?"—which any black person in Britain with any sensitivity (let alone the generous helping fate ladled out to Gordon) has to tiptoe his or her way through.

Other Developments

Racism was far and away the most common topic brought up by the interviewees. All the other half dozen topics had about the same number of mentions as each other, each brought up by about a quarter of the interviewees. The first of these topics was positive: that blacks were doing better in Britain these days. No connection was necessarily being made between this and racism—simply, blacks were experiencing some success. Only three of the migrant generation, but six of the eleven younger generation members volunteered this. Max Springer:

I reckon there's now more opportunity than there ever has been, to get into colleges, libraries, books, courses. Practical opportunity, I mean, there's a crèche at my Poly [polytechnic college], for example. Our parents came basically to get a working-class job and stick with it. They've passed it on to their children—but there's a small group of us who have other ideas.

Those of the young who feel, as does Max, that opportunities are there for the taking, strike a different note from some of their parents, who feel they let them slip. Max is a little impatient with his father, Frank, over this. John Simmons offers the migrant generation's frequent explanation:

Most of us wanted to use LT as a route out and up, I mean, for example, to do night school. Then we found we couldn't do shift work *and* go to night classes at the same time, some evenings you couldn't make it at all. You had to be ready to switch shifts to fit traffic demands.

Audley Simmons, who has come to permit me a close rapport with him, revealed that he saw his own shortcomings (or are they?) in this regard.

The nightmare at the back of my mind was to be completely broke. When I was sixteen I was unemployed and hated it. I was at home, I didn't starve, but I couldn't go to the pictures or anything. I hated it.

Having got here, I never tried enormously hard. I'd work within myself, I'd give myself seven out of ten—my old schoolmaster might give me three out of ten! Imagine people in Barbados saying, "You went to England and *drove a bus?!*" [i.e., that's all?] I never made full use of the things this country had to offer. If you wanted to push yourself, there was night school, lots of opportunities. Some Barbadians did, got their qualifications here, then went to America.

Hmm. If I was the pushing type. . . . But would I be happier? . . . England's all right. There's nothing foreign or alien to me in England. I can be quite [i.e., perfectly] happy in England . . .

If the existence of opportunity seemed of more pertinence to the young, then the second topic, the improvement in housing conditions, was of more pertinence to the migrant generation. In the younger generation's eyes their own housing was not poor, nor had they experienced the worst conditions of a quarter century or more ago; six of the migrant generation (as opposed to just two of their children) brought housing up. "That Rachman housing was unbelievable," said John Simmons. "None of that now." "Attitudes to home ownership have changed," said Alan Maycock. "They didn't bother back then: 'Get a nice council flat,' that's all. Home ownership was for the middle class. Then *we* managed it—and that spurred the English to do it too!'' George Farley was in absolute agreement:

> They never used to worry about the houses here, we taught 'em.
> We bought 'em. Now they're doing all this working on the
> house: d.i.y.,[11] pebble-dashing, crazy paving. . . . One thing
> about a Barbadian: he wants his *own* place.[12]

Charles Eastmond was also in no doubt on this score.

> The real change is this: we came in and worked hard. The wages
> weren't great but we managed to save and then *we bought prop-
> erty.* British people didn't do that. They were quite happy in
> council houses. But when they saw what we were doing, they
> thought, maybe they could have a home too. That's Mrs.
> Thatcher, and why she gets the working-class vote. But we
> taught them that first.

And Eulie Eastmond took her husband's point further, nesting it in a general contrast of the generations.

> The young's attitudes are quite different from ours, they see it
> from totally different angles. We came from Barbados as poor;
> we achieved something. Whereas this [Britain] is all they have
> now, they can't shrug off prejudice like we can, they see it as
> their home. That's the long and short of it. So the same rules
> should apply to white or colored. Things should be laid on for
> them. Whereas I felt I had to work for it. This house represents
> an achievement for us; for them it's ordinary, it's simply a
> starting-place.

Virtually the same number of respondents mentioned the remaining topics: that Britain had evidently become more materially rich; that Britain had "woken up" culturally (as detailed at the beginning of this chapter); that Britain had become a somehow less humane society; and that there had been a sea change in the ways of the British working class, and that Margaret Thatcher was at the back of it. "Britain change a lot since Mrs. Thatcher got in," said Beverly Brathwaite. "The rich do well, the poor do poorer."

Audley Simmons's political views are strongly opposed to those of Thatcherism. He expressed himself in forthright terms:

> Britain's really changed for the worse. People are not so caring:
> dog-eat-dog. But materially it's improved by leaps and bounds:
> cars, TV, washing machines, utility things . . . but people aren't
> their brother's keeper anymore. Sod the rest. They're not *solid*
> anymore . . . I'm talking about working people.[13]

Audley became reflective:

> America, yes, we all wanted to go. It was close. Lots of family
> had gone. And then there was a farm labor scheme. In Barbados
> if someone offered you a five pound note in one hand or a dollar
> bill in the other, you'd go for the dollar. I sometimes wish I'd
> gone to America. I had a chance in '61 and '62, my cousin was
> set up over there. But I don't know why I didn't (I mean, I was
> still single then, I could've). There was all that civil rights vio-
> lence on the TV, you know. And I liked England. England can be
> very nice. England was good then. I mean, the English always
> used—maybe not so much now—to support the loser, sort of
> compassionate. In America you've got to be a *winner*. And you
> can be there, it's true the opportunities are there. I think Mrs.
> Thatcher wants us to be like America, she always copies America.

Not one of the young thought the prime minister to be a noteworthy
topic—she has been there all their adult lives, part of the scenery—but the
migrant generation (or to be precise, the quarter of them who mentioned
this) know what transformation she has wrought. Charles Eastmond mir-
rors what reportedly is a most widespread sentiment among the British today (1988):

> I've got to admit Mrs. Thatcher's quite a person, she's got away
> with it the way she has, privatized all these things. I must say
> she's very clever. You can buy your council house, or a car,
> she's made it easier to get a loan from a bank . . . and you will
> *not* strike! She's curbed the power of the unions.

There is little affection for her, but a somewhat grudging admiration for
her gutsiness, her apparently decisive manner, her articulate combative-
ness; if nothing else, she appears a *leader*.

In May 1989 I spent an evening with the Alleynes. The conversation
wandered where it willed. As I imagine would happen in almost any other
household in Britain, the topic of the prime minister and her doings arose.
She was, it seemed, near the peak of her power. Orville gave his opinion.

> "Mrs. T. says what she thinks, she does it, you've got to re-
> spect her, she's really changed this country. I don't agree with
> everything she's done, but she's shaken us up."
> Me: "So England has changed?"
> Orville: "Oh yes. I'd say the sixties, that's when things
> changed. I mean, that's when England started waking up, wearing
> flares and bright colors."
> Me: "And those broad paisley-pattern ties and Pink Floyd?"

Orville: "Yes, they began to get away from all that dark-suit bowler-hat stuff."

Me: "But the other change is Mrs. Thatcher?"

Orville: "Yes, she's the *political* change, in the eighties. The *social* change—know what I mean?—was the sixties.

"Now we've just had her ten-year anniversary, it was on the telly. It's interesting to see the old film. Back then everybody's making a fuss that she's Britain's first woman prime minister, and you see her there at the microphone and there are all these Tory men standing behind her. And then today you see her, she's up there on her own, no men behind her at all."

I pun: "So, she's the only one in the picture?"

Orville smiles: "Yes. . . . I mean, who can replace her? I lean towards Labour, but who can trust Kinnock? This nuclear thing: he says one thing, then he says another.[14] She says it right out, what she thinks. And I think she's tougher because she's a woman, she's had to have been, so no man can think he can put one over on her."

Pauline: "No, I disagree. I don't even *think* of her as a woman. She's become so much taken for granted, she's just *there:* the boss."

Me: "Yes, it's not important anymore. Isn't it like when Kennedy became president, everyone said, 'Oh my God, a *Catholic!*' And that's unthinkable now, to worry about that. Everyone forgot it once he was 'The President.' I bet you—well, I hope— it'd be the same if Jesse Jackson became president. They'd stop noticing he was black after a while."

Both: "Yes, yes!"

Great enthusiasm for that opinion, then Orville continues: "We saw him a lot on the telly here, he was so good, his words, his charisma. The others looked so ordinary. This Bush chap, you can't really tell what he's like at all."

Pauline: "My sister from Barbados went to New York. Oh, she's gone American, she's done well. But they work so hard. Everyone has two, three jobs. It's all money over there. She was throwing out some old household stuff. Her [grown-up] daughter was round there. 'D'you want any of it?' 'Mmm . . . yes.' 'Give me a dollar.' A dollar! From her own daughter! I couldn't believe it. That's the way it's going here, with Maggie. She's making people like that. The, um . . . quality of life's gone down, there's no courtesy anymore; everyone wants money, that's all. With Maggie, everything's 'efficiency.' Like the Health Service. Not 'How much can we provide?' but 'How much does it cost?' She's making us American. That's what she wants."

In closing this section, to give a full and comprehensive account of the interviewees' views, passing mention should be made of a further clutch of topics that only a few people brought up: that criminal behavior and drug-taking were on the rise; that the cost of living had soared; that young blacks had very different attitudes from those of their parents; and that black youth suffered greatly from a scale of unemployment not known in the years when the migrants were arriving. These topics were, like all the rest that have been mentioned under this section's rubric "Other Developments," totally outweighed by the single topic of the previous section: racism. The interviewees brought it up. I didn't ask them. We may fairly assume they are much exercised by it . . . and it is also of note how much relations with the police—the immediate, unambiguous symbols of white authority—figure in their own framing of the issue of racism. The majority of the interviewees, having achieved a measure of success in London, appear in fact relatively sanguine about racism in England. They think things have gotten better. If one adds in all the other topics that they chose to bring up and attempts to do the roughest of summations, it comes out that the thirty-four interviewees as a group feel positive by a margin of three to one[15] about recent changes in English society.

Autobiography in Context

The third and final section of this chapter deals with the interviewees' responses to my invitation to take the long view of their own personal histories, to stand back and look at it all in perspective. For the migrant generation, the question was phrased, "If you had your time over, would you do the same again?" For the British-raised generation, the questions were, "What kind of deal do you think your parents got by coming to Britain all those years ago?" and "Would *you* have been better off if they had stayed in Barbados?"

The migrant generation was pretty satisfied with the way things had turned out for them. Just over half—the most common response—said yes, definitely, they would do it again. Eulie Eastmond, a social worker, felt, "Yes, it was a good experience. It wasn't nasty, or indifferent. I never had anything terrible with race—I'm lucky. I see that drawing on my work, the problems others've had." Orville Alleyne said,

> Yes, I think so. Yes, yes, yes. There's no substitute for personal experience; you learn from all your experiences. I do wish I'd done some more studying. Some of those who came over with me went to college and university here. But I got married, so I had to work. . . . But, oh well . . .

Orville's voice tailed off, it seemed to me not so much regretfully as acceptingly, philosophically: you can't have everything just the way you think you'd like to. He touched in his rumination on two other topics that arose with fellow migrants. One is that all experience can be salutary, broadening one's perspectives. Even some of those who weren't positive about doing the entire thing over again recognized with appreciation that they had learned something of value. In fact, the second most common response was this one of the usefulness of the whole experience. The other point arising from Orville's response is that he felt he hadn't taken proper advantage of all the opportunities Britain afforded for further education. Two other men said exactly the same of themselves. One was Frank Springer, who wrote me a long, complex letter a good year after I had returned to America:

> What about "LE BOOK"? I am really looking forward to see what kind of restoration job you have done on us Bajans . . . [to] cover the gap between our arrival in England in the fifties as rather gauche and naïve young men to our present status as disillusioned senior citizens on the verge of retirement. . . . And from then until now my life has meandered like an unplanned novel. Some highs, some lows, a bit of drama, occasional farce.
> I am aware that I would never achieve the Sacred Sword of Success of being rich and famous.
> My major regret is never continuing with my education. I would have like to taste a bit of university life, and my only interest is the theatre and films. I often wish I had work in a Drama Workshop. Where I could have experimented in attempting to write plays.
> But as Portia said to Nerissa in Scene 2 of the Merchant of Venice, she said: "If to do were as easy as to know what to do, chapels had been churches, and poor men's cottages prince's palaces." It is only the good Divine that follow his own instructions.
> Joan keep telling me that I am overwriting and that my turgid English would bore the faeces out of you . . .

Frank's humor is keeping him on an even keel here, but another woman, rather in character I'm afraid, was altogether more miserable:

> I started as a teacher, I had a good education—but then getting married is no gratitude to your parents when they've given you an education. To be frank, John, I do feel guilty. I did midwifery courses here too, but what with having the children and our problems, now I'm just working till I retire. Probably I should've done better. But people don't help each other up. My husband doesn't feel he's got that far. Oh, but I know, we don't all need to be at the top. You can work for the community from only in

the middle, like us. Or even from the bottom. Some weekends and evenings I've been doing supplementary school for Afro-Caribbean families. A lot of them are single parents, there's such a need. When I get home I'm so tired . . .

There were other negative voices. With almost the same number of mentions as "the value of the experience," there also arose the matter of the unfree choice of thirty years ago, or the wish that one could have done it differently in some way or another: "Perhaps not come for so long a stay," said Marie Pilgrim. "If I had the return fare in my pocket," said her husband. Beverly Brathwaite has not forgotten the bind she and Trevor found themselves in in their youth: "If me and Mr. Brathwaite had our children, if he was in England, *yes.* Otherwise . . . *no,* I wouldn't travel." We talked some more, I prompted her a little, and she said, "Yes, I've worked very hard. I've learned a lot. Once you can live with yourself, you can live anywhere."

Given the way in which events have run their way in the past decade—their rehousing, their council house purchase just before the Docklands boom, the higher education opportunities that some of their children had seized—the Farleys' attitudes stand predictably in contrast. George was asked if he would do the same again, come to England. "Yes. With the experience that I've had now, yes. When I first came I hated it. But, the standard my children have reached, they couldn't've done it there. Two of ours've got to university." "Yes," said the lively Ernestine, "you can't put it down at all. It help us a lot, for all of us."

Would *you* do the same again, Edward Pilgrim? A silence, and a slow, controlled, enigmatic smile. How, Edward seemed to be saying, how can a man answer such a question? "If I could've lived a comfortable life in Barbados, I wouldn't have left anyway. In Barbados, if you haven't got it, then you haven't got it. You can get stuck in Barbados. It's a small island." And Alan Maycock pondered:

Yes . . . I suppose so . . . given the circumstances. One was in a job where one was stagnating. Perhaps one would do some things differently. . . .
Once things had changed for the better in Barbados, there wouldn't have been any great spur to go and live in Great Britain. But it's not solely a question of economics. It's broadening one's outlook. You get a more rounded view, less of an emotional response to things, from living in Britain. You get the varied opinions of the various British newspapers, not just the *Nation* or the *Advocate* in Barbados. You're exposed to a European view of the world. But in Barbados you just get a very potted view.[16]

There were only a couple of other themes that came up. Two persons volunteered that if they had their time again, they would not go to the United States, whereas two said they would. John Simmons:

> The same again? That's a very difficult question. . . . Ye-es.
> . . . I wouldn't go to the States, I've seen Boston and New
> York. And . . . I know London; I'd live *this* side of the world. I
> wouldn't stay in Barbados either. Well, I would maybe, if it was
> as it is now.

Finally, of all the twenty-three migrants interviewed, only two said that they would not come to Britain all over again. And neither of these was absolutely cast-iron in her opinion. One was Beverly Brathwaite, as quoted earlier. The other was Pauline Alleyne, who resented the way she had been hauled over to England by her mother, who had here remarried, and to a man Pauline didn't like: "I came because mum said so." And yet as we have seen in chapter 9, Pauline on another occasion was the one who said she didn't wish to return to live in Barbados, whereas her partner Orville said he did. The Alleynes really do seem to be having trouble deciding what they truly want to do; they are in a perfect quandary.

How do the British-raised offspring of these migrants view their parents' odyssey? As many as nine out of the eleven—six wholeheartedly, three with reservations—felt that their parents had done well. This was far and away the most commonly offered opinion. Trevor Brathwaite, Jr., said, "I still feel they've benefited from the move. They came to work, they achieved a reasonable standard of living. The opportunity was presented. If he'd stayed, would he have got so far—who knows? Probably not." Colleen Wright was of the opinion that her parents had done "very well—better than if they'd stayed in the West Indies. Ken went to Jamaica in 1984 [where Colleen's mother Edith Simmons is from], and said Jamaica was so poor, and that's '84, so how was it thirty years ago?" If, then, most of the young did feel that the bargain their parents had struck turned out well, just a few put in some qualifications: "Dad got a better deal than mum." Or the realization from three young people that their parents had had to put out an unenviable amount of effort: "They didn't have a fun time. . . . They *worked,*" said Nigel Pilgrim.

But what, to conclude this chapter, did the British-raised feel the legacy of their parents' decisions had entailed for themselves? "Would *you* have been better off if they had stayed in Barbados?" Colleen Wright—the only person of all the interviewees who had not been to Barbados—said she really didn't know; but that she'd heard things from her younger brother Jimmy, then living there:

He says they're still fifty years behind the rest of the world in the way they see black people. There're still certain places out there black people can't go: the Yacht Club, and some club where they didn't want to serve my brother (though he's fair-skinned).

The implication of this reply is tolerably clear, that Colleen thinks it's been to her advantage to have been raised in London rather than Barbados. In this Colleen is quite representative of the group of young people, for by a ratio of two to one, the British-raised felt they had indeed benefited by having been in Britain. Susan Maycock speaks for them:

No. I'd've been more narrow-minded. That's what I find with my cousins there. I don't mean to be "horrible" about it. [A nervous but happy laugh.] They've done pretty well, more or less the same as me academically, but they don't have wider horizons, the outlook. They expect to stay in Barbados, except for one going to Canada for college. But me, no doubt about it in my mind, I'm definitely going to travel.

The young, overall, thus line up behind their parents who, overall, are positive about having come to England and about the changes they've seen in their time there. Such a bland, inclusively reassuring evaluation misses, however, the plurality of crosscurrents and even countercurrents. Things can't be summed up so simply, it doesn't do all this experience justice. The same vexatious ambiguity permeates the slippery topic of the next chapter, that most abstract of abstract nouns: identity.

Eleven
Identity

I am Welsh in England, British in Germany, European in Bangkok.

> Ceri Peach, *The Force of West Indian*
> *Island Identity in Britain*

When he was asked what he considered himself, English or American, . . . Wystan would reply, "I am a New Yorker."

> Ursula Niebuhr, *W. H. Auden: A Tribute,* ed. Stephen Spender

Who I am depends on who you are. Identity is almost invariably contextual. So is the notion of "home," the topic of the next chapter. "Depends on who's asking," said an interviewee. Thus, when talking with a Jamaican, an interviewee is a Barbadian; when with an African, most likely a West Indian; and in many circumstances when with a white British person, most likely a black. This doesn't necessarily denote any inconsistency or ambiguity. "Ethnic or other characteristics of social plurality," writes Peach (1984), "can expand or collapse like a sectional telescope, to fit the situation." This appeals commonsensically. In social anthropology a seminal treatment of such notions was that provided by Evans-Pritchard's "segmentary system" in *The Nuer:*

> What does a Nuer mean when he says, "I am a man of such-and-such a *cieng*"? *Cieng* means "home," but its precise significance varies with the situation in which it is spoken. . . . *Cieng* thus means homestead, hamlet, village, and tribal sections of various dimensions. The variations in the meaning of the word *cieng* are not due to the inconsistencies of language, but to the relativity of the group-values to which it refers.[1]

Rather more crisply, Ceri Peach illustrates the matter in the first epigraph to this chapter.[2] It is a simple notion, somewhat analogous to what geographers would recognize as "scale."

That said, complexity enters immediately, because as the asker of the questions about identity I—middle-class white, sort of English, sort of from America, in a sort of friendly situation—am influencing the responses the interviewees give. Not only that, but there is another dimension altogether. That is, even having specified the context first, there may not be just one, exhaustive answer to the question "Who am I?" When I attended her amiably conducted graduate urban ethnography seminars at University College London from 1986 to 1988, Sandra Wallman used to insist that an individual's identity was fashioned from the *triad* of origin, place/community, and occupation. Approaching these fuzzy but fundamental notions at the end of my questionnaire (having already dispensed with all the purely fact-gathering queries), I in part attempted to uncover feelings of identity through the following question: "Which—and you can choose as many as you like—of these words would you use to best describe yourself?" Respondents were also informed that if they did not feel *any* term fitted, then they did not have to choose any; and also that if there was a term I had overlooked that they felt *did* apply to themselves, then please to volunteer it.

The terms fell across all three of Wallman's triad: origin (e.g., "Barbadian"), place/community (e.g., "Londoner"), and, as a kind of surrogate for occupation, "middle class" and "working class." I tried to jumble the various terms up, so that the sequence was self-evidently random and didn't seem to be leading to some preferred outcome—thus, for example, "colored" was not followed directly, in quasi-chronological fashion, by "black." The terms among which one might choose, in the order I presented them, were: English, middle class, British, foreigner, Londoner, Cockney, Barbadian, immigrant, east Londoner, colored, West Indian, north Londoner, black, west Londoner, Afro-Caribbean, black British, south Londoner, working class, and "any other term?"

Given the multiplicity of possible responses, a table does seem apt here (Table 1). For the migrant generation, a full score—where every respondent agrees she or he would call her- or himself this term—is twenty-three; for the British-raised generation, it is eleven. The "partial" score columns in this table indicate the number of responses from interviewees expressing varying degrees of doubt about so identifying themselves. I don't want to make too much of the "scores." The whole inclination of this research is the very converse of sociometric. For example, the notion of giving a half point for all doubting responses, however expressed, seems overly mechanical. Thus to the question "Are you working class?" the attribution of a half point equates one man's response: "no . . . yes; you *work* for a living. Don't give class much thought" with another woman's wordless response: a laugh. Not, however, the kind of peal of laughter that means "Of course I'm not, don't be so preposterous"; but

Table 1. Designations of self

Term	Number of mentions by immigrants			Number of mentions by all British-raised			Number of mentions by Barbados-born British-raised		
	Full	Partial	Total	Full	Partial	Total	Full	Partial	Total
English	0	2	1	3	0	3	0	0	0
Middle class	2	8	6	7	0	7	3	0	3
British	16	1	16.5	6	1	6.5	2	0	2
Foreigner	10	6	13	3	0	3	2	0	2
Londoner	8	1	8.5	10	0	10	4	0	4
Cockney	0	0	0	0	0	0	0	0	0
Barbadian	22	0	22	3	2	4	3	2	4
Immigrant	17	0	17	2	2	3	1	2	2
East Londoner	0	0	0	1	0	1	1	0	1
Colored	8	0	8	3	0	3	1	0	1
West Indian	21	0	21	6	1	6.5	4	0	4
North Londoner	0	0	0	1	0	1	0	0	0
Black	22	0	22	10	0	10	4	0	4
West Londoner	0	0	0	1	0	1	0	0	0
Afro-Caribbean	6	2	7	5	1	5.5	2	0	2
Black British	5	1	5.5	5	0	5	0	0	0
South Londoner	3	1	3.5	1	0	1	0	0	0
Working class	11	5	13.5	4	0	4	3	0	3
Any other term	1	0	1	3	0	3	0	0	0
	(Jamaican)			(1 Rasta, 2 Buppie)*					

*Black Yuppie—a humorous term.

rather, a laugh signifying, it seemed to me, "Oh-ho, now *there*'s a question. . . . "

There is only one unanimous response across both generations: nobody even considered calling themselves "Cockney." Clearly, this is in the respondents' eyes specific to *white* working-class (east?) Londoners. The only other unanimity was all of the immigrant generation terming themselves "Barbadian" (except, naturally enough, Jamaica-born Edith Simmons). Only five of the younger generation—three fully, two with reservations—identified themselves as Barbadian. These, logically enough, were the five who were born in Barbados. Thus all of those born in Barbados of whichever generation assented to the label "Barbadian," whereas none of the half dozen British-born so identified her- or himself. The term "black" came within a whisker of a full score for both generations, only one person in each disagreeing. In the younger set, it was Trevor Brathwaite, Jr., who said he was "doubtful" in a way that meant "no," just as when we reached the term "black British," he said, "Well, I'm British. . . . Very doubtful . . . . *no."* Among the immigrants it was Tony Gill who demurred.

The only other term that came so close to total acceptance was "Londoner" for the British-raised: ten out of eleven. The exception is, entirely logically, a person who came to London already aged sixteen: Trevor Brathwaite, Jr. When one takes into account that five of the British-raised were born in Barbados—just as the W. H. Auden of the second epigraph was born in Britain—it is most impressive that four out of these five voluntarily describe themselves by reference to the metropolis; even Colin and Carol Simmons do, who are clearly hoping to return to Barbados. The younger generation, then, in this small nonrandom sample, have two identities they agree upon: "black" and "Londoner." The latter was evidently known to screenwriter Hanif Kureishi in his follow-up to *My Beautiful Laundrette,* a movie entitled *Sammy and Rosie Get Laid.* (It was released during my year in London, and a lot of it was shot adjoining Westbourne Park Tube station, only two hundred yards from our flat.) In the movie the London-raised protagonist is told by his father, who had eventually returned to South Asia, to come back "to his own country," and that he, the son, isn't English. The son replies that no, he isn't English, he's a *Londoner,* and enumerates to his father the various attractions of the place that make him feel he belongs there: the walks in the parks in the spring, strolling arm in arm with Rosie along the Thames opposite the great buildings on the north bank, going to a psychology seminar with like-minded Londoners, getting cheap returned tickets to the theater . . .

Nigel Pilgrim exemplifies this. Already we have heard him speak approvingly of the *energy* he feels in London (young New Yorkers will empathize). His father Austin had told me,

> We sent my son to Barbados when he was four to see his grandparents. He came back a year later. "Did you like it?" we asked. "Daddy, why does grandma let chickens in the house, that's bad, isn't it?" Oh, he's an Englishman, a *Londoner* he is, my son!

Edward Pilgrim also thinks the world of his nephew for his total and comfortable assumption of the style and the mantle of London. More than any other label, Nigel responded to "Londoner."

> *"Yes,* definitely."
> "South Londoner?"
> "Yeah! The southeast postcode."
> "North Londoner?"
> A gasp of mock horror: "That would be seriously bad news!

North of the Thames I don't know it. Even the southwest sector, not really. You can live quite *insular* here. [He continues on in proprietorial vein about London, and then says,] You always know when winter's coming to an end, once those damn noisy French students start cluttering the place up!" [This is offered with a grin; we both roar with laughter at his Blimpish sentiments.]

Clive Carter is a Barbadian friend of John Simmons whom I met at the latter's house one evening. As we chatted, John opined that his children probably belonged in Britain, even though he "would fly back tomorrow" to Barbados. Clive responded,

My kids didn't like Barbados much. I mean, it was nice, but they missed London. They always say there's so much to *do* in London. No, well, we don't talk about these things very much with them. . . . They like the privacy of London. No one asks your business. But in Barbados, oh yes . . . !

Marie Pilgrim was feeling similar qualms when we met in May 1989, she having recently retired, and wondering for just how much longer Austin will remain in his very good Underground job before they go back to the house they're building overlooking the Atlantic coast of Barbados.

Marie: "I bought Nigel his Barbados passport as a present. He can have the British one too. I'd love him to come out to live."
Austin: "But I can't see it, he's a Londoner. There's so much here. I mean, even me, I've lived the major part of my life in London. When I'm in other parts of England, I think, 'I can't wait to get back to London.' "
Marie: "Yes, he [Nigel] likes the job in Liverpool very much, he's doing well, but he wants to be back in London after three years, he says."

Even upon the immigrant generation London makes its claims. These persons arrived in a virtually white metropolis, remember, at an average age of twenty-four, blacks from distant Barbados. Yet today over one-third of them give approval to their designation as "Londoners" (one being Austin Pilgrim, who's just mentioned his comfortableness with London in the quotation above). Four even give full assent to a *local* London designation: "north Londoner" or whatever. Four also of the British-raised—one being Barbados-born—are specific in this way. This seems to indicate some significant allegiance: "More substantial areas of [people's] identities," writes Anthony Cohen (1985), are met "as you go 'down' this scale,"[3] that is, become ever more local. Still to be kept in mind, however, is the opening theme of this chapter: the context. Thus young Derek Gill, talking with me in Canon's Park, did assent vigorously to "north Londoner"; but he had also earlier said that when he was in New York he "thought back about London *as a whole*" (my emphasis).

Three other terms gain high but not unanimous acceptance: in order, "West Indian," "British," and "immigrant." "West Indian" gains wide approval from both generations. Entirely logically, its weakest appeal is among the British-born young, whereas four out of five of the Barbados-born young assent to being "West Indian" (the exception is unsurprisingly—given his remarks at the end of Chapter 9—once again Trevor Brathwaite, Jr.). All except two of the immigrant generation so assent, nearly all of them in a neutral, straightforward manner; if one is a Barbadian (as one is), then ipso facto one is a West Indian. Tony Gill, the railway rolling stock supervisor, was an exception in actually *stressing* West Indianness over Barbadianness.

> Barbadian, I don't put a lot of emphasis on being a Barbadian. In my job you can't afford that kind of thing, that island rivalry. Everyone should know that Antigua and Trinidad are so different in every way, but so what?
> West Indian, *yes,* that's it. . . . Let me tell you. There was a toilet in a coach that had to be put right. I had it down to be done in one time-slot. When I asked, it hadn't been. I called in the plumber. I knew he was a Barbadian. "Well, I've done *my* bit," he says. Now the job is such that it's first the coach repairer, then the plumber, then the coach repairer again. The repairer hadn't put it together again. Why not? Because the plumber hadn't told him he'd finished. Why not? Because the plumber won't speak to the coach repairer because the plumber's a Barbadian and the coach repairer is a Jamaican and the coach repairer once insulted Barbados!

I wonder if Tony Gill ever chides that closest of all close friends of his, Austin Pilgrim, over the latter's island chauvinism?

With the slightest of smiles, Trevor Brathwaite, Sr., said, "We always called ourselves British." Over two-thirds of the immigrants assented to such a designation. All except one of the British-born young agreed: Colleen Wright, for ideological reasons, said no, the term for herself she was most comfortable with was "Rasta." She would accept "black" and "Londoner" (recall her fondness for Wembley). She gave very qualified assent to another term, "Afro-Caribbean," by adding, "If it's on a form and I had to." For "British" it was "No. Not unless I had to write it on a form." Every other term met a flat negative from her. Of the five Barbados-born but British-raised young, two assented to "British," three eschewed it; of these three, two, logically enough, were Colin and Carol Simmons, ostensibly planning to return to Barbados.

Thus, whether or not they plan to return to Barbados, most of the immigrant generation choose to call themselves "British." All were born "British subjects" in a colonial territory. All, as we have seen in chapter 2, were schooled in things British. Most still, despite some negative experiences in Britain, keep faith with the Union Jack. Neatly illustrating the general remarks concerning context in this chapter's introduction, Alan Maycock told me,

> If I went abroad I'd see myself as British. If I'm living here, I see myself as a foreigner. Because the indigenous British see me as a foreigner. Or half the time I feel like that because of them. The other half you say to yourself, "I pay my taxes, I'm as British as they are."

Edith Simmons laughed at the term "British," but then said, yes, she was. Then she added, "It gets to me, you know. *You never belong.* They change the law, they'll push you back down the ladder. They can change the law and that'll wipe everything out."[4] The particular focus of this resentment and suspicion was the introduction of a stipulation that from January 1, 1988, tightened up British citizenship requirements for resident Commonwealth and Irish citizens. "D-Day Dec. 31: Sign Up for Citizenship," called the *Caribbean Times* (December 11,1987), warning that "many black people living here could be rendered 'residents without status' by a government whose xenophobia knows no bounds." A particular annoyance was the £60 registration fee exacted, for what many considered a right.

To the question, was she British, Beverly Brathwaite replied matter-of-factly, "Well, I *was*. . . . Barbados is independent now. *Yes,* I am." To the next label offered, "foreigner," she replied with more animation: "You're always a foreigner in this country!" Sandra Gill agreed: "British? Yes. But although I have British citizenship I still think of myself as a West Indian. Foreigner? I still think I'm a foreigner. [She laughed lazily, apparently not mightily concerned.] To the British I'm a foreigner." Yet to the next term offered, "Londoner," she was decidedly positive. I wonder if that has anything to do with there being no gatekeepers to officially evaluate one's Londonness; that is, there is nobody who can officially reject that claim (or charge a £60 fee), nobody who can put one down. To see oneself as a Londoner is an entirely voluntary taking on of a mantle . . . which I suppose could be sloughed off again if one wished.

That "foreigner" followed directly upon "British" in the questionnaire list was not in any way contrived. But despite the fortuitous juxtaposition of these antonyms, over one-third of immigrant interviewees assented to *both,* one or two even chuckling at the contradiction they saw themselves immediately getting into. Unlike logically segmentary pairs like "Londoner" and "British," or "Barbadian" and "West Indian"—which depend on the context, à la collapsing or expanding telescope—"foreigner" and "British" *do* seem irreconcilable, inconsistent. This is further suggested by one-quarter of the immigrant interviewees giving *partial* assent to "foreigner." Partial assents are quite revealing. They frequently indicated, it seemed to me in the interviews, uncertainty and uncomfortableness. The only other terms with which so many immigrant interviewees didn't really know how to deal were the "class" terms. One-third of them gave "middle class" partial assent—I got a feeling of "Well, yes, maybe we are, sort of, but it would be a bit uppity to actually come out and *say* it"—and "working class" received five partial assents. George Farley's responses ran thus. Was he English? "No-oh" (without conviction). Middle class? "No." British? "Well, we are English." Foreigner? "Yes and no." Londoner? "Sort of." Here is much confusion, or if that is too judgmental a word, ambiguity.

Of the British-raised generation, three considered themselves foreigners, two being Barbados-born: Carol Simmons, who came aged seventeen, and Paula Farley, who came aged eleven. Even Colleen Wright, the Wembley-born Rastafarian—whose figurative citizenship is elsewhere than in the "Babylon" (a term she hardly used at all) in which she presently resides—was prepared to grudgingly concede "British" on a form. No, the British-born person who did not consider himself British was Max Springer.

> British? No. Foreigner? Yes. . . . It's a strange sort of thing. In England black people have only been here for thirty, forty years, and England has a long history. It's not like America, blacks have been there almost as long as whites. I don't feel British, even though I'm not bothered by it. I'm an immigrant—that's how I feel. And they don't accept me. People—white people— sometimes ask, "Where do you come from?" "England," I reply. "No, where do you *really* come from?" . . . So . . . I feel like a person, well, who's here and you've gotta do the best you can . . .

One other twist the reader will have picked up on in a number of the preceding quotes is that almost none of the immigrant generation consider themselves "English." The term got two partial mentions, that's all; whereas "British" got one partial, and *sixteen* full. "We're not English, oh no! We're *British,* " said Audley Simmons.[5] He spoke for many; "English" for them implies white people. In the younger generation, none of the Barbados-born and only half of the British-born said they were English. Their claim to Englishness, if based on the birthright of *jus soli,* is incontrovertible. But the other three English-born said no, they weren't English. Perhaps they see Englishness more as an attribute ruled by *jus sanguinis,* available only by approved descent, and from which they are therefore barred. (My impressionistically gathered opinion is that a majority of the white English, especially older persons, would be only too pleased to agree with them in this latter interpretation.)

Once again, I believe I perceive here a real ambiguity and inconsistency. That is, for a white using these terms, the logical segmentary-system rule applies smoothly: I am English in Scotland, but British in Germany. The English-British distinction means something altogether different for the black interviewees, however. Belonging is questionable, the unproblematic segmentary rule doesn't apply here. Nor does it hold for them—as it would for a white person—at one step down the scale either: if one is a Londoner, one cannot, does not, ipso facto claim to be English.

The third of the high acceptance terms, after "West Indian" and "British," is "immigrant." There is, unsurprisingly, a generational split here. Three-quarters of the migrant generation assented, whereas only one-third of the British-raised younger generation did. I say "assented" because the term "immigrant" was hardly *claimed* by the interviewees; it was admitted. "Yes. Hmm . . . I have to be. It is true," ruminated Alan Maycock. Everyone knows the burden of this term, the way it is used to deny full participatory rights in a British society that considers itself *not* to be made up of immigrants. As Gerald Marzorati deftly wrote (*New York Times Magazine,* January 29, 1989) of the parallel case of Asian migrants to Britain, " 'Asian' suggests not only the distance the immigrants have traveled but also the distance at which they remain." As Austin Pilgrim complained, with a (to me) novel angle:

> Immigrant? Yes. You're always told. . . . But all these English people here in London, when they came to London they had nothing. They pretended that they'd always had a nice car and a big house and a son at public school,[6] they'd like to pretend that. But they were immigrants here too, but they give themselves superior airs.

Audley Simmons was one of the minority who refused to use the term: "Call me a 'first-class settler' instead!"

And Jeff Bannister really caused me to bend my mind a different way in considering the term. In my liberal manner I'd always, qua Marzorati, felt it to be a mean-spirited, confining label. Jeff rejected the label from a direction I had never thought of: "No. It has connotations of going to a country and having made up your mind to stay there for the rest of your life. And I haven't done that. I always said one day I'd go back." In this matter of the term "immigrant," he was underlining that *he* had the choice, and was maybe choosing to decline the offer made to him by British society; it was *he* who was the nonacceptor, whereas I had always assumed West Indians to be the supplicants, and that British society had the choice to be the nonacceptor.

I wondered, then, should I have included the term "sojourner" in my list of labels from which to choose, implying voluntary distancing? Unfortunately, the Bannisters were the last family I met, in August 1988, and it was too late to revise and redo the question. And the term "sojourner" too, although with justification much used in the academic literature when considering matters ethnic—in, say, the societal position of the Chinese shopkeeper in southeast Asian countries—is not a term used in common parlance and has perhaps a rather disconcertingly biblical ring to it.

Some of the Barbados-born of the younger generation assented to the term "immigrant," whereas only Max Springer did of the six British-born. All the other British-born felt as Nigel Pilgrim did. He reacted this way to "immigrant?"

> "Of course not. It annoys me when white people here say, 'Where are you from?' I of course say 'London.' Then they say, 'Where are your parents from?' They still think we're not really to be accepted—like that phrase 'second-generation immigrant' of theirs, I mean, *really!*
>
> "When I go to Cornwall, or even to York [his university], it's like going back twenty years, to hear it from my parents. I was talking to an older woman, a flower seller, in the center of York. We were chatting for a while, about the weather and things and then she said she'd just come back from holiday in the Bahamas and I said, 'Did you like it?' And she said, 'Oh, the sun was wonderful but you know, there were so many black people.' I was flabbergasted. And she didn't even realize what she'd said!
>
> "Now, that's not so in London. I feel happy for that reason in London. Here there are [considerable] numbers of black people, who are not new, not special, not distinguishable."
>
> "Isn't that part of what makes London London now?"
>
> "Oh yes, absolutely."

London pride welling up again, a solid, spatial base of identity.

Gordon Alleyne reacted to "immigrant" and a number of other terms in a representative manner, but in a more articulate way than most.

"English? Oh God no, definitely not. Middle class? I wouldn't, but others would describe me as that, I know. British? Yes. Foreigner? No. Londoner? Yes. Cockney? No. Barbadian? . . . " He thinks; he came to Britain aged seven. "Yes. Immigrant? That's technically what I am, but it's not part of how I view myself. Colored? Oh God no, I hate that word. West Indian? Yes."

"Isn't that an old-fashioned, colonial term?"

"I don't mind it."

"Others do. Because, I guess, it's a name given to a colonially imposed unity, I mean defined as the *British* West Indies. *And* a name given because of the Europeans' geographical mistake anyway—I mean, they thought it might be to do with India, didn't they?"

"Oh, that's too political, too clever. I think that kind of stuff is counter-productive."

"Would you apply the term 'black' to yourself?"

"Yes. . . . But . . . ah . . . am I naïve because I don't *think* of myself as black? In a way, there's none so oppressed as those who feel themselves oppressed. Paranoia develops, and then you truly *are* oppressed.

"These labels, like 'black,' they're just another way of confining people, of pinning people down, of limiting people's potential. I hate it if people have it in their mind that I'm *exotic,* as a gay *black* person. I hate it if someone comes to chat me up, not because I'm Gordon and I'm 6'1'', but because I'm black."

Thus does Gordon strike out for his own individually won definition of himself, a definition to which gayness is central. Gordon had the most nonblack set of close friends and his partner was white. Gordon saw his parents as belonging to a world, an era, to which he did not belong, and which he said he didn't find interesting: "Their expectations and self-image and hopes and aspirations have been very different from mine. It's difficult if not impossible to compare."

The resounding uncomfortableness of the immigrant generation with class terms has already been noted. (It is a discomfort they share with very many other British people, as I reported of my own parents in chapter 1.) "Middle class" got only two full assents but *eight* partial ones. "Working class" seemed less presuming: eleven full assents, five partial ones. These numbers don't add up. That's because there were six immigrants who equivocated that they were both, or partly, middle class and working class. "I still see myself as working class," said Pauline Alleyne, "but professionally I'm middle class. The kids disagree with me. 'Oh, c'mon mum,' they say, 'you act middle class, think middle class. . . . ' " Similarly, a report in the *Sunday Telegraph Magazine* (October 27, 1985) on

"Britain's New Middle Class," had a photograph of the Eversley family in middle-class repose in their comfortable and substantial living room (the attractive blue and yellow trident-bearing Barbadian flag stood atop a glass-doored, polished-wood cabinet). "But I would prefer," Owen Eversley, Jr., is quoted as saying, "the term 'progressive, thinking black people' to 'middle class'. . . . For a black person to be described as 'middle class' would be construed as opting-out, ceasing to be black." Because the vast majority of the immigrants came to do jobs of working-class tenor and stuck with them if they could, so the modern British Afro-Caribbean community took the designation "working class" as the group's birthright, as it were.

Their children seem less confused, or perhaps it's less embarrassed, about such a discussion. Nobody gave any partial assents. Also, two-thirds of them—British-born or Barbados-born makes no difference—see themselves as middle class rather than as working class, the converse of their parents. Only one of the British-born, but three of the Barbados-born, saw themselves as working class. Once again, however, the numbers didn't add up, but this time it was due to only one person's ambiguous responses: Paula Farley, without batting an eyelid, said yes, she was middle class; and half a minute later, oh yes, she said, she was working class!

Maybe part of the uncertainty over class labels also stems, straightforwardly, from the elusiveness of the terms after nine years of Thatcherism. There was much fluidity: the meaning of well-tried indicators like trade union membership or monetary income or ownership of stocks and shares was less distinct. And certainly in my own mind, there was and is much uncertainty as to just what *I* meant when I asked them whether they were middle or working class. It's not as if there's some threshold, a definite score to achieve from some sociologist's portmanteau of variables (years of formal education, home ownership, domestic meal patterns, etc., etc.), that once reached, tips one over, titrationlike, into "the middle class" from "the working class." And of course the interviewees themselves, although I have fuzzily referred to them all as middle class, do vary along a continuum. Consider Beverly and Trevor Brathwaite, she with that unenviable string of tough jobs and four children, he over thirty years driving buses, living in the only house they've ever owned, on a modest terraced street in Southall. The respectable working class? Yet they sent Trevor, Jr., to a private school in Barbados where he learned "the proper English," and Tommy, their youngest, is now off to college and informs me that one of his favorite recreations is skiing!

The Pilgrims also live in the only home they've ever owned, also on a somewhat middling, but modern, quiet terraced cul-de-sac. Yet their son was sent to a major London-area public school with great success, and you could never get Austin to drive any car other than a Volvo . . . but his greatest joy is vegetable gardening in the nearby council allotment garden. The Maycocks seem by contrast to be indubitably middle class. Alan was perfectly happy with the label "middle class" and gave a definite no to "working class." To which Althea also gave a "no," but to "middle class" just gave a big laugh and said nothing. Their having moved from a house they owned in Croydon to a newer, bigger one in Surbiton in order to be in a better school district; their comfortable leafy Surrey neighborhood from which they both commute to Waterloo station each weekday morning; their daughter off to college; Alan's considerable back garden, its large manicured lawn, flowering borders resplendent, and kitchen vegetable patch partly concealed modestly at the far end, all this to me signifies "middle class"—as does Alan's unselfconscious use of language patterns such as "one asks oneself," delivered in an almost fruity English accent whose Barbadian echoes are very faint.

The last handful of terms to be looked at include the label "colored," which just over one-third of the migrant generation would use of themselves, whereas a slightly smaller proportion of the British-raised generation would. Conversely, the more modern designation "Afro-Caribbean"[7] was accepted by one-half of the British-raised, but by less than one-third of the migrant generation: "I don't go for that one; Caribbean's okay, but not the Afro," harrumphed Sandra Gill. And the term "black British" is acceptable to five out of six of the British-born, but to *none* of the five Barbadian-born of the younger generation. Of their parents, less than one-quarter are prepared to use it—even though overall they were quite well disposed toward "British" and virtually unanimous for "black." Is there some connotation, political or otherwise, with which they are not happy once the two terms are combined? "Don't know why they have to stick the 'black' on it," grumbled Trevor Brathwaite, Sr., who considered himself British, and who, to "Are you black?", responded unenthusiastically, "Suppose so, yes." Perhaps Barbados memories of "black" meaning undesirably dark skin pigment were obtruding. Or perhaps "black British" intimates some second-class, hyphenated, "not truly British" status in their eyes?

A final thought arises on the self-designations people chose. Were these indeed self-designations, or were they too much my suggestions? That is, if one had given the interviewees a pencil and a blank piece of paper and said, "Write down those terms by which you would be pleased to identify yourself," what kind of responses might one have received? One answer I do believe I could with certainty foresee would be "gay" from Gordon Alleyne. During a wide-ranging conversation in June 1988 in Gordon and

Ted's Earl's Court flat, the perceived conservatism of Barbados society weighed on Gordon's mind for a most evident reason:

> I'm better off for having come here. . . . There's more space in London for me to fit into as a gay—less likely elsewhere in the U.K. and, I'd guess, Barbados. . . . I might find I don't like it now. I'm slightly nervous, and slightly looking forward, to going in October . . . . Yes, I *am* apprehensive about going. . . .

A major disappointment in my week's visit to London in May 1989 is that by ill-fortune it coincided with a ten-day vacation Gordon and Ted had taken out of the country, so I couldn't meet them again to hear about their Barbados trip. I did, however, hear about it secondhand, from Gordon's parents.

> "We talked about it quite a bit with Gordon and Ted before-hand. He [Gordon] hadn't been there since 1976. We warned them about the old people, that they'd be conservative. And, funny thing, it was the young who were rude. They'd say things loudly as Ted and Gordon would walk by. Ted said he couldn't understand the dialect but he knew they were sneering. They didn't know if it was because they were gay or because they were black and white together. Ted thought it was racism. He was very hurt about it. 'Well,' I [Pauline] said to him, 'now you know what it was like for us here in the sixties!' "
>
> "Oh, *Pauline!*" I objected, "that wasn't very nice, when the guy's already hurting."
>
> "No . . . Well. . . . " She continued without appearing chastened. She likes Ted, who seems a good, pleasant man; but I got the definite impression that in her view such a lesson wouldn't do any white person any harm.
>
> "But the old people were all right, never said anything, were nice and polite. It was the young. They were staying with my family, it was fine, they didn't ask questions. They hardly saw Orville's family: *they* wouldn't like it, wouldn't know what to do.
>
> "They were out in a country area, that's why. Well, coun-tryish: edge of town, edge of Christ Church. If they'd been in the hotel area along the coast no one would have bothered."
>
> "Isn't that why London's so good for Gordon? No one bats an eyelid here, you can live your own style?"
>
> "Oh yes, you'd never get Gordon out of London! He'll never move. He's a Londoner, absolutely."

To have opened up the range of possible answers in this way—write it down on a blank piece of paper—might nevertheless have been off-track for what I was trying to get at. Suppose somebody were to answer "a socialist," "an old boy of St. Olave's," "a woman," "a sportsman," or whatever—there would have been less focus, too many answers. But one might have gotten, who knows, fewer answers: "immigrant" seems a prime candidate for a term most would have chosen not to mention. Because it was noticeable *how many* designations there were to which these thirty-four interviewees were prepared to assent. The fewest claimed by anybody was John Simmons's three: Barbadian, West Indian, and black—designations that fit crisply and logically into the segmentary system of identity. On the other hand, two persons—the Alleynes, Sr.—assented in whole or in part to eleven designations, and five further persons to ten. I calculated averages and found that in this matter there was absolutely no difference between the migrant generation and their children, nor between the British-born and Barbados-born young: accepted designations for all three sets of people fell around seven and one-half per person.

Of these people I met, the older generation agree among themselves that they are blacks and Barbadians (and thus West Indians) *and* immigrants *and* British. The younger generation's consensus is that they are blacks and Londoners (and the British-born among them, black British). They were not simply one thing, to the exclusion of everything else. In significant part, yes, this straightforwardly depended on context, analogous to the telescope. But in addition to that, there were also ambiguities and complexities. On more than one occasion I recall Sandra Wallman saying, from her extensive experience of work among ethnic groups in London and elsewhere, that people of West Indian provenance had the most *plural* of identities. The foregoing information, although perhaps gathered with a blunt instrument, does strongly seem to back up Wallman's contention.

I close this chapter with a quotation that illustrates the ability of a respondent to surprise the researcher. Not only to come out with an utterly unexpected answer, but also, indeed, to dismiss the researcher's assumptions about what are important questions. This last word is left to Max Springer, veritably one of "Mrs. Thatcher's children." Like his name—which he told me he thinks makes some people, before they meet him, wonder if he's going to be Continental European, perhaps specifically Jewish—Max's views are a little unusual for the British-raised generation, or should I say, they define one end of its spectrum of views. Others of this generation, like Gordon or Nigel or Colleen (by the very ideology she's embraced) evidently find their racial-cum-national identity to a greater or lesser degree problematic. The incomparable Max claims not to, and in the vigor of his claim comes out with one of the most striking *mots* of the entire study:

Would I have been better off if they'd stayed in Barbados? I don't think so. . . . This Barbados-versus-British thing doesn't bother me much. It don't make no difference when you go out there to make things happen. The important thing is to make a living. When you've got loadsamoney[8] that's all that counts. There's no profits in it, there's no benefits, to sitting and worrying if you're Barbadian or British.

No, when they ask you whether you're Bajan or British, you just show'em your Porsche!

Twelve
Home

. . . To put my feet up in the sun. . . .

Edward Pilgrim

Clad in white shirt, white long pants, and white boots, the bowler accelerates toward the wicket. He hurls the ball toward the batsman at the far end. The batsman, a smallish man of athletic gait, moves quickly forward, has perfectly judged flight and bounce, and aligns his flat bat so that the ball hits the middle of it with a solid thunk. The ball is repulsed safely along the ground to mid-off. The fielder retrieves the ball and tosses it back to the bowler, who already is walking back to where he started his run-up. The vast crowd stir a little in their seats, and anticipate the next delivery.

This most mundane of cricketing sequences—seam bowler rebuffed by forward defensive stroke—must have occurred literally millions of times around the world. To North American readers much of the above probably sounds like impenetrable and potentially boring mumbo jumbo, even if they should happen to be devotees of baseball, cricket's cousin. But North American readers will also, having read this far in this book, suspect that some symbolism of importance is about to be pinned to this somewhat arcane scene, that captured in Figure 16.

Indeed it is. We are at the Marylebone Cricket Club's Lord's ground in north London, the Wimbledon of world cricket. The ground is overflowing, no more spectators can be allowed in. Saturday, June 18, 1988: England versus West Indies, a five-day Test Match. Edward Pilgrim and company, including his female friend who has packed a marvelous luncheon hamper, have taken me to the game. Gordon Greenidge, at

Figure 16: Small bowls to Greenidge, Lord's, June 18, 1988

the time the fifth highest run (hit) scorer in the history of West Indies cricket, is batting. He is from Barbados. His opponent, playing for England and doing his utmost to dismiss Greenidge, is Gladstone Small. He is from Barbados. Given the resonance of cricket in the lives of many of those about whom I have written in this study, hardly any better encapsulation of the ambiguities and intimacies of the Anglo-Barbadian relationship could be sought. How can this at first sight utter inconsistency—the man is playing for the "wrong" national team—be accounted for? Again, having read this far, readers will not be surprised to learn of the manner in which Small has come to play for England. In a very neat conceit, the *Observer*'s correspondent refers to Small's home parish and his adopted national side in the same breath, dubbing him "a true son of St. George's." Scyld Berry (July 17, 1988) writes,

> Gladstone's career took a different course when his father gave up working in the sugarcane fields at harvest-time and as a tailor to the village community out of season. In the Sixties Small senior moved to Birmingham (not Alabama). He found a job in the car industry making components, and settled there.
>   When the TCCB [the Test and County Cricket Board: the game's governing body] came to consider Gladstone's status,

they found a case of legal and sociological nicety. He was 15 when he emigrated to England to join his father, and 14 was the age by when a boy had to settle in this country to be classified as an England-qualified cricketer.

As Small said: "My mum used to go to and fro between Birmingham and Barbados, and my twin sisters were born in England. I stayed living with my grandparents in St. George until I was 15. . . . " [The TCCB decided] the family's roots were being well and truly sunk in their adopted country.

. . . He is certainly a shy, gentle soul, and it may be that years of taunting about his appearance [have affected him. . . . He plays] for Warwickshire.[1] . . . Married to a Western Australian girl and contentedly settled in a Worcestershire village, his has been a successful move from the parish to the flag of St. George.

Small and Greenidge were also facing each other on the selfsame cricket field that was the scene, for the migrant generation of Barbadians, of one of the great sporting occasions of the postwar period, the famous Second Test in 1963 when on the last day (the West Indies were led by Frank Worrell of Barbados) the match tipped in the balance. At the game's last gasp Colin Cowdrey, Kent's and England's captain, came out onto the pitch with a fractured arm in order to make up the required two batsmen (although he did not have to face bowling), and the West Indies were denied. This is one of those junctures for sports followers when, like England's 1966 World Cup Final soccer victory at Wembley stadium over this century's rival, Germany, everyone remembers where they were. Austin Pilgrim—in a story I love him for, the mischief in his eyes twinkling as he told it—remembers where *he* was: heading for "the hallowed turf of Lord's":

> The Bakerloo line [which goes to Lord's] had only three trains running out of forty-four. We were down there at the Tube station on our way to the match. "This is a *disgrace!*" we said loudly, "How can public servants *behave* in this manner?" All the motormen [train drivers] were at the match!

Whether that was Austin's designated day off or not I cannot say. In order to furnish a symmetry worth savoring to the tale, I hope it wasn't!

Resonance also obtains in the other great cricket ground of London, Surrey County Cricket Club's Kennington Oval. The Oval happens to be situated in the early Afro-Caribbean destination of inner south London, just two Tube stops from Brixton. "Oh, the Oval," said Frank Springer, "that's the black man's ground." And when asked whether there were any important places in or around London for Caribbean people, Nigel Pilgrim replied: "The Oval. That's a good place to be because that cricket ground is traditionally the home of the West Indies. Many West Indians live nearby in south London. There are more black faces than at Lord's, the 'Establishment'."

On an August summer's day, Alan Maycock takes me to the Oval to watch the first day of the second London Test Match between England and the West Indies. Once again the match is sold out. Police eye the crowds milling outside the gates as ticket touts ply their trade, uncomfortably trying to make their availability evident while maintaining a necessarily low profile. Among the throng are more than a few Rastas, their dreadlocks tucked bulkily under floppy red-yellow-green-and-black[2] knitted tea-cozy hats: the defiant cultural repudiation of colonialism goes to watch the former colonial master's most English of games. On the field is the captain of the West Indies, Viv Richards of Antigua, known for his sympathy to the Rastafarian project, the quest for a dignity undefined by any white criteria. The symbolism of Richards, dubbed "the Master Blaster," slamming as he did Gladstone Small for four successive "fours" (equivalent to triples) in the preceding Lord's Test, need not be underlined.

Alan—he is a member of Surrey County Cricket Club and has a member's pass—and I walk through the pavilion's elegant wood-paneled meeting room and pass beneath a painting of Surrey's Sir Jack Hobbs (a name to conjure with in the history of the game). To one side is an almost painfully stereotypically stiff-upper-lipped memorial (I do not mock) to those of the club who died in the armed services in World War I: "They Played The Game." Passing through the tall glass doors to take our seats in the sun, we move from the pavilion's repository of "traditional" public school values, from intimations of Sir Henry Newbolt's hortatory verse,[3] to a new cricket "tradition" (as Nigel Pilgrim put it): the ostentatious revelry of some black sections of the Oval crowd, steel percussion, the blowing of whistles, and all. So far has this once novel mode of applause and of gestures of support for one's team moved the game from the stereotypical old style of restrained hand-clapping and from the decorous "Well played, sir!" that I even detect its echo in the jaunty theme tune the BBC now uses to introduce televised cricket programs. This new "tradition" has been invented in just the last thirty years. But, given the decline in interest in cricket among the British-raised young blacks—mirroring an alleged, much agonized-over decline of the sport in English high schools in general—the question arises as to how long this new tradition may persist. Its raucousness, groused a couple of the more conservative of the cricket-loving Barbadian interviewees, brought the game into disrepute[4]—as have, in their eyes, the antics of Ian Botham—plus engendering from certain white supporters a boorish alcohol-lubricated counter-cheering, which these days often adopts a distastefully racist tone. (I take it that this is in part what Scyld Berry was referring to in Gladstone Small's being "taunted about his appearance.") Thus is cricket suffused with meaning.

Formerly Prime Minister Thatcher's closest lieutenant, Norman Tebbit caused a furor in April 1990 with his remarks about cricket during a parliamentary debate on the provision of British passports to (and thus potential immigration after 1997 of) 50,000 heads of households from Hong Kong. Speaking out against such immigration, Tebbit asked, for whom do Asian immigrant persons cheer at cricket matches? "Are you still harking back to where you came from, or where you are? . . . Well, you can't have two homes." Tebbit, who was specifically referring to Asians, rather wittily called this "the cricket test." Audley Simmons said to me,

> Norman Tebbit was implying that we were just flying the flag of convenience, but that at cricket we were showing our true colors, shouting for the West Indies. That's silly. We're not being disloyal to Britain. I mean, people born in Yorkshire but living in London for years'll shout for Yorkshire. Same with Scots and Welsh.

Not only is cricket a resonant and contested political symbol, but even the actual way the game itself is played on the field is contested. The very signature of the English summer, "the sound of leather on willow" for which Somerset Maugham's district commissioners in far-flung colonies mistily-eyed used to long, has been transformed by those who learned it at the knee of imperial England: recall "That's a very *West Indian* stroke." Just as the Irish were roughly forced by colonialism to speak English, just as they magicked it, so have the West Indians done with cricket. "The English language brings out the best in the Irish," wrote T. E. Kalem in a review of Brendan Behan's *Borstal Boy:*

> They court it like a beautiful woman. They make it bray with donkey laughter. . . . Rarely has a people paid the lavish compliment and taken the subtle revenge of turning its oppressor's speech into sorcery.[5]

Recall that Trevor Brathwaite, Jr., said of cricket, "We threw it back at them!" This is no side issue. No less a Third World luminary than Jamaican Prime Minister Michael Manley, plotting in opposition his 1988 return to political power, found the time to publish his book of getting on for 600 pages, *A History of West Indies Cricket.*[6]

Just as those from England's first overseas colony, Ireland, have come to live in London and by their settling have transformed it (and of course transformed themselves), so have those from subsequent colonies such as the West Indies come likewise to settle and to transform London. Cricket is the setting for one of the most visible manifestations of London's partial Caribbeanization. Another such manifestation is, as we have seen, the Notting Hill carnival, like The Oval's black spectators a *new* tradition: "It's become a date in the calendar in the summer season," said Trevor, Jr. This settling of West Indians in Britain at the end of the colonial period—"We are here because you were there," in A. Sivanandan's unmatched aphorism—underlines the probably inevitable two-way cultural traffic of a colonial system.

After always at least an hour, the formal interview concluded with "When you use the word 'home,' what are you thinking about?"[7] The initially disconcerting variety of the thirty-four replies to this question began falling into pretty recognizable patterns once I started trying to analyze them. There were the evident elements of generation and birthplace at play. And a further rather obvious factor suggested itself: the interviewees' particular personalities. I had on record their responses to other strongly related questions, such as to where might they have plans to move in the next five years, or what designations they would accept, such as "Barbadian" or "Londoner." In this way, and also by referring back to notes of my various unstructured conversations with them, I was beginning to get a grasp on the *individuality* of at least some of the interviewees, their particular penchants and biases, their particular mix of concerns and predilections. Their faces were in my mind's eye too as I thought and wrote. The reader cannot of course be helped along by this latter aid in the way I am—I can also catch echoes of their voices—but I hope she or he nevertheless by now feels a certain familiarity, is even beginning to know what to expect, from a number of the people of this book who have impressed their characters upon it: the three Brathwaites, the three Springers, the three Alleynes, Alan Maycock, the inimitable Austin Pilgrim and his son Nigel, Audley and Edith Simmons and their daughter Colleen Wright, and others.

As with identity, so with "home." The segmentary system discussed in the previous chapter applies here too. For example, "home" for me is, or *was,* a certain house on a certain Margate street; then, the Isle of Thanet; then, my county Kent; then, my country England—depending on the context. And later (only once I started living in the New World), I realized I was coming to identify myself at a yet more general scale—as one for whom Europe was home. Similarly, for many interviewees, "It depends on the context" was the response given to the question about home, and for a small minority of them the unproblematic segmentary system seemed to apply just as it did once for me: that is, "home" was this house on this Ilford street; then, London; then, Britain.

Having come to live half my life away from Britain, however, "home" for me is no longer unproblematic: it is as likely to be "Syracuse, New York" as "England." "It depends on the context" is no longer a straight-forward matter of scale, of telescoping, but an admission of uncertainty and ambiguity. "Syracuse, New York" isn't a nested geographical subset, or smaller component, of "England." It's a rival. And this is what is im-plied in "It depends on the context" for nearly all those of the immigrant generation who used the phrase. There is London, and there is Barbados, and the one isn't a constituent of the larger other, but rather a contender with it. Contrast this to the eleven of the British-raised generation, only one of whom felt enough uncertainty to use the phrase "It depends on the context"—and she had come to England at age twelve; all the other ten said "London." These various themes will now thread through the detailed information to follow.

What, then, of "home"? The largest single response was "Barbados," given by just over half of both the immigrants and the Barbados-born young. Three of the twelve immigrants in question immediately specified—and by that I mean in the same breath—that that answer really depended on the context, and two of these three said that if it was in prac-tical terms that I was asking, then London was "home." None of the British-born considered Barbados "home," not even Max Springer, who was prepared to denote himself both a "foreigner" and an "immigrant" (but also "black British"!). Although up to half the interviewees seemed to consider Barbados "home" in some more or less untrammeled way, "untrammeled" does not, however, mean that they necessarily felt this home was immediately available to them. Frank Springer said in reply: "Barbados. But, um, I know the majority of us aren't going to get back there; though 90 percent of the West Indians in London talk about going home, it's a myth, an illusion."

Austin Pilgrim replied "Barbados" immediately, and then added,

Even if I'd've loved to call England home, with the early hostility we've received, at least we've had Barbados to fall back on. After twenty years and more I'm still called an immigrant. And that policeman: what kind of newspaper I should buy, what kind of car I should have!

The Pilgrims take the *Guardian*. Apparently one day a policeman—and I cannot now remember the context, I've forgotten the precise story—had stopped Austin and asked him where he'd got that newspaper: "I suppose he expects me to read the *Mirror* or the *Sun,*" harrumphed Austin. Such annoyances do not, however, stop Austin from fully assenting to the label "Londoner," and also even to the local label of "south Londoner."

The car story is something of a cliché in matters racial in Britain (like the Prejudiced Neighbor of earlier accommodation-hunting years). The Pilgrims' Car Story occurred while I was getting to know them, in February 1988. A principal joy of Austin's life is his vegetable garden in the allotments that adjoin the back of the Pilgrims' house, but whose main gate and road access is round three sides of a square via quiet local streets. Marie recounts the tale, not omitting to draw her preferred moral regarding return to Barbados even before she gets to the pith of the story itself:

> Austin likes to work late in the afternoon on the allotment. There're not many people about to bother him, he can unwind from the strain of the day. Anyway, yesterday something happened and John, I think it's the last straw, I think we know we want to retire and to go back home to Barbados by the end of 1989. He drove around to the far entrance to the allotments, left the car [a late-model Volvo station wagon in excellent condition] there. When he'd finished on the plot, it was dusk. He went back to the car and was just sitting in it, with the heater on, to warm up. A policeman comes up, taps on the window, starts asking him questions: "Whose car is this?" "This is my car," he says. "Ho," he says, with a disbelieving smile. He keeps on questioning him. Austin's very calm, you know what he's like. Good job he's not one of those hot-headed young fellas, they carry a knife like I carry a handbag. That's a quiet little dead-end street with just a footbridge over the railway, it was getting dark, he could've done him in, nobody would ever have found out.

I was really astonished to hear this last Agatha Christie-like scenario issuing from the mouth of Marie Pilgrim, who is one of nature's own keepers of the flame of moral rectitude. "Was it a young, inexperienced cop?" "No, I don't think so. Not particularly. Twenties, maybe thirties. He wasn't a youngster." When I next saw Austin and asked him about it, the insult was still rankling. If he wasn't furious, he was doing a marvelous impression of a man much exercised by fury.

Successful businessman Colin Jemmott had a similar story of being closely questioned for no apparent reason at Gatwick Airport as he waited about for his wife to return from a Sorrento vacation—it turned out they suspected him of being a drug-smuggling pickup man. There was also his

> really nice flashy car, a BMW 635. I'd get stopped once a month. Police check. I got to carrying my driving license[8] and even the

receipt of sale for the car in the glove compartment. They were always polite, *cool* though. At the end they would say, "Have a safe journey, sir." Bah! I had to get rid of it. I got a second-hand Datsun. . . . Oh, it's such a waste of time. I get trouble at the banks cashing checks too.

And one midday Gladstone Codrington came round to have lunch with me at the London School of Economics Senior Common Room and he was *fuming.* The young teller at the nearby National Provincial bank had asked for confirmatory identification with such time-consuming, meticulous thoroughness that Gladstone sensed insult: "I'll write to Lord Booth their chairman, I know him from the ad hoc committee. . . . " Chip on the shoulder? I caught myself silently and uncharitably wondering. Whether yes or no, his time was certainly wasted. So was that of the others previously mentioned. And it does not happen just once. Were it to have happened to me, and then again, and then once again, wouldn't *I* begin to suspect I was beginning to be told something, perhaps that because of my blackness I wasn't to take it for granted that this place was my home?[9]

"It depends on the context" was, among the immigrants, the second most common reply to the question about "home." None of the British-raised feel it necessary to introduce this qualification at all, except for Barbados-born Paula Farley's half mention; the British-raised do not feel Barbados to be home. Of the immigrant generation both John and Amelia Simmons, apparently soon to return to Barbados, still felt they wanted to provide that qualification—that Britain was home as well. When you use the word "home," John Simmons, of what are you thinking?

> A very very very good question.[10] When I says "home," it varies. If I'm *here,* I mean Barbados. My land of birth. In another breath I say home is where I spend my working life: London. It's a . . . er . . . dilemma. . . . When I say this, West Indians here immediately know what I'm talking about.

Of what are you thinking, Amelia? (Amelia who was pleased to fully assent to the label of "Londoner"):

> My place of birth, and where I'm planning to spend the rest of my days, to return to my birthplace.
> When I'm in Barbados, I say to one of my friends, I'm going back home tomorrow. I don't say I'm going back to England. No, I'm going back *home,* because I live here. I've spent more of my years outside it [Barbados].

The third most common reply is "I've got two homes, Britain and Barbados." (*None* of the British-raised say this, only members of the immigrant generation.) But with this one could lump other replies, such as "Barbados is my second home; London comes first" or "fifty-fifty" (with five mentions from the immigrant generation, but only one—Trevor, Jr., who came to London aged sixteen—from the British-raised). Furthermore, a little reflection leads me to think that these various replies are all saying much the same thing as the "It depends on the context" category already perused. They're saying, "I'm equivocal." So, were I to combine these "equivocation" categories—and I speak here of the immigrant generation but *not* of the British-raised—the single resultant category would by far outweigh those who had unconditionally said "Barbados," by a margin of at least two to one.

Alternatively, approaching it in a slightly different way, that of individual by individual, I find that only *four* of the immigrants have given a truly unconditional "Barbados" reply for "home": Austin and Marie Pilgrim, Edward Pilgrim, and Frank Springer. Really, their number is five, but Edith Simmons's undoubted home is not Barbados but Jamaica. Looking at each of these five in reverse order, we may first note that Edith is married to an Audley Simmons who does not sound totally put out when he says, "I got two homes now" and "I may never get back there." Furthermore, Audley's Barbadian "there" is not her Jamaican "there," so Edith's chances for a successful, settled return to the Caribbean place of her choice seem uncertain.

We have already heard from Frank Springer about his dilemma concerning return. He knows how proud Joan is of her Ilford house, how content with it. She had said to me,

> What am I thinking about? "Home" is some place where I could be happy, whether it's here or Barbados doesn't matter. Where it's happy, warm, you can have friends come into, can do what you want, can have a laugh and a joke and play a few records or something. In many ways this is more my home, we've worked, saved, got this place, made it what we want it to be. Ours. The Barbados one was my *parents'* home.

Frank also knows how eager Joan is to watch her grandchildren grow, which means staying in London. Indeed, I remember Catherine Brathwaite, Trevor, Jr.'s wife, saying how powerful a "guilt trip" was played by some of the British-born generation in order to induce their immigrant parents to stay on in Britain: "You deprived us of the enjoyment of our own grandparents by bringing us up on the other side of the Atlantic from them, and now you want to do the same to *our* children here by running off back to the Caribbean yourselves!" Yes, Frank seems semiresigned to not getting back to Barbados.

Unlike Frank Springer or Edith Simmons, Edward Pilgrim does not have to take into consideration the possibly contradictory preferences of any spouse. But there are constraints of a different kind being weighed in his mind. As more than one excerpt from our conversations has indicated, he is extremely concerned about having sufficient means to retire to Barbados in the proper style. It is quite possible that he may never gather the substantial sum he feels he needs before he has the confidence to give it a go.

That leaves us with Marie and Austin Pilgrim. My money's on them. After John and Amelia Simmons, I reckon they will be the next to retire in the approved style to Barbados. It is utterly clear that Austin has never relinquished his strong Barbadian pride, and that Marie is eager to return. When I spent a long evening with them in May 1989 out came the detailed and impressive architect's drawings of the house they are planning on a parcel of her family's land, high above the rugged Atlantic coast[11] of Barbados: built-in garage, two stories, arches and iron grillwork for through airflow, low brick walls with pergolas around a patio-atrium. Austin was even talking of taking their Volvo with them. And their son Nigel, *the* young black Londoner par excellence, is himself pretty sure that his parents will soon make the move. So is Nigel's great friend Derek Gill, who—in talking about his own father Tony who "really doesn't know whether to go or to stay here, he really doesn't"—asserted "whereas Austin Pilgrim would go tomorrow if he could." The Pilgrims will thereby achieve what so many Caribbean migrants to Britain must have fantasized about, but which so few, relatively speaking, have actually managed.

Most of the discussion on "home" thus far has been focused on the migrant generation. Now we come to the British-raised. As already noted, three of the five born in Barbados called it home, but they were clearly outweighed by those eight who specified—four with, and four without, reservations—that London was home. Max Springer furnished, not surprisingly, one of the most matter-of-fact replies. For him, home is instrumental to wealth, he'd happily move home to be wherever the money is:

Home? 9^B Ash Grove, West Green, Tottenham.
    You can get bogged down in stuff that doesn't matter—like my dad going on about "Do black stars on TV get a fair crack of the whip?" All I want to know is: What information do you need to earn more money? I'd like to be rich . . . but anonymously, not famous. That way you can enjoy it better. I might think about moving to America—I've got relatives all over the place there: Texas, Mississippi, New York. I met 'em in Barbados and there in the U.S.

Three others of the British-raised, like Max, just mentioned their present London address for "home"; they expressed no confusion. (Charles Eastmond was the only one of the immigrants to simply give his address.) A couple of the British-raised qualified their answers by noting that "in *practical* terms, London is home." Another three introduced a somewhat stronger, or at least a differently based qualification, the gist of which was that "the house in London is home, but not the country." (The words are in fact those of the only immigrant to offer this reply: Eulie Eastmond. In the light of the preceding reference to Charles, it seems once again that spouses do influence the others' independently volunteered opinions.) Recall too from chapter 8 that when asked where they would like to live, only two of the British-raised (both Barbados-born) mentioned Barbados, whereas all of the eleven other responses, except one, were for London. These young black Britons whom I met seem mostly to be sanely looking the practicalities of life—Where is one to live? Near here? Near the London job?—straight in the eye.

Their parents, perhaps projecting their own anxieties, sometimes verbalize concern about their British-born children's alleged lack of belonging.[12] Trevor Brathwaite, Sr., fretted: "I'm scared for the children. We have roots in Barbados. You know what I mean. They don't have anything—just this place [Britain]." His son Trevor, Jr., may have accorded himself five different identity labels—"middle class," "British," and "Afro-Caribbean" (full), plus "Barbadian" and "immigrant" (partial)—but this to me seems to denote not confusion but a firm grasp of reality. And Trevor, Jr., muses in return: "My parents' generation are all mixed up about this. [He holds up two fingers.] Which is home? England or Barbados? For me, it's here. The young have no doubt." A month or so later I was talking with Trevor, Jr., and Catherine again. Trevor, Jr., said:

> "Home is here. England. These four walls. When we go to Barbados, we go to Barbados in the West Indies. I'm half-and-half, but my kids are British; my wife's 99 percent British."
>
> "Somewhat less," demurs the elegant Catherine [but who, as on p. 209, had already claimed herself to be "English"].
>
> "This is the foundation for the kids," insists Trevor. "It's no good hankering after a place five thousand miles away. I wouldn't go in the next five years."
>
> "I said I'd like to go tomorrow, especially because of the weather . . . but, oh, I really don't know," added Catherine, without conviction, but also without visible concern.

I met a similar mutual evaluation between the Farley generations. Ernestine was saying, "then we can go home to Barbados; we're ready to.

The kids might follow when they get fed up with it here." Not if, but when. Ten days later, I was chatting with her husband George, and he says, "This is no place for a black man, England. I'm always scared"—and then goes on to contradict himself by saying how secure they feel, how wonderful the neighbors are to them, the only black family on the block. Their son Hugh, with a university degree but with an utterly unpretentious manner, confided to me with a grin:

> Dad always said he'd never go back, all those years he didn't. "What is there for me there?" he'd say. And I was going back quite a bit[13] and said it was good. Then when he finally *did* go back on a visit he liked it so much that now he's all set on it!

George's tergiversation may be explicable. He went back, in 1981–82, after almost twenty years away. I strongly sense he felt he had not achieved enough to hold his head up high as a returnee, having lived, for example, in council housing that was condemned. Then came the "fairy story"— the opportunity to buy the new replacement council house, the Docklands development, the surge in house prices—and he and Ernestine are freed of the returnee status anxieties about Barbados that are giving Edward Pilgrim pause. I am wagering the Farleys are going to return to Barbados too—where they will proudly tell of the success of their British children, no doubt.

Apart from four mentions of the "sun, warmth, and sea" variety (all by Barbados-born persons), any other associations that were made with the word "home" by either generation were unique to a particular individual. Of two that were particularly evocative, the first was Gordon Alleyne's already-noted regret that home had once been where one had lived contentedly in a long-lasting gay relationship. The second was Colleen Wright's rumination from a Rastafarian perspective. When you use the world "home," what are you thinking about, Colleen?

> "That's hard. Because this is the place I grew up, I don't know no other place—until I travel to other places, which I haven't; so I can't say. . . . Home is where your parents brought you up." (Recall her fondness for Wembley.)
> "Is home Africa?" I probed.
> "The 'Return,' 'one day' may not even be to a physical Africa, we could be moving onto another sphere. We're still debating The Return in Rasta. We're aspiring to something higher.
> "Bob Marley, he first got Rasta through the music, he didn't stay up in the hills, he brought it down for the people. Now there are Rastas all over the world. It's not just a Black Pride thing, it's not a 'cult,' that is political or social. It's a *faith*. . . .

> Yes, there are people who are Rastas who are people who
> haven't had a revelation, but just do the locks. They're a bit like
> hippies, just a cult for them. They're not bringing their children
> into it as a faith, like we have. When we locked the children's
> hair, it caused a great deal of dissension in the family. . . .
> We're a faith; this is mystical, spiritual. There are white people in
> Rasta now . . . ''

Colleen's mother Edith Simmons has maintained good, close relations throughout this excursion of Colleen and Ken's far beyond the bounds of countenanced, conventional behavior. Her father—the tolerant, humane, easy-going Audley—is hurt and mystified and frustrated by it. Some degree of reconciliation has now occurred, centered around Colleen and Ken's recent formal marriage, but in May 1989 Audley said to me, "I can't tell you how disappointed I am about them. She's a bright girl. What a waste! They're not going to get anywhere with that stuff."

If we now refocus onto both generations taken together, we find that the replies to "home" are not patternless or impossibly complex. That is, for the British-born, and to a lesser extent for those raised in Britain, the answer is "here, London." Some introduce qualifications, some not. For up to half the Barbados-born of either generation, the answer is "Barbados." But there is much equivocation in the migrant generation. Indeed, the most common attitude among the immigrants is a striving for some *balance* between Barbados and London. The balance may in fact be attainable, at least to the satisfaction of some of the interviewees. "Home," Jeff Bannister?

> It all depends whether I'm thinking in the context of Barbados or
> England. . . . Um . . . I've been happy to get to Barbados,
> been happy to enjoy my time there, and I've been happy to
> come back, looking forward to coming back to England. Yes. So,
> that must mean, mustn't it, that . . . I have two homes?!

He looked very pleased to have arrived at this insight resultant upon my inquisition, and just as pleased that things should be that way.
"Home," Pauline Alleyne?

> My gut feeling is it's in Barbados—emotionally. Yet this [Sutton]
> is where I live—structurally. If we won the pools tomorrow, if
> we could afford it . . . [I'm anticipating an Edward Pilgrim-like
> fantasy of easeful sunshine and steps down to one's private
> beach] . . . I'd buy a nice detached house with a nice bit of
> lawn, a nice four-bedroom house . . . near Surbiton tennis
> courts. [!]

Pauline was one of the small minority of migrant generation respondents who had replied negatively to "Would you consider going back to Barbados to stay?" Her pro-Surbiton response (where the Alleynes lived for some years) indicates that, at least on the day I interviewed her, her criteria for achievement and contentment were British-oriented, not Barbadian. However, of all the households I met, the Alleynes were among the two or three who were the most unsure of exactly what it was they wanted, or indeed of exactly who they were. They were of all the respondents, for example, the only two who assented to as large a number of possible labels for themselves as eleven. Orville, who said he would consider going back to Barbados to stay, replied to the "home" question in this way:

> Barbados. But it depends on context. I mean, um, I like to think of here [this house] as home. Funnily enough, if I stayed in Barbados for any length of time, I might refer to England as home, I've spent so long living here. It depends who's asking, too!
>   Life's a paradox, really. . . .

Despite all the ambiguities and doubts, my predominant impression from talking with the interviewees was not that they were persons laboring under continuous emotional strain. There was bemusement sometimes, and, a little less often perhaps, I sensed present pain. All had experienced at least a taste of race-related hurt at some time or other—Austin Pilgrim springs immediately to my mind as a man who still smarts—but for this group, pain was not the unifying characteristic. Yes, they had all been bruised, and some of the bruises may never have healed to the point where they were invisible or forgotten. But "warped"? No, they were not. Just how odd a group, then, were these thirty-four persons, in relation to Britain's Afro-Caribbeans as a whole? How cushioned were they— by being Barbadians, by being Londoners, by being mostly relatively financially secure—from the lives of quiet (or unquiet) desperation I had at least half-expected to meet, given the rather dispirited tone of so much of the discourse of British race relations?

When, for example, I talked with Ivan Weekes, this intelligent man of thoughtful mien and measured phrase offered a diagnosis and prognosis of profound gloom. Especially for a man working at a high level in the central office of one of the great British nonconformist churches, his choice of words in the first sentence rocked me back in my seat.

> The whole story of black people here over the past thirty years has been a disaster, a . . . [he finds the word and looks me levelly in the eye] . . . a *crucifixion*. Any black person who tells

you different is not talking freely to you. The anguish that it's cost people. Of course some of them may own houses, and be materially better off than in Barbados, but they've paid for it emotionally.

. . . A friend of mine over in the Home Office says he's heard young black people say they're going to *burn* this city . . .

Or in a play I saw in London that was written by an Afro-Caribbean, a character asks whether we went to England "to better or bitter ourselves." Or the man a little older than me who was returning with his family to Barbados and whom I quoted in chapter 1 about his antennae warning him of passing white youths, he also said to me: "You know what they say in Barbados? That a quarter of those who return from England are mad."[14] Or that uncompromising guru of matters racial in Britain, A. Sivanandan, who in 1985 wrote, "Neither Asian/Afro-Caribbean nor British but afflicted by both, the second generation was adrift of its moorings and rudderless, caught in a cross-current of emotion in its search for identity."[15] Or Ken Wright, who touchingly gave me his self-produced reggae record: "If any of us are really frank with you, we'll say that to live here for us is as bad as living in South Africa."

Is all this easy hyperbole? Something with which to belabor the ears of a sympathetic—and thus perhaps irritating—liberal white investigator? That seems to me to be both overly cynical and overly simple-minded. If the "crisis" was being imagined, if these views had no tenure whatsoever on reality, then those who expressed such opinions would be instantly laughed out of court. Instead, some of them have the status of pundits whose words are attended to—though I own that, outrageously enough, I do suspect in part that a continuing "crisis" is good for the outrage business, too.

On the basis of my encounter with thirty-four persons, I am more inclined to align myself with the conclusion that Colin Jemmott draws at the end of the upcoming quotation—bearing in mind, however, that this very successful London Barbadian businessman's view is these days probably a "top-down" one . . . a caveat that I acknowledge might also be applicable to me.

"There's a widespread attitude among, well, let's say the less successful West Indian people that we're here in Britain to get as much out of it as we can, we'll stay to get it, a sort of 'they owe us' attitude because of slavery. I mean, look around you here at the sights of London. The Tate Gallery with all its pictures they're so proud of, a 'national treasure.' Where did Tate get his money? Sugar. Founded on slaves. And there's that Lascelles who's cousin to the queen, he has estates in Barbados. Bristol is founded on slaves, Liverpool too. . . . "

His thoughts became ever more discursive, and after a half minute or so I tried to get back onto track, tried to put them in a nutshell: "You mean, so these parents who feel negative themselves about England bring their children up to feel negatively about England—and some of these children think they want to return to Barbados?"

"That's right. But in my experience," resumed Colin, *"a majority of Bajans are on balance positive about Britain, and their kids want to stay here. They think they've a chance to rise here"* (my emphasis).

Colin's encapsulation matches very closely what I think I was hearing from those thirty-four persons. They were not randomly drawn, so I presume that they're likely not representative. By contrast, yes, I have read the depressing reports, the negative reports—that, for example, the proportion of blacks held involuntarily in British mental hospitals is at least twice as high as for whites, and that a mentally ill black person arrested by the police is far more likely than a white counterpart to be imprisoned rather than admitted to a hospital. Yes, I am aware that in June 1990 the Employment Institute reported that during the 1980s the rate of unemployment among ethnic minorities had been nearly double that of white workers, that they were out of work longer, and that the evidence suggested that about one-third of private employers would discriminate against people from ethnic minorities. Yes, I did hear that one-third of elderly West Indians in Britain are living alone, and that the Commission for Racial Equality found in Bristol that less than one-quarter were still living together with children and grandchildren in the extended family of popular Caribbean image. And yes, I did take note of an elderly woman's retrospection that she was now "trapped in a country that never liked me except for my work."[16] And I did listen attentively to Ivan Weekes as he told me his concerns for the Afro-Caribbean aged who cannot afford to return, or to the middle-aged Barbadian woman in Haringey who said to me,

I've seen it here, elderly black people don't fit in nursing homes here, they get bitter and disillusioned, very miserable if they can't return. When you're old, you should be among your own. You can't let go of your roots, they're something to hold on to. With retirement and illness, it's better to be there.

In the face of these submissions, which I would not dispute, it may therefore be really pretty facile of me to adopt a somewhat optimistic tone—

facile because those I met, upon whose reports I base my optimism, are playing with a better hand than most.

Indeed, if under Margaret Thatcher's tenure the differentials in wealth among the British have widened, then naturally enough they will have widened among the black British as well. A number of interviewees have alleged that she has made Britain "more American." Maybe, just maybe, it will be to her long years of power that future social historians will point back and say *this* was when the Afro-Caribbean people of Britain really became heterogeneous in social status; when a substantial black middle class first emerged—and so often North American observers (e.g., Cottle [1978], Foner [1987])[17] note the lack of such in Britain—whose early members, perhaps, this book will have rather providentially portrayed; when the largest proportion of British Afro-Caribbeans remained working class as before; but perhaps when also, belatedly mirroring America, a black British urban underclass first emerged: truly disaffected culturally and politically, unwanted socially, unserviceable economically. This very specter was confronted in a fine television program one mid-November evening in 1987. Michael Ignatieff chaired the discussion among Ralf Dahrendorf, Stuart Hall, Lord Harris, and Ray Pahl. The last-mentioned reluctantly foresaw a Britain with "more burglar alarms and more house insurance." More brutal policing was also anticipated: "I rather fear for the future."

But is it a failure of social vision on my part to state that what makes me semiconfident is that the majority of the thirty-four people whom I met are sane and not unhappy?[18] I did not see the purpose of this book to be at all an analytical prognosis of some future black (or indeed, even nonblack-nonwhite) Britain. I simply feel some optimism because, no doubt, it is an attribute of my own personality, but also because I know what the interviewees told me. Most of them aren't floundering in existential doubt, or wallowing in an identity crisis. They are not unaware, most of them, of the complexities and paradoxes of their situation—but they can usually deal with these, rather than be immobilized by them. They have a grasp on reality. Some I think I got to know well enough to say of them that their personalities and identities, though complex or plural, are still all of a piece.

One way of dealing with these unanswerable conundrums is humor. A lot of those whom I met used it to good effect in order to get their points across. John and Amelia Simmons and I have had some laughs—among others, there was Amelia's "the weather changed"! So, here is Amelia again, seemingly almost *celebrating* a plural identity, closing out this section:

When we're in England, Barbados is home. When we're in Barbados, England is home! We had a good laugh over that, John and me.

Yi-fu Tuan critiqued an earlier draft of this work, and among other observations offered the following. It puts the complexities of this chapter into a broader perspective, thereby furnishing an apt conclusion to it:

The question, "What do you have in mind when you see the word 'home'?" can seem a bit baffling, as indeed many interviewees were baffled. The meaning of home itself has changed, as a consequence of modernization: it is being redefined. By whom? Well, by (among others) the Barbadian Londoners themselves, as they become successful cosmopolities at ease in multiple worlds, rather than natives of place torn by new and multiple allegiances. . . .

Thirteen
Islands and Insularities

No man is an island, entire of itself.

John Donne

On one thing his [immigrant] subjects agree: the British are condescending, insular, and ignorant.

The Economist's review of *Them,* by Jonathon Green

"Insular, adj. . . . 3. Of or pertaining to islanders; hence, narrow; circumscribed; illiberal." Old-style geographers would approve of that definition from *Webster's Collegiate Dictionary* at my hand, in its implication that physiographic features (in this case, being proximately surrounded by water) determine or at least influence human behavior and characteristics. These days we are more circumspect; we know there are plenty of examples of societies that do not inhabit islands but that nevertheless exhibit the same allegedly noncosmopolitan traits: Albania would do for a start. Yet I don't believe our language can be totally off-track in such attributions. That is, the notion of the accordance of sensibly bounded space and evidently bounded sensibility has some grain of truth in it: historically, Japan would leap to mind as an example. This study has been about islanders; about Barbadians directly—persons from a very small island; and about the British indirectly, as makers of the context for this study—persons from a somewhat larger island. As we have seen, their intermingling in London over the past thirty or more years has eroded their illiberal narrowness and widened previously circumscribed horizons—at least for some. Two insularities, the one Barbadian, the other British, have been undermined.

For the English—the dominant and most numerous group inhabiting the island of Great Britain—there can be no symbol of "the Island Race" more telling than that of the white cliffs of Dover. How apt, then, that this was the first view of England, as his ferry approached from Calais, for the first-arrived of all the people of this study, Frank Springer. How apt, too, that for the author of this study those cliffs are natal turf, that as a child I gained a rapid appreciation of the nature of quasi insularity by the fact that white chalk cliffs falling to a grey-green sea visibly bounded my world in two and a half of four compass directions. How apt, too, that in Camberwell late one evening in May 1989, during the very last of gathering material for this study, the Pilgrims should have driven me past a pub with that commonest of names, "The Albion." The obligatory hanging pub sign depicted a sturdily built, top-hatted John Bull of florid complexion: a giant, his legs somewhat apart, firmly planted on the greensward capping of the perpendicular white cliffs of Dover.[1] He stared steadily out at me; proprietorship that could quickly turn to defiance, I sensed.

These cliffs are my home ground. As Derek Gill when in New York thinks with pride of his birthright, the "traditional, historical" ensemble that is London, so do I, on such occasions as I am stirred by home thoughts from abroad, see the East Kent cliffs. "The finest walk in England," I claim with effervescent hyperbole as I drag my poor favored visitors—Canadian, American, South African, Welsh—off on the twelve-mile march from Walmer to Dover and on to Folkestone Warren, with views of France and the busy English Channel all the way. What for me is the very essence of childhood home happens to be the essential symbol of English insularity.

I don't suppose W. H. Auden had in mind this same spot when in 1935 he wrote his poem "Look, Stranger, at This Island Now," but the first time I read it, in my bungalow on a Burundi mission station, images of the cliffs of the South Foreland and of the crowded Channel shipping shouldered their way into my mind. I have never been able, nor wished, to keep them out since, for the feel for East Kent these stanzas evoke is at the core of my first identity.

> Here at the small field's ending pause
> Where the chalk wall falls to the foam, and its tall ledges
> Oppose the pluck
> And knock of the tide,
> And the shingle scrambles after the suck-
> ing surf, and the gull lodges
> A moment on its sheer side.
>
> Far off like floating seeds the ships
> Diverge on urgent voluntary errands;
> And the full view
> Indeed may enter

> And move in memory as now these clouds do,
> That pass the harbour mirror
> And all the summer through the water saunter.

Switch the scene. I now by choice live in America and have an additional identity. So in the course of making their way through this book I suppose it may have occurred to readers that a third insularity has been undermined: the author's own. I would never, had you asked me back then in 1972 on my arrival in the United States, have dreamed that I would stay and Americanize. Especially as the first America I lived in was where, of all the other English-speaking places I have inhabited, I felt most foreign: Los Angeles. Like, I'd suppose, most English visitors, I was struck by the multiethnicity that announced itself everywhere. Unlike, I'd suppose, most English visitors, sometime in my first weeks at UCLA I took it upon myself to *walk* a good ten miles or so inland along Pico Boulevard. The cultural kaleidoscope was remarkable, tangy. After the head shop, and the occult bookstore with its heavy scent of Oriental mysticism, came all-American hamburgers and frankfurters (Germany long forgotten); then, likewise, came a pizza parlor (Italy? No—what could be more American than pizza?); then a Mexican restaurant (if southern California is American, then Mexican food must be "native"—thus American—too; here one stood on "occupied Mexico"); then came Kelbo's Hawaiian restaurant (can the fiftieth state be "foreign"?); and so it proceeded.

Many years later, acclimatized by sojourns in the Midwest and on the eastern seaboard, and married to a Philadelphian, I realized how American I had become, at a moment of national horror: the space shuttle disaster in January 1986. In its immediate wake the *Manchester Guardian Weekly,* whose tone and general stance I usually esteem, ran a piece that greatly offended me. Its correspondent referred, it seemed with unnecessary cynicism and offhandedness, to the perished crew as a contrived "advert for the affirmative action programme." Clearly there was an element of truth in the remark—this was no random selection—but at that juncture it seemed too clever by half. It was not an apt moment to snidely make such an observation from overseas. I felt both embarrassed and hurt by it: embarrassed because I was British, hurt because I was American. The crew weren't just an advert, they were people—American people, therefore, naturally, multiethnic.

The next year, a similar intimation from the cinema correspondent of London's *Sunday Times* (April 26, 1987). Philip French reviews one of the most noted films of the year, the Vietnam War movie *Platoon:* "Almost every dramatic element in 'Platoon' is familiar . . . the carefully selected range of ethnic melting-pot American types (as always, we're invited to predict the order of their deaths); . . . " Are such sentiments typical of the British as a whole? Or are they simply the *mots* of the most iconoclastic wits that the "chattering classes" can provide? If the latter was the whole story and if the sentiments expressed were totally idiosyncratic, then surely their authors wouldn't be given space in the "serious" London national newspapers to purvey such odd views? (Here is one of the reasons I might find the continuing media visibility of Enoch Powell disconcerting.) It seems clear, rather, that the British *are* still looking at a multiethnic America with wonderment, when some perhaps don't seem to realize enough that there is a multiethnic London in their own backyard.[2]

A year later, and a third of the "quality" newspapers provides another straw in the wind. In the *Observer* (March 20, 1988), foreign editor Adrian Hamilton writes a morally exercised piece on South Africa. Two-thirds of the way through, we read: "But apartheid stands as a grotesque insult to everything this country, and every other white democracy, believes in." Do I quibble? Britain is a *mainly* white democracy, I don't deny. But how do the Alan Maycocks and Nigel Pilgrims and Joan Springers and other such citizens of worth feel when they read that sentence? Just a shade disenfranchised, I would suspect . . . as Muslims or Jews must feel when confronted by official requests for "Christian names," not "forenames." It seems to me, even among the sentient leaders in British opinion, that the country still takes it for granted that it is essentially white. A few months later I recall in the "birthdays" section (was it the *Guardian* or the *Observer*?) that a certain Salmon Rushdie was forty-one years old. Again, do I quibble? Surely typographical errors happen to us all? I have been referred to in print as both John Weston and John Ester. Carelessness. Nothing else crosses my mind. But Rushdie had a choice of evaluations that I'll wager he'd rather not have had—the "racial minefield" conundrum, again: "Did they misprint it *because* I was black/outlandish?" Mind you, I'd also wager, with the reception *The Satanic Verses* met in the following year, that Rushdie will never again meet that Salmon problem. But neither would he have chosen the particular manner by which his unfamiliarity or name-recognition problem has been resolved.

And yet, there are straws in the wind in the contrary direction. One of the more memorable news photos during the year in Britain sprang from the attempt by the Ford Motor Company at its plant at Dagenham in east London to introduce various flexibilities in work rhythm, in order to bring productivity up to more nearly Japanese levels (perhaps particularly to those levels the Nissan company was shooting for at its plant in Tyne and Wear). The workers went on strike: "We're 'Brits' not 'Nips,' " said their banner. Holding up each end of the twenty-five-foot-long message were . . . two *Afro-Caribbean* strikers. And the black British have the native's feel for that which is viscerally symbolic of Englishness: there's a reggae piece hymning liberty that simultaneously celebrates "the white cliffs of Dover."[3] With unerring aim, black British musicians composed another piece, Asher Senator's 1985 hit, "The Big Match," which portrays an *all-black* England soccer team defeating Germany in the World Cup.[4] I recall only one top-class black soccer player when I was a teenager, Albert Johannessen of Leeds United; I think he was a black South African or Rhodesian by origin. Today, not only the major London clubs—Arsenal, Tottenham Hotspur—but the finest team of the 1980s, Liverpool, *and* the English national side, are inconceivable without their black players (who nevertheless encounter racial crowd abuse). Indeed, the last-mentioned two teams would be today unthinkable without their star 1987 and 1990 Footballer of the Year, Jamaican-born John Barnes, who performed wonders for England in a closely fought World Cup Semi-Final defeat in 1986. After a year in London, my impression is very strong that black people are no longer dismissible as having merely "encamped" (for what he was purposing, Enoch Powell's choice of verb was superb) upon certain sections of the face of England. Formerly immigrants, they are now indubitably—but, I agree, unequally—*part* of England.

England is made up of immigrants, as one supposes the entire ecumene must be. Many aver that it was during the Tudor period, especially in its apogee of the Elizabethan age, that a "national" politicocultural consciousness first began to be formed. After decades of internal strife in the Wars of the Roses, the Tudors found themselves striving to hold together in one central administration not only all of England, but also the colonial conquests of Wales and Ireland. One serviceable constituent element of the desired cohesion proved to be the conscious creating of a "national character" as societal cement, and another the exhortation of "internal" unity against the "foreign" threat. First the French, then the Spaniards, fitted the external bill. And the finest writer in the language's history was there to lend a propagandistic hand, as *Henry V* gloriously affirms.

Wholly appropriate that at the climactic moment of recent British national consciousness—the skin-of-the-teeth survival of World War II—Laurence Olivier should have produced his landmark film of *Henry V*. Shakespeare's "Britannicizing"[5] propaganda, its witting manipulation aimed at forging some national consciousness, encountered in wartime three and one-half centuries later a partly unmanipulated and spontaneous upwelling of national feeling on an occasion of unmatched crisis. One central component of ethnic consciousness is shared memory. That historical moment for the British—the Dunkirk evacuation and the Battle of Britain and the Blitz and Churchill's spine-tingling radio oratory: "blood, toil, tears, and sweat," "very well, alone," "the Few," "their finest hour"—is a memory to conjure with. Subsequent politicians have indeed drummed up "the spirit of Dunkirk," that moment when the national heart reportedly beat as one, as appropriate to more recent but less fraught moments of national travail.

The British, however, did not exactly stand alone, prior to the saving entry of the Soviet Union and then the United States of America. There was the British Empire. From it came not only Canadians (and Newfoundlanders), Australians, New Zealanders, and white South Africans,[6] but also troops from the considerable Indian army . . . and West Indians, among yet others. I recall, again, at the *Empire Windrush* fortieth anniversary celebration in Brixton in June 1988, one man standing up to complain of the ingratitude and amnesia of his white fellow citizens: "My uncle never came back from a bombing raid over Germany." The Afro-Caribbeans were *there,* in it with the white British, at the hour of national emergency: "Barbados is behind you," indeed.

Consider John Betjeman's light but piercing satire, "In Westminster Abbey":

> Gracious Lord, oh bomb the Germans.
>   Spare their women for Thy Sake,
> And if that is not too easy
>   We will pardon Thy Mistake.
> But, gracious Lord, whate'er shall be,
> Don't let anyone bomb me.
>
> Keep our Empire undismembered
>   Guide our Forces by Thy Hand,
> Gallant blacks from far Jamaica,
>   Honduras and Togoland;
> Protect them Lord in all their fights,
> And, even more, protect the whites.

Betjeman's teasing manner masks a real purpose, that of skewering English xenophobia and racial thinking. Old habits die hard. To return to Britain in 1987 was to find that "the war" was still the datum line: "before the war," "between the wars," "prewar," "postwar." Raised in the 1950s and 1960s, I took on an unconscious anti-Germanism by cultural osmosis. Childhood comics and (still, today!) second-rate war movies always had thin-lipped, peak-capped, killer-shark-eyed Nazis as villains. Three miles away from my home was the Spitfire in camouflaged RAF livery on its plinth at front-line Manston airfield. My father and I would cycle out there, and I gathered from him that this machine was to be regarded with reverence and pride. On the few occasions we went to London, the bomb sites of the Blitz were pointed out with appropriate gravity, especially those all around St. Paul's Cathedral. The express steam engine that hauled us to London was most likely a "Battle of Britain"-class locomotive with a name like "Fighter Pilot," "Lord Dowding," "222 Squadron," or aptly enough, "Spitfire" or "Manston." And if you wanted to put on a "funny accent," it was most likely fake Tchermann. And today I think—having traveled in France and Belgium and, dear God, in Poland and the Ukraine and Russia—that Britain wasn't even *occupied.*

And now we are changing all this. Germany is arguably America's most pivotal European ally (as are the Japanese in the Pacific!). Germany is the locomotive, the economic journalists instruct us, of the European economy. Britain has joined Europe in the EEC. From January 1, 1993, most tariff barriers are to melt away. In just the way that much British official propaganda of the fifties and sixties was concerned with the importance of "moral leadership" and the Commonwealth, now there seems to be a focus on the fraternity of all (Western?) Europeans. The Germans are being, have been, rehabilitated into partners. If, on behalf of the British people, officialdom can devote energies to popularizing a confraternity among those who have indulged in such monstrous bloodletting within living memory, among those whose speech is not intelligible one to another, why can't monies likewise be spent in substantial amounts on propagandizing a positive multiculturalism within Britain? A couple of the more "political" interviewees, indeed, praised former GLC leader Ken Livingstone for his "London Against Racism" propaganda campaigns of the mid-1980s.[7] One of them noted that Livingstone's actions might fairly be seen as a corollary of the not insignificant proportion that black people made up of GLC voters.

In the popular mind the conceptualization of Englishness is indubitably bound up with insularity. And in matters racial, Paul Gilroy considers that a melding has been effected:

> The limits of "race" have come to coincide so precisely with national frontiers. This is a central achievement of the new racism. *"Race" is bounded on all sides by the sea* [my emphasis]. The effect of this ideological operation is visible in the way that the word "immigrant" became synonymous with the word "black." . . .
>
> As part of their ["New Right" writers'] lament that the national heart no longer beats as one, Peregrine Worsthorne has pointed out that "though Britain is a multi-racial society, it is still a long way from being a multi-racial nation." [And Enoch Powell has decreed] "the West Indian does not by being born in England,

become an Englishman. In law, he becomes a United Kingdom citizen by birth; in fact he is a West Indian or an Asian still."[8]

Mr. Enoch Powell is in my eyes to be allowed a certain consistency. He is a self-appointed defender of the essence of English culture. Darker, alien, "New Commonwealth" immigrant hordes threaten this. Additionally—perhaps even more so given the centuries-long British policy of avoiding Continental entanglements—so does Britain's joining the EEC. Now, astonishingly and foolhardily in Mr. Powell's eyes, the British are voluntarily ceding some of their previously allegedly untrammeled constitutional sovereignty to the administrative powers of Eurocrats in Brussels or in Strasbourg. The *Observer*'s television correspondent (July 17, 1988) wrote mischievously on "hearing Mr. Powell spout once again the mystical flapdoodle about the constitution which is his stock in trade. . . . He talked a kind of reverential gibberish, for example, about the 'unexhausted resources of Englishness.' " Margaret Thatcher too, during her decade or more in power, showed little enthusiasm for Europe, unlike former Prime Minister Edward Heath, whom she elbowed out as Conservative leader . . . and who like me could see France from his native Isle of Thanet. "She was scarcely a European at all," judged Peter Jenkins in his benchmark work of political journalism, *Mrs. Thatcher's Revolution.*[9]

But what a change is now being wrought! In 1989 (the year during which the first draft of this book was mostly written) public opinion reportedly turned strongly pro-Europe in Britain, and forced a more positive, less prickly attitude toward her European partners upon the British leader. Most symbolically of all—"because she is looking for monuments," government minister Nicholas Ridley[10] let slip informally—a physical, dry connection is being made with the continent of Europe: the Channel Tunnel. Atop Dover's white cliffs "the greatest castle in England" (in Nigel Nicolson's estimation) takes an implacable, unchanging defensive stance: John Bull on "The Albion" pub sign personified it. Atop the cliffs at adjacent St. Margaret's Bay—geographically the closest point to France, from whose shingle beach the Channel swimmers plunge in, and from where one can easily see the twenty-one-miles-distant clocktower of Calais's Hôtel de Ville—stands a life-size statue of the Churchill of bulldog mien of 1940. Atop the Langdon cliffs, to the immediate east of Dover harbor, stand three radar pylons where, I believe, the very first such towers stood, activated just in time to play a saving role in the aerial Battle of Britain. Rearing up to the immediate west of Dover harbor stands Shakespeare Cliff, making reference to the clifftop scene in *King Lear.* And at its foot, virtually unseen on its far side, are the Channel Tunnel workings. Beneath one's tread on the footpaths over the sea-blown springy downland turf, invisible laborers burrow, pushing out to a mid-Channel meeting. British insularity is literally being undermined. When the first physical connection was made in late 1990, the *Daily Telegraph* front-page headline read: "7.30 P.M., Oct. 30: 'Britain ceases to be an island.' " One was reminded of a contrasting, and celebrated, headline of sixty years earlier: "Fog in the Channel: Continent Cut Off."[11]

In 1988 the only friend from Thanet high school days with whom I am still in touch tried to explain to me what he felt about the Channel Tunnel. He had just asked me about it. I said I thought it was a great idea. So much so that, with my geographer's eye telling me the venture couldn't possibly fail, I had actually bought a share in it. He, conversely, was troubled. Something just wasn't right about it. History and its lessons. 1066. Fear of breaking the defensive line Providence had since then vouchsafed us. Englishness. He could not find the words—this matter was too deep. But Nigel Nicolson has found them. With sly, mock-Freudian irony he writes in his *Kent* (1988) of one side of the debate:

> The objections to the principle of any fixed link with the Continent continue. There is a deep-rooted regret that Britannia will no longer be *intacta.* The tunnel will be a gigantic French rape. Our history, and the theme that throbs through much of our literature, is pride in our insularity. The Channel is a moat not only defensively, but psychologically. It defines the limits of our culture in a way that no river or mountain barrier between states can equal. It is as divisive as an ocean, and to bridge it, even submarinely, is to lose something of our national virtue. These fears, seldom explicitly stated, underlie opposition on more practical grounds. The tunnel will expose us to every Continental ill. Vermin will cross dryshod, bringing rabies. . . . Xenophobia surfaces . . . [it's a] plot to drain away our substance and fill our shops with Continental goods.[12]

Nicolson favors the other side in the debate. Whether or not, as the tunnel's true enthusiasts claim, "Once it is built, insular prejudices will be cured by using it," Kent-dwelling Nicolson is basically for it.

Cured is not the verb I would choose, but I am convinced there is a big point here. Britain will in an incontrovertible sense no longer be an island. Somehow I feel that the changes that the soon-to-arrive common European enterprise is going to bring in its train are going to be enormous and irreversible. Thirty-five years ago, facing a shortage of workers, the British government "called for labor, and people came instead,"[13] in Max Frisch's phrase. Although official records now becoming available under the thirty-year confidentiality rule show that the Conservative government of the day *did* discuss the societal undesirability of black residence in Britain, I still get the sense that the ramifications of the Afro-Caribbeans becoming permanent *settlers* and raising black British children were not really foreseen. Indeed, how can such ramifications be truly foreseen? Even the most meticulous social engineering—as I saw firsthand in South Africa—can have the most unanticipated consequences.

From my now-transatlantic vantage point I sense that the European Community project is going to hit the British with far greater changes, over which they will have far less control, than did the arrival of darker-skinned immigrants in the dusk of Empire. If there is any validity in Gilroy's previously quoted point, then the fact that Britain is no longer bounded on all sides by the sea is greatly symbolic for British race relations as well as for relations with "foreign" Europeans. Evidently here, in my concluding remarks, I am reaching for some very broad and very ill-defined generalities. But my intuition is—perhaps because I met mainly comfortably off black Londoners, perhaps even because they were Barbadians?—that the questions their settlement raised and are raising for the British identity are going to pale in comparison with those that the Europeanization of Britain will bring. *On verra.*

A final set of reflections. Recall from the first chapter my remolding of Raymond Williams's insight to make the point that there has never been in any absolute sense one people or ethnic group, however defined, who could claim primordial belongingness on British soil. To feel otherwise is, logically, to introduce a cutoff date after which arrivals are not bona fide Britishers: the Afro-Caribbeans, 1948; the Poles, 1939; then the Ashkenazim, then the Italians, then the Flemings, then the Huguenot refugees. And so it goes on: Will the Saxons please stand and leave the room now? I joke . . . but "there is no such thing as a joke." The point is there. *Who* draws the cutoff line, if one must be drawn? It will be drawn with reference to an officially approved culturohistorical identity, inevitably defined with reference to some unenviably fuzzy grab bag of criteria. So historians and scholars of culture are powerful people; they get to suggest lines of demarcation. Who writes cultural history? It'd better be me, is one response. Therein, specifically, lies the importance to blacks in Britain that some of their number should be writing British-based black cultural history; their voice must be such that it cannot be ignored.

But I do not believe the line will or can be drawn. The ruling of any cutoff line—the way of apartheid—would have to mean the separation out of all those who fall on the disqualified side, prior to their supposed repatriation: penning, then ejection. Intimations of horror here, not three years before I was born: wall them into Jewish ghettos, then send them in trains "to the East." This we do not do, I cannot conceive of it. The only other choice is inclusion. Ours is a common enterprise; let us enrich each other, and build together.

Yet the call for universal human kinship, for John Lennon's "Imagine," runs up against some Gordian knots in no time at all. What is the enforcement of immigration laws if not penning, then selective ejection: Britain, 1962; the U.S.-Mexican border today? Would I repeal those laws? I don't know what to say in response. I wonder, is my inclusivist liberalism really nothing more than a "generosity" I can easily afford, "top-down" again? Suppose all portals of all sovereign states were fully open, both rich and poor worlds? Imagine: an awful lot of the Russians, Poles, and East Germans (see upcoming footnote) would slip their respective countries; and southern California would rapidly founder into yet deeper despoilment; and most of the Hong Kong middle class would arrive on the Pacific coast of North America; and Australia would brace itself for the Javanese just as the peoples of West Irian and East Timor have had to in the recent past; and . . . this becomes immediately a ridiculously anarchic scenario.[14]

But suppose—and this is the point I really want to finish on—we talk not of the physical movement of actual people, but rather of the free movement of cultures in the widest sense, and of equal honor being ascribed to all cultural beliefs: the banishment of insularity? This comes up against some Gordian knots pretty soon too: Are we permitted to say to the Hindu that sati[15] is wrong, to the Dinka that clitoridectomy is anathema, to certain Solomon Islanders that head-hunting just isn't right? Notice that "we" are telling "them," not vice versa. When I witter on about valuing other peoples' cultures, my assumption is understood, that I don't have to surrender my own culture, which I happen to value. My assumption is based on a worldview that presupposes the industrial, native-English-speaking world to be and to remain the economic, military, and cultural powerhouse of the present international system. I was brought up in its nineteenth-century leader, I have moved to live in its twentieth-century leader. English is becoming, they say, the "world language."[16] So of course I can take a munificent cultural stance—because if there is a world culture in the making, then I've already got my seat booked in the front row.

Yet suppose instead it was, say, a Sino-Japanese nexus that was the ascendent world culture? Yes, I would admire and do admire so much of this high culture. But am I not wary, am I not apprehensive that, even if I learn their culture-ways well, as it behoves me to (because I am living in a world they largely orchestrate), my own visible features will always mark me as a cultural parvenu? I bear the mark of a cultural subject. Culture is equated with appearance, just as the *Daily Telegraph* editorial, cited in the first chapter, equated them in May 1989. I fear therefore, with some reason, that I and my round-eyed descendents will be more or less forever denied full inclusion . . . if inclusion is what we want, or should want. Is this part of how the Barbadians might feel in Britain?

And finally suppose that it wasn't just that somehow in the world at large my culture had been trumped by another more powerful Sino-Japanese one, utterly foreign to me. Suppose this had been an armed conflict, and that, losing the fight, I found not only my livelihood and family but also my territory, my place, taken away from me—or myself, the mark of an enemy upon me, taken away from my place? And then I am obligatorily acculturated into the Sino-Japanese way, my English language is demeaned, bestialized, banned. My children no longer speak it, nor my children's children (if I am able even to identify them as such). The tongue is lost, forever perhaps. *Then,* where am I? What am I? What buttresses are there for my self-esteem, or for that of my descendents? And this lasts for hundreds of years. To miss in this the reference to slavery, to the West African diaspora, would be downright obtuse. For this, inescapably, is the backdrop to all the people who are the informants in this book. Consider them, the knocks they've taken, yet their grasp on sanity and humanity and humor amid the ever-changing complexities of London. Are they not—and I am not talking canonization here—an astounding affirmation of the human spirit?

I salute them.

Epilogue

Audley Simmons wrote to me in Syracuse for Christmas 1988:

You must be well away with your book. . . . I can't wait to get my hands on one so get cracking and let's have it done. Say by next Summer.

It's been very nice to have met and talked to you, and I hope we can do so again some time in the future. That's about it except to say The Weather is awful as usual but we BRITS can take it not like some EXPATRIATES whom I shall not name (smile).

Edith and I send our regards to you and Patricia.

Audley

Appendix

Questionnaire for the Immigrant Generation

1. When did you come to the U.K.?
2a. Were you recruited in Barbados?
2b. So did you get an assisted passage?
3. Tell me about your family's history, your parents' backgrounds, etc.
4a. Which parish in Barbados did you live in?
4b. Where?
5a. How much schooling did you get?
5b. At which school?
6. Did you have any family or friends or acquaintances who had previously left Barbados?
7. Why did you leave?
8. How old were you then?
9a. Were you single when you left?
9b. Married since?
10. Where did you meet your partner?
11. Where is s/he from?
12a. Did your partner come with you?
12b. At the same time?
13. What education standard did s/he get?
14. What was s/he doing then?
15. Are you still with that same partner?
16. Did you have children when you left Barbados?
17. Did they stay or come?
18. Have you had children in Britain?
19. Did you send some of what you earned here back to Barbados?
20. Do you still send some back?
21. What jobs, in order, did you have before you came here?

22.   Once you got here, what jobs did you get?

23.   Was it what you expected, the work?

24.   Can you tell me who is in your household? Who's a student, or working, or retired, or unemployed?

25.   Where does each of these persons work?

26.   Tell me your first impressions of life in Britain back then.

27.   When you first came to England, where did you live?

28.   What was it like?

29.   What was good about it?

30.   What was bad about it?

31.   Who ran it/owned it?

32a. And then you moved to?

32b. When?

33.   What was it like?

34.   What was good about it?

35.   What was bad about it?

36.   Who ran it/owned it?

37a. And then you moved to?

37b. When?

38.   What was it like?

39.   What was good about it?

40.   What was bad about it?

41.   Who ran it/owned it?*

42a. So how did you happen to move into this present place?

42b. When?

43.   Who runs/owns it?

44.   Have you any plans to move in the next five years or so?

45.   If yes, where would you like to live?

46.   What would be your main reason for moving?

47.   In general terms, what's it like to live in this area?

48.   What's good about it?

---

* This question followed, to the extent necessary, by further sets of questions identical to 32a to 36.

49.   What's bad about it?

50.   What's the most important quality you'd look for in neighbors?

51a.   Would having Barbadian neighbors make a difference?

51b.   Caribbean?

52.   Are there particular places in and around London which you like, and why?

53.   Are there particular places in and around London which you don't like, and why not?

54.   Are there particular places in and around London which you feel are important for Barbadians, and why?

55.   Are there particular places in and around London which are important for Caribbean people, and why?

56.   Are there particular places around Britain which are important for Barbadian or Caribbean people, and why?

57.   For example, did you ever go to the Notting Hill carnival?

58.   Did you ever participate in it?

59.   What do you like about it?

60.   What do you dislike about it?

61.   Of all your relatives, apart from parents and children, is there anyone who is specially important to you/your household? How are they related to you, and where do they live?

62.   Where does each of your absent parents live?

63.   When and how were you last in contact, by visit, phone, or letter, with any of them?

64.   Do you have children who no longer live with you? Tell me a little about them: Are they married (to whom)? Do they have a family? What work do they do?

65.   Where does each of your absent children live?

66.   When and how were you last in contact, by visit, phone, or letter, with each of them?

67.   Where do your close friends live?

68.   How did you get to know them?

69.   So, are any of them Barbadians, or from families of Barbadian origin?

70.   Are any of them West Indian, or from families of West Indian origin?

71.   When was the last time you had contact, by visit, phone, or letter, with a close friend(s)?

72.   How often do you get to visit them?

73.   How do you get there or they to here?

74a. Do you attend religious services?

74b. How often?

74c. Where?

75.   How do you get there?

76.   Is your religion of particular importance to you?

77.   Did you attend religious services when at your previous address(es)?

78.   Where do you go shopping for food (convenience and/or big shopping)?

79.   How do you get there?

80.   Where do you go shopping for clothes?

81.   How do you get there?

82.   Are there any other shopping trips worth mentioning?

83.   How do you get there?

84.   Where do your children go to school/kindergarten/child minding?

85.   How do you/they get there?

86.   Where do you go to the doctor/hospital/DHSS/Social Services/etc.?

87.   How do you get there?

88.   When and where do you go to play or watch sports/bingo/cinema/dancing/darts/dominos/etc.?

89.   How do you get there?

90.   Is there some other hobby or activity that is important to you?

91.   How do you get there?

92.   Who are you most likely to do the above with?

93.   Do you eat Barbadian food here? (i) Regularly? (ii) Only on special occasions? (iii) Not at all anymore?

94.   Do you belong to any clubs or societies?

95a. Where do you go for holidays?

95b. Have you traveled outside the U.K., e.g., to North America?

96.   Which—and you can choose more than one—of these words
       would you use to best describe yourself?

English	Cockney	West Indian	black British
middle class	Barbadian	north Londoner	south Londoner
British	immigrant	black	working class
foreigner	east Londoner	west Londoner	any other term
Londoner	colored	Afro-Caribbean	

97.   Have people who live in Barbados come and stayed with or
       visited you here in the last few years or so?

98.   Have you been back to Barbados?

99.   How has Barbados changed since you left?

100.   How has Britain changed since you came here?

101.   Would you consider going back to Barbados to stay?

102a. Have you tried it, or known people who've tried it?

102b. How did they find it?

103.   If you had your time over, would you do the same again?

104.   When you use the word "home," what are you thinking about?

Questionnaire for the British-Raised Generation

1.   Where were you born?

2.   Where were you brought up?

3.   How old were you when you came to the U.K.?

4.   So how long have you been in Britain?

5.   Why did you come here?

6.   How much schooling did you get?

7.   Are you married or have a partner?

8.   Where is s/he from?

9.   Tell me a little about her/his family history.

10.   Do you have children?

11.   How many people, then, are in this household?

12.   What jobs, in order, have you done up to now?

13a.   Once you left your parents' house, where did you go and live?

13b.   When?

14.   What was it like?

15. What was good about it?

16. What was bad about it?

17. Who ran it/owned it?

18a. And then you moved to?

18b. When?

19. What was it like?

20. What was good about it?

21. What was bad about it?

22. Who ran it/owned it?

23a. And then you moved to?

23b. When?

24. What was it like?

25. What was good about it?

26. What was bad about it?

27. Who ran it/owned it?*

28a. So how did you happen to move into this present place?

28b. When?

29. Who runs/owns it?

30. Have you any plans to move in the next five years or so?

31. If yes, where would you like to live?

32. What would be your main reason for moving?

33. In general terms, what's it like to live in this area?

34. What's good about it?

35. What's bad about it?

36. What's the most important quality you'd look for in neighbors?

37a. Would having Barbadian neighbors make a difference?

37b. Caribbean?

38. Are there particular places in and around London which you like, and why?

39. Are there particular places in and around London which you don't like, and why not?

---

* This question followed, to the extent necessary, by further sets of questions identical to 18a to 22.

40. Are there particular places in and around London which you feel are important for Barbadians, and why?

41. Are there particular places in and around London which are important for Caribbean people, and why?

42. Are there particular places around Britain which are important for Barbadian or Caribbean people, and why?

43. For example, did you ever go to the Notting Hill carnival?

44. Did you ever participate in it?

45. What do you like about it?

46. What do you dislike about it?

47. Of all your relatives, apart from parents and children, is there anyone who is specially important to you/your household? How are they related to you, and where do they live?

48. When and how were you last in contact, by visit, phone, or letter, with any of them?

49. How often do you contact any other members of your family?

50. Where do your close friends live?

51. How did you get to know them?

52. So, are any of them Barbadians, or from families of Barbadian origin?

53. Are any of them West Indian, or from families of West Indian origin?

54. When was the last time you had contact, by visit, phone, or letter, with a close friend(s)?

55. How often do you get to visit them?

56. How do you get there or they to here?

57a. Do you attend religious services?

57b. How often?

57c. Where?

58. How do you get there?

59. Is your religion of particular importance to you?

60. Did you attend religious services when at your previous address(es)?

61. Where do you go shopping for food (convenience and/or big shopping)?

62. How do you get there?

63.   Where do you go shopping for clothes?

64.   How do you get there?

65.   Are there any other shopping trips worth mentioning?

66.   How do you get there?

67.   Where do your children go to school/kindergarten/child minding?

68.   How do you/they get there?

69.   Where do you go to the doctor/hospital/DHSS/Social Services/etc.?

70.   How do you get there?

71.   When and where do you go to play or watch sports/bingo/cinema/dancing/darts/dominos/etc.?

72.   How do you get there?

73.   Is there some other hobby or activity that is important to you?

74.   How do you get there?

75.   Who are you most likely to do the above with?

76.   Do you eat Barbadian food here? (i) Regularly? (ii) Only on special occasions? (iii) Not at all anymore?

77.   Do you belong to any clubs or societies?

78a.   Where do you go for holidays?

78b.   Have you traveled outside the U.K., e.g., to North America?

79.   Which—and you can choose more than one—of these words would you use to best describe yourself?

English	Cockney	West Indian	black British
middle class	Barbadian	north Londoner	south Londoner
British	immigrant	black	working class
foreigner	east Londoner	west Londoner	any other term
Londoner	colored	Afro-Caribbean	

80.   Do you ever talk to your parents about their experiences in migrating here?

81.   Do you ever compare their experiences to yours, and/or talk with them about it?

82.   What do you see as differences? Do you think Britain has changed since then?

83.   Have you been to Barbados?

84.   How was it?

85. Do you know anybody who has been there?

86. How did they feel about it?

87. What did your parents teach you about Barbados?

88. Is Barbados of interest to you in any way?

89. Have people who live in Barbados come and stayed with or visited you here in the last few years or so?

90. Would you like to visit there?

91. Would you ever think of going to live there?

92. What kind of deal do you think your parents got by coming to Britain all those years ago?

93. Would *you* have been better off if they had stayed in Barbados?

94. When you use the word "home," what are you thinking about?

Notes

Preface

1. Deemed officially by the apartheid laws of the South African government to be of "mixed racial ancestry." The book resulting from this work is *Outcast Cape Town,* published by the University of Minnesota Press in 1981.

2. E. Bowen (pseud. of L. Bohannan). *Return to Laughter.* New York: Harper, 1954.

3. E. Liebow. *Tally's Corners: A Study of Negro Streetcorner Men.* Boston and Toronto: Little, Brown, 1967.

4. U. Hannerz. *Soulside: Inquiries into Ghetto Culture and Community.* New York and London: Columbia University Press, 1969.

5. Mary Louise Pratt encapsulates the paradox nicely: "Fieldwork produces a kind of authority that is anchored to a large extent in subjective, sensuous experience. . . . But the professional text to result from such an encounter is supposed to conform to the norms of a scientific discourse whose authority resides in the absolute effacement of the speaking and experiencing subject." Her essay, "Fieldwork in Common Places," is to be found in *Writing Culture,* J. Clifford and G. Marcus (eds.), Berkeley, Los Angeles, and London: University of California Press, 1986. This volume discusses these issues at length. The above quotation is found on p. 32.

6. Perhaps the wittiest remark à propos of this entire project came from one of the members of this seminar. If you're looking for a title for a follow-up to your *Outcast Cape Town,* Stephen Frenkel suggested, how about *Overcast London?* He knew whereof he spake, having lived a summer in the metropolis.

One   Transatlantic Homes

1. W. Zelinsky. *The Cultural Geography of the United States.* Englewood Cliffs, N. J.: Prentice-Hall, 1973.

2. A parallel that springs to mind is Anne Moody writing of the South of two years later: "I stood there looking and thinking. Yes, Saturday night is Nigger Night all over Mississippi. I remembered in Centreville, when it was too cold for anyone to walk the streets, Negroes would come to town and sit in each other's cars and talk. Those that didn't believe in sitting around or hanging out in bars, like my mother, just sat or moved from car to car for four or five hours. Teen-agers who were not allowed in cafés went to a movie and watched the picture three or four times while they smooched."

3. G. Mikes. *How to Be an Alien.* London and New York: Wingate, 1946. Quotation on p. 8.

4. "His book includes Vietnamese boat people, South American dissidents, Jews fleeing Nazi Germany, Cypriots fleeing poverty. The larger Commonwealth migrations from the Caribbean, India and East Africa are well-represented too" (*The Economist,* November 10, 1990).

5. Note, again, an American comparison in the experience of celebrated psychologist Kenneth B. Clark, who received his B.S. and M.A. degrees from historically black Howard University. He then "applied to graduate schools at Columbia and Cornell Universities. He says Cornell officials refused to admit him, saying that although his academic record was

good, he would not be happy there. 'I wrote them back a short little note, saying that I was not applying to Cornell to be happy,' he says. 'I told them that I could take care of my own happiness, thank you. I was applying for a Ph.D.' " (*Chronicle of Higher Education,* May 21, 1986). Clark subsequently gained his doctorate from Columbia.

6. C. W. Mills. *The Sociological Imagination.* Harmondsworth, Mddx.: Penguin, 1970. Quotation on p. 14.

7. Olivia Manning. *The Balkan Trilogy.* Harmondsworth, Mddx.: Penguin, 1970. J. G. Ballard. *Empire of the Sun.* London: Gollancz, 1984; S. Rushdie. *Midnight's Chidren.* New York: Knopf, 1981.

8. B. Richardson. *Caribbean Migrants: Environment and Human Survival on St. Kitts and Nevis.* Knoxville: University of Tennessee Press, 1983. Quotation on p. 55.

9. Frank Springer's father was a white estate supervisor.

10. M. Berman. *All That Is Solid Melts into Air: The Experience of Modernity.* New York: Viking, 1988. Quotation on p. 326.

11. J. Enoch Powell held ministerial positions in the Conservative government from 1960 onward, and was a member of Edward Heath's "shadow cabinet" in opposition from 1965. On April 20, 1968, Powell gave his famous "Rivers of Blood" speech, which warned of a future of racial conflict were Britain to continue to permit black immigration. Although ejected forthwith from the shadow cabinet by Heath, and never holding government office thereafter, Powell's uncompromising opposition to black settlement made him one of the most visible British politicians through to the 1980s. See also chapter 10, footnote 4.

12. "Home from Home," BBC Radio 4, May–June 1988. Rita Payne, producer.

13. T. S. Eliot. *Murder in the Cathedral.* London: Faber and Faber, 1935. Quotation on p. 33 (1968 edition).

14. R. Williams. *The Country and the City.* St. Albans, Herts.: Paladin, 1975. Quotation on p. 21.

15. M. Barker. *The New Racism: Conservatives and the Ideology of the Tribe.* Westport, Conn.: Greenwood Press, 1981.

16. P. Fryer. *Staying Power: The History of Black People in Britain.* London: Pluto, 1984.

17. A widely employed British contraction of "quasi-autonomous non-governmental organisation": such as the (British) National Parks Authority, or the BBC. The characterization of the CRE as "toothless" was taken further by A. Sivanandan: "It has no gums." *New York Times*, March 31, 1991.

18. V. Woolf. *Mrs. Dalloway.* Harmondsworth, Mddx.: Penguin, 1964 (reprint; originally published 1925). Quotation on p. 116.

19. N. Glazer. *Ethnic Dilemmas 1964–1982.* Cambridge, Mass., and London: Harvard University Press. Quotation on pp. 294–295.

20. Brave words, but, not surprisingly, Barbadians who have subsequently settled in other lands have indeed been "forced to change" culturally. Perhaps the clearest example has been in Panama. Here, those who went to build and to operate the Americans' canal from the early years of this century onward, later found themselves objects of racial and cultural suspicion. English-speakers, they were obliged in 1941 by the heavy-handedly nationalist Panamanian government of Arnulfo Arias to learn Spanish or to lose citizenship rights, even if Panamanian-born.

21. "Home from Home," BBC Radio 4, May–June 1988. Rita Payne, producer.

22. This is so frequent an observation of black behavior in white-dominated societies that it is close to being a stereotype. A particularly fine expression of it is that by Zora Neale Hurston, writing of the United States of sixty years ago:

The Negro, in spite of his open-faced laughter, his seeming acquiescence, is particularly evasive. You see we are a polite people and we do not say to our questioner, "Get out of here!" We smile and tell him or her something that satisfies the white person because, knowing so little about us, he doesn't know what he is missing . . . The theory behind our tactics: "The white man is always trying to know into somebody else's business. All right, I'll set something outside the door of my mind for him to play with and handle . . .

(The quote is taken from pp. 4–5 of *Mules and Men*. Bloomington: Indiana University Press, 1978 [reprint; originally published 1935].)

23. In "Zora Is My Name!" *American Playhouse,* Public Broadcasting System, February 14, 1990. For sad stories, South Africa under apartheid also offered an ideal arena. In a 1980 meeting with a high-level American investigative commission, Zulu leader Gatsha Buthelezi admonished them, "You must do more than cry for us. We can drown in your tears."

24. "Salo W. Baron, 94, Scholar of Jewish History, Dies," *New York Times,* November 26, 1989.

Two   *The Island Relinquished*

1. Henry Coleridge wrote this in 1825. He is quoted on p. 175 of H. Beckles, *White Servitude and Black Slavery in Barbados, 1627–1715*. Knoxville: University of Tennessee Press, 1989.

2. Might perhaps the fate of the "Red Legs" stand, salutary, as a kind of parable for those white South Africans truly pessimistic about their future? One can emigrate; one can stay and fight in some long-foreseen "race war" and lose and be bloodily annihilated; one can stay and be "annihilated" by racial amalgamation, becoming "Coloured." Or, as in this case, one can stay and remain white, but at the bottom of the heap in a black-ruled Third World country. Whether this specific visceral phantom fear really exists I of course don't know—I mean, have any conservative, change-fearing white South Africans actually heard tell of the "Red Legs"?

3. Beckles, *White Servitude and Black Slavery in Barbados, 1627–1715* (1989), p. 175.

4. Paule Marshall, of Barbadian parentage, treats this issue in her novel *The Chosen Place, the Timeless People* (New York: Harcourt, Brace, and World, 1969). Instances of runaway slaves and runaway servants are also documented by Hilary Beckles in *White Servitude and Black Slavery,* including the 1701 case of a slave woman who escaped and hid for one whole year.

5. I.e., fee-paying private school.

6. "I saw history through the sea-washed eyes / of our choleric, ginger-haired headmaster, / beak like an inflamed hawk's, / a lonely Englishman who loved parades, / sailing, and Conrad's prose." Thus wrote the English-speaking Caribbean's most eminent contemporary poet, Derek Walcott, of his St. Lucia school days in *Another Life.*

7. Audley was a convinced Black Power sympathizer twenty years ago.

8. Sir A. W. (Winston) Scott was the first Barbadian to be governor-general, from 1967 to 1976. He was preceded briefly in the post, from independence in late 1966 until 1967, by the Englishman Sir John Stow, whom Jemmott (wittingly or unwittingly) has overlooked in these remarks.

9. C. L. R. James. *Beyond a Boundary.* London: Stanley Paul, 1969. Quotations on pp. 101, 110–111, and 233.

10. One of London's two great cricket grounds is the Kennington Oval.

11. C. L. R. James honored Wanderers, H. B. G. Austin's old club, as "the originator of the great tradition of Barbados batting."

12. Q. Crewe. *Touch the Happy Isles: A Journey through the Caribbean.* London: Michael Joseph, 1987.

13. Many Barbadian men worked on the construction of the canal in the early years of this century, but exactly why this sister lived there some decades later, I don't know. See Bonham Richardson's fine study, *Panama Money in Barbados, 1900–1920.* Knoxville: University of Tennessee Press, 1985.

14. D. Brooks. *Race and Labour in London Transport.* London and New York: Oxford University Press, 1975.

15. There were twenty-two immigrant-generation Barbadians: twelve men, ten women. The eleventh, final woman was a Jamaican, now married to a Barbadian. She was therefore not eligible for the Barbadian recruitment scheme. Thus she is omitted for this particular statistic. Later, however, for the more general question, "Why did you leave?" it does not seem necessary to exclude her experience. Throughout this book, then, her presence or absence—depending upon the degree of specificity to Barbados of the matter under consideration—will cause totals to be either twenty-two or twenty-three overall respondents, and either ten or eleven women.

16. This, along with a number of other themes in this chapter, is given consideration by Sutton and Makiesky-Barrow in their 1987 (1975) article on migration from Barbados. C. R. Sutton and S. R. Makiesky-Barrow. "Migration and West Indian Racial and Ethnic Consciousness," in C. R. Sutton and E. M. Chaney, eds., *Caribbean Life in New York City: Sociocultural Dimensions.* Staten Island, N.Y.: Center for Migration Studies, 1987, pp. 92–116.

Three   *The Island Attained: Newcomers to England*

1. Successful 1950s author of a number of books that were made into films, such as *Make Me an Offer.* One of his book titles is particularly famous: *My Old Man's a Dustman*—an enormously popular hit record by Lonnie Donegan.

2. F. Raveau. "The Use of Minorities in the Social Sciences." *The New Atlantis* 2: 1, 159–72, 1970. Quotation on p. 159.

3. S. Patterson. *Dark Strangers.* Bloomington: Indiana University Press, 1964. Quotation on p. 4.

4. Although I've just noted that some interviewees remembered the precise date of arrival in Britain "as one of the most significant in their lives," cross-checking with the *Hubert*'s log reveals that Mr. Eastmond is a few days off here.

5. St. Thomas's Hospital, in central London.

6. He rented in a long row of identical four-story terraced houses in Shepherd's Bush.

7. This is not necessarily an incidence of racism pure and simple. Thirty years ago it would be just "not done" to address strangers thus in a doctor's surgery. There's a hilarious parallel in Gerard Hoffnung's 1956 mischievous advice to foreigners in England, part of which was "On entering a railway compartment, make sure to shake hands with all the other passengers"!

8. Ten shillings, i.e., half of one pound sterling.

9. Runs away as fast as possible.

10. Until the passage of the Race Relations Acts of 1965 and 1968, it was perfectly legal to openly discriminate against blacks, or anyone else, in both accommodation and in public houses. The "saloon bar" in a pub is the more expensive, more plushly upholstered, and perhaps more decorous bar, as opposed to the more plebeian "public bar."

11. Teddy Boys were so called because their affected distinctive "uniform"—long

velvet-lined frock coats, bootlace ties, drainpipe trousers, and four-inch shoe soles—was borrowed from the Edwardian era. They appeared in the mid-1950s, were of working-class provenance, behaved in an "antisocial" and violent manner, and gave rise to (in Stuart Hall's celebrated phrase) a moral panic.

12. E. Pilkington. *Beyond the Mother Country: West Indians and the Notting Hill White Riots.* London: I. B. Tauris, 1988. Quotation on p. 115.

13. Ibid. P. 116.

14. J. A. Lukas. *Common Ground: A Turbulent Decade in the Lives of Three American Families.* New York: Knopf, 1985.

15. Pilkington, *Beyond the Mother Country*, p. 122.

16. Sir Oswald Mosley (1896–1980) founded a British fascist party in 1932, organizing anti-Semitic and antiblack rallies. Members of this party gave speeches to and leafletted the crowds during the Notting Hill disturbances.

Four   *A Roof over My Head . . .*

1. Dr. Richard Beeching was brought in from private industry in 1961 in order to streamline the nationalized British Railways. He went at it with a will, especially in the matter of lopping off unremunerative branch and (as in this case) cross-country lines. Hence the coining, "Dr. Beeching's Axe."

2. State registered nurse, as opposed to the lower-grade state enrolled nurse.

3. I.e., three pounds and three shillings.

4. The *Guardian,* May 31, 1988.

5. R. Glass, assisted by H. Pollins. *London's Newcomers: The West Indian Migrants.* Cambridge, Mass.: Harvard University Press, 1961. Quotation on p. 40.

6. T. R. Lee, *Race and Residence: The Concentration and Dispersal of Immigrants in London.* Oxford: Clarendon Press, 1977. Quotation on pp. 38–39.

7. A. G. Bennett. *Because They Know Not.* London: Phoenix Press, 1954. Quotation on p. 22.

8. This is not to imply that such attitudes have somehow obligingly faded away in the ensuing thirty years. See chapter 8.

9. E. Pilkington. *Beyond the Mother Country: West Indians and the Notting Hill White Riots.* London: I. B. Tauris, 1988.

10. M. Holland. *Report of the Commission on Housing in Greater London.* London: Her Majesty's Stationery Office (HMSO), Cmd. 2605, 1965. Quotation on p. 252.

11. A. Cohen. "A Polyethnic London Carnival as a Contested Cultural Performance." *Ethnic and Racial Studies* 5:1, 23–41, 1982. Quotation on p. 27.

12. Not unrepresentative. In 1958 over one-third of all British households had no bath, and just under one-third no hot water.

13. I take it that this meant, "I didn't want to make life more difficult for her, that's why I let her do it."

14. On March 6, 1957, the formerly British-ruled Gold Coast became the first black African-ruled ex-colonial territory, and renamed itself Ghana.

Five   *. . . And Bread on the Table: Employment*

1. Some of the persons in this study are not quite sure whether they should accord this status to themselves or not; see chapter 11.

2. A. Clarke. *Growing Up Stupid Under the Union Jack.* Toronto: McClelland and Stewart, 1980. Quotation on pp. 70–71.

3. In Britain these were the standard government-sanctioned measures of high school achievement in any one subject: O stands for ordinary level, A for advanced level. Two years of study commonly separated A from O levels.

4. I.e., "now that I reflect upon it."

5. Blacks in South Africa have allegedly shared similar perceptions of the English for decades. The stereotype is that at least you know where you stand with Afrikaners; Boers let you know they're against you. Whereas the English are hypocrites; they don't let on. And at the fortieth anniversary of the *Empire Windrush* at Lambeth Town Hall in Brixton on June 22, 1988, I recall with absolute clarity the tone of Baron Baker's voice as he addressed the meeting: "The English are *conniving*, they talk from both corners of their mouth." There were loud murmurs of approval from the floor.

6. I take this to mean, "I found I could relate to them."

7. Heavy Goods Vehicle; i.e., truck-driver's license.

8. I.e., "stick up for me."

9. I.e., Ph.D.s.

10. In the early evening of November 18, 1987, thirty-one people were burned or asphyxiated to death at the busiest Underground station, King's Cross, as a result of improper maintenance and cleaning of an escalator. Fire precautions were revealed as woefully inadequate.

11. The term "Asian" is used in the conventional contemporary British sense throughout this study: persons whose ancestry lies in those lands composing the former British Indian Empire. In this work I do not include "Asians" under the rubric of "blacks." The latter are considered to be those whose ancestry visibly lies at least in part in sub-Saharan Africa, thereby including all the Barbadian Londoners whom I met.

12. C. Brown. *Black and White Britain: The Third Policy Studies Institute Survey.* Aldershot: Gower, 1984. Quotation on p. 164.

13. Some of the most embarrassing occurrences during fieldwork were making the mistake, virtually inevitable sooner or later, of telephoning interviewees during the day to set up a meeting, and waking them up because they were on night shift.

14. The top deck of the double-decker bus was for smokers. From February 14, 1991, smoking was banned on the London buses.

15. As had the murderer of the Ghanaian female student (p. 96), who was apprehended over a year later. (Austin told me of this in May 1989.)

16. A cricketing metaphor, in this case meaning "to apply oneself resolutely."

17. Homes for the severely disabled founded by Leonard Cheshire, a World War II Royal Air Force hero.

18. I.e., "as if they were family."

19. I.e., central London.

20. Diesel Multiple Units: passenger trains powered by a built-in diesel unit. They replaced the steam trains on commuter services.

Six   *Making It: From Flat Rental to Home Ownership*

1. Elizabeth Burney, in her critical *Housing on Trial* (Oxford: Oxford University Press, 1967), opined, "If one had to name one thing which more than anything else has helped the housing of coloured people in Britian it would be the GLC mortgage scheme, the largest and most generous of all" (p. 50).

2. The police finally caught up with this character. He had, all in all, defrauded twenty-four people, both blacks and whites. He was declared bankrupt. The Brathwaites lost their savings.

3. The reader is reminded at this juncture of the account of Beverly Brathwaite's employment history in chapter 5.

4. A pseudonym.

5. A new industrial and commercial development in the zone of what had been the main London docks, which, having become a technological anachronism, were in economic decline. Government grants and tax-free incentives have effected a transformation here since the mid-1980s. The edge of the "enterprise zone" is close to the Farleys.

6. A character in the immensely long-running British TV soap opera "Coronation Street," who was a one-person neighborhood watch!

7. This road.

8. And yet, he is not too keen on living among Asians, *and* he is going home to a Barbados that is much less ethnically diverse than London (see the conclusion of this chapter).

9. Liquor and beer outlet.

Seven   *Valued People, Valued Places*

1. A presentation Christmas hamper, I presume.

2. I presume (and I may be wrong) that such a cutback is in response to Margaret Thatcher's rate-capping policies. Local authorities have been placed recently under much more stringent, and parsimonious, central government supervision as to the level of local taxes they may levy. This has especially hit relatively more generously spending Labour party-led councils, such as Brent—often pilloried as "loony left" by a popular press whose political complexion is to the right of them.

3. I am aware that there are some totals that do not add up here. I think the main problem is likely an unspecifiable measure of double counting. My apologies. The trend, however, is not in doubt.

4. Six Jamaicans were specified. But another respondent said "a few" of his London-met friends were Jamaican. Omitting to press for precision at the time of the interview, I now take it that one could fairly calculate this in as "at least two."

5. My assumption is that when the interviewees said "English" or "Irish," they also meant "white"; and that when they said "Barbadian," they meant—if I may use the term—"nonwhite." A white Barbadian would surely be unusual enough to be specified as such, as D'Arcy Holder mentioned of the man in the Barbados Tourist Office?

6. *Daily Telegraph,* June 17, 1988.

7. Three persons said they had holidayed in Barbados "oh, lots of times" or "many times," and were unable to be more specific; I counted in two for each, and could only add "at least" to the Barbados total when I finally arrived at it. Another somewhat misleading factor is when a husband and wife take multiple vacations to the same place jointly. Suppose they have each made seven trips together to Barbados, and two to Torquay. By the way I have reckoned it up here, Barbados thereby gets fourteen, Torquay four. The ratio stays constant, but the impression is given that Barbados is "ten in front" of Torquay in frequency, whereas it is only five, as it were. Also there is the factor of multiple-destination trips. The destination mentioned of St. Vincent can hardly, it seems to me, have been a trip from London exclusively to that little island—surely it was a side trip off a Barbados-bound journey? Or Edward Pilgrim, now able to take a big vacation once every eighteen months or so, always describes a triangle, going first for a couple of weeks to his brother's in Boston, then to New York, and then stopping by Barbados for ten days or more on his way back to Britain. One other factor is that the interviewees clearly could not possibly recall the exact number of day-trips out of London they had made over the years. They just knew that they had been

to Southend a good few times, and to Walton-on-the-Naze once, and to Brighton at least twice, and . . .

8. One was to Guyana.

9. Through my oversight I omitted to ask this of seven interviewees.

10. S. Smith. "Residential Segregation: A Geography of English Racism?" in P. Jackson, ed., *Race and Racism: Essays in Social Geography.* London: Allen and Unwin, 1987, pp. 25–47.

11. S. Smith. *The Politics of 'Race' and Residence: Citizenship, Segregation, and White Supremacy in Britain.* Cambridge, Eng.: Polity Press, 1989.

12. The arresting adjective in Nicholas Lemann's, in *The Promised Land: The Great Black Migration and How It Changed America.* New York: Knopf, 1990 (p. 23).

13. A church youth organization.

14. A tendency within the Church of England toward liturgical opulence (the use of censers, candles, rich vestments, bells, and so on), and which at the time of which Mrs. Brathwaite is speaking was associated (perhaps unfairly) with a certain stuffiness.

15. Score recorder, simultaneous to the game.

16. Some children have to bear for their entire lives their parents' enthusiasms at the time of the children's births. In Cape Town the anticolonial, socialist sentiments of one father gave Joseph Stalin Brown his name. The first name of another "Colored" man was Rommel, though whether he was actually defiantly named after the World War II enemy of South Africa's white soldiers I cannot say. His age would mesh well. But *rommel* also means "lumber" or "rubbish" in Afrikaans . . .

17. The kind of hit they would probably be referring to would be a shot of unorthodox, powerful athleticism, such as those associated with the "swashbuckling" Rohan Kanhai.

18. A. Cohen. "Drama and Politics in the Development of a London Carnival." *Man* 15, 65–87, 1980; A. Cohen. "A Polyethnic London Carnival as a Contested Cultural Performance." *Ethnic and Racial Studies* 5:1, 23–41, 1982. Quotation on pp. 23, 25; E. Pilkington. *Beyond the Mother Country: West Indians and the Notting Hill White Riots.* London: I. B. Tauris, 1988. Quotation on p. 59.

19. R. Pearson. "Carnival Time." *The Notting Hill Carnival Magazine,* Arif Ali, ed., London: Hansib, 1987. Quotation on p. 12.

20. Pilkington, *Beyond the Mother Country,* p. 59.

21. I.e., a neighborhood shopping center.

Eight   *British-Raised: A Profile*

1. I.e., simple arithmetic; "sums."

2. He doesn't work for AT&T, but for a similar leading communications multinational.

3. Perhaps this was a heavy-handed attempt at humor to console the injured Gordon?

4. As did the African students wish likewise to do to us, especially one young British volunteer with her sixties-style long blond hair.

5. I.e., those of the GLC borough of Harrow.

6. Early agricultural trade unionists who were prosecuted for attempting an "unlawful combination" and transported to the Australian convict colonies.

7. Pseudonym.

8. Royal Air Force.

9. Certificate of Secondary Education: a less advanced level of scholastic achievement than O level.

10. Dahrendorf, German former director of the London School of Economics, left Britain in 1984, to return three years later. He found in 1987 that "the old working-class solidar-

ity of Britain'' was melting away, that there had been ''a real change in people's values and attitudes'' that he would not have thought possible when he left: ''The quick pound, the quick buck, seem to be very much on people's minds'' (The *Independent,* October 9, 1987).

11. Pseudonym for her multinational, one of the biggest companies in Britain.

12. At his parents' home, where we were talking.

13. Department of Health and Social Security (which oversees unemployment benefits).

14. I.e., to catch the commuters' trains. Woking in Surrey is a classic upper-middle-income ''dormitory'' suburb.

15. I assume he is referring to her emphasis upon ''a property-owning democracy.''

16. Shot in Bristol, this followed the efforts of two comparable young men (one black and one white) to obtain rental accommodation. Predictably, there were a number of racially discriminatory acts, whereby the black applicant was denied rooms ''already taken,'' which were then offered to the white applicant when he soon after appeared.

17. I overlooked to ask this of one interviewee.

18. ''Gypsies,'' Romanies.

19. I wasn't sure whether Colin meant they were of Barbadian or whatever ancestry, or whether they were Barbadian-born but raised in part in Britain. I presume the latter.

Nine   *The Island Reconsidered*

1. Chattel houses are still found throughout the island. Their name indicates that their occupants did not own the land upon which the house stood, and so if the lease were terminated, one could up and leave and take the wooden house with one, prizing it off its foundations. Thus these are tiny little houses, in appearance almost like a child's drawing, or a doll's house.

2. Colonial-era establishment in Nairobi, Kenya.

3. J. Bernard. ''In the Clouds.'' *Midweek,* February 11, 1988, 9.

4. At that time the U.S. dollar equivalent for this round trip from Britain would have been approximately $750.

5. Manchester, from where the flights were originating, is in Lancashire.

6. Armed Jamaican drug-running gangs, whose alleged vicious violence was making them good newspaper copy, and thus quite notorious, in 1987–88.

7. ''Oh *come on!*'' objected Alan Maycock when he saw this, ''The whole *island* doesn't wear dinner-jackets for Christmas!''

8. Colloquialism for ''pious.''

9. Another interviewee vigorously disputed the truth of this, at least in the experience of his family and acquaintances.

10. A cricketing metaphor. A batsman abandons defensive circumspection and rashly attempts to hit the ball hard all around the ground . . . and frequently gets himself out.

11. Perhaps an example of Tony Gill's ''a rush of blood to the head''?

12. Soccer sweepstakes.

13. Old-age pensioner, i.e., senior citizen.

14. Rising automatically with the official cost-of-living index.

15. There's a strong parallel here to the words, on a BBC radio program, of the young black British woman quoted on p. 23.

16. A debate within the opposition Labour party was being energetically joined at the time. Should members who were black play a role in all possible committees, etc., but always be in a minority? Or should they form an exclusively black subsection, to speak the more forcefully on behalf of black interests?

17. A direct contradiction, at least terminologically, to her claim a few minutes earlier to be "English."

18. Whose government is led by the redoubtably conservative Eugenia Charles, ideologically kin to Ronald Reagan and one of the instigators of the 1983 invasion of nearby Marxist-led Grenada (in which action Barbados also played an important role).

19. Echoes of the attitudes revealed by the final comment about the Combermere School headship in the colonial era in chapter 2.

20. Pseudonym for a very posh and well-known West End hotel.

21. Catherine, remember, has a beauty business.

22. The precise British equivalent of Archie Bunker.

23. Moira Stewart, Bermuda-born, is mulatto in appearance.

Ten *England Reconsidered*

1. S. Rushdie. *The Satanic Verses.* New York: Viking, 1989. Quotation on pp. 354–55.

2. Upon demobilization at the end of World War II each soldier was provided with a civilian suit of uniform color and cut, which became synonymous with an unadventuresome lack of sartorial style.

3. Perhaps the finest cricketer in Britain of the last decade or more, Botham—depending on whom you ask—is either an ill-mannered, dangerous boor or "his own man," an entertaining sports star in the formerly rather stuffy world of cricket. In a plane in flight over Australia in 1987, for example, a drunk Botham beat up a fellow passenger: thuggery, or engaging "Jack the Lad" naughtiness?

4. On April 20, 1968, J. Enoch Powell, a member of the then opposition Conservative party's "shadow cabinet," gave a speech in which he drew on a classical allusion, "the River Tiber foaming with much blood," to warn of a future of racial violence for Britain, and of vast, potentially swamping increases in the numbers of black people in Britain. An enormous furor ensued. Powell was sacked from the shadow cabinet by party leader Edward Heath. White longshoremen from the East End marched through the streets of London in Powell's support. The repatriation of blacks was mooted. To some, Powell appeared a Cassandra-like seer. He became highly televisual, a status he has maintained for twenty years. In October 1987, on a discussion program on national TV, the interviewer asked: "And what of the future, Mr. Powell?" "Civil War," he replied.

5. Of the 28, 329 Metropolitan Police officers, 1.7 percent are "nonwhite" (*New York Times,* March 31, 1991). As this percentage presumably also includes Asians (among yet others), then the proportion of Afro-Caribbean officers must be far below the 5 percent Afro-Caribbeans constitute of Greater London's total population.

6. "Dixon of Dock Green," a long-running BBC television serial (1953–76), featured actor Jack Warner as the middle-aged P. C. Dixon. This character conveyed the ultimate reassuring image of the fatherly, incorruptible, pedestrian, and unarmed London bobby, guardian of his working-class beat.

7. S. Hall. "Urban Unrest in Britain," in J. Benyon and J. Solomos, eds., *The Roots of Urban Unrest,* pp. 43–50. Oxford: Pergamon Press, 1987. Quotation on p. 49.

8. "Bovver Boys" were adolescent street roughs who in the 1970s beat up members of the public. Their naming comes from "a spot of bother."

9. A justice of the peace, an appointed local magistrate.

10. I.e., "supported my version of events."

11. "Do it yourself."

12. Seeing as George and Ernestine head the household that, of all the twelve, stayed

for by far the longest time in public rental housing (until 1986), it seems faintly disingenuous of him to make so ringing a statement.

13. An almost identical (remarkably so) evaluation to that of Ralf Dahrendorf eight months earlier (see note 10, chapter 8).

14. The Labour party was then split internally over what degree of nuclear deterrent and/or involvement with American nuclear forces a future Labour-led British government ought to espouse. As party leader, Neil Kinnock was trying valiantly to reconcile—or perhaps straddle—both camps.

15. In the most rough-hewn of ways, one could assign a positive, negative, or neutral value to the directional changes for each topic—i.e., "Britain's got more cosmopolitan" is positive; "black youth unemployment" is negative; and "young blacks are different" and "Mrs. Thatcher's brought changes" are designated (the latter is problematic) neutral. It comes out that five topics are positive, four are negative, and two are neutral. However, the positive topics are, in number of mentions, the first through fourth, plus the seventh. And the first topic of all, racism, overwhelms all other mentions in number. Tot it all up, and one gets fifty-one and one-half positive, seventeen and one-half negative, and twelve neutral mentions. But to quantify it thus gives a misleading impression of precision.

16. This implies a prepackaged, "canned" view, of limited horizons.

Eleven *Identity*

1. E. Evans-Pritchard. *The Nuer.* Oxford: Clarendon Press, 1940. Quotation on p. 136.

2. C. Peach. "The Force of West Indian Island Identity in Britain," in C. Clark, D. Ley, and C. Peach, eds., *Geography and Ethnic Pluralism.* London: Allen & Unwin, 1984, pp. 214–230. Quotation on p. 214.

3. A. Cohen. *The Symbolic Construction of Community.* Chicester, Eng.: Ellis Horwood; London and New York: Tavistock, 1985. Quotation on p. 13.

4. I recalled from South Africa the suspicions of so-called Coloured people removed from their previous homes in areas newly designated "White" to areas now formally, ostensibly safely designated "Coloured" by the Group Areas Act. However, one said, "as soon as the houses of the white people appear on the horizon, we wonder if we shall have to shift once more." A similar sense of vulnerability to the other person's seemingly unjust and plastic law obtains here in Edith's words.

5. Recall George Mikes's sally on this point in chapter 1.

6. I.e., fee-paying private school.

7. I'm unsure to what degree a generation or more ago the term "colored" would have included *Indo-*Caribbeans. Clearly, the term "Afro-Caribbean" does not; and whether the term "black" does today is a matter of much contention. On this see, for example, Tariq Modood (" 'Black,' Racial Equality, and Asian Identity." *New Community* 14:3, 397–404, 1988). He also points out that "Indo-Caribbeans of course are defined out of existence by the current idea that the term 'Afro-Caribbean' is simply an update on the term 'West Indian' " (p. 403).

8. In tune with the times, this phrase of contemporary comedian Harry Enfield was immensely popular in the summer of 1988. Enfield's skit was of a brash, grossly insensitive cash-flashing young upstart.

Twelve *Home*

1. Birmingham, to where Small's parents moved, is in the county of Warwickshire.

2. The last three are the colors on the Jamaican national flag, and, more importantly, the first three are the colors of the Ethiopian flag.

3. Many an English reader will know the imperialistic bathos of Newbolt's *Vitae Lampada:* "There's a breathless hush in the Close tonight. . . . Play up, play up, and play the game!" Such things used to be dinned into our memories. We can't escape them—even in our escape to southern California. Christopher Isherwood, having in 1939 pointedly quit a, in his eyes, morally bankrupt post-Munich England for "absolutely free America" (the phrase is his friend's W. H. Auden's), settled in Santa Monica. He writes in *A Single Man* of an Englishman getting drunk at a friend's in Santa Monica Canyon. Slipping ever more deeply into alcohol-induced pleasurable recollection, he calls to mind a previous bibulous occasion: "We both knew Newbolt's *Vitae Lampada* by heart, we'd learnt it at school. So of course we began roaring out, 'play up, play up, and play the game!' And when we got to the second verse, about the sands of the desert being sodden red, I said 'the colonel's jammed and the gatling's dead,' and Rex thought that was the joke of the year, and Jim. . . . "

4. It is also possible that it may be distasteful because it is too close to the white English stereotype during the immigration years of West Indians being carefree, happy, musical people (as in, for example, the Milner Holland report quoted in chapter 4). No one mentioned this, however; nor did I probe.

5. T. E. Kalem, quoted in *The New York Times,* March 16, 1985. (*Borstal Boy* was published in 1959.)

6. M. Manley. *A History of West Indies Cricket.* London: Deutsch, 1988.

7. Once again, a debt to Sandra Wallman. My first thought had been to ask, "Where is home?" I realized, however, that this way of putting it privileged space, that is, that some geographical designation was assumed to be the answer. As I wondered aloud how to rephrase it, Wallman soon came up with this.

8. In Britain this is not the quasi-obligatory identification requirement it is in the United States, nor do people ordinarily carry it about with them.

9. An undisputed tale of racial harassment at the House of Commons was aired in the *Observer* (July 17, 1988); and this was harassment not of some young black temporary worker, but of an MP who happened to be black, and who "was forced out of the public gallery by a messenger, who has now written him a letter of apology." (The first Afro-Caribbean MPs were elected to Labour party seats in London in 1987.)

I am also reminded of the tale Rev. Andrew Young told when, under Jimmy Carter's presidency, Young was visiting the South African financier, mover-and-shaker Harry Oppenheimer, in his Johannesburg mansion. Young was up early one morning and was met in the corridor by a black servant, who eyed him, saw he was not wearing the clothes appropriate to a member of the domestic staff, and asked, "Are you new around here?" "I guess you could say I am," Young replied.

Sad to tell, also, that a white English acquaintance said to me that a few years ago she was teaching an urban affairs course at the Police College in Hendon to senior-level trainees: police inspectors in the making. One written test question was, "How would you ameliorate the inner city?" Over one-half replied—although in later discussion admitting the impracticality—"Send all the blacks back home."

10. Yes, "very" was used three times. I counted.

11. "Where," grinned Marie, knowing it wasn't quite the proper thing to say, "we can look down on the Ecky-Beckies."

12. A fascinating parallel to all this, by the way, was pointed to in an article in the *Christian Science Monitor* (October 13, 1988) entitled "IDENTITY CRISIS. After Years Abroad, Turks Find Turkey Isn't Home." One awaits with anticipation the work of a proficient Turkish-speaking, German-speaking social scientist.

13. Interesting that Hugh used "going back" and not "going over."

14. The reader is reminded of the schizophrenia statistic provided on p. 24.

15. A. Sivanandan. "RAT and the Degradation of the Black Struggle." *Race and Class* 26:4, 1–33, 1985. Quotation on p. 11.

16. S. Fenton. "Health, Work, and Growing Old: The Afro-Caribbean Experience." *New Community* 14:3, 426–43, 1988. Quotation on p. 439.

17. T. J. Cottle. *Black Testimony: The Voices of Britain's West Indians.* London: Wildwood House, 1978. N. Foner. "West Indians in New York City and London: A Comparative Analysis," in C. R. Sutton and E. M. Chaney, eds., *Caribbean Life in New York City: Sociocultural Dimensions.* Staten Island, N.Y.: Center for Migration Studies, 1987, pp. 117–30.

18. And, as has been pointed out in previous chapters, a number of them are not at all convinced that somehow they should feel *particular* responsibility for the plight of less fortunate British blacks. A colleague called my attention to a *Time* report (March 13, 1989), "Between Two Worlds," on America's black middle class. Viewing the black underclass, "Patricia Grayson speaks for many affluent blacks when she observes, 'One person can only do so much. I think it's unfair for people to try to make successful blacks feel guilty for not feeling guilty all the time.' "

Thirteen   *Islands and Insularities*

1. The Roman and Greek designation of Great Britain as Albion is from the same root as the Latin *albus* (white). As these southern civilizations first glimpsed Britain (one may surmise) from across the Channel, their view would be of the distant wall of the white cliffs of Dover—as the entry in the *Shorter Oxford English Dictionary* (1973) indicates. This striking local feature thereby gave its name—signifying white—to the entire island: a geographic synecdoche.

2. On November 10, 1987, the London radio news reported that the Inner London Education Authority had children from 172 mother tongues in its public schools, up from 164 the previous year.

3. I am indebted to Michael Bell for pointing out its lyrics to me.

4. And I am indebted to Paul Gilroy's probing and committed *There Ain't No Black in the Union Jack* (1987) for this telling detail.

5. An inelegant neologism. But if one can "Americanize," I assume one could "Britannicize"?

6. "Nonwhite" South Africans were officially enjoined from carrying arms . . . but I met a number in Cape Town's "Coloured" ghettos who claimed they had.

7. In one of her actions that most flew against public opinion, Margaret Thatcher on March 31, 1986, abolished the GLC and the platform it provided the articulate gadfly Ken Livingstone. Livingstone became an MP for the safe Labour seat of Brent East the following year.

8. P. Gilroy. *There Ain't No Black in the Union Jack.* London: Hutchinson, 1987. Quotation on p. 46.

9. P. Jenkins. *Mrs. Thatcher's Revolution: The Ending of the Socialist Era.* Cambridge, Mass.: Harvard University Press, 1988. Quotation on p. 286.

10. Ridley, a close colleague of Margaret Thatcher, was forced to resign in July 1990 after some injudicious comments that exposed him to accusations of unreconstructed anti-Germanism. In an interview with the London *Spectator* Ridley allowed that the prospective domination of the new Eurocurrency by the deutschmark could be "as bad as Hitler," and "this is all a German racket designed to take over the whole of Europe." (He simultaneously disparaged the French as "poodles to the Germans"!)

11. I was delighted to read that the director of the British side of the Channel Tunnel consortium, Alastair Morton, had a framed copy of this hanging on his office wall.

12. N. Nicolson. *Kent*. London: Weidenfeld and Nicolson, 1988. Quotation on pp. 41–42.

13. "Man hat Arbeitskräfte gerufen, und es kommen Menschen."

14. Writing this first in August 1989, the adverb "ridiculously" seemed perfectly apt. The remainder of the year, however, proved a veritable *annus mirabilis* in Eastern Europe. For example, three months later, the monolithic-appearing authoritarian Communist regime of East Germany was in disarray. After thousands had fled that country, and hundreds of thousands had participated in street demonstrations, the right to travel to the West without a visa was granted: the Berlin Wall was symbolically breached. Euphoria reigned; "freedom" had been grasped by the people. But immediately upon its heels came harder questions, specifically about loss of control, the upsetting of the established (if "unfree") international order. The *New York Times* (November 12, 1989) reported: " 'The Germans on both sides of the wall have really taken charge now,' said a senior Western diplomat, not altogether pleased that events were quickly running out of the grasp of the four occupying powers from World War II—the United States, the Soviet Union, Britain, and France. 'It's wonderful, but how is it going to end?' wondered another. . . . " German reunification seemed a possibility. On December 3 the entire East German politburo resigned. On December 5, after another Monday night of vast street demonstrations, U.S. National Public Radio reported the plaintive request of an East German Communist party leader that the people show discipline lest the state dissolve "into anarchy and chaos. . . . " The postwar Europe totally unraveled; yet four months earlier such a scenario appeared clearly "ridiculous."

15. Sanctioned immolation of a newly widowed woman on her husband's funeral pyre; formerly rendered "suttee" in English.

16. The Hungarian film director Istvan Szabo spoke of the polyglot trials of making *Meeting Venus* with actors from, it seemed, every country in Europe: "We need a common language. This common language is already there, and it is broken English" (*New York Times*, November 10, 1991).

Index

The Author

John Western teaches at Syracuse University, where in 1987 he won the Daniel Patrick Moynihan social science award and in 1990 the College of Arts and Science's prize for undergraduate teaching. In 1991 he won a Distinguished Teaching Achievement award from the National Council for Geographic Education. He previously taught at Temple and Ohio State universities, and is the author of *Outcast Cape Town* (Minnesota, 1981). Raised in England, he lived in Burundi, Canada, and South Africa before settling in the United States. *A Passage to England* is based upon field-work pursued while on leave at the London School of Economics in 1987–88.